THE US PRESIDENCY

In *The US Presidency*, E. Thomas Sullivan and Richard W. Painter examine the evolving state of presidential power in the United States, specifically facilitating discussion and debate concerning the power, responsibility, and accountability of US presidents. How is power acquired? How is it used or misused? How are the President's powers checked and how are they held accountable to and by the people? Rather than promote a single theory of presidential power, Sullivan and Painter answer these questions with a wide range of arguments for and against power in a broad number of circumstances and Supreme Court holdings. Grounded in the intersection of law, politics, and history, this book engages readers across disciplines, helping them understand the remarkable transformation of the United States presidency. Objective and timely, *The US Presidency* makes a case for a democratic model of self-government centered on accountability and the rule of law.

E. Thomas Sullivan is President Emeritus and Professor of Law and Political Science at the University of Vermont; former Provost of the University of Minnesota; Dean Emeritus at both the University of Minnesota Law School and the University of Arizona Rogers College of Law; former Associate Dean of Washington University School of Law, and a Life Member Fellow at Cambridge University, Clare Hall (UK).

Richard W. Painter is a law professor at the University of Minnesota and was the chief White House ethics lawyer for President George W. Bush.

The US Presidency

POWER, RESPONSIBILITY, AND ACCOUNTABILITY

E. THOMAS SULLIVAN
University of Vermont

RICHARD W. PAINTER
University of Minnesota

CAMBRIDGE
UNIVERSITY PRESS

CAMBRIDGE
UNIVERSITY PRESS

Shaftesbury Road, Cambridge CB2 8EA, United Kingdom

One Liberty Plaza, 20th Floor, New York, NY 10006, USA

477 Williamstown Road, Port Melbourne, VIC 3207, Australia

314–321, 3rd Floor, Plot 3, Splendor Forum, Jasola District Centre, New Delhi – 110025, India

103 Penang Road, #05-06/07, Visioncrest Commercial, Singapore 238467

Cambridge University Press is part of Cambridge University Press & Assessment, a department of the University of Cambridge.

We share the University's mission to contribute to society through the pursuit of education, learning and research at the highest international levels of excellence.

www.cambridge.org
Information on this title: www.cambridge.org/9781009521987

DOI: 10.1017/9781009521970

First published 2026

Cover image: Pgiam / E+ / Getty Images

A catalogue record for this publication is available from the British Library

Library of Congress Cataloging-in-Publication Data
NAMES: Sullivan, E. Thomas, author. | Painter, Richard W., 1961- author.
TITLE: The U.S. presidency : power, responsibility, and accountability / E. Thomas Sullivan, University of Vermont; Richard W. Painter, University of Minnesota.
OTHER TITLES: US presidency
DESCRIPTION: Cambridge, United Kingdom ; New York, NY : Cambridge University Press, 2025. | Includes index.
IDENTIFIERS: LCCN 2025026313 (print) | LCCN 2025026314 (ebook) | ISBN 9781009521987 (hardback) | ISBN 9781009521994 (paperback) | ISBN 9781009521970 (epub)
SUBJECTS: LCSH: Executive power–United States–History. | Presidents–United States–History. | United States–Politics and government–History.
CLASSIFICATION: LCC KF5053 .S85 2025 (print) | LCC KF5053 (ebook) | DDC 342.73/062–dc23/eng/20250602
LC record available at https://lccn.loc.gov/2025026313
LC ebook record available at https://lccn.loc.gov/2025026314

ISBN 978-1-009-52198-7 Hardback
ISBN 978-1-009-52199-4 Paperback

Tom Sullivan

For my wife, Leslie Black Sullivan, and for all my research assistants who have supported my scholarship over more than 45 years

Richard Painter

For Karen, Elizabeth, William, and Anne

Contents

Preface

The United States presidency, under Article II of the United States Constitution, is 236 years old. There have been forty-seven presidencies. Two of those presidents, Grover Cleveland and Donald Trump, have served, or are serving, two non-consecutive terms. Twenty-one presidents have served but one four-year term. Another five presidents served their term in office for fewer than four years due to death or other circumstances.

Through their intent and writings, the Founders from the beginning were clear that they were creating a presidency of "shared powers," but not "equal powers." A distinguished scholar called it "separated institutions sharing power."[1]

In this book, we outline through history and examples how the office of the presidency has grown in power and public prominence beyond the intentions of the Founders of the Constitution. History shows that the Founders clearly designed the Constitution and the branches of the federal government, through its design of separation of powers and checking and balancing functions, to ensure that the Congress, under Article I of the Constitution, would predominate over the President. A significant power shift has occurred over the last 236 years from explicit, implied powers under the Constitution or delegated power from Congress to those now exercised by presidents through inherited or "grabbed" powers, through either inaction or acquiescence by Congress.[2]

Readers of this book will be able to trace this remarkable transformation of power from the Founders' intent and written words to the United States Supreme Court's

[1] Richard E. Newstadt, Presidential Power and the Modern Presidents: The Politics of Leadership from Roosevelt to Reagan, 33 (1st ed. 1990). *See also* Theodore J. Lowi, Benjamin Ginsberg, Kenneth A. Shepsle, Stephen Ansolabehere, & Hahrie Han, American Government: Power and Purpose, 3, 77, 285 (17th ed. 2023).

[2] Lowi et al., *supra* note 1, at 58, 111, 117, 118, 284–85. (The constitutional design was a model of "dispersed power ... to protect the nation from tyrannical actions" in both the legislative and executive branches in order to prevent abuses of power.)

recent 2024 opinion granting presidents almost unlimited immunity from criminal prosecution while serving as president except for their personal conduct.[3] The breadth of the immunity defense now suggests, at least indirectly, greater power free from indictment and prosecution.

As we explore in this book, from the founding of the republic to the present, the power of a president has been a subject of vigorous debate. Since the 2024 election, this topic, as we write this book, is being discussed with wonder about the future of the presidency and the power of the institution of the office of the president. This book explores how the Supreme Court has developed doctrinal and legal frameworks over time for deciding questions of presidential power, responsibility, and accountability.

The intent in writing this book is to present a balanced overview of differing views of the presidency, and how power, responsibility, and accountability should be viewed and understood. Consistent with the Founders' intent, this book shows a more balanced approach to institutional power through "checking mechanisms" that guard against abuses of power.

We hope to objectively, accurately, and fairly present differing sides of the debate on these presidential topics so that our readers, the general public interested in this part of our constitutional republic, engaged citizens and voters, legislators, judges, lawyers, along with a scholarly community of faculty and students, can decide for themselves how best, in context, to understand and discuss these critical constitutional and civic ideas. At its core, this book presents readers a rich story of how law, history, and politics intersect to better understand the presidency. In short, we hope this book will be a work of public scholarship – one intended to be accessible and understood by a wide audience for a better comprehension of these important and highly relevant issues.

This book is presented in three parts: Part I on presidential power, Part II on presidential responsibility, and Part III on accountability. Throughout each part, we present, in context, an understanding of the Founders' deliberations about the presidency and their intentions, followed by the doctrinal developments over time of these issues through Supreme Court decisions. Finally, we explore the rich scholarly debate that continues today.

We try to draw conclusions and understanding from weighing the credible evidence, the historical record, and balancing the competing viewpoints so that readers can better understand the state of the law today. Questions are raised in this book about (1) how much power is too much or too little, (2) whether there are sufficient checks on a president's power, (3) whether in some areas the constraints on presidential power are excessive, (4) whether presidents understand their constitutional and civic responsibilities and duties drawn from their oath of office, the text

[3] Trump v. United States, 603 U.S. 593 (2024).

of the Constitution, and federal laws, and (5) whether the Constitution and enacted laws have sufficient mechanisms of accountability and transparency to restrain abuses of power or a loss of trust in a president.[4]

The discussion of presidential "power" in Part I includes the rapidly developing, and now accepted, doctrine of the "Unitary Executive Theory." It includes the President's power to appoint and remove Executive Branch officers, the "advise and consent" nomination process, the President as Commander in Chief over the military, foreign affairs, and emergencies, the President's veto and pardon powers, and the President's role as the "unitary executive" or "manager-in-chief" over the administrative state.[5]

Part II focuses on the duties and responsibilities of a president. It starts with the history of the "Take Care" Clause in the Constitution that requires that the federal laws of the nation are faithfully executed and carried out. It discusses the duties and obligations of a president to understand and follow financial disclosure rules, the Hatch Act covering political activities, federal election laws, and conflict of interest laws.

Part III is centered on transparency and accountability of a president in a constitutional republic. The history of impeachment from its early origins in England to the impeachment of three presidents, and the near impeachment of a fourth, are discussed at length. In addition, we discuss the limitation on presidential terms, under the Twenty Second Amendment, the removal of a president who is disabled, according to the Twenty Fifth Amendment of the Constitution, and the barring from public office, including the presidency, under the Reconstruction-era Fourteenth Amendment of anyone who has engaged in an insurrection or rebellion.

Further, Part III explains when a president can be sued both civilly and criminally, the difference between "official conduct" and "personal conduct," whether there are differences between a president being sued in a federal or state court, and when and to what extent a president can invoke an executive privilege defense in a court's proceedings or in response to a subpoena from Congress.

In conclusion, from its 236 years of US history, this book helps the reader to consider, understand, and ask whether the Founders of the country got the balance of power among the three branches of government right and whether the courts have followed the intent and understanding of the Constitution. Importantly, this book also demonstrates the critical role that the Supreme Court plays in following,

[4] Heidi Kitrosser, Reclaiming Accountability, Transparency, Executive Power, and the U.S. Constitution (1st ed. 2014); Minh Ly, Answering to Us: The Right of Democratic Accountability (Mar 10. 2026), https://press.princeton.edu/books/hardcover/9780691198613/answering-to-us.

[5] Lowi et al., *supra* note 1, at 368.

or not,[6] the notion that we have a constitutional structure and system of "separate institutions sharing power," not "equal powers."[7]

As we finish this book at the turn of the new year, into 2025, we see the United States undergoing significant political, economic, and social change that may well transform society and its political and legal cultures. We hope this book, at this time of polarization and civil discontent, will remind us from where we have come and that the country's foundation rests on important constitutional arrangements and understandings that are rooted in the rule of law and democratic accountability.[8] In the end, the question remains: in a constitutional republic, do presidents have the final word, or do the people?[9]

6 Benedict Vigers & Lydia Saad, *Americans Pass Judgment on Their Courts*, GALLUP (Dec. 17, 2024), https://news.gallup.com/poll/653897/americans-pass-judgment-courts.aspx ("Sharp decline in confidence in judiciary is among the largest Gallup [polling] has ever measured"; "American's confidence in their nation's judicial system and courts dropped to a record low 35% in 2024 . . . The Judiciary stands out for losing more U.S. public confidence than many other institutions experienced between 2020 and 2024").

7 NEWSTADT, *supra* note 1.

8 *See generally* CHARLES HANDY, THE AGE OF UNREASON (1989) (discussing "discontinuous change" from a social philosophy and leadership perspective); LY, *supra* note 4; KITROSSER, *supra* note 4.

9 For an excellent book posing this question *see* COREY L. BRETTSCHNEIDER, THE PRESIDENTS AND THE PEOPLE: FIVE LEADERS WHO THREATENED DEMOCRACY AND THE CITIZENS WHO FOUGHT TO DEFEND IT (2024).

Acknowledgments

Professor Sullivan wishes to thank his research assistant, Phillip Mellon (Class of 2024 University of Minnesota Law School), for his exceptional thoroughness and careful attention throughout this book project. In addition, he extends his appreciation to the University of Vermont for granting him a research leave to complete this book. Special thanks go to Dean Bill Falls and Department Chair Peter VonDoepp. He is also grateful to Dean William M. Treanor for the invitation to be a Visiting Law Faculty member and Dean's Scholar in residence at Georgetown University Law School during the spring semester of 2025. At Georgetown also, he extends appreciation to Professor of Law Austin Williams, Director of the Law Library, and Jeremy McCabe, Head of Library Access Services, for their support, and to his longtime friend and colleague Professor Robert Thompson.

Professor Painter thanks Phillip Mellon, who worked with diligence and precision on this book with both authors from the inception of the project through its completion. He also thanks the University of Minnesota for support of this book and particularly the students in his presidential power seminars in 2023 and 2024 for their invaluable research and provocative classroom discussion of uses and abuses of presidential power. Finally, he thanks the many public servants and former public servants in the executive and legislative branches of federal and state government he has worked with over the years with the hope of restraining unreasonable and excessive exercise of presidential power.

June, 2025

Introduction

In the summer of 1787, the young American republic was in a moment of crisis. After eight years of wars to gain independence from the British, the American experiment, despite its high-minded goals, was close to failing. The United States' first form of government, the Articles of Confederation, had left the thirteen states largely to manage their own affairs as quasi-independent states. The dispersion of power among the states had led to a variety of issues, including dueling foreign policies between the states; each state having its own currency, which made trade between the states and with foreign nations nearly impossible; an inability of the central government to impose taxes to pay off war debts; a reliance on state militias rather than a professionalized military controlled by the central government; and a lack of executive leadership in the central government.[1]

Realizing these issues posed an existential threat to the United States, twelve of the thirteen states sent delegates to Philadelphia to devise a new government. When the delegates arrived in Philadelphia, they brought with them not only their experiences in governing under the Articles of Confederation, but a deep well of knowledge in Enlightenment-era thinking on political rights and government. Among the most formative thinkers in devising a new constitutional government were John Locke, Thomas Hobbes, and Baron de Montesquieu.

The philosophy of Locke and Hobbes was focused on a "social contract" between the government and the governed. But the two thinkers differ in how they reach their conclusion. For Locke, the "state of nature," or how a people-centric society would be in the absence of government, is one of natural freedom and equality.[2] This view, articulated famously in Locke's *Two Treatises on Government* (1689), is

[1] National Constitution Staff, *10 Reasons Why America's First Constitution Failed*, NAT'L CONST. CENTER (Nov. 17, 2022), https://constitutioncenter.org/blog/10-reasons-why-americas-first-constitution-failed.

[2] *Locke's Political Philosophy*, STAN. ENCYCLOPEDIA OF PHIL. (Oct. 6, 2020), https://plato.stanford.edu/entries/locke-political/#StatNatu.

grounded in his belief that humans, as products of the creation of God, have an obligation to obey the commandments of God that inherently will lead to freedom and equality. However, Locke recognized that there are also bad actors in the world, and these bad actors necessitate a government that can protect the "natural rights" of man, including the rights of life, liberty, and property.[3] In Locke's view, the social contract between the government and the governed was the government protecting natural rights in exchange for the governed ceding some autonomy to the government. However, Locke believed that this social contract could be broken, and when it was, the governed had the right to rebel against the government and create a new one that would better uphold the social contract.[4]

The fingerprints of Locke's philosophy are apparent throughout early American history. The catalyst for the Revolutionary War, excessive taxation without colonial representation in Parliament, was viewed as a violation of Locke's social contract. His views were espoused throughout the Declaration of Independence. Additionally, the lack of a strong central government, under the Articles of Confederation, represented a Lockean fear that strong centralized executive power would inherently lead to a break of the social contract.[5]

In contrast to Locke, Hobbes, who wrote his famous book *Leviathan* (1651) decades earlier in the aftermath of the English Civil War, viewed the state of nature in much darker terms. He also saw the state of nature as one of individual liberty, and indeed he was the first political philosopher to recognize that liberty, and the ability of people to enter a social contract. But for Hobbes, the natural state of society was one of war and death as individuals competed for limited resources. Hobbes's social contract, in contrast to Locke, was focused on ridding society of its natural state and imposing civil order so people can live without violence and fear. To achieve this social contract, Hobbes advocated for a strong government whose power would enforce societal order and keep society from reverting to a life of war, scarcity, and early death.[6] The individual liberty inherent in the state of nature thus is voluntarily given up to the government – preferably an absolute monarchy – and citizens have no right to revoke that contract by rebelling against their ruler.

Finally, the writings of Montesquieu informed the Founders' views on the separation of powers. In his treatise *The Spirit of the Law* (1748),[7] Montesquieu argued that the best way to prevent governmental tyranny was to divide the power of government among a legislature, an executive, and the courts. Montesquieu's belief in the separation of powers was based in the ideas that placing the power to write and

3 *Id.*

4 *Id.*

5 *See generally*, The Articles of Confederation.

6 *Thomas Hobbes*, Stan. Encyclopedia of Phil. (Feb. 12, 2021), https://plato.stanford.edu/entries/hobbes/#Aca.

7 *Baron de Montesquieu, Charles-Louis de Secondat*, Stan. Encyclopedia of Phil. (Apr. 2, 2014), https://plato.stanford.edu/entries/montesquieu/#4.

enforce the laws in the same hands would lead to tyranny, and that uniting the power to enforce and interpret the laws would also lead to tyranny.[8] As a result, these three basic functions of government: the powers to write, enforce, and interpret the laws, should be split among three independent branches of government that are self-interested in protecting and preserving their own powers. The influence of Montesquieu's thought is readily apparent in the careful balance of power outlined in Articles I, II, and III of the Constitution.

But before the Constitution was ratified in 1789 came the Declaration of Independence (1776) and the Articles of Confederation (1777). These two documents emphasize rejection of absolute rule by a monarch, and in the case of the Articles of Confederation even the notion of having a separate executive branch of the federal government.

The constitutional story concerning the power, responsibility, and accountability of the presidency started with the debates about governmental "power" which occurred as early as the United States' colonial period. Those same debates continue vigorously today. Political freedom was an early, important value that can be seen clearly in the Declaration of Independence of 1776 as Thomas Jefferson and others set forth grievances, injuries, and usurpations against the despotic rule of the British and as well as advancing underlining political principles to establish a republican form of government.

The Declaration was a call to action setting forth the foundational basis for overthrowing a tyrannical government. Excessive and abusive power by King George III was stated as the grounds for dissolving the political connections between England and the colonies. The underlying philosophical rationales for the declared, required separation were "self-evident truths" that "all men are created equal, that they are endowed by their creator with certain unalienable rights," including "life, liberty, and the pursuit of happiness." In order "to secure these rights," the Declaration proclaimed that "governments are instituted" and derive "their just powers from the consent of the governed." But when the government's powers become "destructive of these ends, it is the Right of the People to alter or to abolish it and to institute a new government."[9] Clearly, the Declaration advanced three political ideas – political equality, natural rights, and the sovereignty of the people. It would serve later as the basis for a constitutional republic as adopted by the Founders in 1787. In short, it was a clarion call for the continuation of the Revolutionary War to overthrow the arbitrary and abusive powers of the British monarchy.

A year after the Declaration of Independence, delivered in Congress in 1776, the colonies, through their Continental Congress, approved the Articles of

[8] *Baron de Montesquieu, Charles-Louis de Secondat*, STAN. ENCYCLOPEDIA OF PHIL. (Apr. 2, 2014), https://plato.stanford.edu/entries/montesquieu/#4.2.

[9] DECLARATION OF INDEPENDENCE, para. 2 (U.S. 1776).

Confederation, the country's first written constitution.[10] The intent was to cooperate with one another, but to maintain each individual state's independence over most matters of governance. The result was a loose confederation with no effective central government and no executive branch to lead the colonies. The power to govern was left to the individual states with little or no enforcement authority within the colonies. By the 1780s it was clear this arrangement was not working: the federal government was out of money; foreign powers sought to take advantage of American weakness; with protection of the British navy gone, American ships and their crews were exposed to plunder, murder, and kidnapping by the Barbary Pirates; and America had no navy.

Despite a common body of philosophical thought from which to draw, the delegates at the Constitutional Convention had dramatic disagreements about how this philosophy should be implemented in practice. The disagreements were between the Federalists, who favored a complete restructuring of executive power that vested it in a singular president, and the Anti-Federalists, who wanted a weak executive and a Congress as the most powerful branch of government. Further divisions existed between Northern and Southern states on the issue of the institution of slavery and the larger and smaller states on the question of representation in Congress.[11]

As a result of these competing values and factions, the final Constitution that emerged from the Convention was a product of compromise. The bicameral Congress, which grants proportional representation in the House of Representatives and two senators per state in the Senate, was a compromise between larger and smaller states. The three-fifths compromise, which counted enslaved people as three-fifths of a person for the purposes of representation in the House, was a compromise between the Northern and Southern states.[12] These states disagreed on a lot, but agreed on one thing, however antithetical this was to the principles in the Declaration of Independence and the political philosophy in which republicanism is grounded: that enslaved persons would have no right to

[10] *See generally* Articles of Confederation of 1777.

[11] *See Three-Fifths Compromise*, Encyclopedia Britannica (Apr. 19, 2024), www.britannica.com/topic/three-fifths-compromise. *See also Connecticut Compromise*, Encyclopedia Britannica (Oct. 18, 2023), www.britannica.com/topic/Connecticut-Compromise.

[12] *Three-Fifths Compromise*, *supra* note 11. The three-fifths compromise arose during the Constitutional Convention between Northern and Southern states regarding how enslaved persons should be counted for the census and apportioning representations in the House of Representatives. To bolster the representation of the Northern states, representatives for those states at the Convention adopted the traditionally Southern position that enslaved people should count as property rather than people for census purposes. Conversely, Southern states adopted the traditionally Northern position that enslaved people should count as people for the census. The two sides ultimately reached a compromise where enslaved people would count for three-fifths of a person during the census count and for apportioning representation in the House of Representatives.

vote or to enjoy any other liberties.[13] Finally, the Bill of Rights, in 1791, was adopted by the Federalists to get the necessary ratifying votes of Anti-Federalists, who were worried that strong centralized presidential power would lead to a trampling of individual rights.[14] These debates were an essential part of the process by which the agreement reached in Philadelphia was "sold" to the state legislatures that ratified the Constitution.[15] As discussed throughout this book, considerable efforts were undertaken to convince the public and legislators voting to ratify the Constitution that the newly created office of the President would not be too powerful, that presidents would be expected to exercise their powers responsibly and would be held accountable when they did not.

In short, the Constitution, rather than representing a uniform view of government by the Founders, was a document of significant compromise, even if it was drafted and ratified by a small group of men, all White, almost all Protestant and property owners, who in fact represented only a small portion of the people living in the United States. Throughout the first six chapters of this book, which examine the powers of the President, we explore how the debates in Philadelphia in 1787 continue to shape the role of the presidency to this day. While the debates of the Constitutional Convention may have ended in September 1787 and the ratification debates in 1989, there continues today to be contentious debates among the public, the elected representatives, and political and legal scholars about the outer limits of presidential power. For example, when presidents should be held accountable for abuse of power. This book seeks to summarize that modern debate and inform the reader about the historical, legal, and political background of these debates.

When the delegates from the states met in 1787 in Philadelphia for the Constitutional Convention, the Founders were aware of the deep defects and weaknesses in the Articles of Confederation. The principles of representative democracy championed by John Locke were essential to the new Republic, but the realism of Thomas Hobbes was necessary as well. The social contract needed some

[13] *See* Kermit Roosevelt III, The Nation That Never Was (2022). While the authors of this book do not necessarily agree with all the sweeping generalizations in Professor Roosevelt's book about the constitutional framework for the original Republic, his point that the Republic fundamentally breached the liberties of enslaved persons is clearly valid and very important. As Roosevelt points out, the Thirteenth, Fourteenth, and Fifteenth Amendments were essential to the modern Republic. With the exception of a very brief period of post-Civil War Reconstruction, however, sustained enforcement of these amendments was not undertaken seriously until the civil rights era of the 1960s. Meanwhile after the Civil War, beginning with President Lincoln and then again from President Theodore Roosevelt until the presidencies of Donald Trump, presidential power has expanded significantly in ways discussed throughout this book, and arguably dangerously so in a manner that departed from the original vision of the Founders.

[14] *Bill of Rights*. Encyclopedia Britannica (Sept. 27, 2024), www.britannica.com/topic/Bill-of-Rights-United-States-Constitution.

[15] *See* Pauline Maier, Ratification: The People Debate the Constitution, 1787–1788 (2010).

measure of executive power, and a new office of the presidency to exercise it, but at the same time nobody, or almost nobody, wanted a president who could become an absolute monarch.

The delegates made many compromises during the Convention in their dominant, focused quest to reach an agreement on adopting a constitution that would unite the states into a United States with the desire of not repeating the mistakes of the weak and failed Articles of Confederation. This "power" question was central to the Founders' concerns because of the long-standing friction between the long reach of British rule and the colonies' political freedom. The "unity" sought by the delegates was ultimately archived, but first, central questions needed to be resolved, including an overriding issue of where the dominant power and authority would lie between the legislative and executive branches of the new government.[16]

Given the Founders' deep fears, concerns, and mistrust that too much power could lead to tyrannical power, as noted in the Declaration of Independence, and as they fought against in the Revolutionary War, the Founders, after considerable, and often bitter and contentious debate, decided that Congress would be the preeminent institution over the presidency.[17] It was not by accident that Article I of the adopted Constitution, the first Article, was designed for Congress as the "first branch," with its powers and responsibilities set forth.

The debates were extensive over how much power should be given to a president considering the grievances the colonies had with the monarchial rule and tyranny of King George III and the lack of "executive" leadership under the Articles of Confederation. In the end, the Founders settled on a system of separation of powers with checks and balances between the branches of government, each acting as a checking agent over the other, and sometimes even as "rivals."[18] As James Madison, one of the authors of the Federalist Papers, observed, "[I]t is not possible to give each department an equal power of self-defense. In republican government, the legislative authority necessarily predominates."[19] Indeed, as one noted scholar has opined, the Founders designed "separated institutions sharing power."[20]

[16] *See* Theodore J. Lowi, Benjamin Ginsberg, Kenneth A. Shepsle, Stephen Ansolabehere, & Hahrie Han, American Government: Power and Purpose, 57, 322, 336, 339 (17th ed. 2023).

[17] H. W. Brands, Founding Partisans: Hamilton, Madison, Jefferson, Adams and the Brawling Birth of American Politics, 1–7 (2023).

[18] *See* Lowi et al., *supra* note 16; Sanford Levinson, An Argument Open to All: Reading "The Federalist" in the 21st Century (1st ed. 2015); *see also* The Federalist Nos. 15, 33, 69, & 70 (Hamilton); The Federalist No. 51 (Madison); Saikrishna Bangalore Prakash, The Living Presidency, 15–40 (1st ed. 2020); Daniel A. Farber, Contested Ground: How to Understand the Limits of Presidential Power, 16–52 (1st ed. 2021); Peter M. Shane, Democracy's Chief Executive: Interpreting the Constitution and Defining the Future of the Presidency, 6–13 (1st ed. 2022).

[19] The Federalist No. 51 (Madison). *See also* Lowi et al., *supra* note 16 at 288–89, 291–93.

[20] Richard E. Neustadt, Presidential Powers and the Modern Presidents: The Politics of Leadership from Roosevelt to Reagan, 33 (1st ed. 1990).

Throughout the debates in the Convention and continued in the Federalist Papers is the "age old problem that faced the [delegates]: how to combine 'stability and energy in government, with the inviolable attention due to liberty and to the republican form.'"[21] The balance struck between these competing concerns expanded "power," although differentially, in both the legislative branch and in the office of the executive. The doctrine of separation of powers, with its checks and balances approach between the two branches, was the Framers' answer to the "age old problem" of the new government maintaining stability and energy while protecting individual liberty in a republican form of government. Although Congress was given greater influence over the presidency, today how much influence is a matter of contention, as this book discusses.

History records that the presidency as an institution has grown and evolved in prominence, power, and authority throughout the years. Several reasons account for this development. A single, unitary, executive decider can lead and make decisions more quickly and efficiently than the lengthy time it takes the 535 decision-makers in the Congress. As this book will trace and analyze, we see a constitutional story unfold on how explicit, implied, delegated, inherited, and acquired powers have flowed between the Congress and the presidency from the country's early beginnings to subsequent events that have shaped current conduct and new tensions.

Historical events are examples of these assertive uses of presidential power: President Jefferson's purchase of the Louisiana Territory; President Polk's annexation of Texas; President Lincoln's Emancipation Proclamation of enslaved people and the suspension of habeas corpus; President Truman's desegregation of the military and attempt to seize the steel mills during the Korean War; President Obama's Paris Agreement on the climate; and President Biden's attempt to cancel college student debt loans, for example.[22]

Other examples of early use of presidential power, include President Washington's suppression of the Whiskey Rebellion in western Pennsylvania, President John Adams's unilateral military actions in the "quasi-war" with France, and President Adams persuading Congress to pass the Alien and Sedition Acts which targeted immigrants and allowed exercise of executive power to restrict political speech contrary to the First Amendment.

History also records that the most assertive leadership styles of presidents started significantly in the twentieth century. Theodore Roosevelt and Woodrow Wilson in the early 1900s, during the Progressive era, were a portend of what was to come in terms of presidential agenda setting. Then came President Franklin Roosevelt's New Deal, his conflict with the Supreme Court, and wartime measures, including the

[21] THE FEDERALIST NO. 37 (Madison).

[22] LOWI ET AL., *supra* note 16.

unconstitutional internment of Americans of Japanese ancestry.[23] President Adams's 1798 Alien and Sedition Acts have been compared to the executive orders and laws passed by Congress after the terrorist attacks of September 11, 2001, and in 2025 President Trump explicitly invoked these Acts in deportation proceedings against aliens whose political speech on the Middle East conflict he deemed threatening to national security.[24] The tension between this use of presidential power and the First Amendment is discussed later in this book. And so on. The story told in this book is one of presidential power almost always expanding, rarely contracting, and sometimes posing a fundamental threat to the principles of liberty and republican government upon which this country was founded.

[23] *See* Korematsu v. United States, 323 U.S. 214 (1944) (upholding President Roosevelt's executive orders resulting in internment of Japanese Americans), Trump v. Hawaii, No. 17-965, 585 U.S. 667 (2018) (disavowing *Korematsu* while upholding President Trump's executive order banning immigration from certain predominantly Muslim countries).

[24] Invocation of the Alien Enemies Act Regarding the Invasion of the United States by Tren de Aragua, 90 Fed. Reg. 13033 (Mar. 14, 2025).

PART I

Presidential Power

1

The Vesting of Executive Power

The executive Power shall be vested in a President of the United States of America.
– United States Constitution, Article II, Section 1, Clause 1

1.1 THE PRESIDENT AS A UNITARY EXECUTIVE

Throughout this book we note frequent references to the "Executive Branch." However, from the text of Article II of the Constitution, which outlines the powers of the Executive Branch, it is unclear who composes the branch. Within Article II, there are two clearly enumerated members of the Executive Branch: the President and the Vice President.[1] Article II, Section 2 references the existence of principal officers who lead executive departments, but it does not define what executive departments should exist.[2]

When George Washington was sworn in as the first US President on April 30, 1789 the question of executive departments was unresolved. Within a month, James Madison, then a member of the House, proposed the first three executive departments. These three departments were the Departments of War, Foreign Affairs, and Treasury.

While these three departments may have been sufficient for the country in the 1790s, it is clear that American society has changed dramatically in the 236 years that followed. Since the 1790s the president's Cabinet has expanded from three departments to fifteen, with the newest being the Department of Homeland Security, established in 2002 in response to the September 11, 2001 attacks. Together these fifteen departments have an annual budget of over $1,500,000,000,000 and employ over 4,000,000 Americans. Additionally, each of these fifteen departments is composed of dozens of executive agencies with their specialized expertise that implement rules and regulations related to laws passed by Congress.

[1] U.S. Const., Art. II, § 1.

[2] *Id.*, § 2.

In addition to the fifteen executive departments, the president has at his (or her) disposal the Executive Office of the President, which provides for the day-to-day support of the president. The Executive Office was established by President Roosevelt in 1939 and is overseen by the President's Chief of Staff. The practice of the president having a Chief of Staff dates back to the Eisenhower administration.[3] In his first day in office, Eisenhower had a simple rule – nothing should come to him without first being screened by someone he trusted.[4] Presidents from Kennedy to Biden and Trump followed Eisenhower's example of hiring a Chief of Staff, with the lone exception of President Carter.[5] During the first two years of his presidency, Carter adopted a "hub and spoke" model of White House management, with himself at the center and a group of six senior advisors acting as the "spokes" with direct access to the President.[6] This model of presidential leadership proved untenable, however, as the six advisors all fought internally for influence and power. In 1979, President Carter appointed Hamilton Jordon to be his Chief of Staff.[7] Unlike the executive department and executive agency officers, who nearly universally require Senate confirmation, Executive Office officials are presidential appointments without the requirement of Senate confirmation.

As we turn to consider the rise of executive power in the White House, we start with Article II, Section 1, Clause I, which states, in part, that "[t]he executive Power shall be vested in a President of the United States of America."[8] Within this short sentence, known as the "Vesting" Clause, there are two elements that have sparked debates over the past 237 years.

First, the Vesting Clause states that the President shall have undefined executive power. From this ambiguous language, two competing theories of the limits of unilateral presidential power have emerged. Proponents of a powerful executive, such as former Justice Antonin Scalia, argue that the undefined nature of executive power within the Vesting Clause means that *all* possible executive power is given to the President.[9] On the other hand, advocates for a restrained executive believe that the Vesting Clause is simply stating to whom the powers belong as enumerated in Article II, Sections 2 and 3.

The earliest views of executive power in America were brought forward in Philadelphia in the summer of 1787 when delegates at the Constitutional Convention debated how to develop a new government from the ashes of the Articles of Confederation. One plan, put forward by James Madison and known as

[3] Chris Whipple, The Gatekeepers: How the White House Chiefs of Staff Define Every Presidency 12 (2017).

[4] *Id.*

[5] *Id.* at 59.

[6] *Id.*

[7] *Id.*

[8] U.S. Const. Art. II, § 1, cl. 1.

[9] Morrison v. Olson, 487 U.S. 654, 726 (1988) (Scalia J, dissenting).

the Virginia Plan, provides insight into Madison's view on executive powers. Article 7 of the Virginia Plan provides that "besides a general authority to execute the National Laws, it [the National Executive] ought to enjoy the Executive rights vested in Congress by the [Articles of] Confederation."[10]

One view of the language of the Virginia Plan is that it must be seen as a grant of general power to the executive. Unlike the Constitution that was ultimately ratified, the Virginia Plan does not enumerate any specific powers to the office of the president. Proponents of a broad approach to executive authority argue that this unspecific language of the Vesting Clause in the Virginia Plan must be seen as a general grant of executive power rather than vesting other enumerated powers with the President.[11]

As observed above, a competing view of the Virginia Plan's Vesting Clause argued that the president's vested power is limited to those powers granted to Congress under the Articles of Confederation. Under the Articles, Congress was a weak body whose powers were limited to declaring war, appointing military officers, signing treaties, making alliances, appointing ambassadors, and managing affairs with Indian nations. Notably, these powers did not include many of the powers commonly associated with the presidency today, including national security, veto powers, pardon powers, and many others. Proponents of an enumerated Vesting Clause under the Virginia Plan argue that the powers vested must be understood through the lens of how the founding generation understood Congress's power under the Articles and that the president's power should be understood to include only those Congress previously had enjoyed.[12] Throughout the tense debates, the issue was whether the vesting Clause was a true "grant of power" or "merely descriptive," to underscore the president's powers in relation to the powers of Congress.[13]

After the Virginia Plan was introduced, vigorous debate ensued about the precise role of the presidency as proposed in Article 7 of the Plan. Charles Pickney, a delegate at the Convention from South Carolina, favored a vigorous executive but feared that granting the power to make and declare war would make the President a monarch in all but name.[14] Similar sentiments were echoed by Roger Sherman of Connecticut, who believed that the president should do nothing more than act as a tool to carry out the will of the legislature.[15] At the same time, other delegates argued that the unitary nature of the presidency required powers that could be exercised

[10] Notes of James Madison from the Constitutional Convention (May 29, 1787), reprinted in THE RECORDS OF THE FEDERAL CONVENTION OF 1787, VOL. 1, 20 (Max Farrand ed., 1911).

[11] *Id.* at 21.

[12] RICHARD W. MCCONNELL, THE PRESIDENT WHO WOULD NOT BE KING 253 (2020).

[13] DANIEL A. FARBER, CONTESTED GROUND: HOW TO UNDERSTAND THE LIMITS OF PRESIDENTIAL POWER (1st ed. 2021), at 8.

[14] Notes of James Madison from the Constitutional Convention (June 1, 1787), reprinted in THE RECORDS OF THE FEDERAL CONVENTION OF 1787, VOL. 1, 64–65 (Max Farrand ed., 1911).

[15] *Id.* at 65.

with vigor and energy when the moment required.[16] Defending the plan he helped draft, Madison argued that there were certain powers that were inherently executive in nature. Madison believed that these included the power to enforce the law, appoint officers, and a number of other powers.[17] But Madison was cautious also in advocating a careful balance of power with appropriate checks and balances between Congress and the presidency.[18]

An early example of this debate in practice came in 1793 when President Washington declared that the United States would remain neutral in a war among France, Great Britain, and their allies. Outside of the federal government declaring neutrality, President Washington's proclamation also made it a punishable offense for private citizens to provide aid and comfort to either side of the conflict. This proclamation by the President brought about significant debate between the Federalists, represented by Hamilton, and the Democratic Republicans, represented by Madison.

In a series of seven essays, known as the "Pacificus-Helvidius debates," the two men debated whether the Vesting Clause of the Constitution granted the power to the president over declaring neutrality or if that power was reserved for Congress under their power to declare war. Writing in favor of a broad vesting of executive power, Hamilton argued that "the general doctrine of our Constitution, is that the executive power of the Nation is vested in the President; subject only to the exceptions and qualifications which are expressed in the instrument."[19] Hamilton reasoned that the expansive nature of both executive power and the office of the presidency meant that discussion of presidential power must be in broad terms so as not to limit the president's authority in moments of great national importance.[20]

The debates over presidential powers in the Virginia Plan were a precursor to the debates over presidential powers in the Constitution and interpretation of the Vesting Clause after ratification of the Constitution. Yet the Virginia Plan, which in its earlier iteration contemplated Congress electing the President for a seven-year term subject only to removal by impeachment (a modified parliamentary system), was different from the Constitution whereby the president is elected directly. The debates over presidential power, however, were much the same, and because the Vesting Clause does not clearly define what powers it is referring to, that debate continues to this day. How much does the Vesting Clause add to the enumerated powers of the President in Article II? Does the Vesting Clause mean the president has lots of other powers besides the enumerated powers (the broad view of presidential power) or does the Vesting Clause only vest in the President the enumerated

16 FARBER, *supra* note 13, at 26, citing THE FEDERALIST NO. 67–77 (Hamilton).

17 THE FEDERALIST NO. 67 (Madison).

18 FARBER, *supra* note 13, at 230–31.

19 7 WORKS OF ALEXANDER HAMILTON 76, 80–81 (J. C. Hamilton ed., 1851).

20 *See* H. W. BRANDS, FOUNDING PARTISANS: HAMILTON, MADISON, JEFFERSON, ADAMS AND THE BRAWLING BIRTH OF AMERICAN POLITICS (2023), at 3 of Preface.

powers (narrow view), or something in between? Different constitutional law scholars, lawyers, and judges have different answers, although presidents and their lawyers almost always invoke the broader view.

Madison, however, took a different approach focused on enumerated powers. Madison argued that Article I, Section 8, which outlined the powers of Congress, included the powers to declare war. Additionally, Madison recognizes that treaty-making and ratification powers are split between Congress and the President in Articles I and II, which he understood to mean that the Constitution places some foreign affairs role for the presidency. Madison ultimately concluded that because the Constitution places some foreign affairs powers with the president, but not the power to declare neutrality, the silence of the Constitution on the president's neutrality powers must mean that that power is best seen as falling under Congress's power to declare war, not the president's.[21]

Another approach to interpreting the Vesting Clause comes from a technique used by constitutional scholars known as intratextual interpretation. This approach, rather than looking at the history of the Constitution, looks inward at the text and considers how similar phrases are used within the document to make conclusions about the relationship between the different contexts.[22] For an analysis of the Vesting Clause, this primarily involves a review of the sections within Article II and the relationship between the Vesting Clauses in Articles I, II, and III.

One of the key intratextual arguments brought forward by advocates of a limited Vesting Clause comes from an analysis of Article II, Sections 2 and 3. Sections 2 and 3 outline a number of presidential powers including the power to act as Commander in Chief, the power to grant pardons, the treaty-making power, the power of appointment, the veto power, and the power to execute the laws of the United States. Advocates of a limited executive argue that by specifically listing these powers in Sections 2 and 3, the Vesting Clause is simply granting the President the power to execute these listed powers rather than granting broad executive powers.[23]

Another intratextual approach compares the Vesting Clauses of Articles I, II, and III. Article I states that "[a]ll legislative powers herein granted [referring to Article I, Section 8] are vested in the Congress." In other words, Article I is granting Congress a specific and limited set of powers that are later enumerated within the article. Similarly, Article III states that "[t]he Judicial Power of the United States shall be vested in one Supreme Court." Similar to Article I, Article III, Section 2 lists nine types of cases, known as "the nine heads of jurisdiction." This argument advocates for a broad reading of the Vesting Clause and that the language of Article II is distinct from the other two articles. Rather than granting specific powers outlined

[21] *See* e.g. 2 Debates in the Several State Conventions, at 378.

[22] Akhil Reed Amar, *Intratextualism* 112 Harv. L. Rev. 791–95 (1999).

[23] *Id.*

later in Article II, some argue that the term "[t]he executive power" should be read as a general grant of authority.[24]

Finally, a third approach can be seen in two landmark cases on executive power, *Youngstown Sheet and Tube Co. v. Sawyer*[25] and *Morrison v. Olson*.[26] They offer competing views on the limits of presidential power. *Youngstown Sheet*[27] arose out of President Truman's nationalization of American steel mills to increase production of supplies needed for the Korean War. While the Court ultimately held that the President alone does not have the power to nationalize industry under his powers as Commander in Chief, this decision is most famous for a concurring opinion by Justice Robert Jackson where he provided a three-part framework to understand how to analyze the powers vested in the President.

First, when the President is acting pursuant to an express or implied authorization by Congress he is at his most powerful. In these cases the President possesses all of the powers of the presidency as well as those delegated by Congress. The President can be viewed as acting for the federal government as a whole. Second, when the President acts in the absence of Congressional approval he acts with his powers alone and none of Congress's powers. Finally, when the President acts against the will of Congress, he possesses only the powers of the presidency minus any powers reserved by Congress.[28]

Another famous passage in the *Youngstown* opinion comes from Justice Felix Frankfurter's concurrence. Justice Frankfurter addressed the limits of executive power under Justice Jackson's three-part framework. Rather than examining the history of the making of the Constitution or using intratextual interpretation, Justice Frankfurter stated that the Constitution should be seen as a framework for governance and that *history* serves as our guide to the limits of presidential power.[29]

A different view of executive power came from Justice Antonin Scalia's dissent in *Morrison v. Olson*.[30] In *Morrison*, the Court grappled with the question whether the Independent Counsel Act, which prohibited the President from removing independent counsels, was a violation of the President's power to remove federal officers. Although the Court held that the Act was constitutional, Scalia's forceful dissent argued that "the constitutional principle that the President had to be the repository of *all* executive power . . . necessarily means that he must be able to discharge those who do not perform executive functions according to his liking."[31] For Justice

[24] *Id.*

[25] Youngstown Sheet & Tube Co. v. Sawyer, 343 U.S. 579 (1952).

[26] Morrison v. Olson, 487 U.S. 654 (1988).

[27] Youngstown Sheet and Tube Co. v. Sawyer, 343 U.S. 579 (1952).

[28] *Id.* at 635–38. *See also* Theodore J. Lowi, Benjamin Ginsberg, Kenneth A. Shepsle, Stephen Ansolabehere, & Hahrie Han, American Government: Power and Purpose (17th ed. 2023) at 288–89, 291–310.

[29] Youngstown Sheet and Tube Co. v. Sawyer at 610–11.

[30] Morrison v. Olson, 487 U.S. 654, (1988).

[31] *Id.* at 726.

Scalia, the Vesting Clause, rather than being a grant of limited enumerated powers, should be viewed as a broad grant of authority.[32]

This debate on the outer limits of the Vesting Clause continues today. The current issues have dramatic implications on the power of the President to confront the challenges of a tumultuous twenty-first century. From the power of the President to unilaterally authorize enhanced interrogation techniques or torture of enemy combatants, to the power of the President to remake the executive branch in his image, these debates are relevant and timely.

Days into his first term of office, President Trump issued Proclamation No. 9645 which restricted entry into the United States for citizens of eight nations that were deemed to present a security threat.[33] In response to this proclamation, the State of Hawaii, along with three individuals and the Muslim Association of Hawaii, sued the Trump administration arguing that the actions were a violation of the Immigration and Nationality Act (INA).

Under the INA, Congress established several statutory grounds for exclusion from the United States, including health concerns, criminal history, terrorist activities, and foreign policy grounds.[34] Additionally, the INA delegates to the President the authority to suspend or restrict immigration for all or any class of aliens when their admission would be "detrimental to the interests of the United States."[35] There were two questions before the Court in *Trump v. Hawaii*.[36] First was whether the proclamation violated the Establishment Clause of the Constitution. On this issue the Court sided with the President. The second issue was whether the President's order fell within this delegation granted by Congress.

First, the Court looked at the statutory language delegating authority to the President. The Court found that the delegating language "exudes deference to the President in every clause. It entrusts to the President the decision whether and when to suspend entry … whose entry to suspend … for how long … and on what conditions."[37]

Next, the Court examined the purpose of the INA. Prior to President Trump's proclamation, immigration from "high risk" countries relied on individual vetting that placed the burden on the immigrant to prove their admissibility.[38] Further, to encourage information sharing with the United States, visa waivers were available for immigrants from thirty-eight countries which met rigorous information-sharing

32 Peter M. Shane, Democracy's Chief Executive: Interpreting the Constitution and Defining the Future of the Presidency 6–13 (1st ed. 2022), at 46–49.

33 Order Enhancing Vetting Capabilities and Processes for Detecting Attempted Entry into the United States by Terrorists or Other Public-Safety Threats, 82 Fed. Reg. 45,161 (Sept. 27, 2017).

34 Immigration and Nationality Act 8 U.S.C. §§ 1182(a) (1952).

35 Immigration and Nationality Act 8 U.S.C. §§ 1182(f) (1952).

36 Trump v. Hawaii, 585 U.S. 667 (2018).

37 *Id.*

38 Immigration and Nationality Act 8 U.S.C. §§ 1187 (1952).

and law-enforcement standards.[39] The Court found that the purpose of these two schemes was to encourage countries to improve their practices and their vetting processes.[40] Under the Trump administration's proclamation, the basis for determination was a lack of data sharing with the United States and inadequate law enforcement practices. By improving their law enforcement and data sharing, countries can, and did, come off the banned list. In the Court's view, the proclamation was a supplement to, rather than an overhaul of, the purposes of the INA.[41]

In March 2020 President Trump declared a national emergency in response to the COVID-19 pandemic. He used his authority as President to place a hold on student loan repayments under the Higher Education Relief Opportunities for Students Act (HEROES Act).[42] When he assumed office, President Biden extended the loan repayment pause under the HEROES Act. In August 2022 he announced a cancellation of $10,000–20,000 in student loan debts for borrowers meeting certain requirements.[43] In response to the loan cancellation, several states that operated student loan entities sued the Biden administration arguing that the President's unilateral decision to cancel a portion of student loan debts under the HEROES Act and 2020 COVID national emergency was a violation of the separation of powers.[44]

President Biden's decision in 2022 to cancel hundreds of billions of dollars in student loan debts for borrowers making less than $125,000[45] was based on the HEROES Act, that allowed the Secretary of Education to "*waive or modify* any statutory or regulatory provision" to protect borrowers affected by "a war or other military operation or *national emergency*."[46]

In 2023, the Supreme Court agreed that the loan forgiveness executive order was a violation of the separation of powers.[47] In its decision, the Court focused on the language and purpose of the HEROES Act. First, the Court looked at the word "modify" in the Act. According to the Court, the word "modify" implies "increment or limitation" and does not authorize "basic and fundamental changes to the scheme designed by Congress."[48] To illustrate this point, the Court examined prior modifications made to the Act by previous Secretaries of Education. It found that

[39] DHS, U.S. Visa Waiver Program (Apr. 6, 2016), www.dhs.gov/visa-waiver-program.

[40] *Id.*

[41] Trump v. Hawaii, 585 U.S. 667 (2018) at 688.

[42] Declaring a National Emergency Concerning the Novel Coronavirus Disease (COVID-19) Outbreak, 85 Fed. Reg 15,337–38 (Mar. 18, 2020).

[43] The White House, Fact Sheet: President Biden Announces Student Loan Relief for Borrowers Who Need It Most, https://bidenwhitehouse.archives.gov/briefing-room/statements-releases/2022/08/24/fact-sheet-president-biden-announces-student-loan-relief-for-borrowers-who-need-it-most/.

[44] Biden v. Nebraska, 600 U.S. 477 (2023).

[45] The White House, *supra* note 43.

[46] Higher Education Relief Opportunities for Students Act of 2003, 20 U.S.C. §§1098aa–1098ee (2003) (emphasis added).

[47] Biden v. Nebraska, 600 U.S. 477 (2023).

[48] *Id.* at 494.

they had made only minor procedural adjustments to loan repayment schemes, such as extending filing periods or changing tax forms used.[49] The Court contrasted these earlier changes with the Biden administration's actions, which it described as "draft [ing] a new section of the Education Act from scratch by 'waiving' provisions root and branch and then filling the empty space with radically new text."[50]

The Court's skepticism of the President's actions only increased when they examined the purpose of the HEROES Act. In arguing that the President's decision was outside what Congress intended when the HEROES Act was passed, the Court invoked a doctrine, known as the "major questions doctrine." The basic concept of the major questions doctrine is that when executive agencies make decisions of incredible magnitude or consequence on matters of earnest and profound debate it must come from a clear delegation by Congress to make that decision.[51]

While certain detractors argue that the major questions doctrine is a creation of the modern conservative Court to limit executive agency power, its basis could arguably be found in Justice Jackson's three-part test on the balance of legislative and executive power.[52] Under Justice Jackson's test, executive (and by extension agency) power is at its peak when Congress explicitly grants the executive some of its power. In this instance, the Court argued, Congress had explicitly granted the Secretary of Education the power to waive or modify statutory or regulatory provisions but it had *not* granted the power to eliminate $469–519 billion dollars in revenue to the federal government.[53] Ultimately, because the Secretary's actions represented a wholesale change of the HEROES Act and because the loan forgiveness represented an encroachment on Congress's power of the purse by an agency without explicit Congressional authorization, the Court found that President Biden had overstepped his constitutional powers.

At times, this book refers to broader theories of presidential power using the phrase "unitary executive theory." The problem is that this phrase appears nowhere in the Constitution or in the Founding documents. Rather it is an invention of the twentieth century. It means different things to different people. Some people refer only to the President's power to appoint and remove federal officers when using the phrase, whereas others use it to describe a broader array of presidential powers to issue executive orders, control foreign policy, decide how, when, and even whether to enforce the laws, and so on. The range of the debate today is about how much power presidents have over and within the Executive Branch.

49 *Id.* at 495.
50 *Id.* at 498.
51 *Biden* 600 U.S. at 504.
52 *See* Youngstown Sheet and Tube Co. v. Sawyer, 343 U.S. 579 (1952).
53 *Biden* 600 U.S. at 502. (Chief Justice Roberts discussing that $469–519 billion accounts for nearly one-third of annual discretionary spending).

Early advocates for a strong empowered executive, known today as the "unitary executive theory," argued that the Constitution vests certain enumerated powers exclusively with *the* President.[54] Using the aforementioned intratextual approach, they note that Articles II and III contain similar "shall be vested" language to grant both the President and the federal courts exclusive powers. Beginning with Article III, Calabresi and Rhodes argue that the vesting language grants the federal judiciary with nine categories of cases. They assert that if you believe that the vesting language of Article III gives federal courts exclusive power to hear certain types of cases, then logically it follows that the similar vesting language of Article II must mean that the President exclusively has the powers vested by Article II.

This idea of exclusive vesting is an important distinction because it removes the power to direct and control federal executive agencies, such as the Environmental Protection Agency (EPA) and the Securities and Exchange Commission, from Congress or the agency heads and places it solely with the President. Advocates of the unitary executive theory claim this power means that the President has the power to direct both policy and personnel of executive agencies.

A recent example of this can be seen in the back-and-forth battles among the Obama, Trump, and Biden administrations over emission standards. In 2012, the Obama administration's EPA issued rules and regulations requiring a gradual increase in average fuel economy for new vehicles that culminated in 2025 with an average fuel economy of 54.5 miles per gallon.[55] In March 2020 the Trump administration's EPA overturned the Obama regulation at the President's direction and implemented a new rule that dramatically reduced the increase in fuel efficiency required year over year.[56] In April 2023 the Biden administration's EPA again reversed the Trump-era regulations and implemented a new series of regulations focused on transitioning American automobiles from internal combustion engines to electric motors.[57]

It is notable that while all three administrations have received criticism within Congress for their changes to emission standards, the focus of the criticism was on the substance of the regulation rather than the use of presidential power to make the changes. In response to President Trump's rollback of the Obama-era emission standards, then Speaker of the House Nancy Pelosi called the change "[an] anti-

[54] Steven G. Calabresi & Kevin H. Rhodes, *The Structural Constitution: Unitary Executive, Plural Judiciary*, 105 Harv. L. Rev. 1153 (1992).

[55] Bill Vlasic, *U.S. Sets Higher Fuel Efficiency Standards*, New York Times (Aug. 28, 2012), www.nytimes.com/2012/08/29/business/energy-environment/obama-unveils-tighter-fuel-efficiency-standards.html.

[56] David Shepardson, *Trump Finalizes Rollback of Obama-Era Vehicle Fuel Efficiency Standards*, Reuters (Mar. 31, 2020, 9:09 AM), www.reuters.com/article/us-usa-autos-emissions/trump-finalizes-rollback-of-obama-era-vehicle-fuel-efficiency-standards-idUSKBN21I25S.

[57] Emma Newburger, *Biden Proposes Toughest Auto Emissions Rules Yet to Dramatically Boost EV Sales*, CNBC (Apr. 12, 2023, 5:00 AM), www.cnbc.com/2023/04/12/epa-proposes-auto-pollution-limits-to-aggressively-boost-ev-sales-.html.

science decision to gut fuel standards [that] will unleash massive amounts of pollution into the air at the worst possible time."[58] Similarly, in response to the Biden administration's changes, six Republican members of Congress signed a joint letter calling for significant decreases in funding to the EPA in an upcoming appropriations bill.[59]

This brings up one of the most important checks Congress has on presidential power – the power of the purse strings. Executive agencies may be controlled completely by the President, but their money comes from Congress through appropriations in legislation enacted under Article I. If Congress doesn't like what the President is doing in a particular agency, whether the EPA or the National Endowment for the Arts or any other, Congress simply refuses the President's request for appropriation in the next year's budget. In recent years, Congress and the President, and sometimes the two houses of Congress, have had frequent showdowns over the budget, leading to brinkmanship against the backdrop of potential shutdown of the federal government when a budget cannot be passed.

1.2 EXECUTIVE ORDERS

While this chapter has focused on the theory of the limits of presidential power, theoretical power is useless without a means to implement it. As noted earlier in this chapter, Article II, Section 1 of the Constitution vests the President with the executive power of the United States.[60] To exercise this executive power, the President may use executive orders to issue statements directing the Executive Branch to implement certain policy goals pursuant to a presidential power under Article II or a power granted by Congress through legislation. While no provision in the Constitution explicitly grants the President the power to issue executive orders, the history of the practice, its acceptance by Congress, and decisions by courts have made the issuance of executive orders generally uncontroversial.

The first executive order was issued just a few months in President Washington's first term in June of 1789. In a simple one-sentence order, Washington ordered his department heads to "submit a 'clear account' of affairs connected with their Departments."[61] Throughout the remainder of the eighteenth century and the first half of the nineteenth century, executive orders were using sparingly and for relatively mundane purposes. As the United States expanded westward, executive orders were used, for example, to establish various forts and military bases in new states and territories under the President's power as Commander in

[58] Shepardson, *supra* note 56.

[59] Chip Roy (@RepChipRoy), X (Apr. 10, 2023), https://twitter.com/RepChipRoy/status/1645473056632995841.

[60] U.S. CONST., Art. II, § 1.

[61] Clifford Lord, List and Index of Presidential Executive Orders, unnumbered series, 1 (1943).

Chief,[62] to set aside parcels of coastal land for naval exercises,[63] and to place executive departments in a state of mourning when former presidents passed away.[64]

During the Civil War, two executive orders by President Lincoln tested the outer limits of permissible power of executive orders. The first test came just six months into the war when Lincoln issued an order to Lieutenant General Winfield Scott, the commanding general of the Union Army, ordering the suspension of the writ of *habeas corpus* within the Union.[65] Article I, Section 9 of the Constitution states that "the Writ of Habeas Corpus shall not be suspended, unless when in Cases of Rebellion or Invasion the public Safety may require it."[66] While the plain language of this clause indicates that Lincoln was acting constitutionally, the problem was the clause's location within the Constitution.

Article I is traditionally viewed as a grant and limit on the power of Congress, not the President. Article I, Section 9, where the *Habeas* Clause is located, is an enumerated list of powers Congress cannot exercise. Because Lincoln was using a congressional power without a delegation by Congress, his order to suspend *habeas corpus* drew immediate scrutiny from the courts. The earliest and most notable challenge to Lincoln's order came shortly after it was issued, in *Ex Parte Merryman*.[67]

In *Merryman*, a prominent Baltimore area farmer was arrested after destroying several bridges used by Union soldiers. After being arrested, Merryman filed a *habeas* petition with the federal courts challenging his detention, and the government refused to either state the basis for his arrest or release him. A few days after Merryman's arrest, his attorney convinced Judge Taney to hear his case. In his decision, Judge Taney held that Lincoln's order was unconstitutional for two reasons. First, Article I is "devoted to the Legislative Department of the United

62 *Id.* at 4, 5 (establishing Fort Gratiot Military Reservation, Nov. 11, 1828; establishing Mount Vernon Barracks Military Reservation, Mar. 10, 1830; establishing Fort Jessup Military Reservation, June 3, 1833).

63 *Id.* at 7 (setting aside Santa Rosa Island, Florida for naval purposes, Apr. 21, 1838).

64 *Id.* at 17 (placing executive departments in a state of mourning for a day upon the death of President Jackson, June 16, 1845).

65 Abraham Lincoln, *Executive Order – Suspension of the Writ of Habeas Corpus Online by Gerhard Peters and John T. Woolley*, The American Presidency Project, www.presidency.ucsb.edu/node/202622 *See also* Noah Feldman, The Broken Constitution (2021); James Oakes, *Was Emancipation Constitutional*, New York Review of Books (May 12, 2022), www.nybooks.com/articles/2022/05/12/was-emancipation-constitutional-feldman-oakes/; Sam Wilentz, *Was the Constitution Pro-Slavery? Jefferson Davis Thought So. Abraham Lincoln Didn't*, New York Times (Nov. 2, 2021), www.nytimes.com/2021/11/02/books/review/noah-feldman-the-broken-constitution.html; James Oakes, *Was Emancipation Constitutional?*, New York Review of Books (May 12, 2022), www.nybooks.com/articles/2022/05/12/was-emancipation-constitutional-feldman-oakes/; Dan Farber, Lincoln's Constitution (2003); Richard A. Posner, *Desperate Times, Desperate Measures*, New York Times (Aug. 24, 2003), www.nytimes.com/2003/08/24/books/desperate-times-desperate-measures.html.

66 U.S. Const., Art. II, § 9, Cl. 2.

67 Ex parte Merryman, 17 F. Cas. 144 (C.C.D. MD. 1861).

States, and has not the slightest reference to the Executive Department."[68] Second, Judge Taney reviewed English history and found that historically the power to suspend *habeas corpus* rested with Parliament, not the crown.[69] In Taney's view, the Constitution embodied this English tradition.

Judge Taney was in fact Chief Justice Taney sitting by designation as a district court judge and the author of the notorious *Dred Scott* decision a few years earlier (1857). Taney was a Southern sympathizer at the outbreak of the war, and Lincoln, perhaps, had a good excuse to ignore his order.

The decision by Judge Taney appeared to have offended the President personally. In an address to Congress in the summer of 1861, President Lincoln argued that his order was constitutional and that

> we have a case of rebellion ... now it is insisted that Congress, and not the Executive, is vested with this power. But the Constitution itself, is silent as to which, or who, is to exercise the power; and as the provision was plainly made for a dangerous emergency, it cannot be believed the framers of the instrument intended, that, in every case, the danger should run its course, until Congress could be called together; the very assembling of which might be prevented ... by the rebellion.[70]

This statement by Lincoln to Congress seemed not to be a post hoc justification for his actions, but a sincere belief in his own powers. In 1863, Congress passed the Habeas Corpus Suspension Act[71] that granted Lincoln the power he already was using under his earlier executive order. Despite this grant of power by Congress, Lincoln continued the practice of suspending habeas corpus under his original executive order, and justified his approach in a widely published letter.[72]

He argued that the Civil War was a clear case of rebellion, and that if the power to suspend habeas corpus was to be left to Congress alone it would act too slowly to end the risk to public safety.[73] In a second letter to Ohio Democrats in 1863,[74] Lincoln reiterated his belief that the power to suspend habeas corpus was his alone. Justifying his decision, Lincoln wrote:

> The constitution contemplates the question [of who can suspend habeas corpus] as likely to occur for decision, but it does not expressly declare who is to decide it. By necessary implication, when rebellion or invasion comes, the decision is to be made, from time to time; and I think the man whom, for the time, the people have,

68 *Id.* at 148.

69 *Id.* at 151.

70 Roy P. Basler et al., eds., The Collected Works of Abraham Lincoln, 9 vols. (1953–1955), 4:430–31.

71 12 Stat. 755.

72 Basler et al., *supra* note 70 at 6:260.

73 *Id.*

74 *Id.* at 6:300.

> under the constitution, made the commander-in-chief, of their Army and Navy, is the man who holds the power.[75]

The second test of presidential authority to issue executive orders came in January of 1863 when President Lincoln issued his Emancipation Proclamation which freed enslaved people in states not under union control.[76] Unlike prior orders, which were clearly within the purview of enumerated presidential powers, the basis of the Emancipation Proclamation were less clear. While Lincoln had argued that the proclamation was necessary to eliminate a vital source of manpower within the Confederacy, it was unclear at the time if the connection between freeing enslaved people in the Confederacy was too attenuated to the President's powers as Commander in Chief.[77]

Even when it was issued, there was deep skepticism about Lincoln's power as President to free the enslaved. In an 1861 letter, Lincoln expressed his skepticism regarding the power of the President, stating,

> it is not for him [the President] to fix their permanent future condition. That must be settled according to laws made by law-makers, and not by military proclamation … Can it be pretended that it is any longer the government of the U.S. – any government of Constitution and laws – wherein a general, or a president, may make permanent rules of property by proclamation?[78]

By the time the proclamation was issued in 1863, Lincoln's reservations about his presidential powers had waned. In a letter issued with the Emancipation Proclamation, Lincoln declared that the proclamation was issued "by virtue of the power vested in [the President] as Commander-in-Chief … and as a fit and necessary war measure for suppressing the rebellion."[79]

Another view on Lincoln's power to free enslaved people under the Commander in Chief power can be found in *United States v. Brown*.[80] In *Brown*, Chief Justice John Marshall wrote that "war gives to the sovereign full right to take the persons and property of the enemy, wherever found."[81] Lincoln used this holding by the Court, in part, to justify his freeing of the enslaved and sidestep the protections of the Fifth Amendment, which prohibits the taking of property without due process.[82] Lincoln did not invoke the argument that is obvious today. The Fifth Amendment right of slaveholders to their "property" is nonexistent because people are not property.

75 *Id.* at 6:303.

76 Emancipation Proclamation, January 1, 1863; Presidential Proclamations, 1791-1991; Record Group 11; General Records of the United States Government; National Archives.

77 Doris Kearns Goodwin, Leadership: In Turbulent Times (2018).

78 Basler et al., *supra* note 70, 4:531–32.

79 *Id.*

80 United States v. Brown, 12 U.S. 109 (1814).

81 *Id.* at 121.

82 U.S. Const., Amend. 5.

Recognition of that principle in the United States would have to await the ratification of the Thirteenth Amendment in 1865.

Because an executive order is an exercise of presidential power, its outer limits are confined to the limits of Article II or an express or implied delegation of authority by Congress. For example, as discussed in Chapter 3, the President has wide authority as Commander in Chief to direct the affairs of the armed forces. This grant of authority under Article II gives the President broad latitude to write executive actions on establishing military forts and bases, enacting changes to the Uniform Code of Military Justice, and directing the nation's intelligence agencies.

In addition, Congress may either explicitly or implicitly delegate authority to the President. An example of this delegation is best highlighted in the Defense Production Act (DPA).[83] Under the DPA, Congress delegated to the President the power to "allocate materials, services, and facilities" in a manner necessary to promote the national defense.[84]

While presidents in the eighteenth and nineteenth centuries used executive orders sparingly and for generally uncontroversial purposes, the practice of "governing" and leading through executive order began in earnest with President Theodore Roosevelt. It continues to this day. From President Washington to President McKinley a total of 1,325 executive orders were issued during the first 112 years of the United States.[85] In contrast, during his seven and a half years in office, President Theodore Roosevelt issued 1,081 executive orders.[86] This shift in the use of executive orders likely came from President Roosevelt's views on executive power. Unlike his predecessors, who generally viewed Article II as limiting presidential power, Roosevelt saw Article II's silence on certain powers as a grant of authority. Since Roosevelt's opening of the floodgates on executive orders, presidents from Franklin Roosevelt to Trump's second term have followed Theodore Roosevelt's example in issuing hundreds of executive orders to bypass Congress. The increased use of executive orders incentivizes the use of presidential powers to remake American society in their image.

During World War II, President Franklin Roosevelt issued two consequential executive orders as Commander in Chief. First, in June 1941 President Roosevelt issued Executive Order 8807[87] that established the Office of Scientific Research and Development (OSRD). The OSRD was given nearly unlimited funding to develop and research cutting-edge munitions, and the Manhattan Project, which developed the atomic bombs that were used in Hiroshima and Nagasaki to end the war, were

[83] 50 U.S.C. §§ 4501 *et seq.*

[84] *Id.* at §§ 4511(a).

[85] Gerhard Peters & John T. Woolley, *Executive Orders*, *in* The American Presidency Project (John T. Woolley and Gerhard Peters eds., 1999–2025), www.presidency.ucsb.edu/node/323876.

[86] *Id.*

[87] Exec. Order No. 8807, 6 Fed. Reg. 128 (1941) at 3207–08.

researched and developed with OSRD funding. Roosevelt's second consequential executive order during the war established "Japanese exclusion zones" along the west coast following the attacks at Pearl Harbor in December 1941.[88]

The use of executive orders under the Commander in Chief power would not end with World War II. Following the end of the war, President Truman established the President's Commission on Civil Rights which issued several recommendations to promote equality for African Americans, including laws against poll taxes, anti-lynching laws, and the desegregation of the armed forces.[89] The Commission's recommendations drew immediate backlash from Southern senators, who threatened to filibuster any civil rights legislation. Undeterred by the senators' threats, President Truman invoked his Commander in Chief power to issue Executive Order 9981 in 1948, which ordered the military to desegregate as rapidly as possible.[90] The effects of this executive order have consequences to this day. In 2023, soldiers of color made up 48 percent of the active-duty army;[91] approximately 15 percent of general officers are African American.[92] In 1989, General (retired) Colin Powell became the first African American Chairman of the Joint Chiefs of Staff.[93] President Biden's Secretary of Defense, General (retired) Lloyd Austin, was the US's first African American Secretary of Defense.

Further, President Truman would invoke his Commander in Chief authority to attempt to nationalize the US's steel mills during the Korean War. In 1951, the steelworker's union threatened to strike after a collective bargaining agreement between the steelworkers and the steel mill owners fell apart. Fearing that a closure of the mills would threaten the war effort, Truman issued an executive order[94] under his Commander in Chief powers that directed the Secretary of Commerce to nationalize the mills to continue their operation. When the Supreme Court considered the constitutionality of Truman's order, it found that he did not have the authority to nationalize the steel mills without express authorization by Congress.[95] The basis of this opinion was the previously mentioned three-part framework in Justice Jackson's concurrence that established a sliding scale for presidential authority which has been used by the courts to evaluate executive orders by later presidents.

88 Discussed in Chapter 3.
89 Exec. Order No. 9981, 13 Fed. Reg. 146 (1948) at 4311–13.
90 *Id.*
91 United States Army FY23 Demographic Diversity, https://api.army.mil/e2/c/downloads/2024/02/20/92ecod8e/army-profiles-fy23-tri-fold.pdf.
92 *Id.*
93 Biographies of the Secretaries of State: Colin Luther Powell (1937–2021), Department of State, https://history.state.gov/departmenthistory/people/powell-colin-luther. Secretary Powell served as Secretary of State in the George W. Bush administration.
94 Exec. Order No. 10340, 17 Fed. Reg. 71 (1952) at 3139–41.
95 Note: this case and the Court's reasoning is examined in greater detail in Chapter 3.

Under the first part of this framework, the President's power is at its maximum when he acts pursuant to an express or authorized delegation of power.[96] When Congress delegates authority to the President, he is said to "personify federal sovereignty," and if a presidential action is unconstitutional in these cases it is because the federal government as a whole lacks the power to act on the issue.[97]

In the second part of the framework, the President's power is diminished because he is acting in either the absence or the denial of a congressional grant of power.[98] In these instances the President can only use his Article II powers and none of Congress's powers. Jackson's framework doesn't fully answer the question of what to do in cases where Congress and the President share an enumerated power, but suggests that congressional inaction in asserting Congress's power weighs in favor of the President's authority to exercise the shared power.

Finally, the President's power is at its lowest when he acts against the express or implied will of Congress.[99] When acting against the will of Congress, the President may only use his Article II powers minus any powers granted to Congress by the Constitution over this matter.[100] Courts are especially cautious when analyzing presidential actions in this third category because of concerns that finding the action constitutional will upset the equilibrium established by the US's constitutional system.[101]

In the aftermath of the Court's landmark decision in *Brown v. Board of Education*,[102] Presidents Eisenhower and Kennedy invoked their Commander in Chief and "take care" powers to enforce the Court's order. Eisenhower issued an order,[103] despite the Posse Comitatus Act prohibiting use of the military for domestic law enforcement, which used his Commander in Chief authority to send federal troops to Arkansas to quell violence and end obstruction by the state's governor in integrating schools. Similarly, in 1962, eight years after the Court had made integrated schools the law of the land, President Kennedy would invoke laws passed by Congress and his authority as President to force the University of Mississippi to integrate.[104]

During the tumultuous 1960s and 1970s, presidents used executive orders to expand the scope and power of the executive branch. In 1961, President Kennedy issued Executive Order 10924[105] that established the Peace Corps under the Department of State. Acting under an implied power granted by Congress in the

96 Youngstown Sheet and Tube Co. v. Sawyer, 343 U.S. 635, 637 (1952).
97 *Id.*
98 *Id.* at 637.
99 *Id.* at 637–38.
100 *Id.*
101 *Id.*
102 Brown v. Board of Education of Topeka, 347 U.S. 483 (1954).
103 Exec. Order No. 10730, 22 Fed. Reg. 186 (1957) at 7628.
104 Exec. Order No. 11053, 27 Fed. Reg. 191 (1962) at 9693.
105 Exec. Order No. 10924, 26 Fed. Reg. 40 (1961) at 1789.

Mutual Security Act, Kennedy viewed the Peace Corps as an expansion of the State Department's power to issue foreign aid. In the summer of 1965, President Johnson used his power as head of the executive branch to prohibit discrimination in federal hiring for both the government and government contractors.[106] This order was consequential because it bypassed the "state action doctrine" of the Fourteenth Amendment.

The state action doctrine arose out of a series of Supreme Court cases[107] following the end of Reconstruction, which held that the Equal Protection Clause of the Fourteenth Amendment applied only to governmental discrimination, not discrimination by private actors such as hotels, restaurants, theaters, and other places of public accommodation.[108] In the Court's opinion in *The Civil Rights Cases*,[109] it held that Congress could pass targeted regulations prohibiting discrimination; however, generalized laws targeting discrimination were too broad an assertion of power.[110] In issuing Order 10924, President Johnson issued a targeted ban on discrimination that remade both public and private government hiring and granted all Americans an equal opportunity in seeking federal jobs.

In the aftermath of the Watergate scandal, President Ford used his pardon power (discussed in detail in Chapter 4) to issue a presidential proclamation[111] granting a blanket pardon to President Nixon for his involvement in the scandal.[112] President Ford's view was that Nixon had suffered enough by resigning the presidency, and that the possibility of him facing a criminal trial for his involvement in Watergate would tear apart the fabric of the nation. For the good of the country, he issued the proclamation pardoning Nixon pursuant to his pardon power under Article II.[113]

During the 1980s, executive orders experienced a "second renaissance" under President Reagan. Reagan sought to rein in what he viewed as governmental excesses and issued hundreds of executive orders that limited government regulations.[114] He revoked and amended hundreds of executive orders issued by his predecessors.[115] He issued an order that required executive agencies to conduct cost–benefit analysis for all new federal regulations.[116] President Reagan's use of

[106] Exec. Order No. 11246, 30 Fed. Reg. 187 (1965) at 12319.
[107] The Civil Rights Cases, 109 U.S. 3 (1883).
[108] *Id.* at 17.
[109] *Id.*
[110] *Id.* at 9–10.
[111] Proclamation No. 4311, 88 Stat. 2502 (1974).
[112] *Id.*
[113] *Id.*
[114] 1981 Ronald Reagan Executive Orders, FED. REG., www.federalregister.gov/presidential-documents/executive-orders/ronald-reagan/1981. This source is a compilation of President Reagan's executive orders issued in 1981. The website contains both where the executive orders can be found in the Federal Register and links to other webpages for President Reagan's executive orders issued from 1982 to 1989.
[115] *Id.*
[116] Exec. Order 12291, 46 Fed. Reg. 12941 (1981) at 13193.

executive orders demonstrated the perils of leadership through executive actions. Unlike laws passed by Congress, which can only be undone by further action by Congress, a constitutional amendment, or a court order finding them unconstitutional, executive orders can be revoked by a president alone without any action by Congress.

Presidents also have used the power of executive orders to expand the scope and power of the executive branch. In 1979, President Carter issued an executive order that established the Federal Emergency Management Agency (FEMA).[117] The purpose of this order was to reassign and reorganize a number of existing agencies across the executive branch and create a unified federal government response to natural disasters. Similarly, in the aftermath of the September 11, 2001 terrorist attacks, President Bush used an executive order[118] to establish the Office of Homeland Security (OHS) to coordinate the nation's homeland security efforts. In 2002 Congress codified the executive order[119] and renamed the OHS to the Department of Homeland Security (DHS). Today, the DHS has a wide-ranging mission including immigration and customs, managing the Coast Guard, the Secret Service, disaster response, and protecting the US's infrastructure. The scope of DHS's mission has made it the third largest federal agency after the Departments of Defense and Veteran's Affairs, with a proposed budget of over $107 billion for fiscal year 2025.[120]

In the early 2000s, President Bush established Guantanamo Bay Naval Base as a detention facility for suspected enemy combatants in the Global War on Terror. During President Bush's two terms, Guantanamo Bay became a flashpoint for human rights watch groups, as many of the detainees were held without formal charges and weren't afforded the protections of prisoners of war.[121] In his first month in office President Obama issued an executive order[122] ordering the Department of Defense to shut down within a year the detainment sites at Guantanamo Bay. While Congress ultimately would override President Obama's order, citing concerns about what to do with the detainees after the closure of the site, the episode demonstrates the broad power of executive orders to overturn decisions by prior administrations.

The two most recent presidents, Trump and Biden, have used executive orders extensively to fulfill campaign promises. During his 2016 presidential campaign, Trump ran, in part, on a platform of banning all Muslims from entering the United

[117] Exec. Order No. 12127, 44 Fed. Reg. 65 (1979) at 19367–68.

[118] Exec. Order No. 13228, 66 Fed. Reg. 196 (2001) at 51812–17.

[119] Homeland Security Act, 6 USC § 101 *et seq*.

[120] FY 2025 Budget in Brief, Department of Homeland Security, www.dhs.gov/sites/default/files/2024-04/2024_0311_fy_2025_budget_in_brief.pdf.

[121] *See generally* United Nations Commission on Human Rights, Situation of Detainees at Guantanamo Bay: Report of the Chairperson-Rapporteur of the Working Group on Arbitrary Detention (2006).

[122] Exec. Order No. 13493, 74 Fed. Reg. 4901 (2009) at 4901–02.

States.[123] During his first month in office, President Trump issued an executive order that barred people from seven Muslim-majority nations from entering the United States under the Immigration and Nationality Act.[124] While this order drew immediate challenges in court and protests across the country, the Supreme Court ultimately upheld key provisions of the order as constitutional.[125] On his first day in office, President Biden issued his own proclamation[126] overturning the travel ban.

The next battle over presidential power and executive orders came from President Biden's orders cancelling student loan debt.[127] Using a series of executive orders, President Biden attempted to cancel billions of dollars in student loans. While so far none of these orders has survived Supreme Court review, Biden's continued attempts to use executive orders, to bypass Congress and act unilaterally, demonstrate how executive orders can be used to fulfill campaign promises.

Throughout the twentieth and twenty-first centuries, executive orders have evolved from a tool and strategy used by presidents to direct the executive branch to carry out these "orders." This makes the President a quasi-legislator. One view of this expansion of executive orders is that divided government (when one or both houses of Congress are not controlled by the political party of the President) and the rise of partisan warfare in Congress have made them a necessity. Under divided government, presidents can either work with the opposing party in Congress or issue executive orders to achieve their goals. This view is perhaps best illustrated by a statement by President Obama in 2014 when he said, "We are not just going to be waiting for legislation in order to make sure that we're providing Americans the kind of help that they need. I've got a pen, and I've got a phone. And I can use that pen to sign executive orders and take executive actions and administrative actions that move the ball forward."[128]

Table 1.1 is a quantitative study of executive orders in the postwar era. It shows who the President was, which party controlled the House and Senate, whether there was divided government in the executive and legislative branches, and how many executive orders the President issued during each congressional term. As of June 2025 President Trump has issued eighty-six executive orders during his second term.[129] These executive orders cover a range of topics including promoting cryptocurrency and the deportation of immigrants. Others target specific individuals and institutions, including law firms and universities, which raises constitutional concerns.

[123] Saba Hamedy, *Everything You Need to Know about the Travel Ban: A Timeline*, CNN (June 26, 2018, 12:42 PM), www.cnn.com/2018/06/26/politics/timeline-travel-ban/index.html.

[124] Exec. Order No. 13769, 82 Fed. Reg. 8977 (2017) at 8977–82.

[125] Trump v. Hawaii, 585 U.S. 667 (2018).

[126] Proclamation No. 10141, 86 Fed. Reg. 7005 (2021) at 7005–07.

[127] *Supra*, Section 1.1.

[128] Rebecca Kaplan, *Obama: I Will Use My Pen and Phone to Take on Congress*, CBS News (Jan. 14, 2014, 12:44 PM), www.cbsnews.com/news/obama-i-will-use-my-pen-and-phone-to-take-on-congress/.

[129] The White House, Executive Orders, www.whitehouse.gov/presidential-actions/executive-orders.

TABLE 1.1 *Executive orders by president and congressional term*

START	END	PRESIDENT	HOUSE DEMOCRATS	HOUSE REPUBLICANS	SENATE DEMOCRATS	SENATE REPUBLICANS	DIVIDED GOVERNMENT?	EXECUTIVE ORDERS ISSUED
1945	1947	**TRUMAN**	244	189	57	38	NO	287
1947	1949	TRUMAN	188	246	45	51	YES	**217**
1949	1951	**TRUMAN**	263	171	54	42	NO	164
1951	1953	**TRUMAN**	235	199	49	47	NO	233
1953	1955	**EISENHOWER**	213	221	47	48	NO	154
1955	1957	EISENHOWER	232	203	48	47	YES	**109**
1957	1959	EISENHOWER	232	203	49	47	YES	**105**
1959	1961	EISENHOWER	282	153	65	35	YES	**116**
1961	1963	**KENNEDY**	264	173	64	36	NO	159
1963	1965	**KENNEDY/JOHNSON**	258	176	66	36	NO	118
1965	1967	**JOHNSON**	295	140	68	32	NO	131
1967	1969	**JOHNSON**	248	187	64	36	NO	130
1969	1971	NIXON	243	192	57	43	YES	**124**
1971	1973	NIXON	255	180	54	44	YES	**118**
1973	1975	NIXON/FORD	243	192	56	42	YES	**133**
1975	1977	FORD	291	144	61	37	YES	**140**
1977	1979	**CARTER**	292	143	61	38	NO	144
1979	1981	**CARTER**	278	157	58	41	NO	176
1981	1983	REAGAN	243	192	46	53	YES	**113**
1983	1985	REAGAN	269	166	45	55	YES	**98**
1985	1987	REAGAN	254	181	47	53	YES	**82**
1987	1989	REAGAN	258	177	55	45	YES	**88**
1989	1991	HW BUSH	260	175	55	45	YES	**74**
1991	1993	HW BUSH	267	167	56	44	YES	**92**
1993	1995	**CLINTON**	258	176	57	43	NO	111
1995	1997	CLINTON	204	230	48	52	YES	**89**
1997	1999	CLINTON	207	226	45	55	YES	**76**
1999	2001	CLINTON	211	223	45	55	YES	**88**
2001	2003	**BUSH**	212	221	50	50	NO	85
2003	2005	**BUSH**	205	229	48	51	NO	86
2005	2007	**BUSH**	201	233	45	55	NO	53
2007	2009	BUSH	233	202	51	49	YES	**67**
2009	2011	**OBAMA**	257	178	57	41	NO	74
2011	2013	OBAMA	193	242	53	47	YES	**73**
2013	2015	OBAMA	201	234	55	45	YES	51
2015	2017	OBAMA	188	247	46	54	YES	78
2017	2019	**TRUMP**	194	241	49	51	NO	92
2019	2021	TRUMP	235	199	47	53	YES	**128**
2021	2023	**BIDEN**	222	212	50	50	NO	106
2023	2025	BIDEN	213	222	51	49	YES	**32 (as of April, 2024)**

Source: Party Divisions of the House of Representatives, 1789 to Present, UNITED STATES HOUSE OF REPRESENTATIVES, https://history.house.gov/Institution/Party-Divisions/Party-Divisions.

1.3 THE PRESIDENT'S POWER TO APPOINT AND REMOVE EXECUTIVE OFFICERS

A clearer view of the unitary executive theory focusing on the power of the President to remove executive officers is best illustrated in an article, *The President and the Administration*,[130] by Professors Lawrence Lessig and Cass Sunstein. They explore the history of the development of executive agencies, arguing that the Founding generation saw a clear distinction between agencies the President had full control over and quasi-independent or fully independent agencies.

To illustrate this point, Lessig and Sunstein explore the debates in the context of the creation of the Post Office. Unlike the earliest three departments, War, Foreign

[130] Cass R. Sunstein & Lawrence Lessig, *The President and the Administration*, 94 COLUMB. L. REV. 1 (1994).

Affairs, and Treasury, which Congress recognized the President had full control over, the Post Office was treated differently. A reorganization of the Post Office by Congress in 1792 removed language that made the Postmaster General subject to the President's direction. In addition, like the Department of the Treasury, Congress explicitly spelled out how these departments should be organized and described the duties of officers within the branch.

Later, in the aftermath of the Civil War and the assassination of Abraham Lincoln, Congress passed a law to restrict presidential removal power. Lincoln's Vice President, Andrew Johnson, was a Democrat with Southern sympathies but loyal to the Union. He was chosen for the 1864 Republican ticket to unify the country after the Civil War. No one foresaw Lincoln being assassinated and Johnson becoming President as head of a Republican administration. Johnson tried mightily to slow the pace of Reconstruction in the South and he was reluctant to use federal troops to protect former enslaved people from retaliation and discrimination by white Southerners. Standing in Johnson's way was Secretary of War Edwin Stanton, a Republican, who wanted federal troops to implement Lincoln's Reconstruction agenda. Johnson wanted to fire Stanton.

To prevent President Johnson from firing Stanton and other federal officers appointed by Lincoln, Congress passed the Tenure of Office Act[131] prohibiting the President from removing officers of the executive branch without the consent of Congress. Johnson insisted the law was unconstitutional and accordingly he fired Stanton. The House responded by impeaching Johnson, who was tried in the Senate and escaped conviction by a single vote.

But was Johnson right – not in his strong Southern sympathies and opposition to Reconstruction – but in insisting that the Tenure of Office Act was unconstitutional? For decades, this question went unanswered because Congress allowed this law – intended to constrain Johnson more than the office of the presidency itself – to expire in the 1880s.

One view of presidential control of executive agencies is best highlighted in a series of Supreme Court cases beginning with *Myers v. United States.*[132] In 1920 Myers, a mid-level postal service officer, was removed from his office by President Wilson. After his removal, Myers brought a lawsuit arguing that his removal was inconsistent with a nineteenth-century law that allowed the President to appoint postmasters confirmed by the Senate, but as a precondition only allowed for the removal of postmasters with the advice and consent of the Senate. In *Myers*, the Court considered whether the President alone had the power to remove executive branch officers or whether he needs the approval of a legislative body. The Court held that the Constitution's silence on the legislative branch's role in removal was intentional. While the Constitutional Convention had considered giving Congress a

[131] Tenure of Office Act, 14 Stat. 430, ch. 154 (1867).

[132] Myers v. United States, 272 U.S. 52 (1926).

role in presidential removal powers, the Court in *Myers* ultimately decided that the Founders considered removal to be an inherently executive power.[133]

As a matter of public policy, federal employees in the Post Office should not be hired or fired for political reasons. There should not be a Democratic or a Republican way of delivering the mail, and a postmaster once appointed should perhaps remain in place unless dismissed for cause, not fired simply for being affiliated with the wrong political party. The problem was that postmasters at the time were presidential appointees, not career civil servants. In passing this law Congress was restricting the President's power to remove an officer appointed by the President. The Court in *Myers* held that Congress's actions restricting the President was unconstitutional. As for the Tenure of Office Act that led to Johnson's impeachment decades earlier, the Court said that, too, probably had been unconstitutional.[134]

In 1935, the Court distinguished *Myers* by adopting a new test for "quasi-legislative" and "quasi-judicial" agencies in *Humphrey's Executor v. United States.*[135] In 1933, President Roosevelt removed Federal Trade Commission (FTC) member William Humphrey because he viewed him as being insufficiently supportive of Roosevelt's New Deal programs. There was a problem, however. Congress earlier had passed a law providing that FTC commissioners could only be removed for cause for the duration of their terms. President Roosevelt believed this restriction on his removal power was unconstitutional and he fired Humphrey. Humphrey argued his firing was invalid. He continued to work and collect a paycheck. He died while in office (or while out of office in President Roosevelt's view). His estate sued the FTC for his back pay. The Roosevelt administration contested the claim.

By 1935, however, the Supreme Court was outright hostile to the presidency, or at least to President Roosevelt, having ruled unconstitutional much of the early New Deal legislation of President Roosevelt that passed through Congress. In Humphrey's case at the FTC, President Roosevelt was going one step further and unilaterally ignoring a constraint on presidential power imposed by an earlier Congress. Without reversing its ruling in *Myers*, the Court found a way to distinguish the two cases.

In breaking from the President's unlimited removal power in *Myers*, the Court held that Congress may impose limits on the executive removal power when the executive agency is "quasi-legislative" or "quasi-judicial" in nature. According to the Court, these quasi-legislative or quasi-judicial agencies are distinct from typical executive agencies in that they are tasked with more than implementing executive branch policy. Quasi-legislative and quasi-judicial agencies possess a specialized expertise, free from political influence and bias, to assist lawmakers and the judiciary

[133] *Id.* at 119–20.
[134] *Id.*
[135] Humphrey's Executor v. United States, 295 U.S. 602 (1935).

with their duties. Ultimately, because these agencies have the power to act independently of the President, they are not purely executive in nature and Congress can impose limitations on removal of these agencies' members, the Court concluded.

Humphrey's Executor is still controlling law as of the time this book went to press, but President Trump's position is that it should be overturned, and in his second term he has sought to remove members of the Federal Trade Commission, the National Labor Relations Board, and other independent agencies. The Court's logic, however, has not convinced critics – including decades later when Justice Samuel Alito, in 2020, suggested that *Humphrey's Executor* should be overruled.[136] For now, at least, *Humphrey's Executor* is hanging on by a thread, carving out a very narrow exception to presidential removal power that allows Congress to protect the job security of members of multi-member commissions such as the FTC. That holding and its reasoning, however, are fragile and could be reversed in the near term.[137]

In other cases, the Supreme Court reaffirmed presidential removal power, striking down acts of Congress that tried to limit it. These cases involved new agencies set up by Congress in the 2000s to regulate public company accountants and consumer financial services in the wake of financial scandals.

In *Free Enterprise Fund v. Public Company Accounting Oversight Board*,[138] the Supreme Court ruled that the Sarbanes–Oxley Act of 2002 violated the separation of powers doctrine by giving broad powers to the Public Company Accounting Oversight Board while preventing the President from appointing Board members or removing them. (The statute had delegated this power to the Securities and Exchange Commission.)[139] Because there were unique features about this case (Board members and employees were not considered government "officer[s] or employee[s]" under the statute 15 USC §§7211(a), (b)), this perhaps was not the best precedent for measuring presidential removal power in other federal agencies, but it was an indicator of where the Court was going.

In 2020, the Court most recently applied the *Myers* rule in *Seila Law LLC v. Consumer Financial Protection Bureau*.[140] In *Seila*, the Court considered whether the "for cause" removal provision for the director of the Consumer Financial Protection Bureau (CFPB) was a violation of the President's removal powers. The Court reaffirmed the *Humphreys* quasi-legislative and judicial exceptions to the *Myers* rule, but added that Congress may restrain the President's removal power in

[136] *See* Alito, J., concurrence in Seila Law LLC v. Consumer Financial Protection Bureau, et al., 591 U.S. 197 (2020).

[137] *See* Trump v. Wilcox, 605 U.S. ___ (2025) (Granting stay of order from the District Court for the District of Columbia enjoining President Trump's removal of a member of the National Labor Relations Board and a member of the Merit System Protection Board).

[138] Free Enterprise Fund v. Public Company Accounting Oversight Board, 561 U.S. 477 (2010).

[139] Sarbanes–Oxley Act of 2002, Pub. L. No. 107–204, 116 Stat. 745.

[140] Seila Law v. Consumer Financial Protection Bureau, 591 U.S. 197 (2020).

instances where the officer is an inferior officer without policymaking authority and limited duties. However, the Court refused to extend this protection to the sole director of the CFPB, which the Court argued wields significant executive power. While there were sharply differing views on the Court, Chief Justice Roberts, writing for the majority, said:

> The Framers deemed an energetic executive essential to "the protection of the community against foreign attacks," "the steady administration of the laws," "the protection of property," and "the security of liberty." Accordingly, they chose not to bog the Executive down with the "habitual feebleness and dilatoriness" that comes with a "diversity of views and opinions." Instead, they gave the Executive the "[d]ecision, activity, secrecy, and dispatch" that "characterize the proceedings of one man."
>
> ... The resulting constitutional strategy is straightforward: divide power everywhere except for the Presidency, and render the President directly accountable to the people through regular elections. In that scheme, individual executive officials will still wield significant authority, but that authority remains subject to the ongoing supervision and control of the elected President. Through the President's oversight, "the chain of dependence [is] preserved," so that "the lowest officers, the middle grade, and the highest" all "depend, as they ought, on the President, and the President on the community."[141]

Pointing to the Decision of 1789,[142] Justice Kagan in dissent said:

> Blackstone, whose work influenced the Framers on this subject as on others, observed that "every branch" of government "supports and is supported, regulates and is regulated, by the rest." ... So as James Madison stated, the creation of distinct branches "did not mean that these departments ought to have no partial agency in, or no control over the acts of each other ... The majority ... [asserts] that its muscular view of "[t]he President's removal power has long been confirmed by history." But that is not so. The early history – including the fabled Decision of 1789 – shows mostly debate and division about removal authority. And when a "settle[ment of] meaning" at last occurred, it was not on the majority's terms. Instead, it supports wide latitude for Congress to create spheres of administrative independence ... The best view is that the First Congress was "deeply divided" on the President's removal power, and "never squarely addressed" the central issue here.[143]

[141] *Id.* at 472–76 quoting THE FEDERALIST NO. 70 (Hamilton) at 471, citing 1 ANNALS OF CONG. 499 (Madison).

[142] For a recent analysis of Congress's deliberations in 1789 about whether to constrain presidential removal power by statute, *see* Jed H. Shugerman, *The Indecisions of 1789: Inconstant Originalism and Strategic Ambiguity*, 171 UNIV. PENN. L. REV. 753 (2023).

[143] Seila Law LLC v. Consumer Financial Protection Bureau, et al., 591 U.S. 197 (2020) (Justice Kagan, dissenting). For a recent analysis of the opinions clause as a vehicle for giving the President information useful in determining whether to remove a superior officer, *see* Ilan Wurman, *The Original Presidency: A Conception of Administrative Control*, J LEGAL ANALYSIS 16 (2024).

The approach of the majority opinion in *Seila Law* is sometimes described as the "unitary executive theory." The concept is simple: there is one executive branch under one president at a time, and that requires the President to be allowed to remove agency heads and other presidential appointees at will. Congress should not be permitted to tie the President's hands by establishing superior offices within the executive branch where the office holder can only be removed for "cause."[144]

An even more extreme version of the unitary executive theory would allow the President to go further and fire inferior officers, even career employees whose positions are protected by civil service laws such as the Civil Service Reform Act of 1978 and the Pendleton Act of 1883. Thus far the Court has not held these laws providing protections to civil service jobs to be unconstitutional. But challenges are pending before the lower federal courts. Most political appointees, however, can be fired by the President. The President directly can fire superior officers appointed by the President, and the President indirectly can fire inferior officers by ordering the head of the agency to fire them.

The aftermath of *Seila* has opened a number of questions about the scope of executive removal power and the power of the President to shape the administrative state. These issues will continue to be debated because of their impact on the power of the presidency. These questions fundamentally impact foundational aspects of the American experience ranging from the quality of drinking water to the Federal Trade Commission stopping anticompetitive monopolies.

While the history, text, and tradition of the Vesting Clause do not ultimately provide us with a clear answer on the outer limits of presidential authority, they do provide insights. Advocates of a strong unitary executive point to the writings of Hamilton, the language of Article II, and a long tradition of presidents, from Washington to Biden, asserting executive power beyond those outlined in Article II to place control of the executive branch in the President alone. According to this unitary executive theory, this control extends from cabinet heads down to low-level executive branch staffers. On the other hand, proponents of restrained presidential powers look to Madison's Helvidius essays, decisions of the Supreme Court, and the skepticism of the Founding generation to executive power in asserting that presidential control over the executive branch is not absolute.

Evidence of this more nuanced position can be found in the deliberations of the First Congress in 1789 over the creation of the first federal departments, and the Court's decisions through *Humphrey's Executor*, but the Court recently has turned quite sharply in favor of presidential removal power being immutable no matter what Congress says in a statute. *Humphrey's Executor* was ninety years ago and rests on very thin ice in today's Supreme Court. The Court's 2020 decision in *Seila* blocked Congress from protecting the tenure of the director of a supposedly independent

[144] Steven G. Calabresi & Christopher S. Yoo, The Unitary Executive: Presidential Power from Washington to Bush 4–9 (2008).

agency, the Consumer Financial Protection Bureau. *Seila* was cited again by the Court in 2024 in *Trump v. United States*, the immunity case, ominously implying that a President might not be subject to prosecution if he removed a federal officer as part of a criminal conspiracy. Ultimately the law today favors the view of a very powerful, and nearly unitary, executive. The independent commissions – the Federal Trade Commission (FTC), Securities and Exchange Commission (SEC), Federal Election Commission (FEC), Federal Communications Commission (FCC), and others – are the remaining area of the Executive Branch where presidents supposedly are not allowed to remove their own appointees without cause until their statutory term has expired. Whether that will remain so – now that President Trump is sending test cases toward the Supreme Court by trying to fire members of both the FTC and National Labor Relations Board (NLRB) – remains to be seen.[145] At this writing, it seems highly likely this issue will be decided by the Court in Trump's second term.

1.4 PRESIDENTIAL APPOINTMENTS AND "ADVISE AND CONSENT"

The Constitution, Article II, Section 2, Clause 2, provides that the President:

> shall nominate, and by and with the Advice and Consent of the Senate, shall appoint Ambassadors, other public Ministers and Consuls, Judges of the supreme Court, and all other Officers of the United States, whose Appointments are not herein otherwise provided for, and which shall be established by Law: but the Congress may by Law vest the Appointment of such inferior Officers, as they think proper, in the President alone, in the Courts of Law, or in the Heads of Departments.

Nomination and confirmation of judges are addressed elsewhere in this book. The focus in this section is on nominations and confirmations of "Officers of the United States" in the Executive Branch.[146] Principal officers can only be appointed with advice and consent of the Senate, whereas Congress may give the President – or the departmental heads or the judiciary – the power to appoint inferior officers.

[145] *See* Trump v. Wilcox, 605 U.S. ___ (2025) supra (allowing President Trump to remove a NLRB member temporarily while the Court rules on the constitutionality of statutory mandated terms for members of the NLRB and other independent commissions). For a more general discussion of the underlying issue of the President's power to control the executive branch, *see* THE FEDERALIST NO. 67–77; FARBER, *supra* note 13 at 3–8, 14, 26, 31, 36–38, 41–43, 41–51, 49–53; BRANDS, *supra* note 20 at 18, 77, 111–12, 195; SAIKRISHNA BANGALORE PRAKASH, THE LIVING PRESIDENCY 15–40 (1st ed. 2020) at 29–30, 42; HEIDI KITROSSER, RECLAIMING ACCOUNTABILITY: TRANSPARENCY, EXECUTIVE POWER, AND THE U.S. CONSTITUTION at 3, 10, 14, 15, 205 (2015); Shane, *supra* note 32 at x, xi, 6–10, 8, 17, 46, 63, 81, 109, 137. *But see* Trump v. United States, 603 U.S. 593 (2024).

[146] *See* Jennifer Mascott, *Who Are "Officers of the United States"?* 70 STAN. L. REV. 443 (2018); Officers of the United States within the Meaning of the Appointments Clause, 31 Op. O.L.C. 73, 77 (2007) (an officer is an official who "hold[s] a position with delegated sovereign authority" and whose office was "continuing," rather than "incidental" or "ad hoc").

Article II, Section 2, Clause 1 refers to "principal officers." It states that the President may require the written opinion of "the principal Officer in each of the executive Departments," on subjects relating to the duties of their respective offices.

The Constitution, however, does not provide explicit guidance on the difference between a principal officer and an inferior officer. As the Court explained in 1988 in *Morrison v. Olson*:[147] "The line between 'inferior' and 'principal' officers is one that is far from clear, and the Framers provided little guidance into where it should be drawn."[148] The Supreme Court later held that an inferior officer is an officer "whose work is directed and supervised at some level by others who were appointed by Presidential nomination with the Senate's advice and consent."[149]

The Senate confirmation process for a principal officer is a critically important check on abuse of presidential power. As Chief Justice Roberts explains:

> The Senate's advice and consent power is a critical "structural safeguard … of the constitutional scheme."[150] The Framers envisioned it as "an excellent check upon a spirit of favoritism in the President" and a guard against "the appointment of unfit characters … from family connection, from personal attachment, or from a view to popularity."[151]

But presidents cannot always get their chosen nominees confirmed by the Senate. It is here that presidents look to other options.

1.4.1 *Recess Appointments*

Article II, Section 2, Clause 3 of the Constitution provides: "The President shall have Power to fill up all Vacancies that may happen during the Recess of the Senate, by granting Commissions which shall expire at the End of their next Session."

Two issues arise. First, when is there a "Recess of the Senate"? Between biennial elections, the Senate has two annual sessions with a recess in between during late December and early January. But the Senate can also go into recess during a session.

[147] Morrison v. Olson, 487 U.S. 654, 671 (1988) (upholding the constitutionality of the Independent Counsel law, observing that the independent counsel was an inferior officer who could not be removed by the President).

[148] *See e.g.* 2 J. Story, Commentaries on the Constitution §1536, pp. 397–98 (3d ed. 1858) ("In the practical course of the government, there does not seem to have been any exact line drawn, who are and who are not to be deemed *inferior* officers, in the sense of the constitution, whose appointment does not necessarily require the concurrence of the senate").

[149] Edmond v. United States, 520 U.S. 651, 652 (1997). *But see* Morrison v. Olson, 487 U.S. 654, 722 (Scalia, J, dissenting) (stating that even an officer who is subordinate to a department head – in the case an Independent Counsel – can be a principal officer.)

[150] Edmond v. United States, 520 U.S. 651, 659 (1997).

[151] The Federalist No. 76, p. 457 (C. Rossiter ed. 1961) (A. Hamilton); National Labor Relations Board v. SW General, Inc, 580 U.S. 288 (2017) (opinion by Chief Justice Roberts).

In *National Labor Relations Board v. Noel Canning*[152] the Court, with three dissenting justices, held that the phrase "recess" in the Recess Appointments Clause applies to both types of recesses. The Court also held that a recess of fewer than ten days is presumptively too short to allow the President to make an appointment under the clause.[153]

For purposes of the Recess Appointments Clause, if the Senate says that it is in session and not in recess under its own rules the Court will defer, because the Constitution provides that "Each House may determine the Rules of its Proceedings."[154] In *Noel Canning*, between December 2011 and the end of January 2012, the Senate met in very brief pro forma sessions every three business days, with almost no senators present, meaning there would be no recess. The Obama administration argued that these pro forma sessions were illusory and that the President could make recess appointments. But the Supreme Court in *Noel Canning* unanimously rejected this argument, saying it was up to each House of Congress to determine whether it is in session or in recess.

1.4.2 *Can the President and the House Force a Recess of the Senate?*

Article II, Section 3 of the Constitution provides that the President may "on extraordinary Occasions, convene both Houses, or either of them, and in Case of Disagreement between them, with Respect to the Time of Adjournment, he may adjourn them to such Time as he shall think proper."

The focus here is not on the power of the President to convene both Houses on extraordinary occasions, but on the power to adjourn. If there is a disagreement between the House and Senate with respect to the time of adjournment, can the President simply adjourn them for as long as he wants for whatever reason, including to make recess appointments? Can the President, with only the House voting for adjournment, simply adjourn *both* Houses of Congress until such time as the President requests them back? The implications of such a maneuver for representative democracy are dire for many reasons. No President has ever used this power under Article II; this possibility will be discussed here because it apparently was contemplated for early 2025 to enable recess appointments by President Trump.

Edward Whelan, a former Justice Department lawyer under President George W. Bush and a conservative commentator, expressed consternation and alarm at this idea. Writing in the *Washington Post*, he observed that House Speaker "Mike Johnson should not be complicit in eviscerating the Senate's advice-and-consent

[152] 573 U.S. 513 at 522–50 (2014).
[153] *Id.*
[154] National Labor Relations Board v. Noel Canning, 573 U.S. 513 (2014), at 55 quoting U.S. Const. Article I, Section 5, Clause 2.

role. He should promptly make clear that the House will abide by its usual schedule of recesses and will not attempt to engineer a recess of the Senate."[155]

Even if the House can do this, in effect allowing the President to adjourn the legislative branch, potentially indefinitely, it would be extraordinarily dangerous to do so. Whether the intent is to enable recess appointments or for any other reason. This kind of adjournment is not so different from the modus operandi of aspiring dictators or strongman leaders who adjourn the legislature to take whatever unilateral action they like.

The Supreme Court, however, might invalidate recess appointments made under such circumstances. Recall that in *National Labor Relations Board v. Noel Canning*,[156] the Court in 2014 held that the Recess Appointments Clause allows appointments when recesses occur during sessions of Congress as well as recesses between the two sessions. But the Court also said that it was deferring to the Senate's determination of when it was in recess *under its own rules* because "Each House may determine the Rules of its Proceedings." An adjournment of the Senate forced by the President, after the House votes to adjourn under pressure from the President, is *not* a recess under the Senate's own rules.

Furthermore, Justice Scalia authored a powerful concurring opinion in *Noel Canning*, joined by Justices Thomas and Alito, stating that they would restrict the President's recess appointments even more than the majority and only allow the appointments in the recess between sessions. Based on the plain language of the Constitution and its history, Scalia wrote: "I would hold that 'the Recess' is the gap between sessions and that the appointments at issue here are invalid because they undisputedly were made during the Senate's session."[157]

Justice Scalia went on to observe:

> All Presidents have a high interest in expanding the powers of their office, since the more power the President can wield, the more effectively he can implement his political agenda. . . . And when the President wants to assert a power and establish a precedent, he faces neither the collective-action problems nor the procedural inertia inherent in the legislative process. The majority's methodology thus all but guarantees the continuing aggrandizement of the Executive Branch.[158]

Justice Scalia has passed away, but Justices Alito and Thomas remain. Would they be of the same opinion when the "recess appointments" the Court is asked to invalidate are not those of President Obama, but appointments by a Republican president during a recess of the Senate?

[155] Edward Whelan, *Mike Johnson Must Block Trump's Scheme on Recess Appointments*, Washington Post (Nov. 14, 2024), www.washingtonpost.com/opinions/2024/11/14/trump-gaetz-cabinet-appointment-johnson/.

[156] National Labor Relations Board v. Noel Canning, 573 U.S. 513 (2014).

[157] *Id.* (Scalia J, concurring).

[158] *Id.*

1.4.3 *Acting Appointments*

The President sometimes appoints persons to temporarily hold offices, including offices requiring presidential appointment and Senate confirmation (PAS offices). This is done so the duties of those offices can be performed while another officer awaits nomination and confirmation by the Senate. These appointments are different from recess appointments and can be made whether or not Congress is in recess.

The Vacancies Act of 1868 increased the number of PAS offices that the President could fill with acting officials.[159] Congress amended the Vacancies Act in 1988.[160] Finally, in 1998 Congress replaced the Vacancies Act with the Federal Vacancies Reform Act of 1998 (FVRA).[161]

The FVRA permits the President to choose from among three categories of officials to temporarily to fill a vacant PAS office: (1) the first assistant to the vacant office; (2) a person who already serves in another PAS office; and (3) a person who has served in a senior position in the same agency for at least ninety days within the year preceding the vacancy.[162]

A person may not be appointed as an acting officer if the President also nominates that person for the same vacant PAS office and the person did not serve in the position of first assistant for at least ninety days.[163] This means that the President cannot simply fill the office with his nominee serving in an acting capacity pending Senate confirmation. The President must choose someone else.

The question presented in *National Labor Relations Board v. SW General, Inc.*[164] was "whether that limitation applies only to first assistants who have automatically assumed acting duties, or whether it also applies to PAS officers and senior employees serving as acting officers at the President's behest." The Court held that this restriction in the FVRA "applies to all three categories of acting officers."[165] In short, the President must choose someone other than his nominee for Senate confirmation to be the acting official.

The FVRA also establishes a time limit on acting service of "210 days beginning on the date the vacancy occurs"; but tolls that time limit while a nomination is pending. A new 210-day time limit starts if the nomination is "rejected, withdrawn, or returned."[166] If the President nominates another person for the position, the acting officer can serve while the nomination is pending in the Senate plus an

159 Act of July 23, 1868, ch. 227, 15 Stat. 168.

160 Presidential Transitions Effectiveness Act, §7, 102 Stat. 988 (1988), amending 5 U.S.C. § 3348.

161 5 U.S.C. § 3345 *et seq.* (1998).

162 5 U.S.C. § 3345.

163 *Id.*

164 NLRB v. SW General, Inc., 580 U.S. 288 (2017).

165 *Id.* (holding that a person became "ineligible to serve as Acting General Counsel [of the NLRB] once the President nominated him to be General Counsel").

166 5 U.S.C. §§ 3346(a)–(b)(1).

additional 210 days if the second nomination is rejected, withdrawn, or returned.[167] This construct means that for practical purposes, the President can indefinitely fill PAS positions with acting officers, so long as the acting officer is chosen from among those persons eligible under the FVRA and a nomination of a different person is pending with the Senate or there are no more than 210 days between nominations.

This statutory scheme creates an unfortunate loophole for a President who wants to fill vacancies with people whom the Senate is not willing to confirm. This practice of appointing acting officials for lengthy periods of service, while technically permissible under FVRA, undermines the constitutional intent in requiring advice and consent of the Senate. As Chief Justice Roberts explains in *National Labor Relations Board v. SW General, Inc.*, quoted at the beginning of this section, the Framers did not intend to allow the President to fill a principal office with anyone he pleases.

In summary, as recess appointments and acting appointments are being hotly debated following President Trump's reelection in 2024 as a way to circumvent the constitutional role of the Senate in the confirmation process to "advise and consent," we should remember the Founders' fear that too powerful a President could interfere with the carefully planned checks and balances system envisioned in the Constitution. Is the Senate on the verge of forgoing and abdicating its Senate prerogative and constitutional duties in the confirmation process?[168]

1.4.4 *Federal Advisory Committees and Other Appointments of Persons outside the Government*

Sometimes the President would like to rely on the advice of people who were successful in their careers outside the government and want to stay outside the government. This may be because they have too many private sector commitments to accept a presidential appointment or because they do not want to divest from business interests creating conflicts of interest prohibited under federal ethics laws.[169]

[167] *Id.* § 3346(b)(2).

[168] David French, *Donald Trump Thinks He Won't Have Enough Power*, New York Times (Nov. 11, 2024), www.nytimes.com/2024/11/24/opinion/trump-recess-appointments-constitution.html (citing The Federalist No. 1 (Hamilton), "Of those men who have overturned the liberties of republics, the greatest number have begun their career by paying an obsequious court to the people; commencing demagogues, and ending tyrants"; The Federalist No. 76 (Hamilton), "[Senate confirmation] would be an excellent check upon a spirit of favoritism in the President, and would tend greatly to prevent the appointment of unfit characters from State prejudice, from family connection, from personal attachment, or from a view of popularity." "French supra."

[169] *See e.g.* 18 U.S.C. Section 208 (imposing criminal penalties on federal officials who participate in matters affecting their own financial interests).

Some presidents have relied in part on advice from an informal "kitchen cabinet" of friends and supporters from outside the government. Provided such consultations are informal and are not held on a regular basis, and provided these advisors do not perform the functions of federal employees, these consultations are permissible without the advisors actually becoming federal employees, subject to specific Federal Advisory Committee Act (FACA) ethics rules and laws.

More formalized arrangements involving advisors from outside the government can be established under the 1972 FACA.[170] These committees can include private sector members who are not federal employees. These private sector committee members thus are not subject to the financial conflict of interest laws, ethics laws, and other requirements for federal employees. FACA, however, requires open meetings, meetings scheduled in advance to allow public involvement, disclosure of work product and reporting by the committee.[171] Presidents and their private sector advisors do not always like these restrictions and have sometimes tried to find ways to involve private sector advisors without forming a committee governed under FACA.

Some commentators believe that FACA is unconstitutional. Jay Bybee, who later became a Justice Department lawyer[172] and then a federal judge, in 1994 wrote that "[p]roperly construed, FACA violates separation of powers by limiting the terms on which the President can acquire information from nongovernmental advisory committees."[173]

In 1982, President Reagan established the President's Private Sector Survey on Cost Control in the Federal Government, under the leadership of businessman J. Peter Grace (the "Grace Commission). Reagan's Executive Order[174] specifically stated that the Grace Commission was being established under FACA. Mr. Grace oversaw a group of over 100 business leaders who volunteered their time with the Commission's Task Forces that recommended cost-cutting measures in the government.

Not all private sector committees advising the President are covered by FACA. In *Public Citizen v. Department of Justice*,[175] the Supreme Court in 1989 ruled that an American Bar Association (ABA) Committee that advised the Justice Department on appointment of federal judges was not a federal advisory committee and did not have to meet the requirements of FACA. Even if a literal reading of the statute might suggest that it covered the ABA Committee, the Court, in an opinion by Justice

[170] Federal Advisory Committee Act (FACA) is Pub. L. 92–463, § 1, Oct. 6, 1972, 86 Stat. 770.

[171] *Id.*

[172] While serving as a lawyer in the Justice Department, Bybee demonstrated his embrace of presidential power in a more ominous area by signing his name to some of the "torture memos" discussed in Chapter 3, Section 3.6 on presidential power.

[173] Jay S. Bybee, *Advising the President: Separation of Powers and the Federal Advisory Committee Act*, 101 YALE L.J., 51, 54 (1994–95).

[174] Executive Order 12369 (June 30, 1982).

[175] 491 U.S. 440 (1989).

Brennan, observed that the intent of FACA was to "cure specific ills, above all the wasteful expenditure of public funds for worthless committee meetings and biased proposals; although its reach is extensive, we cannot believe that it was intended to cover every formal and informal consultation between the President or an Executive agency and a group rendering advice."[176] Justice Kennedy, in a concurrence, disagreed. He found that the language of FACA did include advisory bodies such as the ABA Committee, but that applying FACA in this context was unconstitutional under the Appointments Clause because it interfered with the President's discretion in exercising his power to appoint federal judges.[177]

In 1993, President Clinton established the President's Task Force on National Health Care Reform and named his wife, Hillary Clinton, as the chair of the Task Force. The Task Force sought to keep its records secret from the public, fearful that the health insurance industry would lobby Congress against its proposals even before they were announced. The Task Force's proposals in 1994 were rejected by Congress in part for this reason. Besides Hillary Clinton, all the other members of the Task Force were federal officers. The Court of Appeals for the District of Columbia Circuit, in *Ass'n of Am. Physicians Surgeons v. Clinton*,[178] held that the Task Force was not a FACA merely on account of Hillary Clinton's participation because she, as First Lady, also functioned as a federal employee for this purpose.

Days after being elected to a second term as the 47th President, Donald Trump announced a "Department of Government Efficiency" (DOGE) under the leadership of Elon Musk, who had played an important role in the campaign that returned Trump to the presidency, and another billionaire businessman, Vivek Ramaswamy, who had run for President against Trump in the Republican primary but later endorsed Trump. The Trump transition team announcement said that, despite the odd choice of the label "Department," the entity would be outside the government.[179] This was probably necessitated by Musk and Ramaswamy both seeking to avoid the divestiture of financial assets that would be required for them to comply with ethics rules were they to enter the government as presidential appointees. If so, however, DOGE will very likely be required to function as a FACA, including the need to have public meetings and records. The Trump administration, however, could refuse to comply with these transparency requirements and other provisions of FACA. Instead it could go to court to argue that FACA is an unconstitutional constraint on the President's ability to get private sector advice in the performance

[176] *Id.* at 453.

[177] *Id.* at 469 (Justice Kennedy concurring).

[178] 997 F.2d 898 (D.C. Cir. 1993).

[179] Trump–Vance Transition, Statement from President Donald J. Trump, November 12, 2024 (stating that "the Department of Government Efficiency will provide advice and guidance from outside the Government and will partner with the White House and Office of Management & Budget to drive large scale structural reform, and create an entrepreneurial approach to government never seen before").

of official duties under Article II. The argument that Jay Bybee made over thirty years ago, that FACA is unconstitutional, could become soon a question presented to the Supreme Court. With the acrimonious departure of Elon Musk from the Trump administration in May 2025, and Ramaswamy having bowed out of DOGE months earlier to run for governor of Ohio, the Trump administration shifted gears yet again and brought DOGE inside the Executive Office of the President. FACA will still apply, however, if DOGE includes advisors from outside the government.

1.5 REMOVAL OF FEDERAL PROSECUTORS

Removal of federal prosecutors presents unique challenges. Prosecution of crimes should not be partisan. Indeed prosecutors' ethics rules specifically prohibit politics being factored into prosecutorial decisions.[180] The Department of Justice (DOJ), however, is appointed by and under the control of the President. What can Congress do to prevent a President from firing a prosecutor for investigating the President?

In October 1973, during the infamous "Saturday Night Massacre," President Nixon ordered the firing of Watergate Special Prosecutor Archibald Cox.[181] Nixon was angry at Cox for issuing a subpoena for the White House tapes. Special Prosecutor Cox was not a superior officer appointed by the President, so Nixon ordered the Attorney General to fire him. Attorney General Elliott Richardson refused, as did Deputy Attorney General William Ruckelshaus, who both resigned rather than be fired for insubordination. Solicitor General Robert Bork became the Acting Attorney General. He fired Cox on Nixon's orders.

The House threatened to impeach Nixon.[182] Shortly after he allowed the DOJ to install another special prosecutor, Leon Jaworski, and then the Supreme Court ordered Nixon to hand over the same tapes.[183] Congress responded to the Watergate crisis with the Ethics in Government Act of 1978.[184] A key provision of that law was the Independent Counsel statute, creating an Office of Independent Counsel within the DOJ, that would not be supervised by the Attorney General but by a three-judge panel of the United States Court of Appeals for the District of Columbia Circuit. The law specifically allowed removal of the independent

[180] United States Department of Justice, Justice Manual, Principles of Federal Prosecution, Title IX, § 9-27.260, www.justice.gov/jm/jm-9-27000-principles-federal-prosecution – Initiating and Declining Charges – Impermissible Considerations "In determining whether to commence or recommend prosecution or take other action against a person, the attorney for the government may not be influenced by: 1. The person's race, religion, gender, ethnicity, national origin, sexual orientation, or political association, activities, or beliefs."

[181] Cox was not a principal officer appointed by the President, rather an inferior officer serving under the supervision of the Attorney General, a distinction made in the Appointments Clause of the Constitution. *See* Douglas Kneeland, *Nixon Discharges Cox for Defiance; Abolishes Watergate Task Force; Richardson and Ruckelhaus Out*, New York Times (Oct. 20, 1973).

[182] Jules Witcover, *Pressure for Impeachment Mounting*, Washington Post (Oct. 21, 1973), at A01.

[183] United States v. Nixon, 418 U.S. 683 (1974).

[184] Ethics in Government Act of 1978, Pub. L. 95-521.

counsel by the Attorney General only for "good cause." The President could not simply fire the independent counsel.

This law was in direct conflict with the unitary executive theory – the view that the President, as head of the entire Executive Branch, has an absolute right to remove a superior federal officer as well as to order a superior federal officer to fire an inferior federal officer. But could Congress carve out a statutory exception for a special prosecutor who is investigating the President?

In an 8–1 ruling, the Supreme Court answered this question in *Morrison v. Olson*[185] – reasoning that the Office of the Independent Counsel was an exception to the unitary executive theory. Congress, the Court said, had the power to protect the Special Counsel from dismissal upon orders of the President:

> This case does not involve an attempt by Congress itself to gain a role in the removal of executive officials other than its established powers of impeachment and conviction. The Act instead puts the removal power squarely in the hands of the Executive Branch; an independent counsel may be removed from office "only by the personal action of the Attorney General, and only for good cause."[186]

Justice Scalia, in dissent, argued:

> This is what this suit is about. Power. The allocation of power among Congress, the President, and the courts in such fashion as to preserve the equilibrium the Constitution sought to establish – so that "a gradual concentration of the several powers in the same department," can effectively be resisted. Frequently an issue of this sort will come before the Court clad, so to speak, in sheep's clothing: the potential of the asserted principle to effect important change in the equilibrium of power is not immediately evident, and must be discerned by a careful and perceptive analysis. But this wolf comes as a wolf.[187]

The Supreme Court has changed substantially in the thirty-five years since the *Morrison* holding. The Court might not rule the same way today. Even some liberal-leaning constitutional law experts, including Professor Akhil Amar, have suggested that Justice Scalia may have been right.[188]

The Court has not decided the issue again. After the Clinton investigation by Independent Counsel Kenneth Starr, the votes just weren't there in Congress to renew the Independent Counsel statute. It expired in 1999.[189] The DOJ, through the

[185] Morrison v. Olson, 487 U.S. 654 (1988).

[186] United States v. Nixon, 418 U.S. 683 (1974) at 686.

[187] *Id.* at 699, citing FEDERALIST NO. 51, p. 321 (J. Madison).

[188] *See Special Counsels and the Separation of Powers: Hearing before the Comm. on the Judiciary*, 115th Cong. 1–2 (2017) (statement of Akhil Reed Amar, Sterling Professor of Law and Political Science, Yale Law School, stating, among other things, that a proposed bill protecting Special Counsel Mueller from being fired by Trump would be unconstitutional).

[189] Ethics in Government Act of 1978, Pub. L. 95-521.

Attorney General, reverted to the Watergate-era practice of appointing special counsels for investigations of presidents, among others.

But as the Attorney General can appoint a special counsel at any time, so too can the Attorney General fire them at any time. Americans were reminded of this point during 2017 and 2018 when President Trump constantly berated his Attorney General, Jeff Sessions, whom he appointed, for refusing to fire special counsel Robert Mueller or to interfere with Mueller's investigations of Russia's interference in the 2016 election. Americans were again reminded of this removal power when, after the 2024 election, Special Counsel Jack Smith dropped both criminal indictments he had filed against Donald Trump, and then resigned his position before Trump was inaugurated in January 2025. It was obvious that if Smith had not done so, he would have been fired on or shortly after Inauguration Day by President Trump's new Attorney General.

We will return to this problem later in this book in Part III on presidential accountability. Without an Independent Counsel statute, it may be very difficult for the justice system to hold a president accountable. And today, with a Supreme Court ever more committed to the unitary executive theory, there is genuine doubt about whether such a law, even if again enacted by Congress, would be held constitutional.

Putting aside independent and special counsels, the question remains whether the ninety-three United States attorneys around the country who are appointed by the President can be removed. Can they be removed for any reason? The answer, apparently, is yes. United States attorneys do not serve for a fixed term and Congress has not tried to restrict their removal. If Congress were to do so, presidents would no doubt challenge the law under a separation of powers theory.

The question is whether the United States Attorney is more like the agency head in *Free Enterprise Fund* and *Seila Law*, who can be removed by the President at will, regardless of what Congress says. Or, is a United States attorney more like the independent counsel in *Morrison v. Olson*, to whom the Court – at least then – said Congress could authorize job protection? Also, there is the elusive question, discussed earlier, whether the Supreme Court today would agree with *Morrison*, which was decided almost forty years ago.

Under at least three recent presidents – Clinton, George W. Bush, and Trump – firings of United States attorneys have been controversial. Clinton fired all the United States attorneys upon becoming President in 1993, leading to charges that he was politicizing the prosecutorial process. Clinton also replaced most agency heads and political appointees in other agencies. Some thought the changeover in United States attorneys' offices appeared too political for the prosecutorial role.

President George W. Bush dismissed a handful of United States attorneys who were his own appointees after several Republican senators complained about the

United States attorneys not taking "election fraud" prosecutions seriously. The unitary executive theory has never been challenged in the context of United States attorneys' firings – but that did not stop Congress from demanding answers. Attorney General Alberto Gonzales gave incomplete testimony before Congress on the firings. Democrats in Congress claimed he lied to them, leading to his resignation.[190] Later, in Section III of this book, we expand on the theme of how Congress can hold presidents accountable. This was an instance where that appears to have worked. The President could fire United States attorneys for any reason, but Congress could demand to know why, and insist on truthful answers.

But what if a United States attorney is removed by the President to stop a particular investigation when the investigation also involves the President? At a certain point, firing the prosecutor might be "obstruction of justice." Can the President do it anyway?

In June 2020, President Trump fired Geoffrey Berman, United States Attorney for the Southern District of New York.[191] Berman's office at the time was investigating Rudy Giuliani and Lev Parnas,[192] Jeffrey Epstein and Prince Andrew,[193] Deutsche Bank's loans to Trump,[194] Halkbank, a Turkish government-owned bank that Trump had discussed with Turkish President Recep Tayyip Erdogan;[195] Trump's presidential inauguration committee's finances;[196] obstruction of justice by the

[190] *Attorney General Gonzales Resigns*, ABC News (Jan. 8, 2009, 12:06 AM), https://abcnews.go.com/TheLaw/Politics/story?id=3421219&page=1.

[191] *See* Claire O. Finkelstein & Richard W. Painter, *"You're Fired": Criminal Use of Presidential Removal Power*, 25 N.Y. Univ. J. of Leg. & Pub. Policy (2023); *See also* Claire O. Finkelstein & Richard W. Painter, *This Friday Night Massacre Spells the End of William Barr*, Newsweek (June 23, 2020, 5:08 PM), www.newsweek.com/friday-night-massacre-spells-downfall-william-barr-opinion-1512935 (discussing the firing of United States Attorney Geoffrey Berman).

[192] *See* Rosalind S. Helderman & Tom Hamburger, *As Impeachment Trial Ended, Federal Prosecutors Took New Steps in Probe Related to Giuliani, According to People Familiar with Case*, Wash. Post. (Feb. 14, 2020, 11:00 PM), www.washingtonpost.com/politics/as-impeachment-trial-ended-federal-prosecutors-took-new-steps-in-probe-related-to-giuliani-according-to-people-familiar-with-case/2020/02/14/7893bfb0-4e8a-11ea-bf44-f5043eb3918a_story.html.

[193] *See* Statement of U.S. Attorney Geoffrey S. Berman Responding to Statement Issued Today by Law Firm Representing Prince Andrew, Department of Justice (June 8, 2020), www.justice.gov/usao-sdny/pr/statement-us-attorney-geoffrey-s-berman-responding-statement-issued-today-law-firm.

[194] *See* Michael Riccardi & Jane Wester, *Geoffrey Berman Resigns as Manhattan US Attorney, Ending Standoff With William Barr*, Law.com (June 20, 2020), www.law.com/newyorklawjournal/2020/06/20/uncharted-waters-standoff-looms-after-purported-ouster-of-geoffrey-berman-as-us-attorney-in-manhattan/?slreturn=20250618213257.

[195] Alexander Mallin, *Bolton Suggests Possible "Obstruction" by Trump in SDNY Turkey Investigation*, ABC News (June 20, 2020), https://abcnews.go.com/Politics/bolton-suggests-obstruction-trump-sdny-turkey-investigation/story?id=71362785.

[196] Kenneth P. Vogel & William K. Rashbaum, *Donor to Trump Inauguration Charged with Obstructing Investigation*, New York Times (Jan. 7, 2020), www.nytimes.com/2020/01/07/us/politics/imaad-zuberi-trump-inauguration.html.

Russian agent who had visited Trump Tower in 2016;[197] and payoffs to porn star Stormy Daniels by "Individual-1," aka Donald Trump.[198]

After he was fired, Berman wrote a book about his experience. He said that he was pressured to prosecute former Secretary of State John Kerry on a weak accusation that Kerry had violated the Logan Act prohibiting carrying on unauthorized diplomatic relations with foreign nations.[199] Berman said DOJ political appointees told him that "it's time for you guys to even things out and indict a Democrat before the midterm election."[200] Berman refused.[201]

Is removal of a prosecutor to obstruct an investigation itself a crime?[202] A president, and persons acting on the orders of a president, presumably should be subject to criminal law like everyone else, or so most Americans thought before 2024.[203] For example, the President has the power to remove a prosecutor, but if he does so in exchange for a bribe, he commits the crime of bribery.[204] If the President removes the prosecutor to obstruct an investigation, particularly of the President himself or of the President's close associates, he could violate the obstruction justice statute. This statute imposes criminal penalties on "[w]hoever corruptly … obstructs, influences, or impedes any official proceeding, or attempts to do so."[205]

197 Statement, United States Attorney's Office for the Southern District of New York, Russian Attorney Natalya Veselnitskaya Charged with Obstruction of Justice in Connection with Civil Money Laundering and Forfeiture Action, (Jan. 8, 2019), www.justice.gov/usao-sdny/pr/russian-attorney-natalya-veselnitskaya-charged-obstruction-justice-connection-civil.

198 Grace Panetta, *Michael Cohen Says There Is an Investigation Regarding Trump That Has Not Been Publicly Disclosed*, Business Insider (Feb. 27, 2019, 1:15 PM), www.businessinsider.com/michael-cohen-testimony-prosecutors-sdny-trump-investigation-2019-2.

199 Geoff Berman, Holding the Line: Inside the Nation's Preeminent U.S. Attorney's Office and Its Battle with the Trump Justice Department (2022).

200 George Stephanopoulos & Aaron Katersky, *Justice Department Pressured Former U.S. Attorney to Bring Cases against Trump Enemies, Geoffrey Berman Says*, ABC News (Sept. 12, 2022, 9:20 AM), https://abcnews.go.com/Politics/justice-department-pressured-us-attorney-bring-cases-trump/story?id = 89745338.

201 *Id.*

202 One of the authors of this book, Professor Richard Painter, and Professor Claire Finkelstein have argued that it can be a crime if the removal amounts to obstruction of justice. *See* Finkelstein & Painter, *supra* note 191.

203 Black's Law Dictionary 1448 (9th ed. 2009) (Defining "rule of law" as the doctrine that every person is subject to the ordinary law within the jurisdiction). *See also* Tom Bingham, The Rule of Law, 3–10, 55–56 (2010); Brian Z. Tamanaha, On the Rule of Law: History, Politics, Theory, 3–60, 91–102, 137 (2004); Jothie Rajah, Authoritarian rule of Law: Legislation, Discourse, and Legitimacy (2012); Building the Rule of Law: Firsthand Accounts from a Thirty-Year Global Campaign (James R. Silkenat & Gerold W. Libby eds., 2021). *But see* Trump v. United States, 603 U.S. 593 (2024).

204 *See* 18 U.S.C. §201 – Bribery of Public Officials and Witnesses

205 18 U.S. Code §1512(c) ("Whoever *corruptly* – (1) alters, destroys, mutilates, or conceals a record, document, or other object, or attempts to do so, with the intent to impair the object's integrity or availability for use in an official proceeding; or (2) *otherwise obstructs, influences, or impedes any official proceeding,* or attempts to do so, shall be fined under this title or imprisoned not more than 20 years, or both" (emphasis added)).

Only an extreme version of the unitary executive theory would posit that presidential removal power is so broad that the President can commit a crime with immunity and be free from prosecution. But then again, President Nixon famously said that "if the President does it, it's not a crime."[206] We discuss later in Section III of this book a different case in which a former president, in *United States v. Trump* successfully made an analogous immunity argument before the Supreme Court in early 2024.

1.6 OTHER REMOVALS

We consider next "retaliatory" firings of whistleblowers after a president is impeached by the House and survives a trial in the Senate. In 2020, Trump fired the United States Ambassador to the European Union, Gordon Sondland, a witness against him in the House impeachment hearing over the Ukraine scandal.[207] Michael Atkinson, the Inspector General of the intelligence community, was fired because he told Congress about the whistleblower complaint that led to Trump's impeachment.[208] Inspectors general are required by law to report credible whistleblower complaints to Congress,[209] so Atkinson was fired for doing his job. Nonetheless, Atkinson's dismissal had the explicit approval of Attorney General William Barr.[210] Trump also fired agency inspectors general including Mitch Behm (Department of Transportation), Glenn Fine (Department of Defense), Christi Grimm (Department of Health and Human Services), and Steve Linick (Department of State).[211] Trump fired dozens of inspectors general in multiple agencies at the beginning of his second term in 2025; he also fired the head of the Office of Special Counsel and Director of the Office of Government Ethics.

[206] Richard Nixon Interview with David Frost (1977), www.congress.gov/116/meeting/house/110331/documents/HMKP-116-JU00-20191211-SD408.pdf; *Transcript of Frost Interview*, New York Times (May 5, 1977), www.nytimes.com/1977/05/05/archives/transcript-of-frosts-television-interview-with-nixon-about.html.

[207] Peter Baker, Maggie Haberman, Danny Hakim, & Michael S. Schmidt, *Trump Fires Impeachment Witnesses Gordon Sondland and Alexander Vindman in Post-Acquittal Purge*, New York Times (Feb. 7, 2020), www.nytimes.com/2020/02/07/us/politics/alexander-vindman-gordon-sondland-fired.html.

[208] Jeremy Herb, *Trump Fires Intelligence Community Watchdog Who Told Congress about Whistleblower Complaint That Led to Impeachment*, CNN (Apr. 4, 2020), www.cnn.com/2020/04/03/politics/trump-fires-inspector-general-michael-atkinson.

[209] Statement of Michael K. Atkinson, Inspector General of the Intelligence Community, on his Removal from Office, April 5, 2020, https://int.nyt.com/data/documenthelper/6865-atkinson-statement-on-removal/339e56bc31e7c607c4b9/optimized/full.pdf#page = 1.

[210] Charlie Savage, *Endorsing Trump's Firing of Inspector General, Barr Paints Distorted Picture*, New York Times (Apr. 10, 2020), www.nytimes.com/2020/04/10/us/politics/barr-inspector-general-firing.html.

[211] Melissa Quinn, *The Internal Watchdogs Trump Has Fired or Replaced*, CBS News (May 19, 2020, 11:43 AM), www.cbsnews.com/news/trump-inspectors-general-internal-watchdogs-fired-list.

Does the unitary executive theory allow a president to fire all these people simply because they did their jobs and/or provided truthful testimony to Congress about the President's own acts that might very well be a crime? An extreme version of the unitary executive theory would answer this question in the affirmative, yet a more nuanced and balanced approach would examine whether each of these firings violated existing criminal law or other applicable law, including the obstruction of justice statute. The President's exercise of the removal power under Article II and rule of law principles should comply with other applicable law, particularly criminal law.[212]

Where could abuse of removal power go from here? We were given a taste of that in the Trump administration when an October 2020 executive order, creating Schedule F in the Excepted Service, sought to transfer tens of thousands of career civil service employees having job protection under civil service laws to a new Schedule F category of employees that could be dismissed by political appointees of the President.[213] The transferred employees would be those in "positions of a confidential, policy-determining, policy-making, or policy-advocating character." Critics alleged that this would destabilize the United States government.[214] President Biden rescinded Schedule F in January 2021.[215] A second Trump presidential term has raised the same issues. Trump pledged that if reelected he would purge career civil servants from the federal government, particularly the Department of Justice.[216]

An international comparison from the past is illustrative. Germany's March 1933 Enabling Act allowed the Chancellor and Cabinet to decree laws without the approval of the Reichstag.[217] The first of these laws was the Law for the Restoration of the Professional Civil Service of April 7, 1933, providing that "to restore a national professional civil service and to simplify administration, civil

[212] *See* Finkelstein & Painter, *supra* note 191. *But see* Trump v. United States, 603 U.S. 593 (2024).

[213] Exec. Order No. 13957, 85 Fed. Reg. 67631 (2020) at 67631–35.

[214] *See* Troy Cribb, *Politicizing the Civil Service: How a New Executive Order Destabilizes the U.S. Government*, Just Security (Nov. 2, 2020), www.justsecurity.org/73213/politicizing-the-civil-service-how-a-new-executive-order-destabilizes-the-u-s-government/.

[215] *See* Exec. Order No. 14003, 86 Fed. Reg. 7321 (2021) at 7231–33.

[216] Isaac Arnsdorf, Josh Dawsey, & Devlin Barrett, *Trump and Allies Plot Revenge, Justice Department Control in a Second Term*, Wash. Post. (Nov. 6, 2023, 1:27 PM), www.washingtonpost.com/politics/2023/11/05/trump-revenge-second-term/. According to the *New York Times*, President Trump's Schedule F plan is a part of his "Agenda 47" to convert civil service protected employees to "at will" employees who could be terminated and replaced with his political appointees. He proclaimed during the 2024 election cycle "either the deep state destroys America, or we destroy the deep state." Donald P. Moynihan, *Trump Has a Master Plan for Destroying the "Deep State,"* New York Times (Nov. 27, 2023), www.nytimes.com/2023/11/27/opinion/trump-deep-state-schedule-f.html.

[217] *See* Law to Remove the Distress of the People and the State (The Enabling Act), March 24, 1933, https://ghdi.ghi-dc.org/sub_document.cfm?document_id=1496.

servants may be dismissed from office in accordance with the following regulations, even where there would be no grounds for such action under the prevailing Law."[218] The law, with narrow exceptions, also banned Jews, other non-Aryans, and politically unreliable people from the civil service.[219]

The German example is not a unitary executive theory. That's fascism. Preventing the former from gravitating toward the latter is the job of responsible presidents and federal courts. In some circumstances, the federal courts must be willing to say no to a president.

In sum, from the clear intent of certain Founders and subsequent Supreme Court opinions, the weight of evidence regarding the unitary executive theory comes down to the judgment that the power of a president is not absolute, nor was it intended to be. The historical record and the common law court decisions demonstrate that the Founders wanted a strong, energetic presidency but an even stronger Congress with appropriate balance between the branches and an understanding that the boundaries and line drawing necessary for governance are not always clear.[220]

To accomplish this design and the certain tensions and competition that would follow between the Congress and presidents, the Constitution, with purpose and clarity, explicitly established separate institutions "sharing" power with specific checks and balances on both institutions as a "checking function" on each other's extreme tendencies and abuses of power. The designed separation of powers principle, with its elaborate checks and balances, belies the notion that a single president would have a claim of absolute power, together with the fact that the country had fought a war against tyrannical power. Such an absolute executive power theory ignores all the "accountability" provisions on a president embedded in the Constitution and discussed throughout this book, including Section III on presidential accountability.

While this ongoing debate focuses on the *limits* of executive power, the Founders debated with *whom* executive power rests. Does the Vesting Clause place any power with the Vice President as an executive officer? What powers do cabinet secretaries have over the structure and day-to-day operations of their departments? Why did the Founders adopt a system that places a singular president, rather than multiple executives, as the head of the executive branch. The answer to these questions can be found in an exploration of the debates of the Founding generation when creating the constitutional republic.

[218] Gesetz zur Wiederherstellung des Berufsbeamtentums, April 7, 1933, Reichsgesetzblatt, I, 1933, p. 175, www.yadvashem.org/odot_pdf/Microsoft%20Word%20-%202146.pdf.

[219] *Id.*

[220] Farber, *supra* note 13 at 230–31. *But see* Trump v. United States, 603 U.S. 593 (2024) (where a majority of the Supreme Court embraced an excessively broad view of power within the Executive Branch).

1.7 THE VESTING CLAUSE AND THE SINGULAR PRESIDENT

The second, and less controversial, phrase of the Vesting Clause placed executive power in a singular president. While today we take for granted that the office of the President is occupied by a single person, the Founders did not take this assumption for granted. The Founders, skeptical of centralized power from their experiences as colonists in the 1760s and 1770s, were hesitant to reestablish a king in all but name for the United States. However, despite this skepticism, and the failure of the Articles of Confederation in the 1780s, the delegates acknowledged the reality that some national executive was needed to bring leadership and direction to the new national government.[221]

The earliest plan considered at the Convention, known as the Virginia Resolutions, proposed that "[a] National Executive be instituted." This resolution, primarily written by Madison, far from bringing clarity to the nature of the presidency, began a debate early in the Convention about its composition. The ambiguity of the Virginia Resolutions led the delegates to debate a variety of forms for executive power, including (1) a council that would serve as an advisory board to a singular president but have no authority to overrule presidential decision-making; (2) a power sharing between three executives; and (3) a sole executive.[222]

When considering their options, the Convention looked, in part, to their English roots for inspiration. One option considered was to pair a singular president with an executive council of advisors. This idea likely came from the British Privy Council that served as an advisory board to the English monarch.[223] While this idea initially drew support from several delegates, its momentum slowed as they debated the finer details of the plan. One point of contention was the extent of the Council's power. Would it have the power to override a presidential decision or was its power purely advisory? Some, like Madison, argued that the Council should be purely advisory because otherwise it would be no different than a multi-person executive. However, others argued that a powerless advisory Council would lack the necessary power to safeguard against presidential abuse of power.[224]

An influential voice in the creation of the modern, singular President is a largely forgotten, but important, delegate from Pennsylvania, James Wilson. Unlike many of his contemporaries at the Convention, who harbored a deep skepticism of

[221] THE FEDERALIST No. 67 (Hamilton).

[222] Notes of William Pierce from the Constitutional Convention (June 1, 1787), reprinted in THE RECORDS OF THE FEDERAL CONVENTION OF 1787, VOL. 1, 74 (Max Farrand ed., 1911).

[223] *The Privy Council: History, Functions and Membership*, UK PARLIAMENT, https://commonslibrary.parliament.uk/research-briefings/cbp-7460/.

[224] Calvin C. Jillson, *The Executive in Republican Government: The Case of the American Founding* IX PRESIDENTIAL STUD. Q. 387–88 (1979).

consolidating executive power in a single individual, Wilson believed that a large country such as the United States required an efficient national government centered on a strong and energetic president who had the power and responsibility necessary to lead the nation.[225] This idea, unsurprisingly, was controversial at the time and according to contemporaneous accounts led to "[a] considerable pause" which was broken when Benjamin Franklin stated that this issue was of great importance and asked the other delegates present to state their views.[226] While other delegates at the Convention wanted the President to share power with a Council chosen by Congress, Wilson believed that this would weaken the executive, lead to self-promotion and infighting that would limit the presidency, and ultimately lead to confusion among the people. These arguments in favor of a singular and empowered presidency would later be echoed in Hamilton's *Federalist* 70.[227]

Among the other plans considered in the ensuing debate were Virginia delegate Edmund Randolph's plan to place the executive power among three co-equal executives. Randolph considered Wilson's plan for a single executive to be "a foetus of monarchy" and, more practically, one that the states would never ratify in the final draft of the Constitution.[228] In response to this argument, Wilson noted that every state in the union placed the executive power in a single person and that these examples at the state level made his idea of a single president both practical and politically feasible. Additionally, Wilson looked to history to argue that a single executive, rather than being a "foetus of monarchy" was the best protection against unaccountable executive power. Wilson argued that the examples of the thirty Tyrants of Athens and the Decemvirs of Rome (a ten-man council during the Roman Republic) showed that diffused executive power leads to decreased accountability and slow decision-making.[229]

Roger Sherman of Connecticut argued that the whole debate over the makeup of the presidency was entirely outside of the scope of the convention. He proposed that rather than stating in the Constitution the makeup of the presidency, this decision should be left to Congress to decide. Sherman's proposal ultimately gained little traction at the Convention.[230]

Another alternative proposal came from New Jersey delegate William Paterson's New Jersey Plan introduced in June of 1787. In the early days of the Convention, delegates of smaller states were alarmed by the Virginia

[225] Daniel J. McCarthy, *James Wilson and the Creation of the Presidency*, 17 PRESIDENTIAL STUD. Q. 655, 690 (1987).

[226] 9 THE PAPERS OF JAMES MADISON, 9 April 1786–24 May 1787 at 370 (Robert A. Rutland et al. eds., 1975).

[227] *See also* FARBER, *supra* note 13 at 230–315; PRAKASH, *supra* note 145 at 62.

[228] ROBERT E. DICLERICO, *James Wilson's Presidency*, 17 PRESIDENTIAL STUD. Q. 301, 303 (1987).

[229] Notes of James Madison from the Constitutional Convention (June 1, 1787), reprinted in THE RECORDS OF THE FEDERAL CONVENTION OF 1787, VOL. 1, 66, 71, 74 (Max Farrand ed., 1911).

[230] *Id*. at 65.

Resolutions scheme to tie representation in both the House and Senate to a state's population. Fearing that the Virginia Resolutions would effectively leave their states powerless in Congress, Paterson, along with delegates from Maryland, Connecticut, and New York, proposed the New Jersey Plan that would have affected both Congress and the presidency. Notably the New Jersey Plan, in contrast to the Virginia Resolutions, had a concrete idea of organizing the executive branch that called for multiple single-term presidents.[231] While some parts of Paterson's New Jersey Plan exist today, such as the equal apportionment for each state in the Senate, the idea to have multiple presidencies did not make it into the ratified Constitution.[232]

Less than a month into the Constitutional Convention, consensus began to emerge; amended Virginia Resolutions were introduced and debated in June of 1787. Among the changes were a clarification that "a national Executive be instituted to consist of a Single Person."[233] This change from the original Virginia Resolutions represented a dramatic coalescing around Wilson's ideas. It would go largely uncontested for the remainder of the Convention.

In July 1787, the delegates sent their first draft of resolutions to the Committee of Detail. It provided that "a national Executive be instituted to consist of a Single Person."[234] A second draft to the Committee of Detail, just one month later, reaffirmed the Convention's commitment to a single executive with more power, but also accountability and transparency, now would be the focus. It stated that "[t]he Executive Power of the United States shall be vested in a single person."[235] Three months into the Convention, the delegates largely had agreed to a single person as president.

1.8 THE PRESIDENT AND THE MEDIA

The media, commonly referred to as the "press" at the time of the Founding, is the so-called fourth power,[236] holding in check the first three: the legislature, the

[231] Notes of James Madison from the Constitutional Convention (June 15, 1787), reprinted in THE RECORDS OF THE FEDERAL CONVENTION OF 1787, VOL. 1, 244 (Max Farrand ed., 1911).

[232] U.S. CONST. Art. II, §1.

[233] Journal of the Constitutional Convention (June 13, 1787), reprinted in THE RECORDS OF THE FEDERAL CONVENTION OF 1787, VOL. 1, 225–26 (Max Farrand ed., 1911).

[234] Notes of Robert Yates from the Constitutional Convention (June 16, 1787), reprinted in THE RECORDS OF THE FEDERAL CONVENTION OF 1787, VOL. 1, 258 (Max Farrand ed., 1911).

[235] Notes of Rufus King from the Constitutional Convention (June 16, 1787), reprinted in THE RECORDS OF THE FEDERAL CONVENTION OF 1787, VOL. 1, 266 (Max Farrand ed., 1911).

[236] The media is sometimes also referred to as the "Fourth Estate" juxtaposed to the three estates recognized in pre-Revolutionary France: the clergy, the nobility, and the commoners. In the United States the free press is juxtaposed to the political power of Congress, the President, and the federal judiciary, as well as the power of the states. *See* Erin C. Carroll, *Platforms and the Fall of the Fourth Estate: Looking Beyond the First Amendment to Protect Watchdog Journalism*, 79 MARYLAND L. REV. 529–89 (2022).

executive, and the judiciary. An independent media is essential to an accountable democracy. The First Amendment explicitly mentions freedom of the press in addition to freedom of speech and the freedom to peaceably assemble.[237]

Government control over the media is characteristic of absolute monarchy and dictatorship, not democracy. Diversification of the media is also important, as too much power over news outlets in the hands of too few people can lead to an oligopoly of politicians and media barons. The famous Orson Welles movie *Citizen Kane* was based on newspaper magnate William Randolph Hearst, who aspired to be president.[238] Today, other billionaires control powerful news outlets. Rupert Murdoch controls the reliably Republican Fox News channel and the *Wall Street Journal*. Jeff Bezos, the founder of Amazon, owns the *Washington Post*, which, for the first time in decades, along with the *Los Angeles Times*, refused to endorse a presidential candidate in the 2024 election.

The FCC is an independent agency charged by Congress with limiting industry concentration under the Communications Act of 1934[239] and the Telecommunications Act of 1996.[240] The FCC, however, is part of the Executive Branch, which means that the President appoints the FCC commissioners subject to confirmation by the Senate. The President can remove the FCC Chairman at will. As discussed in this part of the book, on presidential power, it is unclear whether this removal power extends to the other commissioners of an independent agency.[241] Since the Reagan administration caused the FCC to abandon the "fairness doctrine" in the 1980s,[242] the FCC has been a relatively weak counter-force to the power of those who control the media and who prefer their own views over others.

Presidential use of power also can implicate litigation regarding defamation claims. The Supreme Court has ruled that public officials and figures, including

[237] U.S. Const. Amend. I ("Congress shall make no law . . . abridging the freedom of speech, or of the press; or the right of the people peaceably to assemble, and to petition the Government for a redress of grievances").

[238] *See HEARST FOR 20 YEARS HAS SOUGHT POWER; Got a Newspaper in 1886; Now Has Nine and Two Magazines. ONLY 4 YEARS IN POLITICS Personality of the Nominee Is Veiled in Mystery and Men Widely Disagree On It*, New York Times (Sept. 27, 1906), www.nytimes.com/1906/09/27/archives/hearst-for-20-years-has-sought-power-got-a-newspaper-in-1886-now.html ("His political ambition has ranged from a seat in the House of Representatives to the Presidency of the United States, with the Mayoralty of Greater New York and the Governorship of the State thrown in as incidentals").

[239] 47 U.S. Code § 151 *et seq*. Codified in Chapter 5 of Title 47 of the United States Code.

[240] Pub. L. No. 104-104, 110 Stat. 56 (1996).

[241] *See* discussion in Section 1.3 on presidential removal power and whether the Supreme Court is likely to overrule Humphrey's Executor v. United States, 295 U.S. 602 (1935) (upholding a federal statute that prevented the President from removing a Federal Trade Commission Commissioner without cause).

[242] *See* Steven J. Simmons, The Fairness Doctrine and the Media (1978) (detailing the history of opposition to the fairness doctrine which required radio stations and other media outlets to broadcast and publish alternative viewpoints).

candidates and presidents, who sue for defamation are subject to very high burden and pleading standards in order to win.[243] The Supreme Court has said these pleading standards are necessary to protect First Amendment rights. But when a plaintiff is elected president, potential defendants may be more hesitant to express opinions. In December 2024, ABC's parent company Disney Corporation agreed to pay $15 million to President Trump's presidential library to settle a defamation suit Trump had brought after anchor George Stephanopoulos asserted on air that Trump had been found civilly liable for rape.[244]

In the same vein, reporting shortly before President Trump's second inauguration in 2025 shows that Paramount Global, parent company of CBS News, was considering settling a lawsuit brought by the then-President elect seeking $10 billion in damages.[245] The reason that Paramount in June 2025 settled the news case is likely not because they believe that the President will win the case. Rather, reporting shows that senior executives at Paramount are worried about Trump's influence over the FCC which among other things could deny approval of Paramount's merger with Skydance Media.

Social media – where the users generate their own content – is sometimes referred to as the "fifth power."[246] Social media is the primary news source for many young voters, which means that social media will become, if it is not already, the primary media outlet that influences elections.

Defamation suits against the social media industry would be more frequent and even bigger but for the liability shield provided by Congress under Section 230 of the Communications Decency Act.[247] A problem may be that a president, with a politically aligned Congress, can amend Section 230. Even acting alone, the Executive Branch could try to influence the way Section 230 is interpreted by the courts.

The social media industry appears increasingly unwilling to challenge the President. Mark Zuckerberg, who was not close to Trump before the 2024 election,[248] pivoted toward Trump afterwards. Shortly after the 2024 election,

[243] New York Times v. Sullivan, 376 U.S. 254 (1964).

[244] Michael R. Sisak, *ABC Agrees to Give $15 Million to Donald Trump's Presidential Library to Settle Defamation Lawsuit*, AP (Dec. 14, 2024), https://apnews.com/article/abc-trump-lawsuit-defamation-stephanopoulos-04aea8663310af39ae2a85f4c1a56d68.

[245] Jessica Toonkel & Drew FitzGerald, *CBS Owner Discusses Settling Trump Suit, With Merger Review on Tap*, Wall Street Journal (Jan. 17, 2025), www.wsj.com/business/media/cbs-owner-discusses-settling-trump-suit-with-merger-review-on-tap-a5916925.

[246] *See* William H. Dutton, *The Fifth Estate Emerging Through the Network of Networks*, 27(1) Prometheus 1–15 (2009).

[247] 47 U.S.C. §230 – Protection for private blocking and screening of offensive material.

[248] After the assassination attempt on Trump in July 2024, Zuckerberg said that Trump's response with a raised fist was "one of the most badass things I've ever seen in my life." Victoria Feng, *Mark Zuckerberg Praises Trump's Response to Assassination Attempt*, NBC News (July 19, 2024), www.nbcnews.com/tech/tech-news/mark-zuckerberg-praises-trumps-response-assassination-attempt-rcna162777.

Zuckerberg met with Trump at Mar-a-Lago,[249] a sharp reversal of their strained relations only a year earlier when Trump was threatening Zuckerberg with life in prison if he "interfered" in the election.[250] It is not clear what was said at this meeting or any subsequent meetings or phone calls between Trump and Zuckerberg.

Zuckerberg's most significant concession to Trump was to abolish fact checking at Meta.[251] Zuckerberg, after the election, in January 2025, went so far as to blame Meta's own fact checkers, agreeing with Trump that they were politically biased.[252]

Conservative Trump supporters were added to Meta's Board,[253] and Meta donated $1 million to the 2025 presidential inaugural fund.[254] Zuckerberg also co-hosted a reception for Republican billionaires at the inauguration.[255] Zuckerberg was invited to sit with Elon Musk, and next to Jeff Bezos, owner of the *Washington Post*, at the inauguration[256] The *Post* had brought down President Nixon fifty years earlier. But the medium now is different.

Moreover, the social media industry may become even more concentrated after the Supreme Court, in January 2025, refused to strike down a statute requiring divestiture of TikTok's US platform from Chinese ownership.[257] The Court ruled that regulation of the ownership of TikTok is content neutral.[258] The 2024 statute does not disproportionately burden TikTok or users of its platform, the Court held. Furthermore, there is a national security interest of the United States since the Chinese government has been a declared foreign adversary, the Court concluded. Congress and President Trump, and President Biden, simply decided to require new ownership of the company. But with presidents and other politicians deeply

[249] Tom Gerken, *Mark Zuckerberg dines with Donald Trump at Mar-a-Lago*, BBC (Nov. 28, 2024), www.bbc.com/news/articles/c87x98q8yo8o.

[250] *Id.*

[251] Huo Jingnan, Shannon Bond, & Bobby Allyn, *Meta Says It Will End Fact Checking as Silicon Valley Prepares for Trump*, NPR (Jan. 7, 2025), www.npr.org/2025/01/07/nx-s1-5251151/meta-fact-checking-mark-zuckerberg-trump.

[252] Stuart A. Thompson, *Meta Says Fact-Checkers Were the Problem. Fact-Checkers Rule That False*, New York Times (Jan. 7, 2025), www.nytimes.com/2025/01/07/business/mark-zuckerberg-meta-fact-check.html.

[253] Kelvin Chan, *Meta's New Board Includes UFC Boss Dana White, a Familiar Figure in Trump's Orbit*, AP (Jan. 7, 2025), https://finance.yahoo.com/news/meta-adds-three-board-members-112433087.html.

[254] Liv McMahon, *Mark Zuckerberg's Meta Donates $1m to Trump Fund*, BBC (Dec. 12, 2024), www.bbc.com/news/articles/c8j9e1x9z2xo.

[255] *Mark Zuckerberg Will Cohost Reception With Republican Billionaires for Trump Inauguration*, AP (Jan. 14, 2025), www.usnews.com/news/us/articles/2025-01-14/mark-zuckerberg-will-cohost-reception-with-republican-billionaires-for-trump-inauguration.

[256] Jake Traylor & David Ingram, *Elon Musk, Jeff Bezos and Mark Zuckerberg to Attend Trump's Inauguration*, NBC News (Jan. 14, 2025), www.nbcnews.com/politics/donald-trump/elon-musk-jeff-bezos-mark-zuckerberg-attend-trump-inauguration-rcna187642.

[257] Tik Tok Inc. v. Merrick B, Garland, Attorney General, 603 U.S. ___ (2025), www.supremecourt.gov/opinions/24pdf/24-656_ca7d.pdf.

[258] *Id.*

concerned about social media's influence on elections, the change in ownership of TikTok or any other platform can influence the choice of who buys TikTok.

After going dark for a few hours on January 19, 2025, a day before Inauguration Day, TikTok restored service to American users after getting assurance from Trump that he would exercise his discretion under the statute, as President, to delay enforcement while the Chinese parent company, ByteDance Ltd., finds a buyer in the United States. The buyer could be one of the President's supporters, as Trump named several, including Elon Musk, as the likely buyer of TikTok.

In February 2022, Donald Trump became the first President to control his own social media platform. He probably will not be the last. Until they had a falling out in June 2025, Trump had a strong alliance with Elon Musk,[259] who owns X, one of the largest social media platforms in the world. If newspaper and cable television barons thought themselves to be the "Citizen Kane" of American politics, the titans of the social media industry could likely soon replace them.

Consider what happens when the President's control over the FCC and other regulatory agencies is combined with control over social media, in the hands of either the President himself or his close supporters. The FCC is supposed to be an independent agency, but as mentioned earlier, the President's appointment and removal power undermine this expected independence.

It is here – the interaction between the White House and social media platforms – that the Biden administration embarked on a problematic path which is illustrated in *Murthy v. Missouri*.[260] In *Murthy*, the Court denied standing to plaintiffs who claimed that the Biden administration was exerting "soft pressure" on social media platforms to discourage "disinformation." Contextually, in the aftermath of the upheaval of January 6, 2021, the administration directly contacted social media platforms – including Twitter, Facebook, Instagram, and YouTube – to urge them to take down content that was allegedly misleading or incited violence.

[259] *See e.g.* Commonwealth of Pennsylvania v. Musk (2:24-cv-05823) (E.D. Pa 2024) (suit by Philadelphia District Attorney alleging that Musk's pro-Trump America PAC, by virtue of awarding registered voters $1 million in return for signing a petition supporting the First and Second Amendments, violated Pennsylvania's lottery laws, unfair trade practices laws, and consumer protection laws), www.govinfo.gov/content/pkg/USCOURTS-paed-2_24-cv-05823/pdf/USCOURTS-paed-2_24-cv-05823-0.pdf.

[260] Murthy v. Missouri, 144 S. Ct. 1972, 1997 (2024). The Court in *Murthy v. Missouri* declined to decide the case on the merits, and instead observed that "The plaintiffs assert standing based on the 'direct censorship' of their own speech as well as their 'right to listen' to others who faced social-media censorship. Notably, both theories depend on the *platform's* actions – yet the plaintiffs do not seek to enjoin the platforms from restricting any posts or accounts. They seek to enjoin *Government agencies and officials* from pressuring or encouraging the platforms to suppress protected speech in the future." The Court refused the plaintiffs' standing, holding that to "establish standing, the plaintiffs must demonstrate a substantial risk that, in the near future, they will suffer an injury that is traceable to a Government defendant and redressable by the injunction they seek. Because no plaintiff has carried that burden, none has standing to seek a preliminary injunction."

As commendable as this goal might be, for the President's senior officers to exert pressure of this sort on social media platforms may raise serious First Amendment issues. This is a use of presidential power that could easily be abused by other administrations even more intent on controlling the content of social media.[261] The Supreme Court, by refusing to decide the merits of the claim in *Murthy*, left this use of presidential power unchecked, at least for the time.

Consider also another related issue; Where the President's social media accounts become de facto official accounts of the United States government. What if the President controls who is allowed to post comments on those accounts and who gets blocked? The social media account of a cabinet member or other high-ranking official also can be used to communicate government policy to such an extent that it, too, becomes an official account. This means that, among other things, the platform could be a "designated public forum" for the purposes of the First Amendment and blocking dissenters from commenting on it would not be permitted.[262] A court could order a government official, including a president, to stop blocking public access to such a social media account, although it is not certain that such an order would be obeyed or how it could be enforced.

Yet another issue is what happens when official United States government communications on social media are mixed with partisan politics. In the case of an appointed official, but not for a president, the Hatch Act[263] would prohibit the co-mingling of official communications with partisan messaging intended to influence elections.[264] The Office of Special Counsel (OSC) investigates Hatch Act violations and the Director of the OSC, like the heads of other federal agencies, is appointed by the President.[265] Apparently, this Director can be removed by the President with or without cause, and in 2025 President Trump did in fact fire the director of the

[261] *See* Richard W. Painter, *The Question Not Presented: Government and Social Media Corruption after Murthy v. Missouri*, 129 PENN. STATE L. REV. 427, 462 (Feb. 2025).

[262] *See* Knight First Amendment v. Trump, 928 F.3d 237 (2d Cir. 2019). The court ruled that the @realDonaldTrump Twitter account is "a presidential account as opposed to a personal account," and blocking people from it violates their rights to participate in a "designated public forum."

[263] 5 U.S. Code § 7323 – Political activity authorized; prohibitions.

[264] *See* Office of Special Counsel, Report of Prohibited Political Activity under the Hatch Act, OSC File Nos. HA-19-0631 & HA-19-3395 (Kellyanne Conway), May 30, 2019 at 2 ("OSC's investigation determined that Ms. Conway violated the Hatch Act during media appearances and by engaging in both official and political activity on her Twitter account, '@KellyannePolls'").

[265] 5 U.S. Code § 1211(a) and (b) ("(a) There is established the Office of Special Counsel, which shall be headed by the Special Counsel. (b) The Special Counsel shall be appointed by the President, by and with the advice and consent of the Senate, for a term of 5 years").

OSC.[266] The OSC also has no enforcement power, only the power to investigate. If the President so desires, the Hatch Act, like other laws, might simply be ignored, notwithstanding the Article II requirement that the President "shall take care that the Laws be faithfully executed."[267]

In sum, the combined power of the presidency, including the President's control over the FCC, the Justice Department, and other agencies under the "unitary executive theory," and industry concentration of social media in the hands of allies of the President and perhaps the President himself, means the United States faces, arguably, the very real prospect of de facto state control of social media.

Government content-based pressure on social media platforms that do not conform could be part of a plan to consolidate such control, as could be blocking dissenters from posting on platforms aligned with the President and using official government accounts for partisan political messaging. Whether the law can stand up to such abuses remains to be seen.[268]

[266] The statute provides that "The Special Counsel may be removed by the President but only for inefficiency, neglect of duty, or malfeasance in office." 5 U.S. Code § 1211(b). But as discussed in Section 1.3 on presidential power, the Supreme Court has struck down statutes that infringe on the President's power to remove the heads of federal agencies. Seila Law LLC v. Consumer Financial Protection Bureau, 591 U.S. 197 (2020).

[267] U.S. Const., Art. II, § 3.

[268] *See* Painter, *supra* note 261, discussing this problem in more detail.

2

The President and the Administrative State

The Constitution establishes the President as the head of the Executive Branch where virtually all the administrative capacity of the federal government lies.

How much power the President has affects the size and power of the federal government. In the early days of the Republic, the Federalist Party was the proponent of a strong centralized government, while Anti-Federalists and Jeffersonian Democrats distrusted centralized power.

One side wanted centralized political power, taxation, and economic regulation where the other side distrusted the federal government. Presidents, regardless of which side they say they are on, have taken advantage of opportunities to expand their own power and sometimes to undo accomplishments of their predecessors.

A specific area where this debate plays out in the economic sphere has been repeated political battles over whether the United States should have a central bank and if so, who should control it and what it should do. The early controversies over the First and Second Banks of the United States were emblematic of two competing visions for the role of the federal government in regulating the economy.

The Bank of England was founded in 1696. Alexander Hamilton, the first US Treasury Secretary under President George Washington, wanted the United States also to have a bank of its own. The First Bank of the United States was founded in 1791. The Anti-Federalists were firmly opposed. After the Democrats came to power with the election of President Thomas Jefferson in 1800, they allowed the charter of the Bank to expire in 1811. Under President James Madison, with mounting federal debt from the War of 1812, in 1816 Congress established a Second Bank of the United States, this time under the leadership of Philadelphia banker Nicholas Biddle. Once again, agrarian populists vowed to eliminate the Bank. With the election of President Andrew Jackson in 1828, a battle ensued in Congress over whether the Bank's federal charter would again be allowed to expire. It did in 1836.[1]

Corruption scandals fueled opposition to both banks, which Jeffersonians and then Jacksonians described as being beholden to speculators and other moneyed interests in coastal cities.[2] The impact of corruption on the debate over the First and Second Banks of the United States is discussed further in Chapter 11 on financial and political conflicts of interest, along with other examples of corruption of presidential power.[3]

The United States did not get a central bank until 1914 under the presidency of Woodrow Wilson. Although relatively few Americans today want to abolish the Federal Reserve, some of the sentiment of the Jeffersonian and Jacksonian era remains. Anti-Fed sentiment was fueled by the Fed's 2008 financial bailouts of Wall Street, then by broader "deep state" conspiracy theories about the administrative state that emerged in the Trump era, followed by unpopular interest rate increases, intended to curb inflation, introduced by the Federal Reserve during the Biden administration. Although the Fed is independent and sets interest rates without influence or interference from the President, in 2024 candidate Trump said that as President he would use his power to set interest rates in a second term.[4] Whether the President can do this – for example, by firing the Fed Chairman and members of the Federal Reserve Board – is a subject connected with the broader discussion in Chapter 1 of presidential removal power. The Supreme Court in 2025 suggested that Congress may have the constitutional power to insulate Federal Reserve governors from removal. In *Wilcox v. Trump*, the Court appeared inclined to allow President Trump to remove a member of the National Labor Relations Board (NLRB), but the Court specifically noted that Trump's argument for removal power generally did not "necessarily implicate the constitutionality of for-cause removal protections for members of the Federal Reserve's Board of Governors or other members of the Federal Open Market committee ... The Federal Reserve is a uniquely structured, quasi-private entity that follows in the distinct historical tradition of the First and Second Banks of the United States."[5]

1 Andrew T. Hill, *The Second Bank of the United States*, Federal Reserve History (Dec. 5, 2015), www.federalreservehistory.org/essays/second-bank-of-the-us.

2 *Id.*

3 *See also* Richard W. Painter, *Ethics and Corruption in Business and Government: Lessons from the South Sea Bubble and the Bank of the United States* (published by the University of Chicago Law School as the 2006 Maurice and Muriel Fulton Lecture in Legal History) (discussing the role of alleged corruption in political opposition to the First and Second Banks of the United States).

4 Andrew Restuccia & Nick Timiraos, *Trump's Plans Stir Fears for Fed Independence, Inflation: In Donald Trump's First Term, Fed Chair Jerome Powell Resisted His Demands to Lower Rates, but if Re-elected, Trump Could Replace Him in 2026*, Wall Street Journal (Aug. 8, 2024), www.wsj.com/politics/elections/trumps-plans-stir-fears-for-fed-independence-inflation-689bc113.

5 Trump v. Wilcox, 605 U.S. ___ (2025), slip op. at 2.

Thus, even if the President can remove a member of the NLRB, or another other independent board or commission, such would not necessarily be true in the case of the Federal Reserve because of the unique historical position and importance of an independent central bank.

The debate over the size and scope of the administrative state, however, extends far beyond the question of a central bank. In other areas as well, the early American administrative state grew under the Federalists and then the Whigs. Revenue was limited because there was no federal income tax until the Sixteenth Amendment of the Constitution was ratified in 1913. The principal source of revenue was from tariffs on imported goods – a highly contentious political issue then and now. Federalists and then Whigs championed high tariffs to fund construction of canals, bridges, roads, and other infrastructure projects, also arguing that tariffs protected domestic manufacturing from foreign competition. Many Democrats argued that tariffs hurt farmers and that the United States did not need more tariff revenue to pay for a bigger centralized government.

The Federalists' broad concept of presidential power evolved from the doctrine of "implied powers" championed by Alexander Hamilton. He argued that Article I, Section 8 of the Constitution, that bestowed enumerated powers on Congress, also implied that Congress could use the means necessary to these ends. In *McCulloch v. Maryland*,[6] the Supreme Court recognized such implied powers. The Court, in an opinion by Chief Justice John Marshall, ruled that the Constitution gave Congress the power to pass laws necessary and proper to facilitate full exercise of its enumerated powers. In that case, the Court upheld a law Congress had passed establishing a Bank of the United States that could not be taxed by the states. This was the same Bank whose charter Congress later allowed to expire.

The implied powers debate initially was about the power of Congress, but once federal agencies and entities are created by Congress, they reside in the Executive Branch under control of the President. With the expansion of the administrative state, we see the expansion of the powers of the President.

The Civil War was another watershed moment for presidential power. President Lincoln's suspension of habeas corpus is discussed in Chapter 1 and again in Chapter 6. The administrative apparatus of the Executive Branch under Lincoln was focused first on winning the Civil War and then, with Republican domination in Congress, administering the Reconstruction project in Southern states occupied by the Union army. Democrats continued to oppose a strong national government, although this changed later during the Progressive Era when the need for national economic regulation was increasingly acknowledged by both political parties.[7]

6 McCulloch v. Maryland, 17 U.S. 316 (1819).

7 *See* Mark Tushnet, *Introduction: The Pasts and Futures of the Administrative State*, 150(3) Daedalus 5–16 (2021) (discussing the political background of the emergence of the American administrative state beginning in the late nineteenth century).

Economic regulation to counter the enormous power of big business then became the focus of the administrative state. In 1887, the Interstate Commerce Act was passed by Congress and established the Interstate Commerce Commission to regulate the railroads that were accused of overcharging farmers and driving up the cost of food and other goods. In 1890, the Sherman Antitrust Act empowered the federal government to prosecute monopolies and price fixing, significantly expanding the power of the Justice Department over American business. In 1914, the Federal Trade Commission was established also to enforce civil antitrust law and protect consumers.

The Food and Drug Administration (FDA) was founded in 1906 in response to shocking revelations about unsanitary conditions in food processing plants. President Theodore Roosevelt read Upton Sinclair's 1905 novel *The Jungle*, describing conditions in Chicago meat-packing plants. He ordered an investigation and then supported the 1906 Pure Food and Drug Act.

President Roosevelt helped build the administrative state during his term from 1901 to 1909, angering business interests which then supported replacing him with William Howard Taft as the Republican nominee in the 1908 election. Taft's presidency marked the ascendancy in the Republican Party of skeptics of federal regulation, whereas the Democrats retreated from their near century-long opposition to federal power to rally behind a new group of progressives who favored federal intervention in the economic affairs of the nation.[8]

The most noted champion of the modern administrative state in the Progressive Era was Woodrow Wilson, a Democrat, who first was a political science professor and President of Princeton University, then Governor of New Jersey, and then, from 1913 to 1921, President of the United States. Wilson not only studied the administrative state as an academic but also helped build it.

In an 1887 article "The Study of Administration" published in *Political Science Quarterly*, Wilson reviewed the history of public administration and argued for implementation of new administrative methods in American government.[9] Wilson believed that public administration should execute laws and regulations with efficiency and impartiality, like gears and wheels in a machine, with elected leaders making the policy decisions and civil servant administrators implementing them.

[8] While President Taft pursued many of the progressive policies, including antitrust enforcement, embraced by his predecessor Theodore Roosevelt, Taft's presidency moved the Republican Party closer to the business community. A high-profile scandal arose in 1909 when Taft's Secretary of the Interior, Richard Ballinger, approved the sale of millions of acres of federal land to a company for which he had previously been employed. Gifford Pinchot, Chief of the Forest Service, publicly criticized this conflict of interest, and Taft fired Pinchot. Former President Roosevelt took the side of Pinchot and ran as an independent progressive candidate against Taft in 1912, splitting the Republicans in an election won by Democrat Woodrow Wilson. *See* James Penick, Jr., Progressive Politics and Conservation. The Ballinger–Pinchot Affair (1968).

[9] Woodrow Wilson, *The Study of Administration*, 2 Pol. Sci. Q. 2 (1887).

Wilson observed that "the object of administrative study was . . . to discover, first, what government can properly and successfully do, and, secondly, how it can do these proper things with the utmost possible efficiency and the least possible cost either of money or of energy."[10]

Useful models for efficient administration Wilson found in Europe, particularly in Prussia and before that in Napoleonic France. Of Prussia, he writes:

> Such was the case in Prussia, for instance, where administration has been most studied and most nearly perfected. Frederic the Great, stern and masterful as was his rule, still sincerely professed to regard himself as only the chief servant of the state, to consider his great office a public trust; and it was he who, building upon the foundations laid by his father, began to organize the public service of Prussia as in very earnest a service of the public. His no less absolute successor, Frederic William III, under the inspiration of Stein, again, in his turn, advanced the work still further, planning many of the broader structural features which give firmness and form to Prussian administration to-day. Almost the whole of the admirable system has been developed by kingly initiative.[11]

The problem for Wilson was that Prussia and many other countries in Europe where administrations were supposedly so efficient were not democracies. Wilson believed that for the United States the challenge was to take their model of efficient government administration and democratize it. He also recognized that the United States was more decentralized than the European powers, meaning the administrative burden would be shared by the federal government and the states.

As noted earlier, public administration had been expanding in the United States long before Wilson became President. Federal and state laws for protection of public health, wage and hour laws, antitrust laws, and more, all required a government apparatus to implement them. Wilson saw that method of implementation as a science that must be studied as rigorously as any other.

And it was during the Wilson administration that the United States established a new way to pay for the expanding administrative state. The Internal Revenue Service (IRS) was established in its present form in 1918 to administer the federal income tax that came with ratification of the Sixteenth Amendment in 1913. For opponents of the administrative state, the IRS is, of course, one of the most vilified agencies of the federal government.

Every president has shortcomings. Some presidents' shortcomings undermine what they accomplish. Wilson's shortcoming – indeed a moral flaw – was racism. Born and raised in Virginia, he was the first Southerner to become President since the Reconstruction. During his administration, the United States backtracked from what little progress had been made in improving the lives of African Americans. Many were summarily fired from Post Office and other federal jobs. Wilson fired all

[10] *Id.*
[11] *Id.*

but two of the seventeen Black supervisors in the federal bureaucracy appointed by his Republican predecessor William Howard Taft. Wilson refused to appoint Black officials anywhere in the South.[12]

Historian Sheldon M. Stern writes:

> A delegation of black journalists, led by William M. Trotter of Boston, met with the president at the White House in 1914 to protest the segregation of federal agencies. Trotter brought up Wilson's pre-election promises and insisted that the administration's extension of segregation was humiliating and degrading to black citizens. Wilson countered that segregation was a proven benefit to both races. A shouting match ensued, and the President ordered Trotter to leave the White House, declaring angrily, that he had never been spoken to that way in his life by a Negro and would not tolerate it. Newspaper headlines proclaimed that "President Wilson rebukes Negroes for impudence," identifying Trotter as "particularly offensive." Five years later when Trotter tried to go to Versailles to cover the peace conference for his newspaper, Wilson's State Department denied him a passport.[13]

The increasingly "efficient" administration of the United States government under Wilson was a virtually all-white federal administration. It would change very little in that respect up through the 1960s.

In the 1930s, an enormous expansion of the administrative state came under the New Deal. Dozens of new federal agencies were created, including the Social Security Administration (SSA), the Federal Deposit Insurance Corporation (FDIC), the Federal Crop Insurance Corporation (FCIC), the Securities and Exchange Commission (SEC), the Federal Housing Administration (FHA), and the Tennessee Valley Authority (TVA). President Franklin Roosevelt accomplished much of his New Deal program through legislation in Congress, rather than unilateral executive orders.

Still, he initially faced a hostile Supreme Court that early in his administration ruled that some of New Deal legislation exceeded federal powers.[14] A very upset Roosevelt threatened to pack the Court with additional justices. Thereafter, the Court retreated from blocking the President's New Deal legislation.[15]

[12] Sheldon M. Stern, *Just Why Exactly Is Woodrow Wilson Rated so Highly by Historians? It's a Puzzlement*, History News Network (Aug. 23, 2015), www.historynewsnetwork.org/article/just-why-exactly-is-woodrow-wilson-rated-so-highly.

[13] *Id.*

[14] For example, in United States v. Butler, 297 US 1 (1936), in an opinion written by Justice Owen Roberts, the Court ruled that the 1933 Agricultural Adjustment Act was unconstitutional because it exceeded Congress's Spending Power (Article I, Section 8) and attempted to regulate and control agricultural production, an arena reserved to the states. After President Roosevelt proposed legislation that would add additional Justices to the Supreme Court, Justice Roberts in later cases stopped voting to strike down New Deal legislation.

[15] *See* Jeff Shesol, Supreme Power: Franklin Roosevelt vs. the Supreme Court (2010); James F. Simon, F.D.R. and Chief Justice Hughes: The President, the Supreme Court and the Epic Battle Over the New Deal (2012).

The vast administrative state, under the command of the Executive Branch, had been born. Additional agencies would be added under future administrations. For example, the Environmental Protection Agency (EPA) was created under President Nixon in 1970 and the Department of Education under President Carter in 1979. The pattern was much the same as during the New Deal. Congress would create an agency, given its expertise, to carry out a broadly articulated purpose and then delegate to that agency the power to make specific determinations about the details of regulations within its core area of expertise. Because the heads of federal agencies are political appointees of the President, the vastly expanded administrative state brought with it vastly expanded reach of presidential power.

And it is this aspect of presidential power that a conservative Supreme Court is once again cutting back, albeit using different legal doctrines than the Court did in its feud with FDR in the 1930s.

We begin with the "nondelegation doctrine" and the conservative legal movement's pushback against the modern administrative state. Article I, Section 1 of the Constitution provides that "All legislative Powers herein granted shall be vested in a Congress of the United States, which shall consist of a Senate and House of Representatives." The nondelegation doctrine holds that Congress cannot delegate its legislative powers to administrative agencies or self-regulatory private organizations.

In its extreme form, this doctrine suggests that Congress, not political appointees of the President, should impose legal rules, while agencies should only enforce those rules, having no independent rulemaking power. It's not likely courts would go so far in dismantling the current administrative state, but the current justices have said there are limits on how much legislative power Congress can delegate to the executive branch.[16]

A similar but less extreme approach is the "major questions doctrine" that disallows an agency from using broad discretion granted to it by Congress to promulgate regulations when major policy implications are not clearly authorized by Congress. Such "major questions," the doctrine holds, must be decided by Congress through the legislative process, not unliterally by the Executive Branch. This approach allows agencies to use some policy discretion to resolve less important questions but reserves *major* policy decisions for Congress to decide.

In *West Virginia v. Environmental Protection Agency*,[17] for example, the Court ruled by a vote of 6–3 that under the major questions doctrine, Section 7411(d) of the

[16] *See e.g.* Dep't of Transp. v. Ass'n of Am. R.R., 575 U.S. 43, 61 (2015) (Alito J, concurring) ("The principle that Congress cannot delegate away its vested powers exists to protect liberty. Our Constitution, by careful design, prescribes a process for making law, and within that process there are many accountability checkpoints. … It would dash the whole scheme if Congress could give its power away to an entity that is not constrained by those checkpoints. The Constitution's deliberative process was viewed by the Framers as a valuable feature, not something to be lamented and evaded").

[17] West Virginia v. Environmental Protection Agency, 597 U.S. 697 (2022).

Clean Air Act did not grant the EPA authority to regulate emissions from existing power plants to require "generation shifting" at the grid level – that is, a shift in electricity production from coal to natural gas and then to wind and solar energy. The Court held that in the Clean Air Act Congress did not grant the EPA authority to devise emissions caps based on the generation-shifting approach, although the EPA may continue to regulate emissions through emissions-reduction technologies:

> Capping carbon dioxide emissions at a level that will force a nationwide transition away from the use of coal to generate electricity may be a sensible "solution to the crisis of the day." . . . But it is not plausible that Congress gave EPA the authority to adopt on its own such a regulatory scheme in Section 111(d). A decision of such magnitude and consequence rests with Congress itself, or an agency acting pursuant to a clear delegation from that representative body.[18]

This major questions doctrine narrows the authority of other Executive Branch agencies as well. Consider another example that could someday come before the Supreme Court. Congress has given the Federal Trade Commission (FTC) broad authority to prosecute "unfair methods of competition in or affecting commerce, and unfair or deceptive acts or practices in or affecting commerce."[19] But what are "unfair methods of competition" and "unfair or deceptive acts or practices"? The statute does not say. It leaves it to the FTC to decide what business practices are unfair. Thus far, FTC regulations on unfair trade practices have survived in the courts, but, arguably, this flexible and long-used type of statutory construction arguably violates the major questions doctrine. If so, the FTC regulations would be invalid, and Congress would have to pass new legislation enumerating which specific trade practices are unfair and are prohibited.

A separate but important question is whether federal courts will defer to federal agencies' interpretation of statutes that Congress has passed within their purview. The power of the President as head of the Executive Branch is closely linked to the power of federal agencies to interpret and enforce the law. For forty years, courts paid substantial deference to federal agencies in interpreting acts of Congress which they were tasked with interpreting and enforcing.

In *Chevron v. Natural Resources Defense Council*,[20] the Court stated that the Clean Air Act permitted the EPA in 1981 to define the term "stationary source" to mean whole industrial plants only, which allowed plants to build or modify units within plants without the permit required under the Act. In the first year of the Reagan administration the EPA had reversed from the stricter statutory interpretation it had adhered to in the Carter administration.

The Court in *Chevron* held that the Reagan-era EPA's plantwide definition was a permissible construction of the statutory term "stationary source," and more broadly

[18] *Id.*

[19] 15 U.S.C. § 45 (1914).

[20] Chevron v. Natural Resources Defense Council, 467 U.S. 837 (1984).

that with respect to judicial review of an agency's construction of the statute that it administers, if Congress has not directly spoken to the precise question at issue, the Court will decide whether the agency's answer is based on a permissible construction of the statute and, if so, the agency's view shall prevail.[21] The Reagan administration EPA's statutory construction might not have been the best one and was opposed by environmental groups such as the Natural Resources Defense Council, but it was "permissible" and sustained.

That all changed in 2024. In *Loper Bright Enterprises v. Raimondo*,[22] the Court dramatically overturned forty years of precedent. It abruptly ended the judicial deference to administrative agencies established in *Chevron*. This decision means judges now must themselves interpret legislation enacted by Congress, sometimes with the advice of relevant federal agencies. Portions of highly technical statutes may even have been drafted in the same agencies and then sent to Congress for passage. In the future, those statutes, nonetheless, will be interpreted by courts without regard for the views of the agencies. Judges who defer to agency expertise in interpreting statutes now risk being reversed on appeal.

The Court observed:

> *Chevron*'s presumption is misguided because agencies have no special competence in resolving statutory ambiguities. Courts do. The Framers, as noted, anticipated that courts would often confront statutory ambiguities and expected that courts would resolve them by exercising independent legal judgment. ... The very point of the traditional tools of statutory construction – the tools courts use every day – is to resolve statutory ambiguities. That is no less true when the ambiguity is about the scope of an agency's own power – perhaps the occasion on which abdication in favor of the agency is *least* appropriate.[23]

The *Loper Bright Enterprises* case is not just about statutory construction and administrative law. The decision takes a substantial amount of power away from the President as head of the Executive Branch. Recall that in *Chevron* the Court had deferred to the Reagan administration's interpretation of statutory language in Clean Air Act amendments that passed Congress in 1977 during the Carter administration.

The Court's ruling in *Chevron* enabled President Reagan's EPA to adopt more pro-industry rules while courts deferred to the EPA's expert interpretation of underlying statutes. Many liberal constitutional and administrative law scholars praised the *Chevron* doctrine in the following decades, and decried its reversal by the Roberts court in 2024, but it is easy to forget that *Chevron* deference to agency statutory interpretation enhanced presidential power not just in liberal pro-regulation administrations, but also, as in *Chevron* itself, facilitated the policy agenda of a president

[21] *Id.* at 842–45.
[22] Loper Bright Enterprises v. Raimondo, 603 U.S. 369 (2024).
[23] *Id.*

who favored scaling back federal regulation and reducing the reach of the administrative state.

Yet another question addressed by the Roberts court in 2024 was whether Congress can give administrative agencies the power to adjudicate party matters that otherwise would be litigated before a judge and jury. In *Securities and Exchange Commission v. Jarkesy*,[24] the Supreme Court in 2024 curtailed this type of delegation as a violation of the Seventh Amendment right to trial by jury. A Securities and Exchange Commission administrative law judge (ALJ) had found that hedge fund manager George Jarkesy committed securities fraud, fined him, and required disgorgement of $685,000 in ill-gotten gains. The SEC commissioners upheld this decision. But the Fifth Circuit reversed, holding that under the nondelegation doctrine, Congress does not have power to allow SEC ALJs to adjudicate securities fraud cases. The question then presented to the Supreme Court was: "Does the statutory scheme that empowers the Securities and Exchange Commission violate the Seventh Amendment [right to a jury trial], the nondelegation doctrine, or Article II of the U.S. Constitution?"[25]

The Court ruled only on the first question, holding that when the SEC seeks civil penalties for securities fraud, the Seventh Amendment entitles the defendant to a jury trial. The Court did not rule on the nondelegation doctrine question, although the Fifth Circuit's ruling on nondelegation remains good law, at least in that Circuit.

The implications of this case are very broad. They extend well beyond the SEC. There are almost 2,000 ALJs in the Executive Branch agencies who conduct administrative hearings and adjudicate cases between the agencies and private parties. The Court in *Jarkesy* sharply curtailed the power of these ALJs. They no longer can try facts and adjudicate cases as Article III federal courts do.

This is not a book on administrative law. Rather our focus is on presidential power. Yet the power of presidents rises or falls with the power of the federal agencies under the President's control. While the Supreme Court has expanded presidential power in some ways, including holding that presidents have nearly unlimited power to remove superior federal officers,[26] the Court also has reduced the power of the Executive Branch though its embrace of the "major questions" doctrine, and now the reversal of *Chevron* deference to federal agencies in statutory interpretation. These developments shift power back toward the courts and Congress, while reducing the power of presidents. It has done so by reversing decades of legal precedents.

The Roberts court, therefore, has upended the law in many areas relevant to presidential power, but not in one direction. The Court in some ways has increased

24 Securities and Exchange Commission v. Jarkesy, 603 U.S. 109 (2024).

25 *Id.*

26 *See e.g.* Seila Law v. Consumer Financial Protection Bureau, 591 U.S. 197 (2020), discussed further in Chapter 1 of this book.

the scope of presidential power, but in other ways has reduced sharply the domestic powers of the Executive Branch.

The political furor surrounding the administrative state and presidential power is understandable. The country has experienced not only the benefits of a vastly expanded, and more efficient, administrative state, but the drawbacks, including the cost, with much of it covered by the federal income tax or deficit spending, and the politicization of agencies run by appointees of the President. Nonetheless, who gets to balance the pros and cons of the administrative state and decide? Should long-established and well-settled practices in administrative law, including congressional delegation of rulemaking power to federal agencies, judicial deference to statutory interpretations of federal agencies, be reversed so suddenly by five or six of the nine unelected justices of the Supreme Court? Such a fundamental overhaul of administrative law, arguably, should be undertaken, if at all, by the two elected branches of government that are fully capable of using legislation to narrow or expand the powers of federal agencies as needed.

A separate question is how feasible it is for the President to exercise power over the administrative state to accomplish a policy agenda. Can federal agencies quickly and efficiently implement a policy agenda the way Woodrow Wilson envisioned they should in his work on the administrative state?

This is the question of administrative capacity and competence – how good are federal agencies at doing what they are delegated to do? The large volume of workload required in the modern administrative state at times might make it difficult for changes to be implemented quickly. A 2024 study demonstrated that insufficient capacity in federal agencies prevents presidents from achieving their policy agendas and faithfully executing the law:

> Drawing on a survey of federal executives engaged in rulemaking, a dataset of over 190 million federal personnel records, and a dataset of over 5,000 rulemakings from three presidencies, it contributes three core findings to our understanding of presidential power. First, new measures of capacity show wider variation across federal agencies than people often assume. Second, a new survey of federal executives shows that presidents and their proxies have the greatest degree of control over agency rulemaking agendas. Third and finally, multivariate models demonstrate that a low-capacity agency is less likely to complete a rulemaking than a high-capacity agency, controlling for factors that influence both presidential control and presidential priorities. Most importantly, Presidents struggle to implement their agendas in low-capacity agencies regardless of whether they have significant control over those agencies. Traditional markers of presidential control prove ineffective in low-capacity agencies, and, therefore, control and capacity are complements – not substitutes.[27]

[27] Nicholas R. Bednar, *Presidential Control and Administrative Capacity*, 77 Stan. L. Rev. 823 (Apr. 2025); Elaine C. Kamarck, Why Presidents Fail and How They Can Succeed Again (2016).

Another important question is whether this lack of agency capacity is symmetrical in that it affects presidents of both parties equally, or asymmetrical in that agencies have more capacity to dismantle regulations than to promulgate and implement new ones. If so, presidents whose political agenda is to cut back federal regulation and to reduce the size of the administrative state, may accomplish their policy objectives more quickly than presidents who seek to expand regulation to achieve policy goals. The dramatic changes to the administrative state inflicted by President Trump's Department of Government Efficiency (DOGE) in 2025, including mass firings of career civil servants and dismantling of entire agencies such as the United States Agency for International Development (USAID), suggests that this may be the case, although as this book goes to press multiple cases are pending in federal courts that will determine how far these changes can go without legislation passing Congress.

Meanwhile, despite laws protecting the job security of the civil service, civil servants are vulnerable to abuse at the hands of the President and his appointees. Direct constitutional removal power of the President applies only to officers appointed by the President, but those superior officers can be ordered by the President to fire others. This theory of presidential removal power – today often referred to as the "unitary executive theory" – is discussed in Chapter 1 of this book. It not only gives the President the power to build a more efficient civil service, but also to fire people for the wrong reasons. As Black federal workers found out during the Wilson administration, even lower levels of government, supposedly protected by civil service laws, are not always exempt from the whims of the President and his political appointees. And now, in his second term in 2025 Donald Trump has vastly overhauled the federal government with executive orders compelling many agencies to reduce their scope of operations, as well as with pressure from DOGE, a newly created entity within the Executive Office of the President, to force thousands of career civil servants into retirement.

Finally, we turn to a provision of the Constitution that defines an important part of the relationship between the President and the heads of the executive departments. The Opinions Clause. Article II, Section 2, Clause 1, provides: "The President . . . may require the Opinion, in writing, of the principal Officer in each of the executive Departments, upon any Subject relating to the Duties of their respective Offices."

Presumably an opinion provided to the President by the head of an executive department should be an honest opinion made in good faith, even if the President disagrees with it. There also is no requirement in the Constitution that heads of departments follow the orders of the President. However, as discussed in Chapter 1 of this book, the Supreme Court has upheld the President's power to fire the officers he appoints.

As Ilan Wurman writes:

> Congress can insulate inferior officers from removal because they must follow orders. As for principal officers, however, the President can remove but not control

> them, at least not directly. There is no constitutional obligation on the part of principal officers to obey; the only inducement is the threat of removal. The Opinions Clause, far from being superfluous, then assures the President the power to acquire information to intelligently exercise the power to remove. In addition to this account's textual and structural virtues, it appears to have been the understanding of presidential power shared by George Washington, Thomas Jefferson, James Madison, William Wirt, Daniel Webster, William Howard Taft, and the First Congress.[28]

In other words, federal officers outside the military have no legal obligation to carry out the orders of the President. But if they do not obey the President, or even if they express opinions with which the President disagrees, or displeases the President in any other way, the President can respond with two words that Donald Trump was famous for years before he ran for President: "You're fired!" Other scholars, in 2023, argued that this removal power did not entitle a president to fire a federal officer to carry out a crime – for example, the President firing a whistleblower as part of a plan to obstruct justice.[29] But in 2024, the Supreme Court in *Trump v. United States*,[30] remarkedly, bestowed on the President a presumption of immunity from criminal prosecution for any official act, including firing or ordering the firing of someone in the Executive Branch.

28 Ilan Wurman, *The Opinions Clause and Presidential Power*, 16 J. LEGAL ANALYSIS 2024).

29 Claire O. Finkelstein & Richard W. Painter, *"You're Fired": Criminal Use of Presidential Removal Power*, 25 N.Y.U. J. LEGIS. & PUB. POL'Y 307 (2023).

30 Trump v. United States, 603 U.S. 593 (2024).

3

The President as Commander in Chief

Article II, Section 2 of the Constitution states that "[t]he President shall be Commander in Chief of the Army and Navy of the United States, and of the Militia of the several States, when called into the actual Service of the United States."[1] Unlike the vesting clause discussed earlier, which had significant debate during the Constitutional Convention, the Commander in Chief clause was an occasion for little debate at the Convention. Because the Founding generation recently and personally had fought a war to gain their independence from Great Britain, the Founders were acutely aware of the need to vest military command in a single civilian individual.

While there was little debate at the Convention regarding the need for the President to act as Commander in Chief, the application of the President's Commander in Chief powers sparked debate about the outer limits of that power as changes in the technology, tactics, and character of war have forced presidents to adopt eighteenth-century principles to nineteenth-, twentieth-, and twenty-first-century problems.

There are three legal avenues for a president to use military force: (1) a war declared by Congress; (2) authorization by Congress for use of military force short of a declared war; and (3) the President's unilateral use of Article II power as Commander in Chief to defend the United States and its interests.

Deployments of US troops without a declared war are as old as the Republic. Without authorization from Congress, President Jefferson used the Navy to suppress the Barbary pirates who were attacking American shipping. In 1900, President McKinley deployed US troops to China to suppress the Boxer rebellion. The McKinley administration claimed that the operation was necessary to rescue missionaries and other US citizens who were trapped there.[2] Never mind that the

[1] U.S. Const. Art. II, § 2, Cl. 1.

[2] *See Message of the President*, Dept. of State Office of the Historian (Dec. 3, 1900), https://history.state.gov/historicaldocuments/frus1900/message-of-the-president.

United States, and the European colonial powers, all had commercial interests in China too.

The last declared war was World War II. US military engagements since then have been undertaken by the President, claiming express or implied authorization from Congress, an exercise of Article II power to act unilaterally even without consent of Congress, or a combination of the two.

As former Secretary of State Cyrus Vance observed in 1984:

> President Franklin Roosevelt, without consulting Congress, ordered the occupation of Greenland and Iceland and directed the Navy to protect British merchant shipping in the North Atlantic. President Truman committed the U.S. to the Korean War on the recommendation of the United Nations Security Council rather than pursuant to a congressional mandate. President Kennedy ordered a naval blockade of Cuba without congressional endorsement. In 1965 President Johnson dispatched 22,000 U.S. troops to the Dominican Republic without congressional approval.[3]

A lot of miliary operations have been undertaken since, with or without the consent of Congress.

There is no clear definition of "war" as referenced in Article I. Actions taken to defend the United States and its territories or to defend US forces stationed abroad apparently do not require a declaration of war from Congress.[4] Waiting for congressional approval also may endanger national security.[5] On the other hand, military actions taken to defend US economic interests or at the request of a foreign government may exceed the President's authority as Commander in Chief without congressional approval.[6]

In this chapter, we explore the arguments for and against the President's use of war powers.

[3] Cyrus R. Vance, *Striking the Balance: Congress and the President under the War Powers Resolution*, 133 U. PA. L. REV. 79, 80 (1984). Secretary Vance served during the Carter administration, when the Justice Department defined war powers broadly in the wake of the Iran hostage crisis. *See Presidential Power to Use the Armed Forces Abroad without Statutory Authorization, Memorandum Opinion for the Attorney General*, U.S. Dept. of Justice, at 187 (Feb. 12, 1980), www.justice.gov/file/149241-0/dl ("The President's inherent, constitutional authority as Commander-in-Chief, his broad foreign policy powers, and his duty to take care that the laws be faithfully executed generally empower him to deploy the armed forces abroad without a declaration of war by Congress or other congressional authorization. A historical pattern of presidential initiative and congressional acquiescence in emergency situations calling for immediate action, including situations involving rescue and retaliation, confirm this inherent power, and the courts have generally declined to review its use").

[4] *See* Stephen M. Griffin & Matthew C. Waxman, *War Powers: Congress, the President, and the Courts – A Model Casebook Section*, Columbia Public Law Research Paper No. 14-669, at 9 (2020).

[5] *Id.*

[6] David P. Forsythe et al., *U.S. Use of Force Abroad: What Law for the President?*, 26(4) PRESIDENTIAL STUD. Q. 957–60 (1996).

3.1 EARLY USE OF WAR POWERS IN THE ADAMS ADMINISTRATION: THE CONSTITUTIONAL FRAMEWORK

Article I, Section 8 of the Constitution grants to Congress the power "To declare War" and also says that Congress has the power to "grant Letters of Marque and Reprisal, and make Rules concerning Captures on Land and Water." But what did the Founders envision that the President as Commander in Chief would do to defend the country? How much was he expected to consult Congress?

In the late 1790s separations of power were put to the test when the United States entered what became known as a "Quasi-War" with France. France, US's ally in the American Revolution, had deposed and executed its king and under a new government was fighting other European powers including Great Britain. Britain had an important trading relationship with the United States, putting American shipping at risk. Between 1797 and 1799, the French navy seized hundreds of American ships. President John Adams responded by building the US Navy and seeking to authorize American privateers to defend American shipping.

The reaction of the Founders to this military crisis is important because it reflects an early understanding of the respective roles of the President and Congress in defending the nation's interests against a foreign aggressor in the absence of a declared war. Much of the contemporary conversation about the "Quasi-War" was premised on the assumption that Congress had a preeminent role in decisions about war and peace. Still, there was no definitive agreement among the Founders, or holding by the Supreme Court, explicitly saying that the President lacked constitutional authority to act on his own.

The United States has been getting into quasi wars ever since. What's noticeably different today is that presidents more often unilaterally enter into or expand US involvement in foreign conflicts, without explicit or even implicit authorization from Congress. Such does not appear to be the world the Founders envisioned even if they did not insert explicit language in the Constitution prohibiting it.

James McHenry served as Secretary of War from 1796 to 1800. In May 1798 McHenry wrote to Alexander Hamilton asking the critical question of how far the President could go in engaging in hostilities with France without the consent of Congress.

> My dear Hamilton.
>
> I shall in a short time be able to get to sea, one or two of our frigates, and perhaps, in less than six or seven days, Cap Dale, in the Ganges, a lately purchased vessel. Can you spare an hour or two to help me to the instructions that it will be proper to give to their captains. Our ships of war, it is probable, will meet with French privateers, who may be in possession of our merchantmen, or with our merchant vessels having French prize masters on board; or with French privateers cruising upon our coast to capture American vessels. They may also when acting as convoys be

> obliged to employ force to protect their convoy, and may even be obliged to board a French ship of war to terminate a contest and insure its safety. What instructions ought to be given to meet such cases, or enable them to afford competent protection to our merchantmen and preserve the Executive from any future accusation, of having by its orders involved the country in war.[7]

Hamilton's response:

> My Dear Sir
>
> I have received your letter of the instant. Not having seen the law which provides the *Naval Armament*, I cannot tell whether it gives any new power to the President that is any power whatever with regard to the employment of the Ships. If not, and he is left on the foot of the Constitution, as I understand to be the case, I am not ready to say that he has any other power than merely to employ the Ships as Convoys with authority to *repel* force by *force*, (but not to capture), and to repress hostilities within our waters including a marine league from our coasts. Any thing beyond this must fall under the idea of *reprisals* & requires the sanction of that Department which is to declare or make war.
>
> In so delicate a case, in one which involves so important a consequence as that of War – my opinion is that no doubtful authority ought to be exercised by the President – but that as different opinions about his power have been expressed in the house of Representatives, and no special power has been given by the law, it will be expedient for him, and his duty, and the true policy of the Conjuncture to come forward by a Message to the two houses of Congress declaring that "so *far* and no *farther*" he feels himself *confident* of his authority to go in the employment of the naval force; that as in his opinion the depredations on our trade demand a more extensive protection he has thought it his duty to bring the subject under the review of Congress by a communication of his opinion of his own powers – having no desire to exceed the constitutional limits.
>
> This course will remove all clouds as to what The President will do – will gain him credit for frankness and an unwillingness to chicane the Constitution – and will return upon Congress the Question in a shape which cannot be eluded.[8]

If there is one among the Founders who is most often associated with the concept of a strong executive, it is Alexander Hamilton. But at least in matters of war, he seemed to think there were limits on how far a president should go without consent from Congress, "that Department which is to declare or make war." He does not go

7 *To Alexander Hamilton from James McHenry, May 12, 1798*, Founders Online, National Archives, https://founders.archives.gov/documents/Hamilton/01-21-02-0253. Original source: The Papers of Alexander Hamilton, vol. 21, April 1797 – July 1798, 459–61 (Harold C. Syrett ed., 1974).

8 *From Alexander Hamilton to James McHenry, [May 17 1798]*, Founders Online, National Archives, https://founders.archives.gov/documents/Hamilton/01-21-02-0255. Original source: The Papers of Alexander Hamilton, vol. 21, April 1797 – July 1798 461–63 (Harold C. Syrett ed., 1974).

so far as to say that a president *cannot* go further, but the implication is that there are constraints on the President and that the President should not "chicane the Constitution" by going further.

Two months later, on July 7, 1798, Congress did act by rescinding a treaty between the United States and France, sending a clearer signal that Congress embraced strong military action. It never declared war against France. Congress then passed a series of laws expressly facilitating recovery of captured American ships and seizure of ships sailing to French ports, but only under specific circumstances.[9]

There followed before the Supreme Court a series of cases known as the "Quasi-War cases," involving captured shipping. Ordinarily the war powers of Congress and the President do not come before the Court because parties do not have standing to sue. But in these cases, the Court interpreted statutes authorizing the capture of hostile ships or awarding a monetary sum to reward American privateers for recovery of ships that had been seized on the high seas – with a higher sum, up to half the value of the ship, awarded if the ship had been seized by an "enemy" of the United States. Owners of vessels successfully recovering captured ships sued for the reward, under a statutory framework that turned on whether a state of "war" existed with the ship's captors. Owners of vessels improperly seized also sued American privateers for damages.

These cases, in finding a state of war between the United States and France, interpreted acts of Congress, not the President, authorizing a state of hostilities, and determined that France was indeed an "enemy" power within the meaning of federal statutes even though there was no declared war.[10] The cases do not say whether the President acting alone could similarly authorize hostilities with France or any other country if Congress had remained silent.

Of particular interest is a case in which the Court explicitly held that the President did not have authority from Congress to order seizure of ships leaving French ports, only seizure of American ships sailing *to* French ports, and that a Boston privateer's seizure of a Danish ship leaving Haiti had been illegal.[11] However, the Court only decided a dispute between private parties over whether the seizure had been illegal. It was not entering an injunction against the President.

9 *See e.g.* Act to Suspend the Commercial Intercourse between the United States and France, and the Dependencies Thereof, Act of June 13, 1798, ch. 53, 1 U.S. Stat. 565; Act in Addition to the Act More Effectually to Protect the Commerce and Coasts of the United States, Act of June 28, 1798, ch. 62, 1 U.S. Stat. 574; Act Further to Suspend the Commercial Intercourse between the United States and France, and the Dependencies Thereof, Act of Feb. 27, 1800, ch. 10, 2 U.S. Stat. 7.

10 *See* Bas v. Tingy, 4 U.S. (4 Dall.) 37 (1800) (awarding to the captain of the recovering public armed vessel half the value of a ship recovered from the French because France was an "enemy" after Congress appeared to have authorized hostilities even though Congress had not declared war), Talbot v. Seeman, 5 U.S. (I Cranch) 1 (1801) (similar holding concerning salvage rights to a German vessel recaptured by an American vessel from the French).

11 Little v. Barreme, 6 U.S. (2 Cranch) 170, (1804) (holding that the President did not have "any special authority" to order seizure of non-American ships departing French ports).

Some constitutional law scholars in the post-Vietnam era argued that these early cases reflect an understanding that warmaking powers are reserved mostly for Congress, not the President.[12] Others have argued that presidential power is considerably broader[13] and that "these cases concerning the legality of capturing ships belonging to or collaborating with France during the Quasi War do not illuminate how the war powers should be allocated between Congress and the President."[14] The former is probably the better argument. Congress's multiple bills authorizing the Quasi-War suggest that Congress did not think warmaking an issue solely for the President. On the other hand, the United States did not have a navy at the beginning of the Adams administration, and the President depended on Congress for the funding to build one, so he had no choice but to work with Congress to confront the crisis with France. Much of the Quasi War was also conducted by privateers to earn monetary awards Congress provided for by statute.

The Constitution is silent on how far the President can go unilaterally. If Adams had wanted to go it alone against France, without consent of Congress, could he have done so even if Hamilton and others would have objected? Would the Supreme Court have told him he couldn't? As with counterfactual history generally, nobody knows.[15]

3.2 DOMESTIC USE OF COMMANDER IN CHIEF POWERS

Before discussing further in Sections 3.3 and 3.4 how presidents have used their power as Commander in Chief to take military action outside the United States, this Section will briefly address a different issue which is when and how the President can deploy the military inside the United States, a power that has been specifically constrained by acts of Congress. Also it is important to define "the Army and Navy of the United States, and ... the Militia of the several States."[16] While Article II only explicitly enumerates "the Army and Navy," today this list has expanded to six branches including the United States Marine Corps (established in 1775), the United States Coast Guard (established in 1915), the United States Air Force (established in 1947), and the United States Space Force (established in 2019).

[12] *See* Charles A. Lofgren, *War-Making under the Constitution: The Original Understanding*, 81 Yale L.J. 672, 695–97 (1972); Abraham D. Sofaer, *The Presidency, War and Foreign Affairs: Practice under the Framers*, 40 Law & Contemp. Probs. 12, 27 (1976).

[13] Eugene V. Rostow, *Great Cases Make Bad Law: The War Powers Act*, 50 Tex. L. Rev. 833, 850 n28 (1972) (arguing that the War Clause does not give Congress alone the power to initiate military hostility).

[14] J. Gregory Sidak, *The Quasi War Cases – and Their Relevance to Whether "Letters of Marque and Reprisal" Constrain Presidential War Powers*, 27 Harv. J. of L. & Pub. Pol'y. 465 (2005).

[15] *See id.* at 467, arguing that the President's war powers are broad, particularly if Congress has not spoken, citing John C. Yoo, *The Continuation of Politics by Other Means: The Original Understanding of War Powers*, 84 Cal. L. Rev. 167, 294–95 n584 (1996).

[16] U.S. Const. Art. II, § 2, cl. 1.

These six military branches compose the active-duty military. Additionally, each of these military branches, with the exception of the Space Force, has a reserve component as well. Unlike the active-duty military, for whom the military is their primary employment, reservists typically are not full-time service members. However, both active-duty and reservists fall under the exclusive control of the President.

At the state level, every state in the Union has a National Guard that is under the control of the state governor. The National Guards are the modern equivalent of the "Milita[s] of the several States" described in Article II, Section 2, Clause 1. Like federal reservists, national guardsmen typically are not full-time service members. However, despite being a function of state government, presidents may, and have, "federalized" National Guard units.

When might a president need to call the National Guard into federal service if he has the power to control federal forces? The answer to this question lies in a one-sentence statute. In 1878 Congress passed the Posse Comitatus Act[17] that, as amended, prohibits the use of "any part of the Army, the Navy, the Marine Corps, the Air Force, or the Space Force . . . to execute the laws" unless expressly authorized by the Constitution or an act of Congress.[18] However, these Posse Comitatus limitations only apply to service members under *federal* but not *state* control.

When the President federalizes National Guard units, he may do so under two authorities known as "Title 10"[19] and "Title 32."[20] Under Title 10 authority, federalized National Guards and active-duty units are legally indistinguishable from one another. National Guard units federalized under Title 10 receive federal funding, their members receive the same benefits as active-duty service members, and they are subject to the limitation of the Posse Comitatus Act. Typically, Title 10 is invoked when National Guard units are used to support active-duty operations overseas. Throughout the wars in Afghanistan and Iraq during the twenty-first century, presidents regularly invoked Title 10 to support active-duty operations in those theaters.

In contrast to Title 10, Title 32 is a blend of federal and state control. As under Title 10, Title 32 mobilizations receive federal funding and allow the federalized units to perform missions requested by the President. However, unlike Title 10, Title 32 federalization keeps command and control at the state level. The importance of this distinction in command is that it exempts national guardsmen from the limitations of the Posse Comitatus Act.

In June 2025, however, Trump invoked Title 10 to federalize the California national guard to quell violent protests after federal immigration officers conducted

[17] 18 U.S.C. §1385 (1956).
[18] *Id.*
[19] *See generally* 10 U.S.C. §§123011 (1956).
[20] *See generally* 32 U.S.C. ch. 9 (1916).

raids in homes and workplaces in Los Angelese. Trump also deployed U.S. Marines to Los Angeles. He argued federal troops were needed to protect immigration officers in performance of their duties and to protect federal buildings, an exception to the Posse Comitatus Act allowed under Title 10. California Governor Gavin Newsom sued Trump, seeking an injunction against federalization of the national guard for domestic law enforcement on the grounds that state police could restore order and that Trump was illegally using federal troops for more than protecting federal immigration agents and federal buildings in Los Angeles. At this writing, the case was on appeal. Whether in the Los Angeles case or another case somewhere else, there is a good chance that Trump will bring this issue to the Supreme Court during his second term.[21]

Throughout the twenty-first century, presidents have used this Title 32 "loophole" for several domestic missions. President George W. Bush invoked Title 32 in the aftermath of the September 11 attacks to use National Guard troops as airport security,[22] to assist with disaster relief after hurricanes Katrina[23] and Rita[24] in 2005, and to support the Border Patrol at the southern border.[25] President Trump invoked Title 32 in 2018 to send 4,000 federalized National Guard troops to the southern border,[26] and again in 2020 to support the Federal Emergency Management Agency's (FEMA's) COVID-19 operations.[27] President

[21] *See* Gavin Newsom v. Donald Trump, No. 25-3727, 3:25-cv-04870-CRB (9th Cir. June 19, 2025), on appeal from the United States District Court for the Northern District of California (Order staying pending appeal the district court's temporary restraining order "(1) enjoining the President of the United States, the Secretary of Defense, and the Department of Defense from deploying members of the California National Guard in Los Angelese; and (2) directing defendants to return control of the California National Guard to California"). President Trump had invoked 10 U.S.C. § 12406(3), which authorizes federalization of the National Guard when "the President is unable with the regular forces to execute the laws of the United States." The 9th Circuit panel determined that, although Trump was wrong to assert that federal courts could not review his decision, he was still likely to prevail on the merits because courts are highly deferential to the President in such instances.

[22] Kelly Wallace, *Bush Expands Natl. Guard Role at Airports*, CNN (Nov. 9, 2001, 4:33 PM), www.cnn.com/2001/US/11/09/rec.bush.airportsecurity/index.html.

[23] Scott Shane & Thom Shanker, *When Storm Hit, National Guard Was Deluged Too*, New York Times (Sept. 28, 2005), www.nationalguard.mil/Features/2015/Remembering-Hurricane-Katrina/.

[24] The White House, *Fact Sheet: The Federal Government's Hurricane Rita Preparations*, https://georgewbush-whitehouse.archives.gov/news/releases/2005/09/20050923-3.html.

[25] The White House, *Fact Sheet: Operation Jump Start: Acting Now to Secure the Border*, https://georgewbush-whitehouse.archives.gov/news/releases/2006/08/20060803-7.html.

[26] United States Department of Defense, *National Guard Troops Deploy to Southern U.S. Border*, www.defense.gov/News/News-Stories/Article/Article/1487387/national-guard-troops-deploy-to-southern-us-border/.

[27] The White House, *Memorandum on Providing Federal Support for Governors' Use of the National Guard to Respond to COVID-19*, https://trumpwhitehouse.archives.gov/presidential-actions/memorandum-providing-federal-support-governors-use-national-guard-respond-covid-19/.

Biden used Title 32 in 2021 to extend the Trump-era COVID-19 support operations.[28]

In addition to the Title 32 exception, Congress has made an explicit carve-out to the Posse Comitatus Act that allows the President to use the military to enforce the Fourteenth and Fifteenth Amendments.[29] Known as the "Enforcement Acts," a combination of three laws passed in 1870 and 1871 allow the President to use federal troops to enforce the Equal Protection Clause of the Fourteenth Amendment and right to vote enshrined in the Fifteenth Amendment.

The Enforcement Acts were invoked in 1957 when President Eisenhower used active-duty troops to enforce the Court's desegregation order in *Brown v. Board of Education*.[30] After the Court ordered the swift desegregation of America's schools, Arkansas Governor Orval Faubus used the state's National Guard to prevent a group of nine Black students from enrolling in Central High School in Little Rock, Arkansas. In response to this blatant disregard of the Court's desegregation orders, President Eisenhower invoked the Enforcement Acts exception to the Posse Comitatus Act to federalize the Arkansas National Guard under Title 10. One thousand active-duty troops were sent to Little Rock to restore order.[31]

This episode, however, was not the first time a president would use their Commander in Chief powers to enforce civil rights. In an expansive, creative use of a president's executive power, we turn to President Lincoln's use of an executive order in issuing the Emancipation Proclamation in 1863. This book previously discussed the Emancipation in Chapter 1 under the topic of executive orders, but we return to it here because executive orders historically have been broad when the President is acting as Commander in Chief.

In 1863 the Union army's effort in the civil war was not going well, "which threatened the survival of the Union and the Constitution itself."[32] While Congress also was considering the issue of emancipation of enslaved people through discussion of two Confiscations acts,[33] Lincoln had ample wisdom and experience that the institution of slavery was central to the economy of the Confederacy, and as such it was the engine that supported the South's war effort and successes on the battlefield.[34] Enslaved people were used in many ways with their labor to fortify the

[28] The White House, *Memorandum to Extend Federal Support to Governor's Use of the National Guard to Respond to COVID-19 and to Increase Reimbursement and Other Assistance Provided to States*, https://bidenwhitehouse.archives.gov/briefing-room/presidential-actions/2021/01/21/extend-federal-support-to-governors-use-of-national-guard-to-respond-to-covid-19-and-to-increase-reimbursement-and-other-assistance-provided-to-states/.

[29] Enforcement Act of 1870, 16 Stat. 140–46 (1870), Second Enforcement Act of 1871, 16 Stat. 433–40 (1871), Ku Klux Klan Act, 17 Stat. 13 (1871).

[30] Brown v. Board of Education of Topeka, 347 U.S. 483 (1954).

[31] Exec. Order No. 10730, 22 Fed. Reg. 186 (1957), at 7628.

[32] Doris Kearns Goodwin, Leadership in Turbulent Times, 215, 240 (2018).

[33] Daniel A. Farber, Lincoln's Constitution, 153 (2003).

[34] *Id.*

needs of the Confederacy.[35] The use of "slave labor gave the Confederacy a real war advantage."[36] If slavery could be ended, and the enslaved population freed, the South's rebellion could be ended.

Thus, Lincoln saw that ending the institution of slavery was a "military necessity" to winning the Civil War and "restoring the Union."[37] He saw an emancipation declaration as the instrument and means to justify the Union's weakening of the Confederacy and a "fit and necessary war measure for suppressing said rebellion."[38] This was so, he argued, because if the enslaved were freed, Southern landowners would not be available to join the Confederacy's war effort.[39]

In short, Lincoln was able to justify the issuance of the Emancipation Proclamation through an executive order as a necessary war effort through his Article II constitutional war powers as Commander in Chief of the military. As a military strategy, this was viewed as a "legitimate exercise of the President's constitutional war powers."[40] While this underlying war powers rationale was compelling, it surely was an expansive but a successful expansion of presidential power during a domestic war.

Historians continue to consider whether Lincoln's Emancipation Proclamation declaration was based primarily on uniting the Union or promoting civil rights and dignity for enslaved people.[41] Regardless of the historical debate, the issuance of the Emancipation Proclamation achieved (1) a compelling societal good, (2) the expansion of presidential war powers, and (3) the ending of the war.

Another creative action of the Commander in Chief power by Lincoln can be seen in the decision to suspend habeas corpus and establish military tribunals for civilians during the Civil War. This book previously discussed Lincoln's suspension of habeas corpus in Chapter 1, as well as Chief Justice Taney's ruling against Lincoln in another case, *Ex parte Merryman*. Here, more detail on the controversy is appropriate considering the rationale for Lincoln's action that in a civil war he had to exercise his power as Commander in Chief. In October of 1864, a military trial was convened in Indiana to determine whether four men, including Lambdin

[35] MARIA M. CUOMO & HAROLD HOLZER, LINCOLN'S DEMOCRACY, 326 (1990). *See also* FARBER, *supra* note 33, at 153; DORIS KEARNS GOODWIN, TEAM OF RIVALS: THE POLITICAL GENIUS OF ABRAHAM LINCOLN, 459, 462–63 (2005).

[36] GOODWIN, *supra* note 35.

[37] GOODWIN, *supra* note 32; CUOMO & HOLZER, *supra* note 35; GOODWIN, *supra* note 35; FARBER, *supra* note 33, at 153–54.

[38] FARBER, *supra* note 33, at 154–56; GOODWIN *supra* note 35.

[39] GOODWIN, *supra* note 35, at 462.

[40] *Id.* at 462–65. *See also* FARBER *supra* note 33, at 154, 156.

[41] GOODWIN, *supra* note 35, at 215, 471–72; CUOMO & HOLZER, *supra* note 35, at 326; GOODWIN, *supra* note 32, at 215. *See also* generally, MICHAEL BESCHLOSS, PRESIDENTS OF WAR 204 (2018); SARA BURNS, THE POLITICS OF WAR POWERS: THE THEORY AND HISTORY OF PRESIDENTIAL UNILATERALISM, 2–3, 105, 114–20 (2019); JON MEACHAM, AND THERE WAS LIGHT: ABRAHAM LINCOLN AND THE AMERICAN STRUGGLE, 289 (2022). *See also* ARTHUR M. SCHLESINGER JR., WAR AND THE AMERICAN PRESIDENCY (2004).

Milligan, were guilty of conspiring against the government of the United States, inciting rebellion, and supporting the Confederates. Milligan was found guilty of the charges and was sentenced to hang. Following his sentencing, Milligan's attorney filed a petition for a writ of habeas corpus to contest Milligan's detention.[42] In 1866 the Supreme Court considered Milligan's case. The questions, however, were whether the military tribunal that tried Milligan had the jurisdiction to do so.

In *Ex parte Milligan*,[43] the Court held that while Lincoln's Commander in Chief powers generally vested in him the authority to establish military tribunals, he did not have the authority to do so in this case. The Court's decision rested on two important distinctions – Milligan's status as a noncombatant civilian and the location of the tribunal in Indiana. The Court held that the President may try civilians in military trials, but only in theaters of active military operations where the regular civilian courts cannot function. Military tribunals could only operate when civilian government could not be reestablished.

A counterpoint to *Milligan* can be seen in a similar case, *Ex parte Quirin*, from World War II.[44] In June 1942 a squad of eight German saboteurs traveled in a German submarine from occupied France to landings in New York and Florida under the cover of darkness. Upon exiting the submarine near New York, four of the saboteurs, including Richard Quirin, an American citizen who had returned to Germany to fight for the Nazis, were stopped by a Coast Guard patrol boat. After making contact with the Coast Guard, the four saboteurs abandoned their military uniforms and changed into civilian dress. They were ultimately detained by military authorities when they reached land.

The following month the saboteurs were sentenced to death by a military tribunal established by President Roosevelt under his Commander in Chief powers. In his defense, Quirin's lawyer argued that the precedent set in *Milligan* meant that Quirin's tribunal was unconstitutional and outside of the President's Commander in Chief powers. The Court found that Quirin's defense was without merit. New York was not an active war zone in 1942, the traditional civilian courts were open and operational, and Quirin was, at best, an amateur saboteur. He had received no formal training in sabotage, had limited contacts with the Nazi government, and had expressed no plans to return to Germany after the war. Despite these arguments, the Supreme Court held that Quirin's case was different than Milligan's, concluding that the President had the power to try Quirin in a military tribunal.[45]

Why did the Court come to this decision and how did it distinguish it from *Milligan*? The Court's decision relies on the distinction between lawful and unlawful combatants. The Court defined lawful combatants as those who fight in a

42 Ex parte Milligan 71 U.S. 2, 2 (1866).

43 *Id.*

44 Ex parte Quirin 317 U.S. 1 (1942).

45 *Id.* at 26.

uniform. Lawful combatants fight under the laws of armed conflict and enjoy the rights of the laws of armed conflict, including the right to be held as prisoners of war until the conflict ends. Unlawful combatants, on the other hand, work undercover, clandestinely, and operate outside of the laws of armed conflict. Because unlawful combatants operate outside of laws of armed conflict they do not enjoy the legal protections afforded to lawful combatants. As a result, they may be sentenced to death following a military tribunal. The Court reasoned that Quirin became an unlawful combatant when he abandoned his German uniform following detection and when he changed into civilian clothing prior to reaching the shore.

Despite the distinctions in *Milligan* and *Quirin*, some scholars[46] find unsatisfying distinction between the two cases. Both Milligan and Quirin were nonuniformed, unlawful combatants, traditional courts were operational in both cases, both men were United States citizens, and neither Indiana or New York were active theaters of war during the Civil War or World War II, respectively.

The distinctions may rest on a timing context. By the time Milligan's case reached the Supreme Court in 1866, the Civil War had ended. The threat that the Confederacy posed to the stability and unity of the Union had been suppressed, and the nation was in the process of reconstruction. At the time, it was not a controversial decision for the Court to limit presidential power and to hold that the President's power to convene military tribunals was limited.

On the other hand, Quirin was tried in the summer of 1942. The national wounds of the Japanese attacks on Pearl Harbor were still fresh, Nazi Germany was opening concentration camps across Eastern Europe, and Americans had reasonable concerns about the war expanding into the American homeland. Arguably, against this backdrop the Court had no "politically" feasible choice but to find the tribunal that sentenced Quirin to death was within the President's Commander in Chief powers.[47] Perhaps, if Quirin's case had reached the Court in 1946, rather than 1942, the Court would have come to a different conclusion. Similar issues arose in a more recent case of *Hamdi v. Rumsfeld*,[48] holding that although Congress authorized detention of combatants in the circumstances alleged in the case, due process required that a US citizen held in the United States as an enemy combatant be given a meaningful opportunity before a neutral decision-maker to contest the factual basis for that detention.

While *Milligan* and *Quirin* deal with the question of military tribunals and enemy combatants, they don't address the power of the President, as Commander in Chief, to manage the affairs of civilians at home. In a pair of cases, *Korematsu v. United States*[49] and *Hirabayashi v. United*

[46] *See generally* Beverly E. Bashor, *The Liberty/Safety Paradigm: The United States' Struggle to Discourage Violations of Civil Liberties in Times of War*, 41 W. STATE UN. L. REV. 617 (2014).

[47] *Id.*

[48] Hamdi v. Rumsfeld, 542 U.S. 507 (2004), discussed in Section 3.3.

[49] Korematsu v. United States, 323 U.S. 214 (1944).

States,[50] the Court considered the power of the President as Commander in Chief to exclude Americans from areas of the United States in the interest of national security.

Following the attacks on Pearl Harbor in December 1941, President Roosevelt issued Executive Order 9066 that authorized the Secretary of War to designate areas within the United States to "prescribe military areas in such places and of such extent as he . . . may determine, from which any or all persons may be excluded."[51] In response to this order, Lieutenant General John Dewitt, Commander of the Western Defense Command and responsible for defending the Western United States, declared large portions of the west coast as military areas. He imposed strict curfews on the declared military areas and eventually ordered relocation for thousands of Japanese Americans and non-citizen Japanese immigrants.

In May 1942, Gordon Hirabayashi was arrested for violating the military curfew and subsequently was found guilty. On appeal, the Supreme Court held that that the President's issuance of Executive Order 9066 and the implementation of curfews across the west coast was constitutional. The Court found that

> [t]he war power of the national government is "the power to wage war successfully" . . . It extends to every matter and activity so related to war . . . The power is not restricted to the winning of victories in the field and the repulse of enemy forces. It embraces every phase of the national defense . . . Where, as they did here, the conditions call for the exercise of judgment and discretion and for the choice of means by those branches of the Government on which the Constitution has placed the responsibility of warmaking, it is not for any court to sit in review of the wisdom of their action or substitute its judgment for theirs.[52]

In 1944, the Court reexamined the constitutionality of Executive Order 9066 as it related to the relocation of Japanese Americans. Following the issuance of the Order, Fred Korematsu was arrested when he chose to stay in his home in California rather than relocate to an internment camp. Relying on their decision in *Hirabayashi*, two years earlier, the Court held that the Order was based not on racial animus toward Japanese Americans, but a strategic imperative to keep the United States safe within the President's Commander in Chief powers.

Writing a concurring opinion, Justice Frankfurter found that the war powers vested in the President as Commander in Chief are exceptionally broad, but not unlimited.

> [T]he war power of the Government is "the power to wage war successfully." . . . The war power of the United States, like its other powers . . . is subject to applicable constitutional limitations. If a military order such as that under review does not

50 Hirabayashi v. United States, 320 U.S. 81 (1943).
51 Exec. Order No. 9066, 7 Fed. Reg. 1407 (1942) at 1407–09.
52 Hirabayashi v. United States, 320 U.S. 81, 93 (1943).

> transcend the means appropriate for conducting war, such action by the military is as constitutional as would be any authorized action by the Interstate Commerce Commission within the limits of the constitutional power to regulate commerce.[53]

Although today *Korematsu* is often cited as one of the Court's worst decisions,[54] along with *Dred Scott v. Sandford*[55] (holding that the descendants of enslaved people were not United States citizens) and *Plessy v. Ferguson*[56] (holding that segregation was not unlawful discrimination) for ignoring the clear racial discrimination, it still demonstrates some important principles of presidential power. Most importantly, the President's decisions as Commander in Chief during times of war enjoy broad deference. Despite that broad deference, the President's power does not go unchecked in courts. The Supreme Court decades later in *Trump v. Hawaii* repudiated *Korematsu*, although ironically at the same time as affirming President Trump's ban on immigration from predominantly Muslim countries. *Trump v. Hawaii* was discussed earlier in this book in Chapter 1.

Since the late 1700s, warfare has changed dramatically. In the early 1800s Napoleon revolutionized warfare with his policy of *Levée en masse*, or mass conscription, that made national defense a shared responsibility.[57] By the late 1800s the development of automatic weapons and machine guns brought the industrialization of war to the forefront. World Wars I and II introduced the concept of "total warfare" – that wars extended outside of traditional battlefields to include factories, farms, and noncombatants not directly related to combat.

Despite these changes in how wars are fought since the signing of the Constitution, the Court has declined to expand the definition of "battlefield" to these outer limits. The Court held that the Commander in Chief powers stop at home when not directly related to the war.[58]

The most famous example is a presidential power case already discussed earlier in this book but revisited here to discuss how the President's role as Commander in Chief is not unlimited off the battlefield. During the Korean War, steelworkers across America threatened to strike due to a wage dispute. Steel products such as ammunition, armor, and vehicle components were vital to the war. President Truman, fearing that a strike could disrupt the war, ordered nationalization of the nation's steel mills to keep production running.

In response to this seizure, a steel mill in Ohio sued the Secretary of Commerce, Charles Sawyer. During oral argument before the Supreme Court, the government argued that a strike by steelworkers, regardless of length, would pose a grave threat to the security of the nation. Because of this threat, the government argued, the

[53] Korematsu v. United States, 323 U.S. 214, 225 (1944).
[54] Trump v. Hawaii 585 U.S. 667, 710 (2018).
[55] Dred Scott v. Sandford, 60 U.S. 393 (1857).
[56] Plessy v. Ferguson, 163 U.S. 537 (1896).
[57] Alan Forrest, The Legacy of the French Revolutionary Wars 1787–1802, 18–21 (2009).
[58] Youngstown Sheet & Tube Co. v. Sawyer, 343 U.S. 579, 587 (1952).

President, as Commander in Chief, had the inherent power to order the nationalization of the steel mills to protect the nation. Writing the majority opinion, Justice Black reaffirmed the President's Commander in Chief powers under the Constitution. But, despite this broad breadth, the Court drew a distinction between the President's powers on and off the battlefield. In short, if the President wanted to nationalize private property to continue the war effort, he must reach an agreement with Congress rather than acting unilaterally.[59] This case, and Justice Jackson's three-part test for assessing the extent of presidential power, was discussed in more detail in Chapter 1 of this book.

3.3 CONGRESS'S ROLE

Under the Constitution, Congress alone has the power to declare war. Article I, Section 8, Clause 11 states that "[t]he Congress shall have Power . . . [t]o declare War . . . and make Rules concerning Captures on Land and Water."[60] In the nineteenth and early twentieth centuries, this was a war power that Congress would exercise regularly. From 1812 to 1942, Congress had declared war against eleven nations across five major wars, including the War of 1812, the Mexican–American War of 1846, the Spanish–American War of 1898, and World Wars I and II.[61] Since World War II, Congress has not exercised its duty to declare war despite major overseas combat operations in Korea, Vietnam, Iraq, and Afghanistan. This history raises the question: to what extent may the President exercise his Commander in Chief powers *absent* a formal congressional declaration of war?

Sometimes Congress affirmatively authorizes the President to use military force even without a declared war. The 1964 Gulf of Tonkin Resolution, for example, authorized use of military force in Vietnam in 1964. The Joint Resolution stated: "Congress approves and supports the determination of the President, as Commander in Chief, to take all necessary measures to repel any armed attack against the forces of the United States and to prevent further aggression." Congress left the end date for the authorization up to the President.[62] "This resolution shall expire when the President shall determine that the peace and security of the area is reasonably assured by international conditions created by action of the United Nations or otherwise, except it may be terminated earlier by concurrent resolution of the Congress." The war dragged on for years. President Nixon expanded it to Laos and Cambodia before it finally ended with North Vietnamese victory in 1975.

Not all presidents, however, seek consent of Congress, even before a major military operation. President Truman entered the Korean War in 1950 without

[59] *Id.*

[60] U.S. Const. Art. I, § 8.

[61] *About Declarations of War by Congress*, www.senate.gov/about/powers-procedures/declarations-of-war.htm.

[62] Tonkin Gulf Resolution; Public Law 88-408, 88th Congress, August 7, 1964.

seeking congressional authorization, relying instead on a United Nations Security Council resolution and his powers as Commander in Chief to defend South Korea against invasion from the North. The Department of State in a legal memorandum of July 3, 1950 justified this intervention.[63] Congress acquiesced and subsequently funded the Korean War. This sequence of events implicitly expanded presidential power. It also may have emboldened Truman in 1952 to seize domestic steel mills in the face of a strike that would have crippled the war effort. The Supreme Court's famous ruling in *Youngstown Sheet and Tube Co. v. Sawyer*,[64] rebuffing Truman's seizure of the steel mills, is discussed earlier in this chapter and also in Chapter 1 of this book. This case is an illustration of how war powers and domestic power of the President are often intertwined.

When Congress does authorize use of miliary force, presidents often go to the outer limits of what Congress authorized, relying on an expansive interpretation of the congressional resolution and the President's Article II powers to justify whatever Congress did not authorize.

The 2001 Authorization for Use of Military Force (AUFM) in Afghanistan and the subsequent 2002 AUFM in Iraq are cases in point. The 2001 AUMF was a joint resolution passed by both Houses of Congress intended to allow the President to take military action against nations and organizations responsible for the terrorist attacks of September 11, 2001. The AUMF states:

> The President is authorized to use all necessary and appropriate force against those nations, organizations, or persons he determines planned, authorized, committed, or aided the terrorist attacks that occurred on September 11, 2001, or harbored such organizations or persons, in order to prevent any future acts of international terrorism against the United States by such nations, organizations or persons.[65]

This language was a compromise between the Bush administration, that wanted more open-ended authorization to use military force against terrorism, and Congress, that wanted to limit the AUMF to nations and organizations with ties to the terrorist attacks of September 11.[66]

Nonetheless, the past four administrations have relied on the 2001 AUMF to conduct airstrikes, drone attacks, and other operations against countries in the Middle East and Northern Africa. President Bush relied upon the AUMF for operations in Afghanistan and Iraq. A second 2002 AUMF discussed later in this section also applied to Iraq.[67] President Obama relied upon the same 2001 AUMF

[63] Department of State Memorandum, Authority of the President to Repel the Attack in Korea, July 3, 1950.

[64] Youngstown Sheet & Tube Co. v. Sawyer, 343 U.S. 579 (1952).

[65] Authorization for Use of Military Force, PL 107–40, September 18, 2001, 115 Stat 224.

[66] Jennifer Daskal & Stephen I. Vladeck, *After the AUMF*, 5 Harv. Nat'l Sec. J. 115 (2014).

[67] *Global War on Terror*, George W. Bush Presidential Library, www.georgewbushlibrary.gov/research/topic-guides/global-war-terror.

for operations against Syria, Libya, Somalia, and Pakistan;[68] President Trump relied upon it in Syria, Somalia, and Afghanistan;[69] and President Biden in Yemen and Syria.[70]

In all these instances there are strong arguments for and against US military involvement. But the legal and political question is whether Congress today should have a say in whether presidents can deploy American troops based on an AUMF over two decades old.

The United States has also conducted military operations against the Islamic State of Iraq and Syria (ISIS). The United States has very good reasons to fight ISIS, but the relevant question is whether Congress should pass a separate AUMF for that purpose, or whether presidents properly continue to rely on the 2001 AUMF to fight ISIS.

ISIS is a terrorist group[71] responsible for attacks all over the globe. Its origins can be traced to Jaish al-Ta'ifa al-Mansurah, another terrorist group that fought in the Iraqi insurgency of 2004.[72] But ISIS did not exist until three years after the attacks of September 11, 2001. While the 2002 AUMF, discussed later in this section, probably authorizes US operations against ISIS inside Iraq, it is a stretch to argue that the 2001 AUMF authorizes operations against ISIS outside Iraq when ISIS didn't even exist on September 11, 2001.

Yet another curious invocation of the 2001 AUMF is for US military intervention in Yemen, which has lasted from the Obama administration to the present. A summary of the conflict in Yemen reveals understandable policy reasons for the United States to intervene, yet the 2001 AUMF provides a weak legal case because the present conflict in Yemen has little to do with Al-Qaeda.[73]

Nonetheless, in 2016 the United States began conducting strikes also against Houthi rebels, a very different group not aligned with AQ-AP (al-Qaeda in the Arabian Peninsula).[74]

[68] Harriet Agerholm, *Map Shows Where President Barack Obama Dropped His 20,000 Bombs*, Independent (Jan. 19, 2017, 1:19 PM), www.independent.co.uk/news/world/americas/us-president-barack-obama-bomb-map-drone-wars-strikes-20000-pakistan-middle-east-afghanistan-a7534851.html.

[69] Stephanie Savell, *Costs of War, The 2001 Authorization for Use of Military Force: A Comprehensive Look at Where and How It Has Been Used*, https://watson.brown.edu/costsofwar/files/cow/imce/papers/2021/Costs%20of%20War_2001%20AUMF.pdf.

[70] The White House Briefing Room, *Statement from President Joe Biden on U.S. Military Operation in the Middle East* (Feb. 2, 2024), https://bidenwhitehouse.archives.gov/briefing-room/statements-releases/2024/02/02/statement-from-president-joe-biden-on-u-s-military-operation-in-the-middle-east/.

[71] Rachel Elbaum, *What Is ISIS? What You Need to Know about Islamic State in Iraq and Syria*, NBC News (Apr. 18, 2018, 3:39 AM), www.nbcnews.com/storyline/smart-facts/what-isis-what-you-need-know-about-islamic-state-iraq-n859996.

[72] *Id.*

[73] Portions of this summary of US operations in Yemen are based on research by Ryan Murray in Professor Richard Painter's University of Minnesota Law School Spring 2024 seminar on Presidential Power.

[74] *Yemen Conflict: US Strikes Radar Sites after Missile Attack on Ship*, BBC (Oct. 13, 2016), www.bbc.com/news/world-middle-east-37639565.

The Houthis had been organized in the 1990s to oppose the Yemini government.[75] Houthi membership primarily consisted of Zaydi Muslims, a Shia sect of Islam[76] that opposed the Yemini government's alliance with Saudi Arabia.[77] The Houthis have since ousted a Saudi-backed government and have captured much of Yemen, including its capital, Sanaa.[78]

Later, in 2024, President Biden authorized "Operation Poseidon Archer,"[79] military strikes in Yemen[80] in response to Houthi attacks on commercial shipping vessels in the Red Sea.[81] The US operation began with an attack on seventy-two Houthi targets,[82] and the Biden administration then continued to strike Houthi targets for the next several months.[83]

The justification for this response was that Houthi attacks on shipping seriously disrupted global trade passing through the Red Sea. Some members of Congress opposed the strikes on Yemen and urged President Biden to withdraw US naval forces from the Red Sea.[84] However, Congress did not authorize or condemn the strikes. Congress did nothing.

Clearly hostilities with the Houthis do not align with the purpose of the 2001 AUMF, which was to fight Al-Qaeda. The Houthis, a predominantly Shia group, and Al-Qaeda, a Sunni group, have nothing to do with each other. The Houthis, like Al-Qaeda, engage in acts that could be characterized as "terrorism" but there the similarity ends. As the Obama administration acknowledged, the 2001 AUMF does not authorize the President to take military action against all terrorism. The focus of the AUMF is on Al-Qaeda and forces allied with Al-Qaeda.

Regardless of the merit of President Biden's intervention in Yemen, it seems that he, like Presidents Obama and Trump before him, should have asked Congress for a

[75] Tomi Pulkkinen, *Yemen and the Houthi Rebellion in the Context of the Global War on Terror*, 10 History in the Making No. 5 32–36 (2017).

[76] 2022 *Report on International Religious Freedom: Yemen*, U.S. Dept. of State (2022), www.state.gov/reports/2022-report-on-international-religious-freedom/yemen.

[77] Pulkkinen, *supra* note 75, at 32–44.

[78] *Id.*

[79] Eric Schmidt, *U.S. Strikes against Houthis in Yemen for Second Day, as Conflict Escalates*, New York Times (Jan. 13, 2024), www.nytimes.com/2024/01/22/us/politics/houthi-yemen-strikes.html.

[80] The White House, *Statement from President Joe Biden on Coalition Strikes in Houthi-Controlled Areas in Yemen* (Jan. 11, 2024), https://bidenwhitehouse.archives.gov/briefing-room/statements-releases/2024/01/11/statement-from-president-joe-biden-on-coalition-strikes-in-houthi-controlled-areas-in-yemen.

[81] *Id.*

[82] *Id.*

[83] *See* Nayera Abdallah & Enas Alashray, *Houthis Attack Four Ships in Indian Ocean, Red Sea*, Reuters (Apr. 29, 2024), www.reuters.com/world/middle-east/container-ship-reportedly-targeted-with-missiles-near-yemens-mokha-ambrey-says-2024-04-29/.

[84] Yasmeen Abutaleb & Abigail Hauslohcr, *House Members Tell Biden He Must Seek Authorization for Yemen Strikes*, Wash. Post. (Jan. 26, 2024, 8:49 AM), www.washingtonpost.com/politics/2024/01/26/congress-biden-houthis-war-powers/.

separate AUMF to authorize military operations against the Houthis. President Biden didn't do that, but instead relied upon a strained interpretation of the 2001 AUMF to proceed.

The Biden administration said that strikes were conducted to "protect and defend our personnel who are in Iraq and Syria conducting military operations pursuant to the 2001 Authorization of Use of Military Force. The strikes were intended to degrade and disrupt the ongoing series of attacks against the United States and our partners and to deter Iran and Iran-backed militia groups from conducting or supporting further attacks on United States personnel and facilities."[85] The goal was to protect US and partner forces from third-party attacks while these forces were conducting operations pursuant to the 2001 AUMF.

In other words, once US military personnel are deployed under the 2001 AUMF, presumably to fight groups aligned with Al-Qaeda, the President has the power under the AUMF or under Article II, or both, to attack other groups that pose a threat to those same personnel. Acquiring additional power without congressional authorization? Perhaps, but presidents do it because they can.

A second post-9/11 authorization passed by Congress was even more controversial. The 2002 Authorization for Use of Military Force against Iraq was premised on the since discredited claim that Iraq possessed weapons of mass destruction. The 2002 AUMF "authorizes the President to use the U.S. armed forces to: (1) defend U.S. national security against the continuing threat posed by Iraq; and (2) enforce all relevant Security Council resolutions regarding Iraq."[86] The AUMF authorized the operation to topple Saddam Hussein. Unlike the 2001 AUMF, the 2002 AUMF only authorizes military action in Iraq.

Although the Iraq war began over twenty years ago, and most US forces have left Iraq, the 2002 AUMF is still in effect. It is cited to justify military action "to defend U.S. national security against the continuing threat posed by Iraq," which is interpreted to allow for military action in Iraq whenever there is a threat posed from somewhere in Iraq.

On January 2, 2020, President Trump ordered an airstrike inside Iraq targeting Qassem Soleimani, commander of Iran's Islamic Revolutionary Guard Corps-Qods Force ("Qods Force" or "IRGC-QF"). Soleimani was visiting Iraq. The Iraqi government was not consulted before the attack.

The Department of Justice (DOJ) Office of Legal Counsel (OLC), in keeping with past practice during previous administrations, prepared a memo to justify the

[85] *Letter to the Speaker of the House and President pro tempore of the Senate consistent with the War Powers Resolution (Public Law 93-148)*, The White House (Nov. 22, 2023), https://bidenwhitehouse.archives.gov/briefing-room/presidential-actions/2024/01/05/letter-to-the-speaker-of-the-house-and-president-pro-tempore-of-the-senate-consistent-with-the-war-powers-resolution-public-law-93-148-9/.

[86] H.J. Res. 114 (2002).

targeted killing.[87] The OLC observed that, "Although the primary focus of the 2002 AUMF was the threat posed by Saddam Hussein's regime, the statute has long been read to authorize the use of force for the related purposes of helping to establish a stable, democratic Iraq and addressing terrorist threats emanating from Iraq." And then, "As the United States has sought to establish stability in Iraq and to address terrorist threats emanating from the country, Iran has remained a malign presence there and throughout the Middle East."[88]

All this may be true. But it's a heavy challenge for OLC to rely upon the 2002 AUMF to conduct a targeted killing of an Iranian general temporarily inside Iraq in 2020, all without the consent of the Iraqi government that the United States installed in place of Saddam Hussein pursuant to the same AUMF eighteen years later.

Yet another problem with the original 2002 AUMF is that Congress approved it relying on faulty information provided by US military and intelligence agencies. The Bush administration insisted that Iraq was developing weapons of mass destruction, but when the invasion was concluded no weapons of mass destruction were found.[89]

Early in the Global War on Terror, the outer limits of the President's power under these post-9/11 authorizations would be tested. Soon after the initial 2001 occupation of Afghanistan, the military captured Yaser Esam Hamdi, an American citizen, in Afghanistan.[90] Although Hamdi claims he was in Afghanistan doing relief work, the government alleged he was in Afghanistan fighting for the Taliban.[91] While he was under military detention at the United States naval base in Guantanamo Bay, Cuba, Hamdi's father filed a habeas corpus petition on his behalf alleging that his son was under indefinite detention without formal charges or access to legal counsel.

When the Supreme Court accepted Hamdi's case in 2004, it considered two questions: (1) whether the language of the 2001 AUMF which authorized the President to "use all necessary and appropriate force" in the Global War on Terror granted him the power to indefinitely detain combatants and (2) if the AUMF did not grant him that power, did the President have a plenary power under his Commander in Chief powers.[92] Beginning with the first question, the Court reviewed the history of prisoners of war in the United States.

87 *See Memorandum for John A. Eisenberg Legal Advisor to the National Security Council*, U.S. Dept. of Justice Office of Legal Counsel, at 20 (Mar. 10, 2020).

88 *Id.* at 4.

89 *See* Richard A. Clarke, Against All Enemies: Inside America's War on Terror (2004). *See also* Seymour Hersh, Chain of Command: The Road from 9/11 to Abu Ghraib (2004); Dennis Ross, The Missing Piece: The Inside Story of the Fight for Middle East Peace (2004); Hans Blix, Disarming Iraq (2004); Philip Bobbitt, Terror and Consent: The Wars for the Twenty-First Century (2009).

90 Hamdi v. Rumsfeld, 542 U.S. 507, 507 (2004).

91 *Id.*

92 *Id.* at 516–17.

Citing *ex parte Quirin*,[93] the Court recognized a legitimate government interest in the capture, detention, and trial of unlawful combatants to prevent them from returning to the battlefield and taking up arms.[94] In addition, the Court acknowledged that the detention of United States citizens was not necessarily unconstitutional. A plurality of the Court held, however, that the Fifth Amendment due process guarantees that a US citizen held in the United States as an enemy combatant has the right to contest his detention before a neutral decision-maker. The citizen detainee is not entitled to the same due process as in a civilian court, but is entitled to a meaningful opportunity to show that he is not an enemy combatant:

> We therefore hold that a citizen-detainee seeking to challenge his classification as an enemy combatant must receive notice of the factual basis for his classification, and a fair opportunity to rebut the Government's factual assertions before a neutral decisionmaker .... These essential constitutional promises may not be eroded. ...
>
> At the same time, the exigencies of the circumstances may demand that, aside from these core elements, enemy combatant proceedings may be tailored to alleviate their uncommon potential to burden the Executive at a time of ongoing military conflict. Hearsay, for example, may need to be accepted as the most reliable available evidence from the Government in such a proceeding. Likewise, the Constitution would not be offended by a presumption in favor of the Government's evidence, so long as that presumption remained a rebuttable one and fair opportunity for rebuttal were provided. Thus, once the Government puts forth credible evidence that the habeas petitioner meets the enemy-combatant criteria, the onus could shift to the petitioner to rebut that evidence with more persuasive evidence that he falls outside the criteria. A burden-shifting scheme of this sort would meet the goal of ensuring that the errant tourist, embedded journalist, or local aid worker has a chance to prove military error while giving due regard to the Executive once it has put forth meaningful support for its conclusion that the detainee is in fact an enemy combatant.[95]

History thus shows that in several ways the 2001 AUMF caused controversy. The 2003 invasion of Iraq that led to the toppling of Saddam Hussein and his Baathist party was, in part, grounded in the 2001 Resolution. While Congress ultimately passed a separate resolution authorizing the use of force against Iraq in October 2002, the Resolution made clear that the President's power as Commander in Chief to enter Iraq was part of his larger powers under the 2001 authorization.[96]

This, however, is not the end of the controversial story on the use of presidential power in war. Beginning in 2021, Congress made a concerted and bipartisan effort to repeal the 2002 Resolution. During the 117th Congress (2021–2023), two bills were

[93] *See* ex parte Quirin, discussed in Section 3.1.
[94] *Id.* at 518.
[95] Hamdi v. Rumsfeld, 542 U.S. 507 at 534 (2004).
[96] Authorization for Use of Military Force Against Iraq Resolution of 2002, Pub. L. No. 107–243.

introduced, one each in the House and Senate, to repeal the 2002 authorizations. The House Resolution passed in the lower chamber, but did not come for a vote in the Senate. The Senate bill did not even receive a vote on the Senate Floor. During the 118th Congress four bills were introduced to repeal the Resolution. Two of these bills died before reaching the floor of the House or Senate; one bill each in the House and Senate is currently, at this writing, under deliberation. However, even if one of these bills were to pass both Houses of Congress, the broader 2001 Resolution would remain in place. There is currently no serious effort to repeal this broader grant of authority.

The War on Terror and other conflicts also involve questions about the president's power when multi-country coalitions fight common enemies." For example, during the 1990 Gulf War six nations, including the United States, sent combat troops to Kuwait and Iraq to push the Baathist military out of Kuwait and back into Iraq.[97] In addition to the six nations that sent troops, thirty-three other nations provided material aid and intelligence support to the conflict. This broad coalition did not happen by accident. Then Secretary of State James A. Baker III traveled the globe building consensus and support for the war before the first troops were staged in Saudi Arabia.[98] Despite the impressive political, military, and diplomatic advantages and successes of coalition warfare, it raises important questions about the power of the President and whether he can command both American and coalition forces.

As Commander in Chief, the President always retains, and cannot relinquish or delegate, his power to command United States forces.[99] In addition, the President during coalition warfare retains the power to withdraw US forces and terminate the nation's participation at any time.[100] Similarly, coalition members retain "national command" over their nations' forces. While the unique nature of each coalition will dictate who has command over the coalition, the Department of Defense recognizes broadly two organizational structures for coalition warfare.

The first organizational structure, seen most vividly in the 2001–2021 war in Afghanistan, is a lead nation command structure. As the name suggests, under this organizational structure, one nation state, in this instance the United States, serves as the lead for overall command and other coalition nations place their militaries under the command and control of the lead nation. Under a lead nation command structure, in instances where the United States serves as the lead nation, the

97 CNN Editorial Research, *Gulf War Fast Facts*, CNN (July 13, 2023, 2:02 PM), www.cnn.com/2013/09/15/world/meast/gulf-war-fast-facts/index.html.

98 Peter Baker & Susan Glasser, The Man Who Ran Washington: The Life and Times of James A. Baker III, 393–416, 429, 432, 443, 464, 479 (2020). *See also* Jon Meacham, The American Odyssey of George Herbert Walker Bush: Destiny and Power, 437, 442, 464–65, 466 (2015).

99 JP 3-16, Multinational Operations Joint Chiefs of Staff, *Multinational Operations*, JP 3-16 (2021), II-1, https://irp.fas.org/doddir/dod/jp3_16.pdf.

100 *Id.*

President becomes the de facto commander of both United States and coalition forces due to the United States' status as lead nation.[101]

The second coalition organizational structure is a parallel command structure. Under this scheme, each coalition member retains overall command over its own nation's forces, but coordination occurs between each member nation. In these conflicts the President, as Commander in Chief, retains exclusive control over the United States Armed Forces, but the broader coalition decision-making is divided between the members.[102]

3.4 USE OF MILITARY FORCE WITHOUT CONSENT FROM CONGRESS

Finally, we address the difficult, and largely unanswered, constitutional question of what the President can do *unilaterally* to deploy American military forces without any authorization from Congress. This is an important question even when a President claims authorization from Congress because, as discussed in the preceding section, the White House's interpretation of congressional authorization is often strained. But this does not matter if the President has the constitutional power to act anyway.

Article I, Section 8 of the Constitution provides that Congress has the power to declare war.[103] Article II, Section 1 provides that the President has the power to repel attacks against the United States and that the President is Commander in Chief of the armed forces. How do we balance the two?

For instance, what is the result if one applies the framework of *Youngstown Sheet and Tube Co. v. Sawyer*, to a president's use of military force against the background of both an ambiguous congressional authorization for use of military force and Article II of the Constitution? Recall that the Court in *Youngstown* held that the President did not have the ability to seize the nation's steel mills to prevent a strike that would cripple steel supply during the Korean War.[104]

Justice Jackson's opinion carved out a tripartite framework for assessing presidential power in three situations: (1) when the President acts pursuant to express or implied authorization of Congress his authority is at its maximum; (2) when the President acts in absence of either a congressional grant or denial of authority he can only rely upon his own independent powers, but there is a zone in which he and Congress may have concurrent authority, or in which distribution of authority between the President and Congress is uncertain; and (3) when the President takes measures incompatible with the express or implied will of Congress his power is at

[101] *Id.*
[102] *Id.*
[103] U.S. CONST., Art. I, § 8.
[104] Youngstown Sheet & Tube Co. v. Sawyer, 343 U.S. 579, 635 (1952).

its lowest ebb. There are some scenarios where Congress cannot prohibit the President from carrying out his Article II duties, for example to defend the country against an attack. The steel mills case and Justice Jackson's three-part test for assessing the extent of presidential power was discussed in more detail in Chapter 1 of this book. Here its relevance is to a specific issue which is the topic of this section, the use of military force without consent from Congress.

Many situations fall in the second category described above because Congress does not explicitly approve or disapprove of military action. In 1999, for example, President Clinton authorized air strikes against Yugoslavia.[105] Clinton did not obtain congressional approval.[106] Legislation that would have allowed the President to conduct air and missile strikes against Yugoslavia had failed in the House via a tie vote.[107] However, Clinton proceeded regardless, stating: "the actions were justifiable under [my] constitutional authority to conduct foreign relations."[108] Clinton cited the need to curtail genocide against ethnic Albanians in Kosovo.[109] Congress, then, failed to pass a resolution requesting that Clinton stop military action in Yugoslavia.[110]

The consequences of Clinton's unilateral military action were not insignificant. Russia, which has long been close to Serbia and entered World War I to defend Serbia in 1914, was humiliated in its inability to defend an ally against NATO bombing in 1999. This may have been a factor in the rise of Russian nationalism, Vladimir Putin coming to power, and Russian hostility to both NATO and the Clintons. Russia's reignited feud with the West continued into the twenty-first century, culminating with the 2022 Russian invasion of Ukraine. Wars have consequences. The early history of the United States summarized in Section 3.1 suggests that the Framers intended such a momentous decision to intervene in a foreign war to be made not by the President alone, but by Congress.

Applying the *Youngstown* framework in more recent times, there is clear authorization from Congress for some operations under one or both post-9/11 AUMFs (the first *Youngstown* category). However, by stretching the 2001 AUMF from Al-Qaeda and the Taliban to other terrorist organizations, presidents are essentially adding words to the text of the AUMF that never existed. This puts most of today's military operations in the second category, where Congress has been silent. The principal restriction imposed by Congress is under the War Powers Resolution of 1973, discussed later in this chapter. If its provisions are complied with, the President at

[105] William J. Clinton, *Message to Congress*, U.S. DEPT. OF STATE ARCHIVE (May 26, 1999), https://1997-2001.state.gov/regions/eur/990525_clinton_ksvo_letter.html.

[106] *Id.*

[107] Bill Miller, *Clinton's War Powers Upheld*, WASH. POST. (June 9, 1999), www.washingtonpost.com/wp-srv/national/daily/june99/dismiss09.htm.

[108] Clinton, *supra* note 105.

[109] *Id.*

[110] Miller, *supra* note 107.

least will be acting in the second category of Justice Jackson's framework, rather than in the third category doing that which Congress has expressly told him he may not do.

As a practical matter, presidents can conduct military operations in this second category with fear only of political ramifications, not interference from courts. Domestic orders of the President, such as Truman's seizure of the steel mills, however, are different, and more likely to be litigated, and may subject the President's actions to more scrutiny.

Article II presidential power to use military force without authorization from Congress is at its height when the action is purely defensive. The *Prize* cases, for example, addressed the President's blockade of ports actively involved in armed rebellion against the government during the Civil War.[111] The Court held that a president, under Article 2, may use force against rebelling states without the need for congressional approval. "If a war be made by invasion of a foreign nation, the President is not only authorized but bound to resist force by force. He does not initiate the war. He is bound to accept the challenge without waiting for any special legislative authority."[112]

Consider also a more dubious 2011 opinion by OLC authorizing President Obama to conduct operations to support the overthrow of longtime dictator Muammar al-Gaddafi in Libya.[113] The OLC opined that the President has broad power to commit United States troops abroad, as well as to take military action to protect important national interests, even without specific prior authorization from Congress.

First, OLC pointed to UN Security Resolution 1973, that authorized member states to use military force in Libya after Gaddafi began to massacre civilians. The United States was not required to take military action to enforce Resolution 1973 but was authorized by the UN to do so.

Second, OLC observed that the President had complied with the War Powers Resolution in which Congress had said what the President must do when taking military action, for example reporting to Congress within forty-eight hours and a maximum operation of 60–90 days. The implication from this part of the OLC opinion is that anything Congress has not explicitly prohibited is permitted.

Third, the OLC memo relied on past military action by past presidents in Yugoslavia, Haiti, Somalia, and Bosnia, among others.[114] In other words, other presidents ordered similar operations, and nobody stopped them, so the current President can do so too under the prior precedents.

[111] The Prize Cases 67 U.S. 635 (1863).
[112] *Id.* at 668.
[113] Opinion of Caroline Krass, Principal Deputy Assistant Attorney General, Department of Justice Office of Legal Counsel, April 1, 2011.
[114] Haig v. Agee, 453 U.S. 280, 291 (1981).

The fourth issue addressed in the OLC memo is the definition of "war" within the meaning of the Declaration of War clause of the Constitution. Defining a "war," the OLC said, was a "fact-specific assessment of the 'anticipated nature, scope, and duration' of the planned military operations." In short, there is no clear definition of a war that would require a declaration of a war by Congress. Under the construction of the meaning of the word "war," the conflicts in Korea, Vietnam, Afghanistan, and Iraq presumably were not "wars" because Congress never declared war. Veterans of those wars might beg to differ.

In sum, OLC yet again found a way to legally justify a military intervention that the President believed necessary, even if he was acting without consent of Congress. And, as many times before in American history, for better or for worse, that is exactly what presidents have done.[115]

The issue arose yet again in June 2025 when President Trump unilaterally, without consent of Congress, entered the war between Israel and Iran by bombing nuclear facilities inside Iran where Israel and the United States have long feared Iran could be making nuclear weapons. Iran's nuclear program has been known about for decades, and presidents including Trump could have gone to Congress for an authorization for use of military force (AUMF) to stop it, but none has done so. Trump apparently informed a few Congressional Republicans immediately before the bombing, but this hardly meets the War Powers Act requirement that a president consult Congress whenever possible before taking military action. Some commentators claimed the bombing of Iran was legal, observing that Clinton, Obama, and other presidents have similarly taken military action without consent of Congress.[116] Others rejected this "practice makes principle" approach, insisting the American attack on Iran was illegal under both US law and international law.[117]

The extent of the damage to Iran's nuclear program is disputed. The Trump administration claimed it was obliterated, but some intelligence reports suggest otherwise. This will make it very difficult for Trump to explain any further US strikes against Iran and indeed could complicate matters if he were to go to Congress in the future for an AUMF premised on the need to stop Iran's nuclear program. Recall the controversy over the 2002 AUMF authorizing the invasion of Iraq, premised on false intelligence about weapons of mass destruction. With Iran, Congress may be skeptical about the underlying intelligence the President relies on to justify the use of military force, which may explain why Trump did not approach even a Republican-controlled Congress for authorization to bomb Iran.

[115] *See* Michael Beschloss, Presidents of War (2018); Sarah Burns, The Politics of War Powers (2019).

[116] Geoffrey Corn, Claire Finkelstein, & Orde Kittrie, *Why Trump Didn't Have to Ask Congress Before Striking Iran: It has Been Presidential Practice for Decades to Unilaterally Undertake Similar Military Action*, Wash. Post. (June 23, 2025).

[117] Oona A. Hathaway, *Trump's Strikes on Iran Were Unlawful. Here's Why That Matters*, New York Times (June 23, 2025).

But what next? Would defenders of bombing Iran agree that if war were to break out elsewhere, perhaps between Taiwan and China, the President could join the war and launch military operations without the consent of Congress, or is the Middle East conflict somehow different? At some point, a line needs to be drawn. Over the years presidential war power has expanded vastly. Some would argue presidential war power has expanded dangerously from where it was when Alexander Hamilton carefully explained what he believed President Adams could and could not do to defend American shipping. Adams himself understood this was impermissible without the consent of Congress, to take sides and intervene in the war – one of many – between France and Great Britain (see Section 3.1).

3.5 IS THE WAR POWERS RESOLUTION CONSTITUTIONAL?

The 1973 War Powers Resolution provides that if the United States engages in a military conflict overseas, it "shall be reported within 48 hours in writing by the President to the Speaker of the House of Representatives and the President pro tempore of the Senate, together with a full account of the circumstances under which such hostilities were initiated, the estimated scope and duration of such hostilities, and the constitutional and legislative authority under which the introduction of hostilities took place."[118] The President must then obtain congressional approval unless the use of force is to: "(a) to repel an armed attack upon the United States, its territories and possessions … (b) to repel an armed attack against the Armed Forces of the United States located outside of the United States, its territories and possessions … or (c) pursuant to specific statutory authorization."[119] The President also must provide Congress with "periodic updates" every six months.[120]

The War Powers Act followed decades of presidents ordering military operations, and even entering full-scale wars, without consent of Congress. In June 1950, President Truman, during a press conference on the growing conflict in Korea, stated that "we are not at war" and suggested that the United States' involvement in the conflict was part of a "police action under the United Nations."[121] Despite the President's distinction between war and a police action, the reality on the ground looked very much like a war. President Truman's deployment of military assets to the peninsula encompassed the full spectrum of the nation's military might, including ground troops, artillery, and intelligence from the army, warships from the United States Navy's Seventh Fleet, and airpower from the newly formed United States Air Force. In addition, the total number of casualties, both American and

[118] 50 U.S.C. 33 § 4 (1973).
[119] 50 U.S.C. 33 § 2(c) (1973).
[120] 50 U.S.C. 33 § 4(c) (1973).
[121] United States Department of State, Office of the Historian, https://history.state.gov/departmenthistory/short-history/koreanwar.

other, from the conflict looked like a war, with over 36,000 Americans dead and over 2.5 million people killed in total.[122]

Despite the large deployment of combat power, Congress did not significantly push back on Truman's Commander in Chief powers. While some Republicans at the time – including Senator Robert Taft, who described Truman's actions as "a complete usurpation by the President of authority to use the armed forces of the country"[123] – criticized Truman's decision, Congress implicitly authorized the continuing use of the President's Commander in Chief powers by providing appropriations needed to run the war.[124]

Despite President Truman's public confidence that he had the authority as Commander in Chief to send American forces into the Korean peninsula, his internal deliberations tell a more nuanced story of a president who struggled with the constitutionality of his decision. Soon after American forces landed in the Peninsula, Truman sought counsel from congressional and State Department leaders about using legislative backchannels to have Senator Scott Lucas, then Senate Democratic Leader, introduce a war resolution on the Senate floor on Truman's behalf.[125] Despite Truman's insistence on seeking the Resolution, Lucas refused, fearing that lengthy debate on the Senate floor would erode public support for the war, and that Senate Republicans would use the debate as an opportunity to cast doubt on Truman's wider East Asia strategy.[126] Ultimately, without Lucas's support for the resolution, Truman withdrew his plan for seeking a war resolution.[127]

Further complicating matters was Truman's basis for deploying force to the Korean peninsula. As noted, the involvement of the United States was based on a United Nations Security Council resolution, not an act from Congress. In 1945, the same year the United Nations was formed, Congress passed and Truman signed into law the United Nations Participation Act.[128] This Act, in part, affirmed that a UN-sanctioned military action was not enough for the President to commit forces overseas.[129] Rather, if the President wished to send American forces abroad he *must* go through the traditional constitutional procedure of seeking and receiving a formal authorization from Congress.

In the early 1970s, President Nixon faced a similar predicament. By the late 1960s, the war in Vietnam had expanded from a few hundred advisors sent to South Vietnam to train and equip the South Vietnamese Army to a complex multination

[122] A. R. Millett, *Korean War*, Encyclopedia Britannica (Jan. 23, 2024), www.britannica.com/event/Korean-War.

[123] Gary R. Hess, Presidential Decisions for War Korea, Vietnam, the Persian Gulf, 34 (2009).

[124] Mutual Security Act of 1951, Pub. L. No. 82-165 (1951).

[125] Hess, *supra* note 123, 35.

[126] *Id.*

[127] *Id.*

[128] United Nations Participation Act, Pub. L. 79-264.

[129] *Id.*

conflict including deployment of the Army, Navy, Marines, and Air Force working in concert to destroy both the regular North Vietnamese Army and the guerilla Vietcong forces.[130]

Earlier in 1964, five years before Nixon became President, Congress passed the Tonkin Gulf Resolution.[131] This Resolution granted President Johnson three important powers as Commander in Chief. First, it gave the President, as Commander in Chief, the power to "take all necessary measures to repel any armed attack against the forces of the United States." The plain language of this passage of the Resolution seemed to give the President plenary power over the war as Commander in Chief. It did not place any restrictions on the number of troops deployed to Vietnam or how they should be used once deployed. Second, the Resolution gave the President the power to "take all necessary steps, including the use of armed force, to assist any member or protocol state of the Southeast Asia Collective Defense Treaty requesting assistance in defense of its freedom."[132] This passage reinforced the President's plenary power by providing him with broad and unilateral authority to conduct the war as he saw fit. Finally, the Resolution gave the President, not Congress, the power to determine when his own powers should expire *unless* Congress should pass another act eliminating the President's powers under the Resolution.[133]

In 1973, Congress withdrew the power it ceded with the Tonkin Gulf Resolution when it passed the War Powers Resolution of 1973 over a Nixon presidential veto.[134] The 1973 Resolution limited, but did not entirely eliminate, the President's power to deploy combat troops overseas without a declaration of war by Congress. The 1973 Resolution marked an important and critical milestone in the tension between Congress and the President. It allowed Congress to retake some of its constitutional powers in the decision to go to war, while still providing the President broad authority to handle the *conduct* of war as the nation's Commander in Chief.

In part, the 1973 Resolution required the President, as a precondition before deploying combat troops overseas to: (1) in every possible instance consult with Congress before deploying armed forces to overseas hostilities and (2) to provide a report to congressional leadership within forty-eight hours of deployment that included the circumstances of the hostilities, the estimated scope and duration of the conflict, and the constitutional or legislative authority under which the introduction of hostilities took place.

In the years following the Vietnam War, presidents from both parties relied on the War Powers Resolution to deploy troops overseas in support of both major and minor conflicts. Since 1973, the War Powers Resolution has been used over 100

[130] Max Hastings, Vietnam: An Epic Tragedy, 1945–1975, 275–78 (2018).

[131] Tonkin Gulf Resolution, Pub. L. No. 88-408.

[132] *Id.*

[133] *Id.*

[134] War Powers Resolution, Pub. L. No. 93-148.

times, including to deploy troops to Cambodia in 1975, Lebanon in 1982, Iraq and Kuwait in 1991, Kosovo in 1999, and Libya in 2011.[135]

But are the constraints the War Powers Resolution imposes on the President's power as Commander in Chief constitutional? The text of the Constitution says in Article I, Section 8 that Congress declares war, not the President, so it seems that Congress should have the power to limit military operations substantial enough that they could provoke other nations to declare war on the US. On the other hand, Article II grants broad powers to the President as Commander in Chief. Surely the Framers would not have intended to constrain the President acting to prevent or repel an attack on the United States. The Supreme Court has not yet ruled on the constitutionality of the War Powers Act, but the text of the Act seems to strike a reasonable balance between the shared powers of Congress and the President in the conduct of war. This should be constitutional provided it is interpreted in a way that allows the President to take military action unilaterally when there is an imminent threat to national security or to repel an attack on an ally that the United States is under a treaty obligation to defend.

The 2001 AUMF, and the 2002 AUMF authorizing the invasion of Iraq, are discussed in Section 3.3. For those who believe the President can always use military force without consent of Congress, AUMFs such as these are superfluous, and the War Powers Act is unconstitutional in the constraints it imposes on the President. In most instances, however, presidents have acted as if they should get some type of consent of Congress and have gone through the motions of complying with the War Powers Act, when they commit United States troops to combat operations of significant duration. With shorter missions, including Clinton's bombing of Serbia in 1999 and Trump's bombing of Iran in 2025, presidents have dispensed with congressional authorization altogether, as discussed in Section 3.4.

3.6 THE PRESIDENT AND TORTURE

The Eighth Amendment of the Constitution prohibits the federal government, and later state governments through the Fourteenth Amendment, from imposing "cruel and unusual punishment" during criminal sentencing.[136] During the Constitutional Convention there was broad consensus that there needed to be limits on the government's right to impose punishments, but there were concerns about how to limit the government without making criminal punishments toothless.

The Eighth Amendment's limit on cruel and unusual punishments began to receive scrutiny in the early twentieth century in a series of Supreme Court cases that questioned whether the death penalty was cruel and unusual. In *Weems*

[135] H.J. Res. 542, 93rd Cong. (1973).
[136] U.S. Const. Amend. VIII.

v. United States,[137] the Court held that the cruel and unusual should not be seen as only what would be considered cruel and unusual in the late eighteenth century, but rather it is based on what society at the time views it, as society evolves. During the Global War on Terror in the early twenty-first century the Eighth Amendment would come back into the national spotlight as the George W. Bush administration used a variety of interrogation techniques such as stress positions, waterboarding, and sleep deprivation on alleged terrorists to gather intelligence.

One of the most shocking developments after the September 11, 2001 terrorist attacks was a series of OLC memos advising the Central Intelligence Agency (CIA) and the Department of Defense that they could torture detainees under color of presidential authority.[138] The misrepresentation of law and fact in these memos was multifold, embracing arguments that the "enhanced interrogation" methods (for example, waterboarding) did not inflict sufficient lasting physical or psychological harm to amount to torture, and that torturers could invoke a self-defense or "necessity" defense if criminally charged.[139] The memos cited no evidence that torturing prisoners helps interrogators obtain useful intelligence information. Also, it did not acknowledge that there is very little support for that view among intelligence experts.

Also troublesome was OLC's conclusion that under the Constitution the President's Article II powers take precedence over both criminal laws prohibiting torture[140] and US treaty obligations such as the Convention Against Torture.[141] This essentially casts the President as being above the law. According to this theory, presidential power supplants the law; the President, and presumably even inferiors acting under presidential authority, can redefine the law.

These OLC memos were later rescinded and widely condemned.[142] Some ethics experts opined that the OLC lawyers who authored the torture memos should be prosecuted.[143]

As pointed out in Chapter 1 of this book, senior OLC lawyers are almost always political appointees of the President. The OLC all too often tells a president how to do whatever the President, or a political appointee of the President, wants to do. Yet the OLC's client is not the President; it is the United States government. A conflict of interest surely arises when lawyers represent the government and at the same time

[137] Weems v. United States, 217 U.S. 349 (1910).

[138] *See e.g.* John C. Yoo, Office of Legal Counsel, Memorandum to Alberto R. Gonzales, Counsel to the President, August 1, 2002, www.justice.gov/sites/default/files/olc/legacy/2010/08/05/memo-gonzales-aug1.pdf.

[139] *Id.*

[140] *See* 18 U.S.C. §§ 2340 and 2340A (prohibiting torture).

[141] Yoo, *supra* note 138.

[142] *See e.g.* Richard W. Painter, Getting the Government America Deserves: How Ethics Reform Can Make a Difference 121 (2009), ch. 5, "When Lawyers Work for the Government" (discussing the illegality of the DOJ torture memos).

[143] *See* Claire Finkelstein & Michael Lewis, *Should Bush Administration Lawyers Be Prosecuted for Authorizing Torture?*, 158 U. Pa. L. Rev. 195 (2010).

help the government evade the law. If the Supremacy Clause means what it says, then both federal statutes and treaties prohibiting torture are the "supreme law of the land." It is difficult to escape the conclusion that the OLC lawyers who advised the CIA and the Defense Department on torture betrayed their client, the United States government, and the people of the United States.[144]

The Justice Department Office of Professional Responsibility investigated and concluded that the OLC lawyers who drafted the torture memos should be referred to their state bar associations for violating professional conduct rules.[145] A superior lawyer at the DOJ, however, disagreed and these lawyers were not referred by the DOJ for professional discipline.[146]

But twenty years later the Supreme Court's 2024 decision in *Trump v. United States*,[147] discussed in more detail later in Part III of this book, ruled that a president has absolute immunity from criminal prosecution for official acts within his core constitutional duties, of which the Commander in Chief role is surely a part. Does this mean that the President could order torture of detainees with impunity? If so, could subordinates order torture of detainees and escape prosecution, claiming they were acting on orders of the President? If *Trump v. United States* is to be interpreted this broadly, the vision of Article II power in the OLC memos, long ago repudiated by the Justice Department, is now enshrined in an opinion of the Supreme Court. This, of course, would mean, at least in the view of the present Court, that the President is indeed above the law. These implications for the foundational historical principle of the "rule of law" are deeply troubling for a constitutional republic.

3.7 THE PRESIDENT AND THE MILITARY-INDUSTRIAL COMPLEX

As emphasized elsewhere in this book, the President's core constitutional powers include those as Commander in Chief. The Army and Navy at the time of the founding of the United Sates were small, but over 230 years have grown to be the

[144] *See* discussion of the OLC torture memos in Richard W. Painter, *Avoision: When Government Lawyers Turn the Sovereign against Itself*, 75 Case W. Univ. L. Rev. 473 (2024).

[145] *See* July 29, 2009, Department of Justice Office of Professional Responsibility, Report: *Office of Legal Counsel's Memoranda Concerning Issues Relating to the Central Intelligence Agency's Use of "Enhanced Interrogation Techniques" on Suspected Terrorists* (finding that OLC lawyers John Yoo and Jay Bybee engaged in professional misconduct because they had failed to provide "thorough, candid and objective" analysis in the memoranda concerning interrogation of suspected terrorists). The OPR indicated an intent to refer the matter to the bar disciplinary authorities in the states where Yoo and Bybee were licensed.

[146] *See* January 5, 2010, Memorandum for the Attorney General and Deputy Attorney General from David Margolis, Associate Deputy Attorney General https://irp.fas.org/agency/doj/opr-margolis.pdf (overruling OPR's determination and finding that the torture memos showed "poor judgment" instead of a violation of rules of professional conduct).

[147] Trump v. United States, 603 U.S. 593 (2024).

most powerful military force in the world; and the most expensive. In 2024, the defense budget was almost $1 trillion.[148]

The United States government could design and manufacture its own weapons, but it doesn't. It relies on private military contractors. The defense industry is driven by pursuit of profit.[149] President Eisenhower recognized this problem in his famous 1961 speech on the rise of a military-industrial complex. His fear was that the weapons industry and the military would push the government to spend more and more on defense at the expense of domestic priorities.[150]

> This conjunction of an immense military establishment and a large arms industry is new in the American experience . . . Yet we must not fail to comprehend its grave implications . . . In the councils of government, we must guard against the acquisition of unwarranted influence, whether sought or unsought, by the military-industrial complex. The potential for the disastrous rise of misplaced power exists and will persist.[151]

Given the enormous size of the military budget, members of Congress often want a say in fixing its total size, appropriation of funds to their district, and specifying which weapons programs should be funded. National security and costs presumably are the primary considerations, but political factors such as whether a project is in a representative's district, and perhaps even campaign contributions from the defense industry, also come into play. The President has political considerations as well.

Each year Congress passes a National Defense Authorization Act (NDAA) specifying the budget for the Department of Defense with detailed conditions attached to specific acquisitions programs.[152] Congress also passes more general laws aimed at cost controls. An example is establishing a preference for the acquisition of commercial off-the-shelf items instead of items specifically manufactured for a government contract as a means to cut costs.[153]

Congress has delegated to the President broad powers over defense contracting. These include the power to modify the terms of contracts "without regard to other

[148] Agency Profile, Department of Defense, www.usaspending.gov/agency/department-of-defense?fy=2024.

[149] Richard W. Painter, *Fiduciary Duties of Military Contractors: Shareholder Primacy or Loyalty to the United States*, *in* Ethical Dilemmas in the Defense Industry (Daneil Schoeni, Tobias Vestner, & Kevin Govern eds., 2023).

[150] President Dwight D. Eisenhower's Farewell Address (Jan. 17, 1961), www.archives.gov/milestone-documents/president-dwight-d-eisenhowers-farewell-address.

[151] *Id.*

[152] *See e.g.* Public L. 118-31 – Dec. 22, 2023, 137 Stat. 136 (118th Cong.), "National Defense Authorization Act for Fiscal Year 2024." The law addresses detailed issues for specific equipment contracts. For example, three programs for the Army: e.g. Sec. 111. "Limitation on availability of funds pending assessment of Army Trackless Moving Target systems," Sec. 112. Strategy for Army tactical wheeled vehicle program, Sec. 113. Report on acquisition strategies for the logistics augmentation program of the Army. By contrast the Act has twenty-two provisions imposing restrictions on the Air Force.

[153] *See e.g.* 10 U.S.C. §3453 – preference for commercial products and commercial services.

provisions of law ... whenever [the President] deems that such action would facilitate the national defense."[154] In some situations the President may use this power to increase the cost of the contract, paying the contractor more than originally contracted. In other scenarios, however, the President could use this authority to modify a defense contract to recoup unjust profits from the contractor, particularly in egregious circumstances of equipment failure.[155] Such downward revisions have fallen out of favor. Throughout American history, the Executive Branch has compelled ex post, or after the fact, price reductions to military contracts.[156] Perhaps presidents should do so more assertively today.

Military contractors in the United States sell weaponry to the United States government, and to other countries. In 1936, the Supreme Court in *United States v. Curtiss Wright Corporation*[157] ruled that Congress could delegate control over foreign arms sales to the President. The Curtiss–Wright Export Corporation sold fighter planes and bombers to Bolivia during the Chaco War. This was in violation of a proclamation issued by President Franklin D. Roosevelt banning US weapons manufacturers from aiding either side of the war. Curtiss–Wright argued that a statute authorizing the President to impose such a ban had violated the nondelegation doctrine in allowing the President to make decisions that in each instance should be made by Congress. But the Court ruled that in foreign affairs, "the President alone has the power to speak or listen as a representative of the nation."[158] Congress could also delegate to him broad discretion, in this case to determine which foreign arms sales shall be permitted and which prohibited.

The United States frequently provides military aid for a foreign nation for political or national security reasons. Sometimes the President acts without consent of Congress and sometimes not. For example, a series of neutrality acts passed by Congress in the 1930s prohibited arms sales to foreign belligerents.[159] When war broke out in Europe, President Roosevelt persuaded Congress to pass the Neutrality Act of 1939, which loosened the arms embargo and allowed Britain and other nations at war with Germany or Japan to purchase arms and other war materiel from the United States, but only on a "cash and carry" basis.[160] After Germany

[154] 50 U.S.C. §1431(a), Pub. L. No. 85-804, § 1, 72 Stat. 972 (1958).

[155] *See* Tucker Ring, *Presidential Power over Defense Contracts: How an Existing Statute Authorizes the Executive Branch to Recoup Profits from Defense Contractors*, 99 N.Y. Univ. L. Rev. __ (Apr. 2024), https://nyulawreview.org/issues/volume-99-number-1/presidential-power-over-defense-contracts-how-an-existing-statute-authorizes-the-executive-branch-to-recoup-profits-from-defense-contractors/.

[156] *Id.*

[157] United States v. Curtiss-Wright Export Corp., 299 U.S. 304 (1936).

[158] *Id.*

[159] *See e.g.* 49 Stat. 1081 (Pub. Res. 74-67) (Aug. 31, 1935) ("JOINT RESOLUTION Providing for the Prohibition of the Export of Arms, Ammunition, and Implements of War to Belligerent Countries"), www.govinfo.gov/content/pkg/STATUTE-49/pdf/STATUTE-49-Pg1081.pdf#page = 1.

[160] Pub. Res. 76-54, 54 Stat. 4 (Nov. 4, 1939), https://govtrackus.s3.amazonaws.com/legislink/pdf/stat/54/STATUTE-54-Pg4.pdf.

invaded Poland and France, with Britain running out of money, Roosevelt in September 1940 acted unilaterally in approving a "destroyers for bases" deal with Great Britain.[161] Roosevelt then went to Congress with a similar proposal that became the Lend–Lease Act of March 1941,[162] allowing the President to supply arms to Great Britain and other allies on credit in exchange for Britain leasing its overseas military bases to the United States. The United States did not enter World War II until the attacks on Pearl Harbor, Hawaii on December 7, 1941.

During the Cold War, presidents sometimes acted unilaterally in supplying military aid to other countries without express consent from Congress. Presidents Eisenhower and Kennedy sent advisors and military equipment to South Vietnam to combat communist incursions from the North.[163] Congress did not give its formal approval for United States combat operations in Vietnam until the Gulf of Tonkin Resolution of 1964. The important point here is that US involvement in a war sometimes begins with providing weapons and military training to belligerents, with combat operations coming later. Providing weapons made in the United States to a country at war may be the first step in getting the US into that war.

On occasion, presidents or their senior aides have orchestrated military aid in violation of laws specifically prohibiting it. For example, in the Iran–Contra scandal, the Reagan administration violated a clear statutory mandate prohibiting military aid to belligerents in Nicaragua.[164] This was accomplished by secretly selling weapons to Iran and using the proceeds to assist "Contra" rebels fighting the communist

[161] Letter Agreement dated September 2, 1940 between Secretary of State Cordell Hull to the British Ambassador (Lothian) Right Hon. The Marquess of Lothian, C.H., British Ambassador to the United States (specifying military bases and airfields throughout the British empire to be leased to the United States and that "In consideration of the declarations above quoted, the Government of the United States will immediately transfer to His Majesty's Government fifty United States Navy destroyers generally referred to as the twelve hundred-ton type."

[162] An Act further to promote the defense of the United States, and for other purposes, Pub. L. 77-11. 55 Stat. 31 (Mar. 11, 1941).

[163] The Southeast Asia Treaty Organization (SEATO) was formed in 1955 to prevent Communist expansion after communists took control of North Vietnam. As President Kennedy explained in a letter to a woman whose brother was killed in Vietnam, President Eisenhower in 1955 had established an advisory group to provide South Vietnam "with adequate weapons and equipment and training in basic military skills" and by 1963 "forty-five American soldiers, including your brother, have given their lives in Vietnam." Letter, dated March 6, 1963, from President John F. Kennedy to Bobbie Lou Pendergrass, www.docsteach.org/documents/document/letter-president-kennedy-bobbie-pendergrass. By the time this war was over, over 50,000 American soldiers had been killed. *See* Vietnam Conflict Extract data File of the Defense Casualty Analysis System (DCAS) (records of 58,220 United States military fatal casualties of the Vietnam War). National Archives, Vietnam War United States Military Fatal Casualty Statistics, Electronic Records Reference Report, www.archives.gove/research/military/vietnam-war/casaulty-statistics.

[164] Public Law 98-473, 98 Stat. 1935–37 (Oct. 12, 1984), §8066 (providing that: "During fiscal year 1985, no funds available to the Central Intelligence Agency, the Department of Defense, or any other agency or entity of the United States involved in intelligence activities may be obligated or expended for the purpose or which would have the effect of supporting, directly or indirectly, military or paramilitary operations in Nicaragua by any nation, group, organization,

regime in Nicaragua. This led to congressional investigations, a special prosecutor's investigation, and criminal indictments of high-ranking Reagan administration officials. During the Reagan years there were also calls for impeaching President Reagan.[165] Eventually many of the people were pardoned by President George H. W. Bush on Christmas Day 1992, after he had lost reelection.[166]

More recently, the United States has sent military aid to Ukraine and Israel. President Biden took some steps unilaterally to help Ukraine when Congress held up additional military aid in 2023. More substantial aid required appropriations by Congress, which were approved in 2024.[167] The Russia–Ukraine conflict is less contentious at home than the Middle East conflict but involves the United States providing arms used for attacks inside Russia, a nuclear power with an arsenal as large as that of the United States.

Other nations can afford to pay billions to buy weapons without US military aid. The United States is by far the largest arms exporter in the world, followed by France and Russia.[168] In approving these sales, the US government may assume that wealthy countries that can afford American weapons will use them for a good purpose, although almost nobody comes out and says it that way as a moral proposition.[169] Such an argument – that a nation's wealth translates into moral superiority – is absurd and contradicted by history. One should consider the arms buildup in Germany in the 1930s.

Consider also Saudi Arabia. United States arms sales to Saudi Arabia are politically justified as Saudi Arabia is an important counterweight to Iran. This is the "enemy of my enemy is my friend" theory of arms dealing. During the Trump administration, Jared Kusher, the President's son-in-law and a senior White House

movement, or individual"), www.govinfo.gov/content/pkg/STATUTE-98/pdf/STATUTE-98-Pg1837.pdf.

165 Seymour M. Hersh, *The Iran–Contra Committees: Did They Protect Reagan?*, New York Times (Apr. 29, 1990), www.nytimes.com/1990/04/29/magazine/the-iran-contra-committees-did-they-protect-reagan.html.

166 *See* David Johnston, *Bush Pardons 6 in Iran Affair, Aborting a Weinberger Trial; Prosecutor Assails "Cover-Up,"* New York Times (Dec. 25, 1992).

167 Pub. L. No: 118-50 (Apr. 12, 2024) (providing supplemental appropriations to federal agencies for assistance to Ukraine, Israel, and United States allies in the Indo-Pacific region).

168 Trends in International Arms Transfers, 2023, Stockholm International Peace Research Institute, Fact Sheet (2024) (reporting that the United States had 42% of global arms exports and France and Russia each 11%), www.sipri.org/sites/default/files/2024-03/fs_2403_at_2023.pdf.

169 *But see* Duncan MacIntosh, *The Sniper and the Psychopath: A Parable in Defense of the Weapons Industry*, *in* Ethical Dilemmas in the Defense Industry (Daniel Schoeni, Tobias Vestner, & Kevin Govern eds., 2023) (arguing that wealthier nations are presumptively morally superior to others and that arms dealers achieve good ends even if motivated by psychopathic greed when selling to the highest bidder). A Lockheed Martin executive wrote a short essay for the same edited volume. One author of this book (Richard Painter) also contributed an essay to the volume. Many of the other essays in the published volume were critical of the defense industry. The MacIntosh essay, however, not only is wrong in its assertions about the moral superiority of wealthy arms-buying nations, but did not mention specific examples that contradict that proposition, such as Saudi Arabia and other arms buyers in Western Asia.

staff member, coordinated negotiations of a $110 billion arms sale to Saudi Arabia, which included a missile defense system sold by Lockheed Martin.[170] Saudi Arabia at the time had been accused of war crimes in Yemen,[171] not to mention the murder and dismemberment in Istanbul of a journalist who had criticized the Saudi regime.[172]

The ability to pay for billions of dollars of US-made weapons does not imply the moral judgment to use them responsibly. Meanwhile, the private defense industry spends millions on campaign finance and lobbying. This sector contributed roughly $50 million to political candidates and committees during the 2020 campaign cycle.[173] Lockheed Martin alone spent $2,770,278 in political contributions in 2023 and 2024, evenly split between the two major political parties.[174] The problem President Eisenhower spoke about in his 1961 farewell address hasn't gone away.

3.8 THE PRESIDENT AND NATIONAL INTELLIGENCE AGENCIES

Defending the security of the United States does not just involve the President's role as Commander in Chief of the armed forces. Also important are the CIA and other agencies in the Intelligence Community (IC). The agencies are controlled by the President, pursuant to the National Security Act of 1947,[175] which also organized the modern Department of Defense.

[170] Kushner allegedly lobbied the CEO of Lockheed Martin to lower the price for the Saudis, and Lockheed Martin apparently agreed. David Reid, *Kushner Reportedly Called Up Lockheed Martin CEO to Cut Cost of Saudi Arms Deal*, CNBC (May 19, 2017), www.cnbc.com/2017/05/19/kushner-called-up-lockheed-martin-ceo-over-saudi-arms-deal-says-report.html. After President Trump left office, the Saudi Sovereign Wealth Fund loaned Kushner family businesses $2 billion in 2021, against the recommendations of its financial advisors but at the urging of the Saudi Crown Prince. David Kirkpatrick and Kate Kelly, *Before Giving Billions to Jared Kushner, Saudi Investment Fund Had Big Doubts*, New York Times (Apr. 10, 2022), www.nytimes.com/2022/04/10/us/jared-kushner-saudi-investment-fund.html?smid=tw-share. The Emoluments Clause of the Constitution, which prohibits federal officers from receiving profits and benefits from foreign governments, and which is discussed more extensively in Part III of this book, did not apply since at the time of the Saudi investment Kushner had left the White House and was no longer a federal officer.

[171] United Nations Human Rights Council. Forty-Fifth Session, Annual report of the United Nations High Commissioner for Human Rights and reports of the Office of the High Commissioner and the Secretary-General: Situation of human rights in Yemen, including violations and abuses since September 2014 (Sept. 28, 2020) (reporting egregious human rights abuses and violations of international law on all sides of the Yemeni civil war including a large number of violations by Saudi Arabia), www.ohchr.org/sites/default/files/Documents/HRBodies/HRCouncil/GEE-Yemen/2020-09-09-report.pdf.

[172] *Saudi Crown Prince Is Held Responsible for Khashoggi Killing in U.S. Report*, New York Times (July 17, 2021), www.nytimes.com/2021/02/26/us/politics/jamal-khashoggi-killing-cia-report.html.

[173] Open Secrets, *Defense Sector Summary*, www.opensecrets.org/industries/indus?ind=D.

[174] *Id.*

[175] (Pub. L. 80-253, 61 Stat.495, enacted July 26, 1947). This Act also created the position of Secretary of Defense to oversee the Department of Defense consisting of the Army (previously the War Department), the Navy, and the Air Force.

After the attacks of September 11, 2001, the National Security Act was amended by the Intelligence Reform and Terrorism Prevention Act of 2004 (IRTPA)[176] that placed the IC under the authority of the Director of National Intelligence (DNI), who is appointed by the President and confirmed by the Senate. The DNI oversees the National Intelligence Program, while the Military Intelligence Program which supports tactical military operations remains under the control of the Department of Defense.

Intelligence operations are covert. Much of what these agencies do is classified information, shared only with persons who have required security clearances *and* a "need to know." Occasionally, some classified information about intelligence operations is shared with select members of Congress, but not often. Without congressional oversight, scrutiny by the news media, or knowledge by the public until an intelligence operation is exposed, the risk of abuse is present.

Abuse of covert operations has a long history. President Theodore Roosevelt, for example, authorized US operatives to instigate a coup in Panama against Columbian rule in 1903 and then used US military force to back it up. The objective was US control of the Panama Canal, thought vital to US national security, but perhaps more important to American corporate interests.[177]

World War II saw both the United States and Britain engage in assassinations of enemy military leaders. These World War II "targeted killing" operations, mostly conducted against enemy combatants inside war zones, very likely were in accordance with international law. They included the assassinations of German SS leader Reinhard Heydrichs in Prague by Czech resistance fighters with aid from British Special Operations Executive (SOE) officers in Operation Anthropoid; the kidnapping of German Major General Heinrich Kreipe in Crete by SOE officers and Greek resistance fighters; a failed attempt by British commandos to assassinate German General Erwin Rommel in North Africa in Operation Flipper; and the American killing of Japanese General Isoroko Yamamoto by shooting down his airplane after code breaker discovered his flight plans in Operation Vengeance.[178]

The effectiveness of these operations during World War II, however, incentivized more legally dubious targeted killing operations during the Cold War and beyond, including drone strikes during President Obama's administration[179] and the

[176] Pub. L. 108458, 118 Stat. 3638 (Dec. 17, 2004).

[177] David McCullough, The Path between the Seas: The Creation of the Panama canal, 1870–1914, 361 (1977) (ch. 13 titled "Remarkable Revelation").

[178] *See* Adam Leong, Killing the Enemy: Assassination Operations during World War II (2015) (discussing in detail these and other assassinations during World War II).

[179] Claire O. Finkelstein, *The Status of State and Nonstate Actors in Postwar Hostilities: Restoring the Rule of Law to US Targeted Killing Operations*, 54 Vand. J. of Transnat'l L. 1163 (2023) (discussing the doubtful legality of many of these targeted killing operations).

Trump's administration's killing of Iranian General Qasem Soleimani inside Iraq in 2020.[180]

The CIA has also been involved in overthrowing foreign governments. President Dwight D. Eisenhower ended the Korean War with an armistice in 1953, but the Cold War then pivoted to covert operations with the aim of stopping the spread of communism. In Iran, a new socialist prime minister, Mohammad Mosaddegh, threatened to nationalize oil fields owned by British petroleum companies.[181] CIA agents, led by Kermit Roosevelt, Jr. (grandson of President Theodore Roosevelt),[182] orchestrated a coup in which supporters of the Shah of Iran, Mohammad Reza Pahlavi, overthrew Mosaddegh, effectively ending democracy in Iran. Even though the 1953 coup involved CIA agents committing multiple crimes inside Iran, including bribing government officials and media outlets, it had tacit approval from the White House.[183] Kermit Roosevelt, Jr. even wrote a book about it.[184]

In 1979, the Shah was overthrown by anti-American Islamic militants who also took hostages in the American embassy during Jimmy Carter's presidency. Iran since 1979 has been ruled by extremists who have made hatred of the United States into an obsession and national rallying point. To this day the Middle East and United States continue to live with the consequences of the CIA's coup in Iran.

Under President Nixon, the CIA overthrew yet more democratically elected governments abroad. This also was with the aim of stopping the spread of communism. Salvador Allende, a pro-Soviet socialist, was elected President of Chile in 1970 and threatened to nationalize US-owned copper mines.[185] The CIA spent $8 million on covert operations designed to destabilize Allende's government,[186] creating a state of political and economic chaos that ended with a military coup led by General Augusto Pinochet in 1973. Although the United States had no known role in the coup itself, the CIA's meddling in Chile's internal affairs helped make it

[180] *Id.* A separate issue is whether this targeted killing operation inside Iraq fell within Congress's 2002 Authorization for Use of Military Force (AUMF) preceding the Iraq War seventeen years earlier.

[181] Ervand Abrahamian, The Coup: 1953, the CIA, and the Roots of Modern U.S.–Iranian Relations (2013).

[182] Irvin Molotsky, *Kermit Roosevelt, Leader of C.I.A. Coup in Iran, Dies at 84*, New York Times (June 11, 2000), www.nytimes.com/2000/06/11/us/kermit-roosevelt-leader-of-cia-coup-in-iran-dies-at-84.html ("It was the C.I.A.'s first successful overthrow of a foreign government, and the shah stayed in power until the Islamic revolution of 1979. 'For an operation to last 25 years is not so bad,' one of Mr. Roosevelt's C.I.A. colleagues, Samuel Halpern, said today. 'It fell apart. Every operation cannot go on forever'").

[183] Abrahamian, *supra* note 181.

[184] Kermit Roosevelt, Jr., Coutercoup: The Struggle for the Control of Iran (1979).

[185] *Covert Action in Chile* 1963–1973, Staff Report of the Select Committee to Study Governmental Operations with Respect to Intelligence Activities, United States Senate (94 Cong. 1 Sess. 1975), at 5, 20 (discussing Allende's plan to nationalize Chile's copper mines), www.intelligence.senate.gov/sites/default/files/94chile.pdf.

[186] *Id.* at 1.

happen.[187] The Pinochet dictatorship ushered in years of political persecution, torture, and the disappearance of political opponents.[188]

Next came domestic spying. When the *New York Times* reported the secret bombing of Cambodia in May 1969, President Nixon responded to the leak by ordering illegal wiretapping of National Security Agency staff, with Secretary of State Henry Kissinger picking those who would be wiretap targets.[189]

The CIA's disregard for the rule of law was later investigated by the US Senate Committee led by Senator Frank Church (D-ID), the "Church Committee," which issued its report in 1976.[190] The Foreign Intelligence Surveillance Act of 1978 (FISA)[191] now requires prior authorization from the Foreign Intelligence Surveillance Court before the intelligence community can conduct surveillance *within* the United States.

Finally, after the attacks of September 11, 2001 came a new low, with the explicit endorsement of torture. The Department of Justice's infamous "torture memos" were discussed in Section 3.6,[192] but a purpose of these memos was to provide legal cover for intelligence officers in the CIA and Defense Department who used "enhanced interrogation" methods to extract information from suspected terrorists detained in CIA "black sites" around the globe and at the US military installation at Guantanamo Bay, Cuba. For years this program was classified, and much of it still is classified information. The DOJ torture memos eventually were declassified. After an investigation, the Senate issued a 2012 report, the Senate Select Committee on Intelligence Study of the Central Intelligence Agency's Detention and Interrogation Program.[193]

To this day, the United States government seeks to protect classified information about the torture program under the "state secrets doctrine," which the Supreme Court affirmed in *United States v. Zubaydah*[194] in 2022. In that case, Abu Zubaydah, a former associate of Osama bin Laden, was captured in Pakistan and then held at a

[187] *Id.* at 29 ("According to CIA documents these efforts played a significant role in setting the state for the military coup of September 11, 1973").

[188] *Id.* at 39 (discussing "torture centers" operating throughout Chile after the 1973 coup).

[189] *Nixon Testifies Kissinger Picked Wiretap Targets*, New York Times (Mar. 14, 1976), www.nytimes.com/1976/03/11/archives/nixon-testifies-kissinger-picked-wiretap-targets-says-he-ordered.html ("Richard M. Nixon said in sworn testimony made public today that he ordered a program of telephone wiretaps in 1969 to locate news leaks, but that it was Henry A. Kissinger, then his national security advisor, who supplied the Federal Bureau of Investigation with the names of the original targets of the program").

[190] *See* Senate Select Committee to Study Governmental Operations with Respect to Intelligence Activities (Report 1976) (94th Cong. 2nd Session).

[191] 50 U.S.C. §§1801–11, 1821–29, 1841–46, 1861–62, 1871. Pub. L. 95–511 (1978).

[192] For further discussion of the Bush-era torture memos see Section 3.5.

[193] S. Rep. 113-288 – Report of the Senate Select Committee on Intelligence Committee Study of the Central Intelligence Agency's Detention and Interrogation Program together with Foreword by Chairman Feinstein and Additional and Minority Views, 113th Congress (2013–2014).

[194] United States v. Zubaydah, 595 U.S. 195 (2022).

CIA "dark site" in Poland, where CIA contractors used "enhanced interrogation techniques" against him. Zubaydah, now held in Guantanamo Bay, Cuba, intervened in a Polish criminal investigation into the CIA's torture program, seeking to compel the US government to disclose evidence to the Polish authorities. The US government asserted the state secrets privilege to protect the information from disclosure.

Seven of the justices agreed with the government. Justice Breyer, writing for the majority, relied on a declaration from the Director of the CIA stating that the discovery requests would significantly harm US national security interests by confirming or denying the existence of a CIA detention site in Poland. The Court held that the government was entitled to invoke the state secrets privilege in response to those requests.

Justice Gorsuch wrote a powerful dissent, joined by Justice Sotomayor:

> They waterboarded Zubaydah at least 80 times, simulated live burials in coffins for hundreds of hours, and performed rectal exams designed to establish "total control over the detainee." Six days into his ordeal, Zubaydah was sobbing, twitching, and hyperventilating. During one waterboarding session, Zubaydah became "completely unresponsive, with bubbles rising through his open, full mouth." He became so compliant that he would prepare for waterboarding at the snap of a finger.

Gorsuch's opinion observed that the President shares foreign affairs powers with Congress, and Congress passed a law providing that US courts could assist foreign tribunals in providing information needed for their proceedings, "including criminal investigations conducted before formal accusation."[195] He noted that Poland's investigation of torture at CIA black sites in Poland fit this description precisely. The Constitution, thus, requires federal courts to apply "independent judgment" and uphold "the ancient right to every man's evidence."[196] Gorsuch also commented that although English monarchs "may have enjoyed the kind of latitude the government sought" in this case, the "Constitution did not create a President in the King's image but envisioned an executive regularly checked and balanced by other authorities."[197]

In some of his opinions, most notably his joining of the majority upholding presidential immunity from criminal prosecution for official acts in *Trump v. United States*,[198] Justice Gorsuch has come down squarely on the side of presidential power and privilege. But for Justice Gorsuch earlier, if not the other justices, concealment of information about torture was a bridge too far.

[195] 28 U.S. Code § 1782 – Assistance to foreign and international tribunals and to litigants before such tribunals.

[196] United States v. Zubaydah, 595 U.S. 195 at 259 (2022).

[197] *Id.* at 250.

[198] *See* discussion of *Trump v. United States* in Chapter 16, Section 16.3.

2025 brought yet another controversial use of the President's Commander in Chief power when President Trump summarily stripped his political opponents of security clearances. These included Joe Biden, Kamala Harris, former Secretaries of State Hillary Clinton and Anthony Blinken, Manhattan District Attorney Alvin Bragg, who had prosecuted Trump, former Ambassador Norman Eisen, who wrote a book about the prosecution of Trump, former Republican Congresswoman Liz Cheney, who supported the impeachment of Trump in 2021, and dozens of others.[199] The President also ordered security clearances suspended of all individuals working at law firms, including Perkins Coie LLP, that had previously represented his political opponents.[200] A federal court later ruled the executive order against Perkins Coie to be unconstitutional.[201]

[199] *Full List of Names Donal Trump Has Stripped of Security Clearance*, NEWSWEEK (Mar. 22, 2025).

[200] The White House, Executive Order of the President, Addressing Risks from Perkins Coie LLP, March 6, 2025.

[201] *See* Perkins Coie LLP v. United States Department of Justice et al. (D. D.C. 2025), Civil Action No. 25-716 (BAH), Order dated May 2, 2025 at 38 ("[i]t is simply not the case that all security-clearance decisions are immune from judicial review," quoting Nat'l Fed'n of Fed. Emps. v. Greenberg, 983 F.2d 286, 289 (D.C. Cir. 1993)).

4

The President in the Lawmaking Process

So far, this book has focused on the power of the President to act. However, the President and the Executive Branch make up just one of the three branches of the federal government, Congress and the federal courts composing the other two. In this chapter we will focus on the relationship between the power of Congress to make laws and the President's power to sign into law a bill Congress has passed, the power to veto a law, and the power to issue statements of interpretation on a bill the President signs into law.

During the Constitutional Convention of 1787, the debates over the veto power took place during a single August day late into the convention.[1] During the debates over the veto power three questions were presented – should the President have a veto power, if so should Congress be able to override the veto, and if the veto can be overridden what percentage of Congress should be required to override it?

On the first question, the mere existence of a veto, two ideas dominated the debate. The first idea, proposed by James Madison of Virginia, proposed that *both* the President and the Supreme Court should have the power to veto any bills passed by Congress.[2] While the records of the Convention don't explain why Madison believed that both the President and the Court should have a veto power, the early history of the United States may provide some clues. Later, after ratification of the Constitution, the Court did assert a type of veto power – the principle of judicial review, by which the Court can strike down a law but only if a majority of the Justices find it to be unconstitutional.

In 1803 the Supreme Court heard the landmark case *Marbury v. Madison*,[3] which involved the question of whether a commission to an executive office signed by

[1] *See generally* Journal of the Constitutional Convention & Notes of James Madison from the Constitutional Convention (Aug. 15, 1787), *reprinted* in THE RECORDS OF THE FEDERAL CONVENTION OF 1787, VOL. 2, 294–302 (Max Farrand ed., 1911).

[2] *Id.* at 298.

[3] Marbury v. Madison, 5 U.S. 137 (1803).

President Adams in the final days of his term must be delivered to the recipient, William Marbury, by Adam's successor, President Jefferson. This case is foundational to American law and governance because it established the concept of judicial review.

In the *Marbury* opinion, Chief Justice Marshall wrote that while the refusal by the Jefferson administration was itself illegal, he also refused to order the commission be given to Mr. Marbury because the Judiciary Act of 1789, which allowed Mr. Marbury to bring his grievance before the Supreme Court, was in conflict with Article III, Section 2 of the Constitution.[4] In making this determination, we see the first instance where the Court expanded its power from merely offering its interpretation of the law to stating that a law itself is unconstitutional.

The Court has used its power of judicial review to rule both federal and state laws unconstitutional. For example, in some of its most controversial decisions, the Court recently has struck down campaign finance laws, including in *Citizens United v. FEC*.[5] State laws were struck down in dozens of landmark cases over the past 220 years, including *Brown v. Board of Education*[6] (holding that segregated schools were a violation of the Fourteenth Amendment's Equal Protection Clause), *Tinker v. Des Moines*[7] (holding that prohibiting students from wearing black armbands protesting the war in Vietnam was a violation of the First Amendment), and *Roe v. Wade*[8] (holding that a law that severely restricted access to abortion was a violation of the Due Process Clause of the Fourteenth Amendment).

Returning to the question of the veto power at the Constitutional Convention, this early use of judicial review in American history indicates that the justices to some extent agreed with Madison, in their later holding that the Supreme Court should have some measure of a veto power because its power of judicial review extended beyond simply saying how the law should be interpreted to also include deciding whether laws are unconstitutional.

In contrast to Madison's idea, Thomas Pinkney of South Carolina argued that the President alone should have the veto power. Pinkney believed that giving the Court the veto power would "give a previous tincture to their opinions" should the Court have to rule on a law they had previously vetoed.[9] Similarly, John Mercer of Maryland cautioned that giving the Court the power to veto bills passed by Congress would violate the separation of powers and act as an oppression on the

4 *Id.* at 303.

5 Citizens United v. Federal Election Commission, 558 U.S. 310 (2010).

6 Brown v. Board of Education of Topeka, 344 U.S. 1 (1952).

7 Tinker v. Des Moines, 393 U.S. 503 (1969).

8 Roe v. Wade, 410 U.S. 113 (1973). After a fifty-year political struggle over abortion in the United States, the Court reversed its decision in *Roe* in *Dobbs v. Jackson Women's Health*, 597 U.S. 215 (2022).

9 Journal of the Constitutional Convention & Notes of James Madison from the Constitutional Convention (Aug. 15, 1787), *reprinted* in The Records of the Federal Convention of 1787, vol. 2, 298 (Max Farrand ed., 1911).

masses through their representatives in Congress.[10] Despite Madison's best efforts to persuade his fellow delegates on the proposal to grant veto power to both the President and the Court, it was voted down 8–3.

After the Convention decided that the President alone would wield the veto power, the question turned to when, if at all, Congress may override the President's veto. Always fearful of governmental overreach, the question before the delegates was whether granting the President the power to veto would lead to executive tyranny or whether Congress had the unfettered power to make laws that would lead to legislative tyranny. The views on this topic varied widely. One view, espoused by Gouverneur Morris of New York, argued that granting the President the power to veto and Congress the power to override the veto would destroy public trust as two branches of government publicly express their differing views on the merits of a law.[11] Roger Sherman of Connecticut expressed doubt that it was wise to place the judgment of a single individual, the President, above that of the entire legislature, and that no presidential veto power should exist at all.[12] James Wilson of Pennsylvania looked to English history to inform his views on the veto power. He argued that when the executive wields formidable power the words "king" and "tyrant" become synonymous.[13]

However, the experience in England's civil war, as demonstrated through the dissolution of the crown, shows that when executive power is at its nadir then the legislature fills the vacuum of power and becomes the tyrant.[14] Left with the possibility of either executive or congressional tyranny, Wilson ultimately concluded that it was best that the President have some power to fight back against congressional overreach.[15] Despite the wide spectrum of views present at the Convention, the delegates by a very narrow margin gave the President the power to veto legislation and Congress the power to override a presidential veto with a vote by two-thirds of both houses of Congress.[16]

Since the ratification of the Constitution all but seven presidents have exercised their veto power.[17] The high watermark of the exercise of the veto power is President Franklin Roosevelt, who vetoed 635 pieces of legislation during his twelve years in office.[18] Since the ratification of the Constitution, however, presidents have found creative means to modify and expand their veto power. Several of these means will be explored throughout the remainder of this chapter.

[10] *Id.*
[11] *Id.* at 299.
[12] *Id.* at 300.
[13] *Id.* at 300–01.
[14] *Id.*
[15] *Id.* at 301.
[16] *Id.* at 302.
[17] *Vetoes, 1789 to Present*, United States Senate, www.senate.gov/legislative/vetoes/vetoCounts.htm.
[18] *Id.*

4.1 PRESIDENTIAL POCKET VETOES

While Congress controls the legislative agenda, once a bill passes both houses, and goes to the President for approval and signature, he has several other veto options including a "pocket veto." In short, the veto power includes the power of the President to veto congressional legislation, and explain his reasons why in a message to Congress, followed by a possible "override" of the veto if a two-thirds majority vote is obtained in both houses of Congress. In addition the President may take no action for a so-called pocket veto during an adjournment of Congress to occur. The President has ten days to approve a bill. If Congress adjourns during this ten-day period, a veto of the legislation automatically occurs if the President takes no action on the bill.

The constitutional basis for this procedural move is found in Article I, Section 7, which states that "he [the President] shall return it, with his Objections to that House in which it shall have originated ... unless the Congress by their Adjournment prevent its Return, in which case it shall not be a law."[19] Without a house of Congress in session to return the bill to, at the end of the ten-day period the bill dies with the President's refusal to sign it. Unlike regular presidential vetoes, which can be overridden by Congress, the only mechanism to "override" a pocket veto is for Congress to pass, again, the legislation when they are back in session, wait for the President to veto the legislation again, then override the second presidential veto.

Since the ratification of the Constitution, thirty-three of our nation's forty-six presidents, from Madison to Clinton, have used the pocket veto block a total of 1,066 bills from becoming law, representing about 40 percent of the 2,594 presidential vetoes issued.[20] Of these 1,066 pocket vetoes, three of them, in 1926, 1936, and 1970, have received scrutiny by the Supreme Court.

The first challenge to a presidential pocket veto came in 1926 to two cases that were heard together, *Okanogan, Methow, San Poelis, Nespelem, Colville, and Lake Indian Tribes v. United States* and *Bands of the State of Washington v. United States* (commonly referred to as "the Pocket Veto Cases"),[21] which involved the pocket veto of a bill that would have allowed certain Indian tribes to bring lawsuits against the United States for the loss of historically tribal land. The bill was presented to the President on June 24, 1926. On July 3, Congress adjourned for the summer and under the Pocket Veto Clause the bill died when President Coolidge failed to sign it into law.

Despite the President's pocket veto, several tribes brought suit against the government, arguing that the law was valid because "adjournment" in Article I, Section 7

[19] *Id.*

[20] *Id.*

[21] Okanogan, Methow, San Poelis, Nespelem, Colville, and Lake Indian Tribes v. United States, 279 U.S. 655 (1926).

referred only to the final adjournment of Congress when a new Congress is sworn into office. In a 9–0 decision, the Court unanimously rejected the tribes' reading of the term "adjournment." Writing for the Court, Justice Sanford's opinion held that adjournment included both final adjournment of Congress as well as interim adjournment within and between sessions of Congress.[22] In Sanford's view, it is a constitutional mandate that "[the bill] is to be returned to the "House" when sitting in an organized capacity for the transaction of business, and having authority to receive the return . . . and proceed to reconsider the bill; and that no return can be made to the House when it is not in session as a collective body and its members are dispersed."[23]

Additionally, the Pocket Veto Cases raised the question of whether the President returning his objections in a veto to an agent of Congress, such as the Secretary of the House or Senate, would suffice when Congress is not in session. Here the Court also said no. The Court reasoned that nothing in the Constitution authorizes Congress to delegate the responsibility to receive a president's objections and that depending on the length of Congress's adjournment it could be weeks or months until Congress can consider the President's objection.[24]

Just over a decade later, the Court would, again, take up the question of a presidential pocket veto. In *Wright v. United States*[25] the Court considered whether a three-day recess by the Senate was sufficient to be considered adjournment. On April 24, 1936 Congress presented to the President a bill that would grant jurisdiction to various claims in the Court of Claims against the United States. On May 4 the Senate adjourned for three days while the House of Representatives remained in session. On May 5 the President vetoed the bill and submitted to the Secretary of the Senate his objections to the bill.

Later in 1936 Wright filed a claim with the Court of Claims arguing that the President had not properly used his veto power under the holding in the Pocket Veto Cases. In short, Wright argued that the Pocket Veto Cases prohibited the President from delivering his objections to an agent.

Writing for the majority, Chief Justice Hughes made two important distinctions with the Pocket Veto Cases. First, unlike in those cases, only one house of Congress was in recess. The Court held that adjournment by *Congress* means both houses of Congress. Second, and most confusingly, the Court held that there were instances where the President *could* return a vetoed bill to an agent of Congress. The Court distinguished the Pocket Veto Cases by reasoning that the recess by the Senate was only three days compared to several weeks in those cases. While declining to draw a bright-line rule on when return of a vetoed bill to an agent becomes impermissible,

[22] *Id.* at 683.
[23] *Id.*
[24] *Id.* at 684.
[25] Wright v. United States, 302 U.S. 583 (1938).

the Court ultimately held that for short congressional recesses the concerns articulated in the Pocket Veto Cases were overcome by the brevity of the recess.[26]

The most recent notable case testing the limits of the pocket veto came from the DC Circuit in 1974. In *Kennedy v. Sampson*,[27] the case involved a bill presented to the President on December 14, 1970. On December 22 both the House and Senate adjourned for Christmas, to return on December 29 and 28 respectively. On Christmas Eve President Nixon issued a statement saying that he would not sign the bill, and on Christmas Day the ten-day window closed with the bill being unsigned by the President.

After the bill did not become law, Senator Ted Kennedy began a lawsuit against the head of the General Services Administration asserting that the President had not vetoed the legislation within ten days and, under the standard set in *Wright*, the week-long adjournment for Christmas should be considered a brief recess during which the President should have left his objections to the law with the Secretary of the House or Senate.

The DC Circuit sided with Senator Kennedy's reading of the *Wright* decision. The Court's opinion held that the pocket veto was an exception to the general rule that Congress may override a presidential veto, and looked to the purpose of the Supreme Court's holding in the Pocket Veto Cases. Here the DC Circuit identified that the reason the Supreme Court had held the pocket veto valid was because of the lengthy recess and uncertainty about when Congress would adjourn again. There was no similar concern here. The recess was only for a week and there was a set date when Congress would reconvene. Based on this, the DC Circuit held that if President Nixon wished to veto the bill he should have given his objections to the Secretary of the Senate and that a pocket veto was inappropriate.

While the pocket veto has fallen out of favor today, no president since President George W. Bush has used it, it remains a valid tool at the President's disposal.[28] As we will see, the President also has other tools under the veto power to affect legislation. Most important, these Article II powers of the President to influence legislation are exercised before a bill becomes law.

4.2 THE LINE ITEM VETO

The act of legislating is an act of compromise. It is not uncommon for the President and Congress to have differing views on legislative priorities, and the final version of a bill that reaches the President's desk for his signature often reflects not just the will of Congress but compromised language that Congress believes the President will

[26] *Id.* at 589–90.

[27] Kennedy v. Sampson, 511 F.2d 430 (D.C. Cir. 1974).

[28] Bush's pocket veto of the National Defense Authorization Act for Fiscal Year 2008 in December 2007 was controversial because the House had designated agents to receive presidential messages before adjourning.

sign into law. This compromise is most visible when Congress passes its annual budget. Modern budgets passed by Congress are a mix of appropriations approved of by both Congress and the President, appropriations only Congress wants, and appropriations only wanted by the President.

Beginning with President Grant in the mid nineteenth century, presidents have sought a constitutional amendment that would expand their power under the Presentment Clause to include the power to veto individual appropriations as well as entire bills. In 1996, Congress met the President halfway and passed the Line Item Veto Act of 1996.[29] While the Act didn't grant the President an absolute veto power, it did give him the power to "cancel … an item of new direct spending" upon a finding that vetoing the spending would reduce the federal deficit, not impair any essential government functions, and would not harm the national interest.[30] After the passage of the Line Item Veto Act, President Clinton used the power delegated to him by Congress to veto eighty-two appropriations from eleven different laws.[31]

Just two years after the Line Item Veto Act became law it was struck down by the Supreme Court as a violation of the Presentment Clause.[32] The case that struck down the Line Item Veto Act, *Clinton v. City of New York*,[33] involves a complex Medicaid scheme where President Clinton vetoed a provision of the Balanced Budget Act of 1997 that would have required New York State to reimburse the federal government for certain Medicaid costs.[34]

In striking down the Line Item Veto Act, the Court considered the language of both Articles II and I. Beginning with Article II, the Court acknowledged that the President has the power to "from time to time give to the Congress Information on the State of the Union, and recommend to their Consideration such Measures as he shall judge necessary and expedient."[35] The Court interpreted this passage to mean that while the President cannot directly recommend measures necessary and expedient by using the line item veto, he may influence the legislative process through his communications, both public and private, with members of Congress and the public. An example of this use of the presidential platform to influence legislation is perhaps best illustrated by both Presidents Roosevelt, who used the mass media of their time and their outsized popularity to compel Congress to pass landmark legislation such as the Pure Food and Drug Act,[36] the creation of the Departments of Commerce and Labor, and the Social Security Act of 1935.[37]

[29] Line Item Veto Act, Pub. L. No. 104-130, 110 Stat. 1200 (1996).
[30] *Id.*
[31] Todd Garvey, Edward C. Liu, & Andrew Nolan, Cong. Rsch. Serv., Whose Line Is It Anyway: Could Congress Give the President a Line-Item Veto? 1 (2018).
[32] U.S. Const., Art. I, § 7.
[33] Clinton v. New York, 524 U.S. 417 (1998).
[34] *Id.* at 417.
[35] *Id.* at 438 (citing U.S. Const., Art. II, § 3).
[36] Pure Food and Drug Act of 1906, Pub. L. No. 59-384, 34 Stat. 768.
[37] Social Security Act of 1935, Pub. L. No. 74-271, 49 Stat. 620.

In addition to Article II, the Court also examined the language of the Presentment Clause in Article I. The key distinction the Court made between a line item veto and a typical veto is on the timing. The Court reasoned that the "return" of a bill to Congress following a typical veto occurs *before* the bill becomes law. On the other hand, a line item veto occurs *after* the bill becomes law. While the before/after distinction is perhaps a legal fiction, the Court also looked to the Constitution's silence on the line item veto. While the Constitution expressly allows a president to play a role in the legislative process, both through the use of his bully pulpit and through a full veto of a bill, it is silent on the ability of a president to unilaterally repeal or amend only a portion of a bill.[38] The Court held that he cannot do so.

4.3 THE LEGISLATIVE VETO

Up to this point, this chapter has focused on the power of the President to influence the lawmaking process through the use of vetoes. But to what degree, if any, may Congress control the Executive Branch through legislation? In 1983 the Supreme Court answered this question in the landmark case *INS v. Chadha*.[39]

Chadha involved a challenge to the Immigration and Nationality Act ("INA")[40] that granted the Attorney General discretionary power to suspend deportation for those who had entered the country illegally or overstayed their visa if the deportation would cause undue hardship on the alien or their immediate family if they were citizens or lawful permanent residents.[41] However, under the INA, the House of Representatives, but not the Senate, could override the Attorney General's decision to suspend the deportation.[42]

This congressional scheme posed two constitutional questions. First, could Congress delegate the power to suspend deportations to the executive branch? Second, was the power of the House to veto the Attorney General's decision proper? Beginning with the first question, the answer is yes.

Under Article I, Section 1 of the Constitution, "[a]ll legislative Powers … shall be vested in a Congress of the United States, which shall consist of a Senate and the House of Representatives."[43] The Constitution in Article I, Section 8 then goes on to enumerate the powers granted to Congress to include the power to declare war, make laws, regulate interstate commerce, lay and collect taxes, and several other powers.[44] Under the "non-delegation doctrine," Congress runs afoul of principles of

38 Clinton v. New York, 524 U.S. 417 (1998) at 439.
39 INS v. Chadha, 462 U.S. 919 (1983).
40 8 U.S.C. § 1254 (1952).
41 *Id.* at § 244(a).
42 *Id.* at § 244(c)(2).
43 U.S. Const. Art. I, § 1.
44 *Id.* at § 8.

separation of powers when it delegates one of the powers in Section 8 to another branch of government.

However, this is not to say that Congress cannot delegate any authority to other branches. This principle is best highlighted when executive agencies are tasked with interpreting statutes passed by Congress. For example, when Congress passed the Clean Air Act of 1970[45] it recognized that pollution was a growing problem and sought to solve the issue through legislation limiting sources of pollution. To implement the Act and develop standards on polluting emissions Congress gave the Environmental Protection Agency (EPA) broad discretion to set rules and standards on pollutants. The idea underlying this decision is that while Congress has enumerated lawmaking power, it lacks the specialized expertise on what pollutants should be regulated and in what quantity, so it delegated the rulemaking authority to the EPA to "fill in the gaps" in congressional knowledge. We should note that the Supreme Court today is increasingly receptive to stricter iterations of the nondelegation doctrine, a topic addressed in Chapter 2, and the Court's recent holding in *West Virginia v. Environmental Protection Agency*.[46]

On the second question of the authority of the House veto, the Court found this scheme unconstitutional as a violation of the principles of bicameralism and the Presentment Clause.[47] In order for a "legislative veto" of an executive branch decision to be constitutionally sound, it must be passed by both houses of Congress, rather just one as seen in *Chadha*.

Despite the seemingly clear holding in *Chadha*, the legislative veto continues today in all but name. A 2005 study by the Congressional Research Service found that most unicameral, or one chamber of Congress, legislative vetoes in the aftermath of *Chadha* were replaced with joint resolutions of approval.[48] Unlike in *Chadha*, where an executive action could be vetoed by a single house of Congress, joint resolutions require that the executive branch receive the approval of *both* houses of Congress before making a proposed action. This however, is a distinction without a difference. A joint resolution of approval can be thwarted by a single house of Congress, which is identical to the scheme in *Chadha*.

Another way that Congress and the President have found to bypass *Chadha* is to create informal agreements that bypass the legislative process altogether. In 1989 Secretary of State James Baker met with congressional leaders and agreed to give four congressional committees veto power of funding to Nicaraguan rebels in exchange for $50 million in humanitarian aid to the rebel group.[49] The release of

45 42 U.S.C. ch. 85 (1955).

46 597 U.S. 697 (2022).

47 INS v. Chadha, 462 U.S. 919 (1983) at 952.

48 *Legislative Veto after Chadha*, Cong. Research Serv., www.everycrsreport.com/files/20050502_RS22132_f3f5994e75ce9c1c1ac4aac4e3b019cfc61f2f38.pdf.

49 John Felton, *Bush, Hill Agree to Provide Contras with New Aid*, CQ Weekly Report (Mar. 25, 1989), at 656.

the aid funding was conditioned on the approval of four committees and party leadership. Despite anger from members of Congress and a lawsuit brought challenging the side deal as a legislative veto forbidden under *Chadha*, a federal court dismissed the suit as being part of the give-and-take of negotiations in representative government.[50]

4.4 PRESIDENTIAL SIGNING STATEMENTS

As discussed throughout this chapter, legislation by Congress is a product of compromise. Unless one party controls the House, the Senate, and the presidency, congressional leaders must work with their colleagues across the aisle to get the votes to have a piece of legislation to reach the President's desk. The President may have his own objections regarding the wording or context of a statute or the constitutionality of a statute entirely.

Article I, Section 7 of the Constitution provides the President with a binary choice to either sign a bill with which he agrees, or to veto a bill with which he disagrees.[51] As discussed throughout Sections 4.1 and 4.2 of this chapter, the President has several ways to veto a bill. However, what should a president do if he believes that a statute is constitutionally questionable or has a different interpretation of a law than Congress?

That answer to this dilemma came in the late twentieth century with the rise of the presidential signing statement. The basic idea of a signing statement is that when a president signs a bill into law he will do one of three things. He will either offer an interpretation of a statutory provision for an executive agency to follow, announce constitutional objections to parts of the law, or declare how the administration will enforce the law.[52]

While a few presidents in the nineteenth century, including President Jackson in 1830[53] and President Tyler in 1842,[54] gave signing statements, the practice exploded in popularity during the Reagan administration. During his eight years in office, President Reagan issued 250 signing statements of which one-third objected to at least one statutory provision that he signed into law.[55] In the words of Samuel Alito, then a member of the Office of Legal Counsel of the Department of Justice, the purpose of these signing statements was to "ensure that the Presidential signing

[50] Burton v. Baker, 723 F. Supp. 1550 (D.D.C. 1989).

[51] U.S. CONST. Art. I, § 7, cl. 2.

[52] *See generally* TODD GARVEY, CONG. RSCH. SERV., PRESIDENTIAL SIGNING STATEMENTS: CONSTITUTIONAL AND INSTITUTIONAL IMPLICATIONS (2012).

[53] *See* Christopher S. Kelley, A *Comparative Look at the Constitutional Signing Statement*, 61st Annual Meeting of the Midwest Political Science Association, at 5 (2003).

[54] LOUIS FISHER, CONSTITUTIONAL CONFLICTS BETWEEN CONGRESS AND THE PRESIDENT 133 (4th ed. 1997).

[55] Curtis A. Bradley & Eric A. Posner, *Presidential Signing Statements and Executive Power*, 23 CONST. COMMENT. 307, 323 (2006).

statements assume their rightful place in the interpretation of legislation."[56] In other words, when a court reviewed one of these statutes, Alito believed that the court should consider not only what Congress intended when it passed the bill, but also how the President interpreted it when he signed it into law.

In 1993 Walter Dellinger, also in the Office of Legal Counsel under President Clinton, wrote a memo to the President on the use of signing statements.[57] Unlike the Alito memo, which unequivocally addressed the presidential signing statement, the Dellinger memo found some uses of signing statements constitutionally appropriate and other uses legally questionable.

In the Dellinger memo, three uncontroversial uses of signing statements were identified. First, the President may use signing statements to inform the public and interested industries about the effects of the bill and how it fits in with the President's views or programs.[58] Second, a president may use signing statements to direct the Executive Branch on how to interpret and implement a statute.[59] As noted earlier, the President, as head of the Executive Branch, controls a vast bureaucracy of fifteen executive departments, and signing statements can provide clarity to those affected departments on how ambiguous language in a statute is read by the President. Third, signing statements can be used by the President to announce his views on any applications that otherwise are deemed unconstitutional, and as a result the Executive Branch will not enforce the law in these unconstitutional cases.[60]

In contrast to the Alito memo, the Dellinger memo found the use of signing statements to create "executive history" that is problematic for two reasons.[61] First, Article I, Section 1 of the Constitution places all legislative powers with Congress, not the President.[62] The view of the Dellinger memo is that Congress alone creates legislative history through committee reports, floor debates, congressional hearings, and other typical legislative methods.[63] Signing statements, on the other hand, occur *after* the legislative process is completed. They should only be granted limited consideration in understanding congressional intent.[64] The second concern of the

[56] Samuel A. Alito, Jr., *Using Presidential Signing Statements to Make Fuller Use of the President's Constitutionally Assigned Role in the Process of Enacting Law*, Office of Legal Counsel Memorandum, February 5, 1986.

[57] The Legal Significance of Presidential Signing Statements, Memorandum Opinion for the Counsel to the President (Nov. 3, 1993), www.justice.gov/file/147336-0/dl?inline=.

[58] *Id.* at 132.

[59] *Id.*

[60] *Id.*

[61] *Id.* at 135.

[62] U.S. Const., Art. I, § 1, cl. 1.

[63] The Constitutional Separation of Powers between the President and Congress, Walter Dellinger, May 7, 1996 at 136, www.justice.gov/file/146951/dl?inline=. This later memorandum was to the general counsels of federal agencies explaining the legal effect of signing statements.

[64] *Id.* at 136, citing to *Regional Rail Reorganization Act Cases*, 419 U.S. 102, 132 (1974).

Dellinger memo is that when the President reinterprets the parts of legislation he disapproves of he is effectively issuing a line item veto.[65]

Despite this skepticism, the Dellinger memo found that when the President played a critical role in the legislative process it may be appropriate for him to offer a signing statement as a means of creating legislative history. The constitutional underpinning for this opinion is rooted in Article II, Section 3,[66] which allows the President to "recommend to [Congress's] Consideration such Measures as he shall judge necessary and expedient," and Article I, Section 7,[67] which allows the President to sign a bill into law or return it to Congress *with his objections*. Viewed together, Dellinger believed that these two sections allowed the President to explain both his and Congress's intention in passing a law when presidential leadership was instrumental in shepherding legislation through Congress.[68]

The skepticism of the Dellinger memo on signing statements would not stop the frequent use of them by either President Clinton or his successors. During his eight years in office President Clinton issued 381 signing statements and President George W. Bush issued 161 signing statements challenging over 1,000 distinct provisions of law.[69]

In contrast to his four predecessors, President Obama took an unambiguously skeptical approach to signing statements. Compared to Presidents Reagan through George W. Bush, who issued over a hundred signing statements each, President Obama only issued thirty-eight statements during his tenure in office. In a March 2009 memo issued by the President, he expressed four principles that he believed would limit his use of signing statements.[70] These four principles were (1) communicating with Congress during the legislative process to minimize the need for signing statements, (2) presume that legislation passed by Congress is constitutional unless it is clearly unconstitutional based on well-founded legal principles, (3) ensure that any signing statements clearly and specifically identify the basis of a constitutional objection, and (4) if issuing a statement to construe a statute to avoid a constitutional problem the construction should be a legitimate one.[71]

Following the Obama-era realignment on signing statements, both Presidents Trump and Biden also have limited their use of signing statements. During his four years in office, President Trump issued sixty-nine signing statements, and as of April

65 Discussed *supra* in Section 4.2.

66 U.S. Const., Art. II, § 3.

67 U.S. Const., Art. I, § 7.

68 Dellinger, *supra* note 63, at 136.

69 *See* Neil J. Kinkopf and Peter M. Shane, *Signed under Protest: A Database of Presidential Signing Statements, 2001–2009*, Public Law and Legal Theory Working Paper Series No. 141 (Jan. 2011).

70 *Memorandum on Presidential Signing Statements*, The White House (Mar. 9, 2009), https://obamawhitehouse.archives.gov/the-press-office/memorandum-presidential-signing-statements.

71 *Id.*

2024 President Biden had given just ten signing statements.[72] Whether this decline in signing statements represents a new skepticism of the power and constitutionality of signing statements, dysfunction in Congress leading to fewer bills requiring signing statements, or some other combination of factors is an open question. Regardless, the nature of the legislative process and inevitable differences between executive and legislative interpretations of the law will likely lead future presidents to continuing to use the signing statement as a means to assert presidential influence and power.

Throughout this chapter we have seen how presidents have tested the outer limits of their veto power to achieve their policy objectives despite congressional objections. While courts have been skeptical of schemes that run afoul of the Presentment Clause, presidents continue to use the power of the pocket veto, signing statements, and negotiations with Congress to limit congressional power and achieve their goals through other means. As we close on this discussion of the interplay between Congress and the President, we will move next to examining the power and limitations of the President's pardon power.

[72] *Signing Statements 2021 President Biden*, Coherent Babble, www.coherentbabble.com/ss2021.htm.

5

Presidential Pardons

For Others and Self?

Article II, Section 2 of the Constitution empowers the President to "grant Reprieves and Pardons for Offences against the United States, except in Cases of Impeachment."[1] The seemingly simple language of this clause in the Constitution obscures a number of complicated questions about the scope and nature of this presidential power. For example – may Congress play a role in a president's decision on pardons? Can the President grant a pardon for both state and federal crimes? Is the President required to fully pardon someone, or may he place conditions on the pardon? And, can a president pardon himself?

To begin with, it is important to think about *why* the Constitution grants the President this broad pardon power. When designing the government structure, the Founders looked to early democratic systems in ancient Greece and Rome as well as the English government for both inspiration and warnings. Under all three systems, the Founders identified that leaders enjoyed the power to pardon.[2] Under English law this power can be traced back to King Ine of Wessex, who ruled in 688–725 CE.[3] During the following 1,000 years, Parliament through statutes would rein in the King's power to pardon and curtail this power in certain instances, such as forbidding the sale of pardons and the use of pardons as bribery to join the military.[4]

For instance, in early English law, pardons by the King were unilaterally issued for mercy, religious, political, or financial reasons. Later, pardons were also given for service, friendship, or loyalty.[5] Throughout traditional English law, the monarch

[1] U.S. Const. Art. II, § 2, cl. 1.

[2] Daniel T. Kobil, *The Quality of Mercy Strained: Wresting the Pardoning Power from the King*, 69 Tex. L. Rev. 569, 583–85 (1991).

[3] 1 Benjamin Thorpe, Ancient Laws and Institutes of England 46 (1840).

[4] Kristen H. Fowler, *Limiting the Federal Pardon Power*, 83 Ind. L.J. 1651, 1654 (2008). *See* Statute of Westminster (1275).

[5] William Blackstone, Commentaries on the Laws of England: A Facsimile of the First Edition of 1765–1769 (1979).

could not be impeached or be charged with a crime under the legal principle of sovereign immunity.[6] King Charles I, in 1649, was the only exception as he was tried by Parliament and executed for high treason and other high crimes during the English Civil War.[7]

Over time, a practice of consent or mutual agreement by the parties, the monarch and the recipient of the pardon, developed, in effect, a bilateral understanding or agreement that became effective when the pardon was accepted with or without conditions. In short, the notion of two parties to the pardon became implicit and commonplace. This was especially true, throughout the common law, when the recipient requested the pardon and accepted the offer. Hence, the modern development of pardons considered the acceptance as an implicit admission of guilt for the pardon to be effective, as evident later in the practice in the United States discussed below.

This history of executive pardons in early democracies and the English tradition almost certainly influenced the drafting of the Constitution. As noted later in this chapter, when the Constitutional Convention convened in Philadelphia, two states, New Jersey and Virginia, brought to the Convention their own dueling plans for shaping the new government. While neither state's plan initially included an executive pardon power, Hamilton was the first to suggest the power in a list of proposed amendments to the Virginia Plan.[8] Hamilton's amendment would have vested with the executive the power to pardon all offenses except for treason, which would have required approval from the Senate.[9]

The reason for Hamilton's treason exception to the executive's plenary pardon power was based on fears of the President using the pardon power as a means of self-pardon.[10] The final language of the clause, which replaced "treason" with "impeachment," was considered to offer similar protections because the Impeachment Clause in Article II, Section 4 lists treason as one of the grounds on which a president can be impeached. Accordingly, if a president committed treasonous acts he could be impeached by Congress and the language of the Pardon Clause would prevent him from self-pardoning.[11]

[6] *See generally* Ketana Krishna, *Development of the Doctrine of Sovereign Immunity in England and India* (Mar. 3, 2012), https://ssrn.com/abstract=2402176.

[7] Daniel Gosling, *Treason against the State: The Execution of Charles I*, THE NATIONAL ARCHIVES (Jan. 30, 2023), https://blog.nationalarchives.gov.uk/treason-against-the-state-the-execution-of-charles-i/.

[8] 1 THE RECORDS OF THE FEDERAL CONVENTION OF 1787, at 292 (Max Farrand ed., 1911).

[9] *Id.*

[10] 2 THE RECORDS OF THE FEDERAL CONVENTION OF 1787, at 626 (Madison's notes, referring to Randolph's arguments that the pardon power could not be used by a president who is guilty of treason and used treasonous individuals to consolidate his own power).

[11] *Id.* (Madison's notes, arguing that an exception to the pardon power for treason was unnecessary because if the President is a party to treason he can be impeached and prosecuted).

Other than the debate on the treason and impeachment exception, the other debate during the Convention was to what extent, if any, the legislature should act as a check on the pardon power. Some early drafts of the Constitution considered a role for the Senate, which would be required to approve any presidential pardons before they were law.[12] However it was Hamilton, echoing the debates on a singular or multi-person presidency, who argued that a single person, rather than a legislative body, would be better able to "balance the motives which may plead for and against the remission of the punishment, than any numerous body whatever" and that the pardon power "should be as little as possible fettered or embarrassed."[13] While the pardon power would receive some limited debate during the remainder of the Convention, ultimately Hamilton's views won out. The Constitution granted the President generally broad pardoning powers.

While the pardon power has received limited scrutiny by the courts, likely due to its plenary nature, there is a limited number of cases that highlight some of the limitations of a president's pardon power. In *Burdick v. United States*[14] President Wilson issued a "blanket pardon" (a pardon for all crimes related to a certain action) to journalist George Burdick to deny him his Fifth Amendment right against self-incrimination after it was suspected that he had bribed a customs official to get a scoop on a jewel smuggling ring. After Burdick refused to accept the pardon, he was fined and jailed until he complied with the investigation into the sourcing for his story. In its ruling, the Court held that while the President could *offer* pardons, recipients, such as Burdick, could elect to refuse the pardon for any reason or no reason at all.[15] The Court reasoned that acceptance of a pardon may have "consequences of even greater disgrace than those from which it purports to relieve."[16] In Burdick's case, perhaps out of a sense of journalistic integrity, he seemed to believe that protecting his sources and suffering the consequences was of greater importance than his own freedom.

In addition, while the President may grant pardons for virtually any federal offense, he may not grant pardons for violations of state law. Under our system of federalism, every state and territory within the United States has its own body of criminal law which largely operates independently of federal criminal law. While state governors generally have pardon authority within their own state, they do not have pardon authority over criminals in other states or over federal law. A similar principle applies to the President. His pardon power extends only to federal law.

[12] *Id* at 419.

[13] THE FEDERALIST NO. 74, at 385–86 (Alexander Hamilton) (George W. Carey & James McClellan eds., 2001).

[14] Burdick v. United States, 236 U.S. 79 (1915).

[15] *Id.* at 90.

[16] *Id.*

He may not pardon state-level offenses or offenses charged under another country's criminal code.[17]

Finally, the President may not condition a pardon on terms that are constitutionally objectionable.[18] In *Hoffa v. Saxbe*,[19] the Court reviewed a conditional pardon granted by President Nixon to union leader Jimmy Hoffa. As part of the conditions for the pardon, Hoffa was prohibited from assuming any union leadership positions for several years. Hoffa argued that this condition was a violation of his First Amendment right to free association. While the Court in Hoffa's case ultimately ruled that the conditions on Hoffa's pardon were constitutional, they also laid out a two-pronged test to examine the constitutionality of conditional pardons.

First, the courts consider the relationship of the condition and the public interest. In Hoffa's case, he was charged and convicted with bribery and fraud in relation to his activities as President of the Teamster Union. The federal appellate court reasoned that the public interest was well served by making Hoffa ineligible for the same types of positions that led to his conviction.[20]

Second, the conditions of the pardon must not unreasonably infringe upon any constitutional rights. While this prong of the two-part test has never seriously been challenged in court, one can imagine a number of conditions a court may find would unreasonably infringe on a constitutional right.

The pardon power also raises questions about *who* a president may pardon. May a president pardon large, similarly situated groups of people? May a president pardon himself? The answer to the first question is a clear "yes." In 1977 President Carter issued Executive Order 11967[21] that granted blanket pardons, or amnesty, to those who had violated the Selective Service Act to evade the draft during the Vietnam War. Similarly, in 2022 President Biden granted amnesty to those who violated the Controlled Substances Act and were convicted of simple possession of marijuana.[22] Additionally, during the last full day of his presidency, President Biden issued a sweeping Executive Grant of Clemency for five of his close family members that covered any nonviolent crimes they may have committed during the previous ten years.[23]

It is unclear whether a presidential self-pardon is constitutional. Although the United States has never encountered a situation where a president has tried to self-pardon, the history of presidents' legal troubles can offer us guidance on how a court might rule.

[17] Hickey v. Schomig, 240 F. Supp. 2d 793, 795 (N.D. Ill. 2002).
[18] Schick v. Reed, 419 U.S. 256, 265 (1974).
[19] Hoffa v. Saxbe, 378 F. Supp. 1221, 1234 (D.D.C. 1974).
[20] *Id.* at 1240.
[21] Relating to Violations of the Selective Service Act 42 Fed. Reg. 4,393 (Jan. 21, 1977).
[22] The White House, A *Proclamation on Granting Pardon for the Offense of Simple Possession of Marijuana*, https://bidenwhitehouse.archives.gov/briefing-room/presidential-actions/2022/10/06/granting-pardon-for-the-offense-of-simple-possession-of-marijuana/.
[23] Executive Grant of Clemency, Office of the White House, January 19, 2025, www.justice.gov/pardon/media/1385756/dl?inline.

The Watergate scandal during the Nixon presidency sheds light on this self-pardon question. In the waning days of the Nixon administration, the President had his legal counsel prepare a memo on the constitutionality of a self-pardon. Most succinctly, the Office's memo states that "This [the pardon power] raises the question whether the President can pardon himself. Under the fundamental rule that no one may be a judge in his own case, it would seem that the question should be answered in the negative."[24] The basis for the opinion in this brief memo was that as a fundamental rule no one may be a judge in their own case, and that by extension of this principle the President cannot pardon himself.

The findings of the Office's memo to President Nixon were reaffirmed on September 8, 1974 when President Ford granted a pardon to President Nixon for "any charges which might be brought against [him] for actions taken during the time I was President of the United States."[25] In a statement released the same day the pardon was issued, President Nixon accepted President Ford's pardon and expressed his regret for his involvement in the Watergate scandal. As noted earlier, in *Burdick* recipients of a presidential pardon are under no obligation to accept the pardon they have been given. If Nixon truly believed he could not be prosecuted for his involvement in the Watergate scandal, why would he choose to accept the pardon and the admission of guilt that came with it?

Just over twenty years after the conclusion of the Nixon saga, President Clinton found himself in a similar predicament. In 1994 Kenneth Starr was appointed as independent counsel to conduct an investigation into President Clinton's alleged involvement in a complex real estate investment scheme that had drawn scrutiny from the Securities and Exchange Commission.[26] After the investigation expanded to cover Clinton's truthfulness in civil proceedings over his alleged sexual misconduct, and after years of litigation, Robert Ray, who had assumed the duties of independent counsel in 1999, closed the investigation into the Whitewater affair in January 2001 and declined to pursue criminal charges against the President.[27] As a condition of Ray not pursuing charges against the President, Clinton agreed to pay a $25,000 fine and have his Arkansas law license suspended for five years.[28] As with Nixon, Clinton's agreement with the independent counsel indicates an implicit acknowledgement that any pardon he gave himself would have been unconstitutional.

[24] Memorandum Opinion for the Deputy Attorney General, Presidential or Legislative Pardon of the President, August 5, 1974, https://www.justice.gov/file/147746/dl?inline=

[25] Presidential Proclamation 4311 – Granting Pardon to Richard Nixon (September 8, 1974). Statement by Former President Richard Nixon (Sept. 8, 1974), www.fordlibrarymuseum.gov/library/document/0019/4520706.pdf.

[26] *Kenneth Starr's Mandate*, Wall Street Journal (Sept. 25, 1996, 12:01 AM), www.wsj.com/articles/SB843603671806139000.

[27] *Remarks by Independent Counsel Robert Ray Closing the Whitewater Investigation*, The American Presidency Project (Jan. 19, 2001), www.presidency.ucsb.edu/documents/remarks-independent-counsel-robert-ray-closing-the-whitewater-investigation.

[28] The Associated Press, *Clinton Pays $25,000 Fine in Arkansas Case*, New York Times (Apr. 8, 2001), www.nytimes.com/2001/04/08/us/clinton-pays-25000-fine-in-arkansas-case.html.

The historical underpinnings of the pardon power can also help illuminate the self-pardon question. As noted above, both of the early templates for the Constitution, the Virginia and New Jersey Plans, excluded *any* presidential pardon power. This skepticism of a broad plenary power was understandable. The Founders had fought a war over unchecked executive power less than a decade before. They were rightfully skeptical that the pardon power would undermine their careful plans of creating a nation of laws, not men.

An early draft of the pardon power included an explicit prohibition for cases involving treason. Edmund Randolph argued that it was "too great a trust. The President may himself be guilty. The Tra[i]tors may be his own instruments."[29] James Wilson argued that prohibiting pardons for impeachment was the proper limitation and that "[i]f the President be himself a party to the guilt he can be impeached and prosecuted."[30] While Wilson's argument facially appears to be more limiting, it is perhaps more restrictive on a president's power than Randolph's. The language of Article II, Section 4 allows for the impeachment of the President for treason, bribery, and other high crimes and misdemeanors.[31]

A careful study of the Constitution and Article II also weighs against the legality of a presidential self-pardon. In *Schick v. Reed*[32] the Supreme Court held that "the pardoning power is an enumerated power of the Constitution ... its limitations if any, must be found in the Constitution itself."[33]

One simplistic way to view this statement from *Schick* is that Article II, Section 2 places only two limits on the pardon power – the President can only pardon "Offences against the United States" and the President cannot grant pardons in cases of impeachment.[34] Under a canon of statutory construction known as "*expression unius est exclusion alterius*" (the expression of one thing is the exclusion of the other) the explicit mention of two limitations on the pardon power implies that there are no other limitations to the power.

However, as others argue, this simplistic reading of the Pardon Clause is just that – simplistic. Michigan State Law Professor Brian Kalt argues that the key phrase in *Schick* is that any limitations on the pardon power must be found in the *Constitution*, rather than the *clause*, and that the search for limitations requires a holistic and structural approach to constitutional interpretation.[35]

29 Notes of James Madison from the Constitutional Convention (Sept. 15, 1787), reprinted in THE RECORDS OF THE FEDERAL CONVENTION OF 1787, VOL. 2, 626 (Max Farrand ed., 1911).

30 *Id.*

31 U.S. CONST. Art. II, § 4.

32 Schick v. Reed, 419 U.S. 256 (1974).

33 *Id.* at 267.

34 U.S. CONST. Art. II, § 2.

35 Brian Kalt, *Pardon Me? The Constitutional Case against Presidential Self-Pardons*, 106 YALE L.J. 779, 793 (1996).

First, he argues that the Constitution is fundamentally structured to prevent abuse of power and self-dealing by officials. To illustrate this point, Kalt points to articles in the Constitution that prohibit members of Congress from holding multiple federal offices, increasing their own pay before a congressional election, and resigning to take federal jobs that were created during the current Congress.[36] Similar prohibitions on self-dealing can be found within Article II. Article II, Section 1, Clause 7 expressly prohibits the President from using the immense power of his office to receive emoluments, or compensation, from the United States besides his salary.[37] Similar to Congress, the President cannot have his salary raised by Congress without a presidential election occurring first.[38] Finally, Article II places the Chief Justice, rather than the Vice President as head of the Senate, as the presiding officer over an impeachment trial.[39]

A more recent article by Professor Al Alshuler[40] has concluded that the President cannot pardon himself and furthermore cannot properly use the pardon power to obstruct justice or for other illegal ends.[41] Whether future presidents will observe such limitations remains to be seen.

Two hundred and fifty years of practice and tradition illustrate deeply held national principles against self-dealing and self-judgment by those in power. In *Federalist No. 10* Madison wrote that "No man is allowed to be a judge in his own cause, because his interest would certainly bias his judgment, and, not improbably corrupt his integrity."[42] An early Supreme Court case, *Calder v. Bull*,[43] reaffirmed this commitment, stating that "a law that makes a man a Judge in his own cause . . . it is against all reason and justice, for a people to entrust a Legislature with such power; and, therefore, it cannot be presumed that they have done it."

Regardless, after *Trump v. United States*, self-pardon may be largely unnecessary as a president has broad immunity from prosecution for official acts. Only a president who committed personal capacity crimes would be interested in a self-pardon.

Finally, a discussion of the pardon power would be incomplete without mentioning President Trump's 2025 pardon of the perpetrators of the insurrection at the Capitol seeking to block certification of the presidential election on January 6, 2021.

36 *Id.* at 794.
37 U.S. CONST. Art. II, § 1, Cl. 7.
38 *Id.*
39 U.S. Const. Art. I, § 3, Cl. 6.
40 Albert W. Alschuler, *Limiting the Pardon Power*, 63 ARIZ. L. REV. 545 (2021).
41 *Id.*
42 THE FEDERALIST NO. 79 (Madison).
43 Calder v. Bull, 3 U.S. 386 (1798).

Trump, on the first day of his second term, commuted the prison sentences of fourteen felons convicted of the most serious offenses relating to the insurrection, and granted a "complete and unconditional pardon to all other individuals convicted of offenses related to events that occurred at or near the United States Capitol on January 6, 2021."[44] At the time of their pardons in January 2025, over 1,500 rioters had been charged with federal crimes related to the event. Of these 1,500 rioters nearly 1,020 had pleaded guilty to the charges, roughly 250 had been convicted by a jury after a trial, and just two were acquitted of the charges brought against them.[45] While none of these defendants had been charged with the crime of "treason," several had been convicted of seditious conspiracy.

These pardons raise concerns like those Edmund Randolph had expressed at the Convention when deliberating how to limit the pardon power in the Constitution, that in cases where the President himself might be guilty, "the Tra[i]tors may be his own instruments."[46] President Trump was never found guilty of any crime in connection with the insurrection, an accountability issue discussed in more detail throughout Part III of this book, but the January 6 pardons suggest that the Framers' final decision to exempt only "cases of impeachment" from the pardon power may not have been enough.

[44] Proclamation Granting Pardons and Commutations of Sentences for Certain Offenses Relating to the Events at or Near the United States Capitol on January 6, 2021, January 20, 2025.

[45] Alanna Durkin Richer & Michael Kunzelman, *Here's Where Jan. 6 Trials Stand on the Fourth Anniversary of the Capitol Riot*, PBS (Jan. 6, 2025), www.pbs.org/newshour/politics/heres-where-jan-6-trials-stand-on-the-fourth-anniversary-of-the-capitol-riot.

[46] Notes of James Madison, *supra* note 29.

6

Presidential Emergency Powers

Since the nation's founding in the late eighteenth century, it has experienced trying times, including a civil war, two world wars, a Cold War with the Soviet Union, acts of domestic and international terrorism, a decade-long economic collapse in the 1930s precipitated by a stock market crash and a global trade war, another economic collapse after the 2008 financial crisis, a violent attempt to overturn a presidential election, civil unrest precipitated by racial tension, anti-war protests, and protests against immigration policy. All of these events, as well as countless others, have required the nation to act quickly and decisively to respond to unprecedented circumstances.

Despite the need for decisive action that emergencies require, the Constitution is silent on what constitutes a national emergency and what powers, if any, the federal government and the President may assume during times of crisis. The Constitution's silence on emergency powers is likely a result of the deep skepticism of the Founders regarding unfettered executive power. As discussed in earlier chapters, the Constitution is a reflection of the experiences of the founding generation under the rule of King George and his belief that all executive power ran through him. As a result of this skepticism, the Founders were hesitant to grant emergency powers to the President, fearing that he would declare emergencies arbitrarily when Congress frustrated his legislative goals.

However, despite the Constitution's silence on the issue, there are several powerful arguments for giving the President emergency powers in time of need. As Hamilton wrote in *Federalist* 70, "energy in the executive is the leading character in the definition of good government."[1] In times of emergency, deliberation and indecision by Congress can paralyze a unified national response. Additionally, as head of the Executive Branch the President is uniquely situated to coordinate a "whole of government" response to emergencies by bringing together various

[1] The Federalist No. 70 (Hamilton).

cabinet secretaries to ensure a comprehensive plan with the input of experts within each department.

A number of statutes since 1792 and 1871, known colloquially as the Insurrection Act of 1807, grant the President the limited authority to use federal military forces *inside* US territory.[2] Importantly, the Posse Comitatus Act of 1878 prohibits the US military from deploying for use in domestic law enforcement within the United States. However, the Insurrection Act permits the President to use the military inside the boundaries of the United States, as an exception to the Posse Comitatus Act, for emergencies where civilian law enforcement is unable to manage local domestic violence, rebellion, or insurrection.

Section 251 of the Act allows the President to deploy troops if a state legislature or governor requests federal assistance to suppress an insurrection. Section 252 allows the President to deploy troops without such a request, "to enforce the laws" of the United States or to suppress rebellion when "unlawful obstructions, combinations, or assemblages, or rebellion" make it "impracticable" to enforce federal law in that state by the "ordinary course of judicial proceedings." Section 253 allows the President to deploy the military without consent of a state to suppress "any insurrection, domestic violence, unlawful combination, or conspiracy" that "deprives any portion of the state's inhabitants of a constitutional right when state authorities are unable or unwilling to protect that right." Section 253 – which is exceedingly broad – also permits the President to deploy troops to suppress "any insurrection, domestic violence, unlawful combination, or conspiracy" in a state that "opposes or obstructs the execution of the laws of the United States or impedes the course of justice under those laws."

Although considered during an early version of the Act, preconditions for triggering the Act would have required congressional and judicial approval. These provisions were removed before final enactment, leaving the President unilateral authority, power, and discretion to implement the statute.[3] The Act does not define what a true emergency is, nor does it set forth checks against an abuse of power by the President,[4] or any due process protections to citizens harmed by military forces.

Over time, there have been many examples of the Insurrection Act being invoked, such as General Andrew Jackson invoking martial law in New Orleans during the War of 1812 and President Roosevelt declaring martial law in Hawaii following the attacks on Pearl Harbor in 1941.[5] More recently, Presidents Kennedy and Eisenhower triggered the Act in the 1950s and 1960s "to enforce desegregations and civil rights laws" in the South. More recently, President Trump threatened to

2 *See* An act to provide for calling forth the militia to execute the laws of the Union, suppress insurrections, and repel invasions and to repeal the act now in force for those purposes (1795). *See also* Militia Act of 1862, 12 Stat. 597 (1862).

3 *Id.*

4 *Id.*

5 David French, *Can Martial Law Happen in America?*, New York Times (Dec. 5, 2024).

use the Act to stop protests in Oregon after the killing of George Floyd in 2020.[6] Again in 2025 President Trump considered invoking the Insurrection Act to respond to riots against his immigration policy in Los Angeles, but he decided on an alternative path of deploying a federalized National Guard under another federal statute allowing deployment of troops to protect federal agents in performance of their duties. The Governor of California's lawsuit against Trump and the legal requirements for National Guard deployments were discussed in Chapter 3.

Since the creation of emergency powers granted to the President, the "Presidential Emergency Action Documents" (PEADs) which are "classified" and "secret," were drafted "in anticipation of a range of emergencies."[7] These are a set of executive orders and communications to Congress that then are ready for implementation for an emergency when it presents itself.

Apparently, there are more than 100 of these emergency action documents that have been used for numerous "emergency" situations. They include: the "detention of alien enemies" and other "dangerous persons" within the United States, suspension of the writ of habeas corpus by Executive Order, establishment of military territories during World War II, and even a declaration of war. From time to time, those emergency power documents have undergone repeal and review by different presidential administrations, including under Presidents Eisenhower and George W. Bush. These emergency power documents are now likely undergoing repeal and review under President Trump who has expressed considerable interest in claiming emergency powers.

There are other statutes that Congress has enacted that give presidents broad power over emergency situations. These are "catch all" emergency statutes granting broad powers which have been invoked more than fifty times.

Throughout the nineteenth and twentieth centuries presidents regularly would take extraordinary action in response to emergencies. As discussed in Chapters 1 and 3, in 1861 President Lincoln suspended habeas corpus without authorization by Congress. President Lincoln claimed that the Civil War created an ongoing emergency that required this severe remedy. While a federal court would later strike down the suspension of habeas corpus in *Ex parte Merryman*,[8] Lincoln chose to disregard the court's ruling and Congress only later suspended habeas corpus in accordance with that ruling. The right to habeas corpus would only resume after the end of the war.

As discussed in Chapters 1 and 3, two other presidents used ongoing wars to expand presidential authority during times of emergency. Following the attacks on Pearl Harbor in 1941, President Franklin Roosevelt unilaterally created "Japanese

[6] *Id.*

[7] *A Guide to Emergency Powers and Their Use*, BRENNAN CENTER FOR JUSTICE (Dec. 5, 2018), www.brennancenter.org/our-work/research-reports/guide-emergency-powers-and-their-use.

[8] Ex parte Merryman, 17 F. Cas. 144 (C.C.D. MD. 1861).

exclusion zones" along the west coast in a belief that Japanese-Americans living there would provide aid and comfort to the Japanese war effort. However, the Supreme Court upheld Roosevelt's decision in *Korematsu v. United States*, holding that the President, as Commander in Chief, had a duty to protect Americans. It was not within the Court's purview to second-guess how the President achieved those goals.[9]

Finally, as noted in Chapters 1 and 3, President Truman attempted to nationalize the nation's steel mills during the Korean War to provide supplies for the war effort. While the Court ultimately would strike down Truman's plan, it is most famous for a concurring opinion by Justice Jackson that outlined a three-part framework for executive power. Under this framework, presidential power is strongest when the President acts with congressional approval, it is limited only to enumerated Article II powers when Congress is silent, and at its weakest when acting contrary to congressional intent.[10]

In 1976, Congress sought to address this tension between the need for the government to respond quickly to national emergencies and the concerns about unfettered executive power when passing the National Emergencies Act.[11] The Act is composed of five components which sought to sunset previously declared national emergencies, set rules for declaring future national emergencies, define the scope of presidential authority under national emergencies, set in place accountability to Congress during emergencies, and declare how emergency powers would interact with conflicting federal law.[12]

The Act declared that all emergencies that were declared prior to September 14, 1976 would be terminated on September 13, 1978.[13] A Senate report prepared concurrently with the Act showed that the purpose of this sunsetting provision was a response to Great Depression and Cold War-era emergency declarations by Presidents Franklin Roosevelt,[14] Truman,[15] and Nixon[16] which, among other things, prohibited the hoarding of gold, organized the national economy toward defense production, threatened to use the National Guard to deliver mail during a postal strike, and imposed import tariffs on consumer goods.[17]

9 Korematsu v. United States, 323 U.S. 214 (1944).

10 Justice Jackson's three-part framework on executive power is discussed in greater detail *supra* in Chapter 1, Section 1.2.

11 National Emergencies Act, 50 U.S.C. §§ 1601–51 (1976). *See also* THEODORE J. LOWI, BENJAMIN GINSBERG, KENNETH A. SHEPSLE, STEPHEN ANSOLABEHERE & HAHRIE HAN, AMERICAN GOVERNMENT: POWER AND PURPOSE, 337 (17th ed. 2023).

12 National Emergencies Act, *supra* note 11.

13 *Id.* at § 1601.

14 Exec. Order No. 6102 (Apr. 5, 1933).

15 Proclamation No. 2914, 3 C.F.R., 1943 Cum. Supp.

16 Proclamation Nos. 3972 (1970) and 4074 (1971).

17 S. Rep. 93-549.

Second, the Act grants the President the power to declare national emergencies by issuing a proclamation to Congress.[18] Once a national emergency has been declared it may be terminated either by a joint resolution of Congress or by the President.[19] Under the Act, Congress must meet at least every six months to consider the need for the ongoing emergency declaration.[20] Notably, earlier drafts of the Act stated that unless Congress explicitly authorized the continuation of the emergency it would automatically terminate after six months. However, at the request of President Ford, this language was struck from the final bill and significantly weakened the power of Congress to terminate an emergency through inaction.[21] Despite this statutory requirement that Congress reconsider current emergency declarations, Congress has rarely done so since 1976.

A president also may unilaterally continue an ongoing emergency. Under the Act, if a president wishes to extend an emergency past one year he may do so by notifying Congress of his intention. If he fails to notify Congress, the emergency automatically expires after one year.[22]

Finally, the Act provides for accountability to Congress for the exercise of emergency powers. This accountability takes two forms. First, the Act requires that the President report to Congress all declarations and orders used to expand executive power during the emergency.[23] This provision is likely a result of fears by Congress that absent some oversight the President could use an emergency as a pretext to usurp power from Congress. Second, and most importantly, the Act requires that the Executive Branch provide Congress with an ongoing accounting of all money spent in the exercise of emergency powers.[24] As the branch of government responsible for raising government revenue, Congress has a uniquely vested interest in ensuring that the President is not taking away congressional spending power under the guise of a national emergency.

Along with the National Emergencies Act, the President also has three other statutes that allow him broad grants of authority during national emergencies. These three statutes are the Public Health Services Act (PHSA),[25] Stafford Disaster Relief and Emergency Assistance Act (Stafford),[26] and Special Authority Act (SAA).[27] Over the past fifteen years use of the PHSA has fallen broadly into three categories – the

18 National Emergencies Act, § 1621.
19 *Id.* at § 1622.
20 *Id.*
21 Patrick A. Thronson, *Toward Comprehensive Reform of America's Emergency Law Regime*, 46 U. Mich. J. L. Reform 737, 750 (2013).
22 National Emergencies Act, § 1621.
23 *Id.* at § 1641.
24 *Id.*
25 Public Health Services Act, 42 U.S.C. § 247(d).
26 Stafford Disaster Relief and Emergency Assistance Act, 42 U.S.C. § 5121.
27 Special Authority Act, 22 U.S.C. § 2381(a)(1).

opioid crisis, limiting the spread of infectious disease, and response to natural disasters.

In 2017 then Acting Secretary of Health and Human Services Eric Hargan issued a declaration that misuse and abuse of opioids such as fentanyl constituted a national emergency.[28] The declaration of the national public health emergency allowed President Trump to access funds to support counter-narcotics actions along the United States/Mexico border from where a large quantity of opioids come.[29] While some at the time saw the declaration of the public health emergency under the PHSA as a way for President Trump to bypass Congress to get funding for his border wall, which was central to his 2016 presidential campaign, the broad discretion of the PHSA allowed him access to money and presidential power he otherwise would not have enjoyed.

Perhaps the most notable example of invoking the PHSA is in response to the COVID-19 pandemic. On January 31, 2020 President Trump declared a national emergency from the rapidly spreading COVID virus.[30] Although there were no reported cases of COVID in the United States at the time the emergency was declared, PHSA allowed the President to invoke a wide range of precautionary measures including a partial shutdown of travel to the United States in March 2020, the use of the Defense Production Act to accelerate the production of personal protective equipment such as face masks and ventilators, and unilateral authorization of funds to prevent the spread of the virus. The COVID-19 emergency authorization was renewed regularly until February of 2023, when the Biden administration finally allowed it to lapse. As discussed in Chapter 1, before declaring an end to the COVID emergency, President Biden had invoked it to fulfill his 2020 campaign pledge to forgive hundreds of billions of dollars in student loans, an executive order struck down by the Supreme Court in *Biden v. Nebraska*.[31]

In addition to the PHSA, the Stafford Act is another tool within the President's emergency powers, with frequent overlap between the two powers. Passed in 1988, the Stafford Act allows the President, at the request of a state governor, to bring federal emergency management money, supplies, and technical assistance into the state. The two most notable examples of the Stafford Act being invoked are in response to hurricanes Katrina and Harvey in 2005 and 2017. In both cases, the Stafford Act was invoked to provide immediate supplies and emergency shelter to the hurricane-battered areas. In addition, PHSA was invoked in response to both hurricanes to provide public health assistance as the hurricanes destroyed vital

[28] Julie Hirschfield Davis, *Trump Declares Opioid Crisis a "Health Emergency" but Requests No Funds*, New York Times (Oct. 26, 2017), www.nytimes.com/2017/10/26/us/politics/trump-opioid-crisis.html.

[29] *Id.*

[30] Alex M. Azar II, *Determination That a Public Health Emergency Exists*, U.S. Dept. of Health & Human Services (Jan. 31, 2020), https://aspr.hhs.gov/legal/PHE/Pages/2019-nCoV.aspx.

[31] Biden v. Nebraska, 600 U.S. 477 (2023).

public health facilities such as hospitals, sewage treatment plants, and water treatment plants.

Finally, the Special Authority Act[32] allows the President to direct obsolete Department of Defense equipment and inventory in support of foreign countries and unilaterally direct up to $100 million annually in military education and training to support US allies. Most recently, in July of 2024 President Biden invoked the Special Authority Act to provide munitions, training, and obsolete artillery weaponry to support Ukraine's defense against the invasion by Russia.[33] Prior to the war in Ukraine, presidents have invoked the Special Authority Act to provide weaponry and training to Taiwan, Saudi Arabia, and other allies.

Taken as a whole, history has shown that the need for rapid decision-making in times of emergency has trumped concerns about unfettered executive power. Throughout the nineteenth, twentieth, and twenty-first centuries, Congress has regularly ceded its power to the President on issues of emergency powers by failing to meet and confer to end emergency declarations. As the events of the twenty-first century continue to demand decisive executive action on a variety of issues, from wars overseas to natural disasters at home, Congress delves deeper into partisan division which will leave more power in the hands of the President. For now, Congress has shown an unwillingness or inability to clearly delineate the meaning of an emergency and how to end emergency situations.

[32] 22 U.S. Code § 2318 – Special Authority Act.

[33] *Use of Presidential Drawdown Authority for Military Assistance for Ukraine*, U.S. Dept. of State (Sept. 6, 2024), www.state.gov/use-of-presidential-drawdown-authority-for-military-assistance-for-ukraine/.

7

Other Presidential Powers

In addition to the more debated presidential powers discussed in the previous chapters of this book, the President can also exercise several less controversial powers. Among these powers are the power to seek the opinions of executive officers,[1] the power to appoint ambassadors, federal judges, and other officers of the United States,[2] and the right to provide Congress information on the state of the union.[3]

Despite the generally noncontroversial nature of these powers, there have been some changes throughout history in how these powers have been used in practice. Early in the nation's history, President Washington directed his Secretary of State, Thomas Jefferson, to send a letter to the Supreme Court seeking the Court's opinion on twenty-nine questions regarding a treaty between the United States and France.[4] In response to Washington's request, the Court observed that the principles of separation of power and the express limitation in Article II on the power of the President to seek the opinions of *executive* departments meant that the Court could not, and would not, provide legal opinions to the Executive Branch.[5]

This refusal by the Court to issue an "advisory opinion" represented a dramatic shift from the English tradition.[6] By the late 1700s, English courts had given advisory opinions to the British monarch for over a century.[7] In their brief reply to Jefferson,

1 U.S. CONST. Art. II, § 2, cl. 1.
2 *Id.*, § 2, cl. 2.
3 *Id.*, § 3, cl. 1.
4 *To George Washington from Supreme Court Justices, 8 August* 1793, FOUNDERS ONLINE, National Archives, https://founders.archives.gov/documents/Washington/05-13-02-0263. Original source: THE PAPERS OF GEORGE WASHINGTON, PRESIDENTIAL SERIES, VOL. 13, 1 JUNE–31 AUGUST 1793 (Christine Sternberg Patrick ed., 2007), 392–93.
5 *Id.*
6 Christian R. Burset, *Advisory Opinions and the Problem of Legal Authority*, 74 VAND. L. REV. 621 (2021).
7 William R. Casto, *The Early Supreme Court Justices' Most Significant Opinion*, 29 OHIO N.U. L. REV. 173, 188 (2002).

the Court was able to reaffirm the importance of separation of powers and affirm that the "executive Departments" language of Article II, Section 2 means *only* executive departments such as the Department of Defense and Department of Treasury. Under Article III of the Constitution, an actual case or controversy must be present before the Court has subject matter jurisdiction.[8]

There is a downside to such strict separation of powers. Instead of advisory opinions from the courts, which could have been a helpful check on executive power, presidents and their appointees obtain legal opinions from the Justice Department's Office of Legal Counsel (OLC), which is not independent of the President and is often staffed with political appointees. OLC opinions are discussed throughout this book where relevant subject matter arises, in areas as different and far-reaching as forgiveness of student loans and war powers, the pattern being that OLC almost always tells the President or his senior appointees that there is a legal basis for them to do what they want to do.

7.1 APPOINTMENT OF FEDERAL JUDGES AND JUSTICES

Although the power of the President to appoint cabinet officers and federal judges with the Senate's advice and consent is uncontroversial, the increasing polarization of American politics has made these confirmations high stakes, and often bitter, affairs.

In 1816 the Senate established the Senate Judiciary Committee as a permanent standing committee. From its establishment until 1868 roughly two-thirds of presidential nominations to the Supreme Court were referred to the Committee.[9] In 1868 the Senate decided that all nominations should be referred to the Committee, and since then all but seven nominations have been referred to the Committee.[10] Throughout the nineteenth and early twentieth centuries these Committee hearings were closed door affairs, but in 1916 the Committee held its first public hearing for the confirmation of Justice Brandeis.[11] The practice of public hearings became the norm with the confirmation of Justice John Marshall Harlan II in 1955. In 1981 the practice of televising the Committee's hearings became the norm with Justice O'Connor.[12]

While the vast majority of modern presidential nominees to the Court are ultimately confirmed, political polarization does occasionally lead to the senate rejecting a presidential nominee. Justice Louis Brandeis was narrowly confirmed

[8] U.S. Const. Art. III, § 2.

[9] Barry J. McMillion, Cong. Rsch. Serv., Supreme Court Appointment Process: Consideration by the Senate Judiciary Committee 1 (2021).

[10] The seven nominations not referred to the Judiciary Committee were Edwin M. Stanton in 1869 (former Secretary of War at time of nomination); Edward D. White in 1894 (sitting Senator); Joseph M. McKenna in 1897 (Attorney General, former US Representative); Edward D. White again, in 1910, nominated to be Chief Justice; William Howard Taft in 1921 (former President); George Sutherland in 1922 (former Senator); and James F. Byrnes in 1941 (sitting Senator).

[11] McMillion, *supra* note 9, at 10.

[12] *Id.*

in 1916 after a bitter debate between supporters of President Wilson's nomination of Brandeis and a group of opponents motivated by hostility to Brandeis's progressive politics, his proposals to regulate banks, railroads, and other businesses, and/or his Jewish faith. At the height of controversy over civil rights and court-ordered school desegregation, President Nixon nominated two conservative southern judges to the Court, Clement Haynsworth and G. Harrold Carswell, in 1969 and 1970 respectively. Both nominations failed. A relatively modern example of this is the Senate's rejection of Judge Robert Bork's nomination by President Reagan for the Supreme Court in 1987. As noted in Chapter 1, Bork was a key player in the "Saturday night massacre" during the Watergate scandal. After President Nixon's Attorney General and Deputy Attorney General resigned in protest and refused to fire the Special Prosecutor investigating the President's involvement in the Watergate scandal, Bork, who was then Solicitor General, became the Acting Attorney General. He fulfilled Nixon's demands.

After news of Bork's nomination by President Reagan reached the Senate, a flurry of controversy surrounded the embattled nominee. Senator Joe Biden (D-DE), then Chair of the Senate Judiciary Committee, questioned the independence of Bork's decisions. "It's a question of whether the Reagan–Meese [President Reagan's Attorney General] agenda is going to be accomplished through the court and whether Judge Bork has been picked to be the vehicle to accomplish that."[13]

Senator Ted Kennedy (D-MA) went a step further with his criticisms, arguing that Bork's confirmation would lead to a dystopian future in which

> women would be forced into back-alley abortions, blacks would sit at segregated lunch counters, rogue police could break down citizens' doors in midnight raids, schoolchildren could not be taught about evolution, writers and artists would be censored at the whim of government, and the doors of the federal courts would be shut on the fingers of millions of citizens for whom the judiciary is often the only protector of the individual rights that are the heart of our democracy.[14]

Bork previously had expressed the opinion that the right to privacy under the Fourteenth Amendment, which was fundamental to the Court's decision in *Roe v. Wade*,[15] did not exist.[16] He also had expressed in 1963 reservations about the constitutional underpinnings of the 1964 Civil Rights Act.[17]

[13] Wash. Post. Staff Writer, *Biden Plans to Oppose Bork*, Wash. Post. (July 9, 1987 1:00 AM), www.washingtonpost.com/archive/politics/1987/07/09/biden-plans-to-oppose-bork/6e5c1c97-5bae-41c5-86f8-9f3444afb3ad/.

[14] Greg Kesich, *The View From Here: Living in Robert Bork's America*, Portland Press Herald (June 19, 2022), www.pressherald.com/2022/06/19/the-view-from-here-living-in-robert-borks-america/.

[15] Roe v. Wade, 410 U.S. 113 (1973).

[16] Ruth Marcus, *Bork on "Judicial Imperialism,"* Wash. Post. (July 1, 1987, 8:00 PM), www.washingtonpost.com/archive/politics/1987/07/02/bork-on-judicial-imperialism/60fb83a3-f529-4751-8066-7a9806883f0e/.

[17] Richard Cohen, *The Civil Rights Thing*, Wash. Post. (Oct. 8 1987, 8:00 PM), www.washingtonpost.com/archive/opinions/1987/10/09/the-civil-rights-thing/4408a0f9-1c9d-44e9-964d-1c539ae9dc69/.

In addition to criticisms of Bork's legal views, his confirmation also had a decidedly undignified air to it. Shortly after Bork's confirmation hearings began, a reporter leaked a copy of Bork's videotape rental history from a DC area video store. In what became known as the "Bork tapes," this list of 146 rentals showed that Bork had a pedestrian taste in movies.[18] Despite the mundane nature of the list, the press latched onto the story with one writer using the list to label Bork as an Anglophile and a "Supreme Couch Potato."[19]

The numerous attacks, on both Bork's judicial philosophy and character, did not go unnoticed by Republicans. In a statement before Bork's nomination was voted on by the Senate, Senator Mitch McConnell (R-KY) stated that if the Bork nomination did not pass there would be a price to pay.[20]

A presidential nomination to the Supreme Court is also not a guarantee that a nominee will receive a hearing by the Judiciary Committee. Since the practice of public hearings was established in the mid twentieth century, four nominations have not received a hearing. In November 1954 President Eisenhower nominated Judge John Harlan II to a vacancy on the Court. However, because of poor timing (the Senate adjourned for the holidays in early December), Harlan did not initially receive a hearing.[21] When the Senate reconvened in early 1955, Judge Harlan was renominated by President Eisenhower and was easily confirmed by a Senate closely divided between Republicans and Democrats with seventy-one "aye" votes and eleven "nay" votes.[22]

One of President George W. Bush's nominees to the Court, Harriet Miers, was scheduled but did not receive hearings with the Judiciary Committee. To fill the vacancy for the seat of retiring Justice O'Connor, President Bush nominated Miers, who was his White House Counsel at the time. Unlike most modern Supreme Court nominees, who are "pulled up" from the federal appellate courts to the Supreme Court, Miers had spent the majority of her career in the private practice of law and had never served as a judge in any capacity. This lack of any judicial experience raised concerns among democratic senators about her fitness for the office. In addition, her answers to questions about basic tenets of constitutional law in private meetings with senators raised concerns with both parties about her ability to receive a passing vote out of the Judiciary Committee or to be confirmed by the entire Senate. Eleven days before her hearings were scheduled to begin Miers requested that President Bush withdraw her nomination for the vacancy. President

[18] *Publication of Bork's Video Rentals Raises Privacy Issue*, Chicago Trib. (Aug. 9, 2021 1:06 AM), www.chicagotribune.com/1987/11/20/publication-of-borks-video-rentals-raises-privacy-issue/.

[19] Neil Richards, Intellectual Privacy: Rethinking Civil Liberties in the Digital Age, 132 (2017).

[20] *Senator McConnell on Bork*, C-SPAN (Oct. 22, 1987), www.c-span.org/video/?c4734304/sen-mcconnell-bork.

[21] McMillion, *supra* note 9, at 11.

[22] Barry J. McMillion, Cong. Rsch. Serv., Supreme Court Nominations During Years with a Closely Divided Senate, 2 (2022).

Bush then nominated Third Circuit Judge Samuel Alito to this seat and Alito was confirmed by a vote of 52-42 in January 2006.[23]

The most recent example of a nominee not receiving a hearing came with the death of Justice Antonin Scalia in 2016. President Obama nominated Judge Merrick Garland to replace him on the Court. The timing of the nomination has become a political flashpoint, with views on the President's power to nominate Judge Garland breaking down largely along partisan lines.[24] Senate Republicans, led by then Senate Majority Leader Mitch McConnell, argued that "[i]t is a president's constitutional right to nominate a Supreme Court justice, and it is the Senate's constitutional right to act as a check on a President and withhold its consent."[25] Republicans at the time argued that with the 2016 presidential election just nine months away the Senate should block Garland's nomination and let the winner of the 2016 election nominate Scalia's replacement.

Senate Democrats, on the other hand, called for a vote in the Senate for Judge Garland, arguing that the Appointments Clause extends from the first to the final day of a president's time in office.[26] While the Constitution makes no "election year exception," the political realities of the Senate ultimately sank Judge Garland's nomination after the Republican Senate majority refused to hold a hearing before the Senate Judiciary Committee or a confirmation vote before the entire Senate.

Judge Garland's nomination was the first Supreme Court nomination since hearings became regular procedure not to receive a hearing under the Constitution's "by and with the Advice and Consent of the Senate" save for nominations withdrawn by the President or whose appointment came later with a hearing.

In an ironic twist, the nation found itself in a nearly identical situation just four years later. Fewer than two months before the 2020 presidential election, Justice Ruth Bader Ginsburg, a longtime liberal jurist on the Court, passed away.[27] This time, a Republican President, Donald Trump, was in office and the parties found

[23] One of the authors of this book, as chief White House ethics lawyer for President Bush, participated in the ethics screening and confirmation preparation of both Chief Justice Roberts and Justice Alito. The shortcomings of this process are discussed further in a forthcoming book, Richard W. Painter, Conduct Unbecoming: The Ethics Crisis in the Supreme Court and How Legitimacy Can Be Restored (2026).

[24] Juliet Eilperin & Mike Debonis, *President Obama Nominates Merrick Garland to the Supreme Court*, Wash. Post. (Mar. 16, 2016 10:30 PM), www.washingtonpost.com/world/national-security/president-obama-to-nominate-merrick-garland-to-the-supreme-court-sources-say/2016/03/16/3bc90bc8-eb7c-11e5-a6f3-21ccdbc5f74e_story.html.

[25] Amita Kelly, *McConnell: Blocking Supreme Court Nomination "About a Principle, Not a Person,"* Nat'l. Pub. Radio (Mar. 16, 2016 12:31 PM), www.npr.org/2016/03/16/470664561/mcconnell-blocking-supreme-court-nomination-about-a-principle-not-a-person.

[26] *Remarks by the President Announcing Judge Merrick Garland as His Nominee to the Supreme Court*, The White House, https://obamawhitehouse.archives.gov/the-press-office/2016/03/16/remarks-president-announcing-judge-merrick-garland-his-nominee-supreme.

[27] *Biography of Associate Justice Ruth Bader Ginsburg*, www.supremecourt.gov/about/biographyginsburg.aspx.

themselves arguing contradictory, but politically expedient, positions from 2016. Fearing a replacement on the Court by a Republican president would lead to a decades-long conservative majority, then Senate Minority Leader Chuck Schumer (D-NY) issued a statement shortly after Justice Ginsburg's death arguing that "[t]he American people should have a voice in the selection of their next Supreme Court Justice. Therefore, this vacancy should not be filled until we have a new President."[28]

The challenge by Schumer did not go unanswered. About a month after Ginsburg's death, and after the beginning of then Judge Amy Coney Barrett's nomination hearing, McConnell issued a statement that said in part: "[t]his confirmation process falls squarely within history and precedent. Neither falsehoods nor strong feelings change that fact. History shows that when Supreme Court vacancies arise in presidential election years, the outcome hinges on whether the same party or different parties control the presidency and the Senate."[29] Ultimately, Senator McConnell went through with his plan to confirm President Trump's nominee, Judge Amy Coney Barrett, to the Supreme Court.

Just nineteen days before the 2020 presidential election, the Senate Judiciary Committee began formal hearings on Judge Barrett's nomination.[30] Ten days after the hearings began Judge Barrett's nomination was sent to the full Senate with the vote out of committee breaking down along partisan lines with all twelve Republicans voting in favor and all ten Democrats abstaining from the vote in protest.[31] Just eleven days before the 2020 election Judge Barrett was confirmed by the Senate in a near party line vote. Fifty-two of fifty-three Republicans voted to confirm Judge Barrett. Senator Susan Collins (R-ME) voted against her confirmation.[32] All forty-five Democrats voted against her nomination, and two independent senators, Angus King (I-ME) and Bernie Sanders (I-VT), both of whom caucus with the Democrats, voted against Barrett's nomination.[33]

[28] Jordain Carney, *Schumer: Ruth Bader Ginsburg Seat Should Be Filled by Next President*, The Hill (Sept. 18, 2020 8:13 PM), https://thehill.com/homenews/senate/517167-schumer-ruth-bader-ginsburg-seat-should-be-filled-by-next-president/.

[29] *McConnell: Proud to Support Judge Barrett's Confirmation and Proud of This Precedent-Backed Process*, www.republicanleader.senate.gov/newsroom/press-releases/mcconnell-proud-to-support-judge-barretts-confirmation-and-proud-of-this-precedent-backed-process.

[30] Kelsey Snell, *"Courts Are Not Designed to Solve Every Problem," Barrett to Say in Opening Statement*, Nat'l. Pub. Radio (Oct. 11, 2020, 7:00 AM), www.npr.org/sections/live-amy-coney-barrett-supreme-court-confirmation/2020/10/11/922305748/senate-judiciary-panel-to-begin-barrett-confirmation-hearings-amid-pandemic.

[31] Alex Rogers, *Supreme Court Judiciary Committee Advances Supreme Court Nominee Amy Coney Barrett Despite Democratic Boycott*, CNN (Oct. 22, 2020, 10:36 AM), www.cnn.com/2020/10/22/politics/amy-coney-barrett-committee-vote/index.html.

[32] *Senator Collins' Statement on Supreme Court Nomination*, Office of Senator Susan Collins (Oct. 25, 2020), www.collins.senate.gov/newsroom/senator-collins%E2%80%99-statement-supreme-court-nomination.

[33] Roll Call Vote 116th Congress – 2nd Session, www.senate.gov/legislative/LIS/roll_call_votes/vote1162/vote_116_2_00224.htm.

While a president can nominate just about anyone to be a Supreme Court justice, the Senate has sole discretion in deciding whether to confirm the nominee. Despite decades of precedent in which every Supreme Court nominee either got a hearing or was confirmed without a hearing, the Senate apparently can refuse to hold a hearing, as they did for Judge Garland in 2016, even if this violates the spirit if not the letter of the Senate's constitutional power and responsibility to "advise and consent." Or the Senate can rush a nomination to confirmation weeks before a presidential election as they did for Justice Barrett in 2020. Votes against a nominee in the Senate can be cast for just about any reason no matter what the senators say about their reasons. For example, how many senators voted no on Brandeis because they did not want a Jewish justice, or voted yes on Gorsuch, Kavanaugh, and Barrett because they would confirm a nominee from a president of their own political party no matter who he nominated? Those are questions for historians and political scientists to examine, but the point relevant to this book is that confirming a judge or justice is a sphere in which the Senate has asserted virtually unlimited discretion. In the highly politicized Senate confirmation process we have today, whether the President's political party controls the Senate makes a critical difference.

Also, Congress by statute sets the number of justices, which has not always been nine, and the number of other federal judgeships. The President cannot decide this alone. A president with large majorities in both houses of Congress could propose expanding the Court, as President Roosevelt did in 1938, although Congress might not go along with such a plan. Indeed, Roosevelt was accused of trying to pack the Court, and after one of the Justices, Owen Roberts, stopped voting to strike down New Deal legislation, Roosevelt over time continued to make his point. His plan never became law.

7.2 SETTING TARIFFS

Tariffs and regulation of trade have long been an area where power is shared by the President and Congress. The Constitution in Article 1, Section 8 states that "The Congress shall have Power To lay and collect Taxes, Duties ... To regulate Commerce with foreign Nations." But Congress in several statutes has delegated to the President the power to impose tariffs in specific situations.

Section 232 of the Trade Expansion Act of 1962 gives the President the power to adjust or regulate imports if there is a threat to national security. A department or agency head or other interested party may request the Department of Commerce to investigate the potential effect of specific imports on national security. The Bureau of Industry and Security (BIS) in the Commerce Department conducts the investigation. The Secretary of Defense is consulted and the Secretary of Commerce prepares a report within 270 days.[34] If the Department concludes there is a threat

[34] *See e.g.* U.S. Department of Commerce, Section 232 Investigation on the Effect of Imports of Steel on U.S. National Security (2018), www.commerce.gov/issues/trade-enforcement/section-232-steel.

to national security, a report is submitted to the President and Congress, and the President may unilaterally restrict imports as deemed necessary, using tariffs or quotas, as President Trump did on steel imports in 2018.[35]

Section 232 arguably is an unconstitutional delegation to the President of Congress's power to set tariffs. That argument, however, has been rejected by the courts. In *American Institute for International Steel, Inc. v. United States*, the Court of International Trade in 2019 upheld the constitutionality of Section 232.[36] The Federal Circuit affirmed.[37]

Section 301 of the Relief from Unfair Trade Practices Act of 1974[38] allows the President to impose tariffs and take other steps to respond to an unfair act, policy, or practice of a foreign government that burdens US commerce. The Office of the United States Trade Representative (USTR) is empowered to investigate foreign trade practices that allegedly violate US rights under trade agreements and burden US commerce.

If the USTR determines that an "act, policy or practice" of a foreign country violates a trade agreement or is unjustifiable and burdens or restricts US commerce, Section 301 requires the USTR to take retaliatory measures "subject to the specific direction, if any, of the President."[39] These measures may include imposing duties or import restrictions on the country in question, withdrawal or suspension of concessions granted under existing trade agreements; or alternatively reaching an agreement with the foreign country where the government agrees to either cease the conduct violating the trade agreement or compensate the United States with corresponding trade benefits.[40]

Section 301 was used to resolve trade disputes before establishment of the World Trade Organization (WTO) in 1995. But even with the WTO in place, a president inclined to bypass international dispute resolution mechanisms might invoke Section 301 more frequently. On September 15, 2020, a WTO dispute panel issued a report concluding that President Trump's Section 301 tariffs against China violated

[35] *See e.g.* Presidential Proclamation 9705 of March 8, 2018, Adjusting Imports of Steel into the United States, 83 FR 11625 – Adjusting Imports of Steel into the United States (Mar. 15, 2018), www.federalregister.gov/documents/2018/03/15/2018-05478/adjusting-imports-of-steel-into-the-united-states.

[36] 376 F. Supp. 3d 1335 (Ct. Int'l Trade 2019).

[37] American Institute for International Steel, Inc. v. United States (Fed. Cir. 2020), Cert denied, No. 19-1177, www.supremecourt.gov/DocketPDF/19/19-1177/142477/20200427145900082_Steel%20Tariffs%20cert-stage%20again.pdf.

[38] Public Law 93-618 (Jan. 3, 1975), www.govinfo.gov/content/pkg/STATUTE-88/pdf/STATUTE-88-Pg1978-2.pdf.

[39] 19 U.S. Code § 2411 – Actions by United States Trade Representative, subsection (a) (Mandatory Action).

[40] 19 U.S. Code § 2411, subsection c (scope of authority).

the General Agreement on Tariffs and Trade (GATT), but the WTO panel also had no power to stop them.[41]

Finally, the International Emergency Economic Powers Act (IEEPA)[42] authorizes the President to regulate international commerce in a national emergency. Unlike Sections 232 and 301, the IEEPA does not require an investigation before the President can act. Before 2019, IEEPA was never used to impose tariffs on imports, but tariffs are among the tools a president is authorized to utilize to confront an international emergency.

In 2019, President Trump announced that "to address the emergency at the Southern Border, I am invoking the authorities granted to me by the International Emergency Economic Powers Act. Accordingly, starting on June 10, 2019, the United States will impose a 5 percent Tariff on all goods imported from Mexico."[43] This executive action was never challenged in the courts because three days before the deadline, the United States and Mexico reached agreement on a Joint Declaration to address the migration problem at the border.[44] President Trump announced that the tariffs were suspended.

Tariffs were an even bigger issue in 2025 when Trump, at the beginning of his second term, announced tariffs against imports from almost every country in the world, some as high as 100 percent, invoking what he claimed to be his authority under several of the above-mentioned statutes. Some of his tariffs did not fare well in the courts, including a ruling by the US Court of International Trade[45] striking down an exceedingly broad presidential order imposing global tariffs which some of Trump's critics jokingly said included imports from penguins in Antarctica. This judicial ruling led Trump to furiously denounce advice he had received from outside consultants, including longtime Federalist Society co-chair Leonard Leo, when he had appointed federal judges during his first term.[46]

41 World Trade Organization, WT-DS543/R, September 15, 2020, United States – Tariff Measures on Certain Goods from China, Report of the Panel, www.wto.org/english/tratop_e/dispu_e/543r_e.pdf.

42 50 USC §§1701 *et seq.*

43 Statement from the President Regarding Emergency Measures to Address the Border Crisis, The White House (May 30, 2019), https://web.archive.org/web/20190531004403/https:/www.whitehouse.gov/briefings-statements/statement-president-regarding-emergency-measures-address-border-crisis/.

44 Joint Declaration and Supplementary Agreement between the United States and Mexico on Migration and Refugees, Signed June 7, 2019, www.state.gov/wp-content/uploads/2019/09/19-607-Mexico-Migration-and-Refugees.pdf.

45 V.O.S. Selections, Inc., et. al. v. United States, et al. (U.S. Ct. Int. Tr. 2025), No. 25-00066, Slip Op. 25-66. See also V.O.S. Selections, Inc. et. al. v. Trump, 2025 WL 2490634 (Fed. Cir. 2025).

46 *See* Charlie Savage, *Trump, Bashing the Federalist Society, Asserts Autonomy on Judge Picks*, New York Times (May 30, 2025). The Federalist Society's role in selecting judges and justices, and the massive spending by special interest groups on Supreme Court confirmation battles, is discussed a length in Painter, *supra* note 23, chapter 1.

Trump apparently could not distinguish between a "conservative" judge of the sort that Leo for decades had recommended that Republican presidents appoint, and a judge who simply does whatever the President who appointed him wants him to do. Meanwhile, the sheer magnitude of Trump's executive orders on tariffs in 2025, frequently changing his mind during volatile trade negotiations with other nations, and the extreme volatility this caused in financial markets, underscored the economic as well as constitutional importance of the question of how far a president can go in imposing tariffs without consent of Congress.

7.3 IMPOUNDMENT OF APPROPRIATED FUNDS

The US Constitution's Appropriations Clause states: "No Money shall be drawn from the Treasury, but in Consequence of Appropriations made by Law."[47] But if an appropriation is made by Congress, does this mean that the President must spend the money? Does the obligation of the President to "take Care that the laws be faithfully executed"[48] require him to spend the money even if he thinks it is not necessary?[49]

With pressure from fiscal conservatives to cut the cost of government, presidents sometimes refuse to spend money appropriated by Congress. Withholding the funds without consent of Congress is called "impoundment."

President Thomas Jefferson's actions are an early example of this practice. In 1803 he refused to spend $50,000 Congress had appropriated to acquire gunboats for the US Navy to use on the Mississippi River.[50]

President Nixon tried impoundment, refusing to spend money allocated for environmental protection under the Federal Water Pollution Control Act Amendments of 1972, which had passed Congress over Nixon's veto. When Environmental Protection Agency (EPA) Administrator Russell E. Train, acting on the President's orders, refused to dispense the appropriated funds, the City of New York sued. The Supreme Court in *Train v. City of New York*[51] held that Nixon had overstepped his statutory authority. This case, however, merely interpreted a single federal statute, the 1972 Water Pollution Control Act Amendments, which the Court held did not permit the EPA Administrator to allot to the states less than the entire amounts Congress had authorized to be appropriated.[52] The Court did not

[47] U.S. Const. Art. I, § 9, cl. 7.

[48] U.S. Const. Art. II, § 3.

[49] For an argument in the affirmative *see* Zachary S. Price, *The President Has No Constitutional Power of Impoundment, Notice and Comment*, Yale J. Reg. (blog) (July 18, 2024), www.yalejreg.com/nc/the-president-has-no-constitutional-power-of-impoundment-by-zachary-s-price/.

[50] *See id.* (discussing President Jefferson's impoundment of the money appropriated for the gunboats).

[51] Train v. City of New York, 420 U.S. 35 (1975).

[52] 420 U.S. 35, at 42–49.

address the constitutional separation of powers arguments that could have been made that Congress had no power to constrain the President in this manner.

To reinforce this point, Congress passed the Congressional Budget and Impoundment Control Act of 1974.[53] This law prohibits the President from impounding appropriated funds without going back to Congress for permission.

But would the Supreme Court rule the same way today as it did fifty years ago in *Train v. New York*? Would the Impoundment Control Act be ruled constitutional? Of the many legal issues that arose when President Trump temporarily withheld military aid appropriated by Congress for Ukraine in 2019 one was whether Trump had violated the Impoundment Control Act.[54] The US Government Accountability Office found that he had, saying that "the President cannot substitute his policy priorities for those that Congress has enacted into law."[55]

Impoundment is yet again being put to the test in 2025 as President Trump unilaterally slashes government spending, as he promised in his 2024 campaign. Trump's Department of Government Efficiency (DOGE) ordered multiple agencies to fire thousands of career federal employees, including the abolition of entire agencies such as the United States Agency for International Development (USAID), a decision drawing strong criticism from former Presidents Bush and Obama who feared a catastrophic impact on global health. Congress has not approved most of these spending cuts, and Trump's unilateral impoundment of funds Congress appropriated is being litigated in multiple lawsuits, including suits by fired federal employees, under both the underlying appropriation statutes and the Impoundment Control Act.

7.4 OTHER POWERS

In addition to other powers, the President has the power to provide Congress with updates on the State of the Union. As times and technology have changed, so too has the tradition of the State of the Union. Our first two presidents, Washington and Adams, delivered their address to Congress in person.[56] However, from 1801 to 1912 presidents simply provided Congress with a written report.[57]

53 Public Law 93-344 (July 12, 1974).

54 This episode involved separate even more serious issues because Trump allegedly withhold the appropriated military aid from Ukraine while seeking to extract political concessions from Ukraine, including an investigation of presidential candidate Joe Biden and his son Hunter. This scandal led to Trump's first impeachment, which is discussed further in Part III of this book, on Accountability.

55 U.S. Government Accountability Office, Office of Management and Budget – Withholding of Ukraine Security Assistance, File No. B-331564 (Jan. 16, 2020), www.gao.gov/assets/b-331564.pdf.

56 About Traditions & Symbols | State of the Union, www.senate.gov/about/traditions-symbols/state-of-the-union.htm.

57 *Id.*

As radio and television revolutionized mass media, presidents adapted to the media of their time and expanded the reach of the bully pulpit. In 1923 President Coolidge was the first president to have his State of the Union address broadcast over radio. In 1947 President Truman gave the first televised State of the Union address.[58] Today, the State of the Union address is a carefully choreographed speech that allows the President to use his power and influence to shape national policy, influence debates on Capitol Hill, and outline his priorities for the coming year. While the pageantry of the modern State of the Union is a distant past from the humble beginnings of the State of the Union over 200 years ago, it still finds its constitutional grounding in a single sentence in Article II.

Finally, we would be remiss not to discuss the powers of the Vice President. While these include a number of informal powers, among them surrogate and sounding board for the President, he or she also has a few enumerated powers. First, Article I, Section 3 states that the Vice President shall be the President of the Senate and serve as a tie-breaking vote.[59] While the responsibility of Senate President does not require the Vice President to physically preside over the Senate, as this responsibility is usually assigned to one of the more junior senators, the Vice President is responsible for being present to cast a tie-breaking Senate vote.[60] The Vice President, as President of the Senate, and also by Amendment XII to the Constitution, opens up the Electoral College certification and presides over the counting of the ballots in a ministerial role without independent discretion.[61]

Almost always this ceremonial role is performed by the Vice President without incident. On January 6, 2021, Vice President Michael Pence was threatened with assassination by a violent mob that stormed the Capitol demanding that Pence reverse the result of the 2020 election and declare President Trump and himself the winner. On that day, it was the Vice President, not the President, who took the important steps necessary to assure peaceful transition of power, which has been an American tradition ever since John Adams conceded the presidency after losing the 1800 election to Thomas Jefferson.

The other, and arguably most important responsibility of the Vice President is to assume the presidency if the President resigns, dies, suffers a temporary incapacitation, or is deemed incapable of discharging the duties of the office under the Twenty Fifth Amendment.[62] Of these four categories, three have been tested. President Ford became the US's thirty-eighth President after President Nixon resigned in disgrace in the aftermath of the Watergate scandal. Eight presidents (Tyler, Fillmore, Andrew Johnson, Arthur, Theodore Roosevelt, Coolidge, Truman,

[58] *Id.*
[59] U.S. Const. Art. I, § 3, cl. 4.
[60] *The Executive Branch*, The White House, www.whitehouse.gov/government/executive-branch.
[61] U.S. Const. Amend. XII. *See also* U.S. Const. Art. I, § 3, cl. 4.
[62] U.S. Const. Amend. XXV.

and Lyndon Johnson) have all assumed the presidency after the presidents they served died in office. Finally, three presidents (Reagan, George W. Bush, and Biden) have invoked Section 3 of the Twenty Fifth Amendment to temporarily transfer the power of the presidency due to a brief incapacitation from medical procedures. In each instance, the transfer of power lasted less than a day.

Finally, Section 4 of the Twenty Fifth Amendment also allows the Vice President and a majority of cabinet officers to find a president unable to discharge the powers and duties of his office.[63] Although this provision has never been invoked, Vice Presidents George H. W. Bush and Mike Pence were asked to consider invoking Section 4 in 1981 and 2021 respectively.

The first time Section 4 was considered occurred on March 30, 1981, when John Hinckley fired several shots at President Reagan with one round becoming lodged in one of the President's lungs.[64] President Reagan ultimately recovered quickly. He was not in serious danger of long-term incapacitation, but the frenzy of the moment, and the Vice President's unavailability while he was on Air Force Two, and given the emotional scars of the assassination of President Kennedy fewer than twenty years earlier, led to a crisis in the White House.

In the pressure of the moment, Secretary of State Al Haig called a press conference to update the nation on the situation. While it is unknown if the comment was off the cuff or part of a prepared statement, the Secretary at the press conference stated, "as of now, I am in control here, in the White House."[65] This comment would jump-start a minor constitutional crisis. The Presidential Succession Act of 1947[66] clearly delineates the order of presidential succession. The Secretary of State is fourth in line after the Vice President, Speaker of the House, and President *Pro Tempore* of the Senate (the most senior Senator from the majority party). With the three men ahead of him in succession in good health and capable of assuming the office of the President, Secretary Haig's pronouncements were seen as an attempt to grab power in a time of crisis.[67]

While Section 4 was not ultimately invoked, discussion on the issue continued in the Situation Room after the Haig press conference. From the portions of the transcripts of the deliberations that have been declassified, officers in the Situation

[63] U.S. Const. Amend. XXV, § 4.

[64] The Learning Network, *March 30, 1981 | President Reagan Is Shot*, New York Times (Mar. 30, 2012, 4:09 AM), https://archive.nytimes.com/learning.blogs.nytimes.com/2012/03/30/march-30-1981-president-reagan-is-shot/.

[65] Richard V. Allen, *When Reagan Was Shot, Who Was "in Control" at the White House?*, Wash. Post. (Mar. 25, 2011, 9:12 PM), www.washingtonpost.com/opinions/when-reagan-was-shot-who-was-in-control-at-the-white-house/2011/03/23/AFJlrfYB_story.html.

[66] An Act to Provide for the Performance of the Duties of the Office of the President in Case of the Removal, Resignation, Death, or Inability of Both of the President and Vice President, Pub. L. 80-264, 61 Stat. 380.

[67] *Who's in Charge? The 25th Amendment and the Attempted Assassination of President Reagan*, The Reagan Library Education Blog (Jan. 8, 2021), https://reagan.blogs.archives.gov/2021/01/08/whos-in-charge-the-25th-amendment-and-president-reagans-assassination-attempt/.

Room considered shifting some, but not all, authority to Vice President Bush.[68] This idea was quickly abandoned as those present in the room believed there was no constitutional basis to shift only some presidential power to the Vice President. Ultimately, the group of officers believed that the Twenty Fifth Amendment was the proper means to temporarily assign presidential authority to Vice President Bush. They went so far as to draft memoranda to congressional leadership invoking Section 4, but ultimately did not send them as President Reagan regained consciousness following surgery to remove the bullet from his lung.[69]

The most recent consideration of Section 4 came following the January 6, 2021 attacks on the United States Capitol. In the aftermath of the attacks two of President Trump's cabinet secretaries (Betsy Devos, Secretary of Education, and Elaine Chao, Secretary of Transportation) resigned.[70] While it is unclear how far discussion progressed on invoking Section 4, reporting from the time indicates that there was at least some discussion by what remained of the President's cabinet on invoking Section 4.[71] In addition, within a week of the Capitol attack, the House of Representatives voted 223–205 to adopt a resolution to compel Vice President Pence to invoke Section 4.[72] While the resolution had no force of law, Vice President Pence sent a letter to Speaker Pelosi saying that he would not consider invoking Section 4. The bipartisan vote expressed the anger of the nation at the time.

To prevent this amendment from leading to a vice-presidential coup, it allows the President to submit to the Speaker of the House and President *pro tempore* of the Senate a declaration that no inability exists.[73] If the Vice President disagrees with the President's assessment of his abilities he or she may submit a second declaration of inability, in which case Congress may find, by a two-thirds majority vote, that the President is incapable of handling the responsibilities of his office.[74]

68 *Id.*

69 Unsigned Letters from President Reagan to Senator Strom Thurmond and Speak Tip O'Neill (Mar. 30, 1981), https://reagan.blogs.archives.gov/wp-content/uploads/sites/18/2017/02/mar-30-1981-25th-letters-unsigned-217731_wormfg001.pdf.

70 *The Trump Administration Officials Who Resigned Over Capitol Violence*, New York Times (Jan. 17, 2021), www.nytimes.com/article/trump-resignations.html.

71 John Santucci, Katherine Faulders, Emily Shapiro, Jonathan Karl, & Benjamin Siegel, *Members of Trump Cabinet Discussing Invoking 25th Amendment: Sources*, ABC News (Jan. 7, 2021, 3:34 PM), https://abcnews.go.com/Politics/lawmakers-call-trumps-impeachment-wake-capitol-hill-violence/story?id=75097032.

72 *House Votes 223–205 to Call on Pence to Strip Trump of Power*, New York Times (Jan. 12, 2021, updated Oct. 29, 2021), www.nytimes.com/live/2021/01/12/us/impeachment-trump-25th-amendment.

73 U.S. Const. Amend. XXV, § 4.

74 *Id.*

8

The President and the Alien Enemies Act

During and after the 2024 election, President Trump said he would lead a mass deportation of undocumented immigrants from the United States. The estimate for undocumented immigrants in the United States is approximately 11 million people.[1] Their deportation, in addition to legal and humanitarian concerns, could destabilize the United States economy by causing a significant labor shortage, increasing food prices, construction, and other sectors that for years have relied heavily on labor of undocumented immigrants.[2] This potentially pits Trump's immigration policy against one of his other 2024 campaign promises, to reduce inflation.

Supporters of this proposal claimed undocumented workers took jobs away from Americans and drove down wages, and that some committed crimes, although no reliable study has shown a higher propensity to criminality among undocumented workers than the general population. Opponents of mass deportation point to the enormous burden on the economy, the cost to the government (the budget bill that passed Congress in July 2025 allocates $45 billion each year to immigration

[1] Office of Homeland Security Statistics, U.S. Department of Homeland Security, Estimates of the Unauthorized Immigrant Population Residing in the United States: January 2018–January 2022. *See also 11 Million: The Number of Undocumented Immigrants Living in the United States*, New York Times (Nov. 17, 2024) at 2.

[2] Paul Krugman (Nobel Laurate), *Immigration Is Great for Jobs, Actually*, New York Times (July 23, 2024), www.nytimes.com/2024/07/23/opinion/immigration-unemployment-inflation.html; Suzanne Blake, *Mass Deportations Could Cause Wage Increases in Five States*, Newsweek (Jan. 29, 2025), www.newsweek.com/mass-deportations-could-cause-wage-increases-five-states-2022942 (Statement by Nancy Vanden Houten, lead US economist, Oxford Economics; Mark Zandi, (Chief Economist, Moody's Analytics), *Stagflation Threatens to Hit the U.S. as It Did 50 Years Ago, Economist Zandi Says*, The Philadelphia Enquirer (June 27, 2025), www.inquirer.com/business/inflation-stagflation-immigration-tariffs-iran-20250627.html; Adam Posen (President, Peterson Institute for International Economics), *Peterson's Posen Sees US Immigration Risk from Election*, Bloomberg (June 26, 2024), www.bloomberg.com/news/videos/2024-06-26/peterson-s-posen-sees-us-immigration-risk-from-election-video.

enforcement), and the impact on families including American citizens whose children or parents are deported. Independent of the question of whether and how the President has the power to deport particular persons, we are left with how prudent the implementation of such a deportation policy is considering the economic, budgetary, and human consequences.

In his second term Trump invoked a 1798 federal statute known as the "Alien Enemies Act"[3] that was signed into law by President John Adams. President Trump invoked the Alien Enemies Act to remove Venezuelan nationals who are alleged to be members of Tren de Aragua (TdA), a designated foreign terrorist organization.[4] This action has been challenged, and the case is heading to the Supreme Court, which only granted very limited temporary relief to the claimants.[5]

The context for the enactment of the statute was a fear in 1798 that naval warfare with France was imminent, that French nationals sympathetic to the French cause were living in the United States, and that they would frustrate the war effort. In order for President Adams to invoke the Act, preconditions required that either there was a *declaration of war* between the United States and a foreign government or a foreign government had *invaded* the United States or threatened to do so.[6] If one of these conditions is met, non-citizen military-age men in the United States could be declared "alien enemies." The Act was amended in 1918, during World War I and the Russian Revolution, at the urging of President Wilson, to expand the reach of coverage beyond the deportation of military-age male foreign nationals to *any* non-citizen.[7]

The President can deport undocumented immigrants without invoking the Act pursuant to immigration laws, as Presidents Obama, Trump, and Biden have all done. But, as discussed in Chapter 3, invoking the Act would be a precursor to using the military for this purpose, and establishing an exception to the Posse Comitatus Act prohibition on use of the military for domestic law enforcement. A sudden mass deportation on the scale contemplated by President Trump might require the military to support the Immigration and Naturalization Service (INS) and other law enforcement agencies, as Trump claimed when he federalized the National Guard in Los Angeles in June 2025 and was sued by the Governor of California, as

3 1 Stat. 577 (July 6, 1798). 50 U.S.C. Ch. 3. There are many broad Executive Branch authority powers under the immigration laws of the United States, including deportation orders (Immigration and Nationality Act (8 U.S.C. 1101 *et seq.*) through the Department of Homeland Security (DHS) and its subdivision, Immigration and Customs Enforcement (ICE), which the President may use to influence a deportation policy.

4 Presidential Proclamation No. 10903, 90 Fed. Reg. 13033 (2025).

5 A.A.R.P. v. Trump, 605 U.S. ___ (2025) (reviewing application for injunctive relief denied by the Fifth Circuit) ("We decide today only that the detainees are entitled to more notice than was given on April 18, and we grant temporary injunctive relief to preserve our jurisdiction while the question of what notice is due is adjudicated.") This case, and the extent of the President's power under the Alien Enemies Act, will be decided on the merits after publication of this book.

6 1 Stat. 577 supra.

7 40 Stat. 531 (Apr. 16, 1918).

also discussed in Chapter 3. This would come at considerable cost to a country that since the end of the Civil War has not experienced military rule.

One issue with this law is that it is unclear who has the authority to declare an invasion or what constitutes an invasion. While the Constitution in Article I, Section 8, Clause 11 gives Congress alone the power to declare war, the only mention of invasion within the Constitution is in Article IV, Section 4 where it states that "[t]he United States shall ... protect each of them [referring to the states] against invasion."[8] History, unfortunately, does not provide much clarity on this question.

An approach to defining what constitutes an "invasion" is to look at how the Founders would have used the term. During the Constitutional Convention and state ratification debates, those present used the term invasion in the most extreme sense. Rather than simply referring to mass migration, the Founders understood the term invasion to refer to hostile armed incursion against the nation.[9] This definition of the term invasion is supported by a report prepared in 1800 by James Madison, where he stated that an invasion is an operation of war.[10]

Only twice in American history has a president declared an invasion. In December 1941 following the attacks on Pearl Harbor, President Franklin Roosevelt declared that the Japanese Empire had perpetrated an invasion on a territory of the United States.[11] President Trump declared a national emergency and an invasion in February 2019 when Congress refused to give him billions of dollars to fund and build his promised border wall.[12] However, during the Biden administration there was also a push by congressional Republicans to declare an invasion at the United States–Mexico border. In 2024 Representative Debbie Lesko (R-AZ), along with forty-one co-sponsors, introduced a bill following the issuance of a federal injunction that blocked a Texas state law that would have allowed Texas law enforcement to arrest and deport undocumented immigrants.[13]

Today, the Alien Enemies Act provides for the possible deportation of "all natives, citizens, denizens, or subjects of a hostile nation or government" of persons who are at least fourteen years old who are not naturalized citizens of the United States and

8 U.S. Const. Art. IV, § 4.

9 Frank O. Bowman III, *Immigration Is Not an "Invasion" under the Constitution*, Just Security (Jan. 9, 2024), www.justsecurity.org/91543/immigration-is-not-an-invasion-under-the-constitution/.

10 *The Report of 1800, [7 January] 1800*, Founders Online, National Archives, https://founders.archives.gov/documents/Madison/01-17-02-0202. Original source: The Papers of James Madison, vol. 17, 31 March 1797–3 March 1801 and supplement 22 January 1778–9 August 1795 (David B. Mattern, J. C. A. Stagg, Jeanne K. Cross, & Susan Holbrook Perdue eds., 1991), 303–51.

11 Pres. Proc. 2525. Issued Dec. 7, 1941.

12 Peter Baker, *Trump Declares a National Emergency, and Provokes a Constitutional Clash*, New York Times (Feb. 15, 2019), www.nytimes.com/2019/02/15/us/politics/national-emergency-trump.html.

13 Expressing the sense of the House of Representatives that the situation at the southern border is an invasion, H.R. 1031, 118th Cong. (2024).

come from a foreign enemy nation.[14] All could be deemed "alien enemies." Interestingly, at present the United States has not declared a war with another government or nation. Nor is there currently a military invasion against the United States or a known or planned invasion. Is such presidential action an abuse of wartime power and due process principles under the Constitution? Is it possible that large-scale, mass immigration, without legal authority and not sanctioned by a foreign government, could be considered as an "invasion" under the statute? Or could the Trump administration successfully argue under the Act that drug cartels or organized crime entities from other countries have facilitated this immigration that amounts to an "invasion" by a quasi-nation state?[15] These are matters that federal courts now will have to decide.

Further complicating the issue is both the quantity and nature of undocumented border crossings. While border crossings in the past four years have been high, they are not unusually high in the larger historical context. Data from the United States Customs and Border Protection from 1960 to the present shows that the United States experienced similar levels of border crossings in the early 1980s and late 1990s.[16] Additionally, over the past twenty-five years there has been a sharp decrease in Mexican citizens illegally crossing the border and a sharp inverse uptick in citizens of "third countries," such as Ecuador, Brazil, Nicaragua, Venezuela, Haiti, and Cuba, who "pass through" Mexico en route to the United States.[17] This raises the question of whether current immigration trends can be truly considered an "invasion" if they are neither uniquely high nor largely originating from a single country.

The history of the Alien Enemies Act that has been invoked on three occasions – all related to a *declaration* of war. First, it was invoked during the War of 1812 by President James Madison. Second, it was invoked by President Woodrow Wilson during World War I. Most recently, it was invoked during World War II by Presidents Franklin D. Roosevelt and Truman. Notably, the Act was not cited as authority during World War II for the internment of Japanese Americans. That authority came from an executive order from President Roosevelt.[18]

[14] *Id.*

[15] Catherine E. Schoichet, *A Little-Known Law from 1798 Could Be a Key Part of Trump's Deportation Plans*, CNN (Nov. 14, 2024), www.cnn.com/2024/11/14/politics/alien-enemies-act-1798-trump-cec/index.html.

[16] John Gramlich & Alissa Scheller, *What's Happening at the U.S.–Mexico Border in 7 Charts*, Pew Research Center (Nov. 9, 2021), www.pewresearch.org/short-reads/2021/11/09/whats-happening-at-the-u-s-mexico-border-in-7-charts/.

[17] *Id.*

[18] Pres. Proc. 2525–27; Executive Order 9066. *See also* Korematsu v. United States, 323 U.S. 214 (1944), Trump v. Hawaii, 585 U.S. 667 (2018) (comments that *Korematsu* was wrongly decided). *See also* Pres. Proc. 2655, giving the Attorney General authority under the statute to decide whether "enemy aliens" within the United States were "dangerous to the public peace and safety of the United States, and if so, order them removed." *See* Ludecke v. Watkins, 335 U.S. 160 (1948).

Clearly, the Act gives a president power to detain and deport non-citizens during times of "declared war." Consider whether outside the context of a declared war or foreign invasion, as required by the Act, how the federal courts might decide the legality of the Act's application to a deportation order under the Act or by executive order of millions of undocumented immigrants as the courts might be pressed to consider a claim of "national security" versus individual liberty.

If the courts found that the preconditions to the Act's coverage – either a declared war or a foreign invasion – are not present, they would not need to balance security interests over civil liberties and due process defenses. And there are, of course, additional questions and concerns how such a presidential order actually would be implemented and enforced with additional Fifth Amendment due process of law issues raised. The practical effectiveness of large-scale, mass deportation orders would be a significant challenge and highly disruptive regarding capacity (facilities), competence, and the size of personnel in Immigration and Customs Enforcement to accomplish the mission.[19] A critical issue regarding the President's power is whether Congress approves or acquiesces in the use of such power under the circumstances, or whether Congress would need to declare "war" in order to the trigger the 1798 Alien Enemies Act to empower the President.

Applying the framework in *Youngstown* (the 1952 steel mills case) to President Trump's construction of the Alien Enemies Act, recall that the concurring opinion by Justice Jackson established the legal test for when a president holds the power: (1) when the President acts pursuant to an express or implied authorization by Congress, the President is at his maximum authority; (2) when the President acts in absence of a congressional grant or denial of authority he may only rely upon his own constitutional powers; and (3) when the President takes measures incompatible with the express or implied will of Congress, the President's power is at its lowest ebb. An exception to the latter is when the nation is under attack and the President has an Article II responsibility as Commander in Chief to defend the nation.[20] And this circles back to President Trump's insistence that there is an "invasion" of the United States, which he then can claim makes the analysis in *Youngstown* less relevant because the border crisis expands his Commander in Chief authority beyond that of President Truman during the Korean War.

Finally, the lessons of the Global War on Terror in 2003 and a 1948 Supreme Court case raise important practical considerations about how and when any

[19] *See* Dara Lind, *How Far Will the Mass Deportation Plan Go?*, NEW YORK TIMES (Nov. 24, 2024).

[20] *See* Youngstown Sheet & Tube Co. v. Sawyer, 343 U.S. 579 (1952). This case illustrates how the "war powers" and "domestic powers" of a president are often intertwined. The Court held that Commander in Chief powers stop at home when not directly related to a "war." And, of course, it is Congress, under Article I, Section 8, Clause 11, that holds the power to declare a war. No war has been declared by Congress since World War II.

declaration of an invasion should end.[21] In 1948 the Supreme Court held in *Ludecke v. Watkins*[22] that even though Hitler's Germany had surrendered to the Allied powers, an order to Mr. Ludecke, a German national in the United States, was valid because there remained an open declaration of war against Germany, and thus there was still an ongoing emergency.

One fear is that once a president declares an invasion and invokes the Alien Enemies Act it will become politically unpopular for his successors to undo that declaration. During the 2010s and 2020s Presidents Obama and Biden promised to undo much of the security apparatus that was implemented by the George W. Bush administration. However, once they took office neither President was able to accomplish that goal. The detention facility at Guantanamo Bay remains open, and President Trump now threatens to use it for illegal immigrants. Much of the post 9/11 Patriot Act remains in place, and as discussed in Chapter 3 of this book, the current Authorizations for Use of Military Force issued in 2001 and 2002 remain in place. Once there is an emergency there will always be an emergency, and with respect to the Alien Enemies Act, once we characterize illegal immigration as an "invasion" it will always be in invasion. Whether courts will accept that argument remains to be seen.

[21] For background on the Iraq war, *see* Hans Blix, Disarming Iraq (2004); Richard A. Clarke, Against All Enemies (2004); James R. Clapper, Facts and Fears: Hard Truths from a Life in Intelligence (2018); Seymour M. Hersh, Chain of Command: The Road from 9/11 to Abu Ghraib (2004); Ron Suskind, The One Percent Doctrine: Deep Inside America's Pursuit of Its Enemies since 9/11 (2006); Bob Woodward, Bush at War (2002).

[22] Ludecke v. Watkins, 335 U.S. 160 (1948). According to a new report by the US Immigration and Customs Service, "nearly half of the 1.4 million people in the United States" who have pending deportation orders cannot be returned to their home countries. Nick Miroff, *Many Targeted for Removal by Trump Can't Be Deported, ICE Data Show*, Wash. Post. (Dec. 8, 2024), www.washingtonpost.com/immigration/2024/12/06/mass-deportation-obstacles-trump-migrants/.

9

Does the President Have the Power to Void Birthright Citizenship?

On the day of his second inauguration, on January 20, 2025, President Trump signed an executive order challenging the Fourteenth Amendment's Citizenship Clause which grants United States citizenship to anyone who is born in the United States. This right of citizenship always has been considered as an automatic vesting of citizenship upon birth in the United States.

The Fourteenth Amendment states: "All persons born or naturalized in the United States, and subject to the jurisdiction thereof, are citizens of the United States and of the state wherein they reside."

In a 1898 decision the Supreme Court in *United States v. Wong Kim Ark*[1] interpreted this clause of the Fourteenth Amendment when it ruled that it conferred citizenship at birth. This decision has never been reversed or criticized by the Supreme Court since it was decided 127 years ago.

Moreover, even before the Fourteenth Amendment was ratified in 1868, Congress by federal statute enacted a statutory right to citizenship at birth.[2] Thus, a court challenge to the Fourteenth Amendment may be decided without addressing the constitutional issue by basing the decision on the plain meaning of the federal statute. Either approach would result in invalidating the President's executive order as a violation of the Civil Rights Act of 1866 or of the Constitution. Subsequent Supreme Court cases and government legal opinions have affirmed the ruling in *Wong Kim Ark* and by application that there is no exception to "birthright citizenship" on the grounds that the parents were resident aliens or undocumented immigrants at the time of birth.[3]

Finally, turning to the language of "subject to the jurisdiction thereof" in the Fourteenth Amendment, the implied exception was to exclude from birthright

1 United States v. Wong Kim Ark, 169 U.S. 649 (1898).

2 Civil Rights Act of 1866.

3 Plyler v. Doe, 457 U.S. 202 (1982); INS v. Rios-Paneda, 471 U.S. 444 (1985); United States Department of Justice, Legislation Denying Citizenship at Birth to Certain Children Born in the United States (Dec. 13, 1995), www.justice.gov/file/147026-0/dl.

citizenship children born to diplomatic appointees from other countries, Native American children born in the United States on reservations subject to tribal government sovereignty,[4] and children of alien enemies during a wartime hostile invasion.[5] None of these has application under the sweeping executive order signed by President Trump. Nor is the United States in a war "declared" by Congress, or a wartime invasion by a hostile enemy. No court to date has ruled that an "invasion" means anything other than "operation of war," as James Madison stated in his Report of 1800.[6] In short, an immigrant without legal documentation is not an invasion. And, without question, all those born in the United States, with or without the benefit of the federal statute and the Fourteenth Amendment are, at birth, subject to the jurisdiction of the United States and the state they are born in. This is clear whether they are born of parents who are US citizens, legal aliens, or undocumented immigrants.

The day after President Trump signed his "birthright" executive order, it was challenged by twenty-four states in federal court and the judge issued a temporary restraining order blocking the President's order, ruling that Trump's order was "blatantly unconstitutional."[7]

On February 6, 2025, a preliminary injunction was issued against the executive order.[8] The district court judge issuing the restraining order was appointed to the federal judiciary by President Ronald Reagan.

In July 2025, the Supreme Court held that a federal district court could not enter a nationwide injunction against President Trump's executive order. The Court's holding did not address substantive interpretation of the Natural Born Citizen Clause of the Fourteenth Amendment, but instead the power of federal courts to issue nationwide injunctions against the President, which the Court held in most instances, including this one, a federal judge could not do. The Court left open the possibility that the plaintiffs – persons born in the United States to undocumented parents – could bring a nationwide class action to seek relief, but the Court did not address the underlying merits of such a lawsuit.[9] The underlying issue, the construction of the Fourteenth Amendment, is likely to be decided by the Court at some point in 2026.

4 Under the language of the Fourteenth Amendment, Native American born on reservations were originally not granted birthright citizenship because the reservations were not subject to the jurisdiction of the United States. However, in 1924 Congress passed and President Coolidge signed into law the Indian Citizenship Act of 1924, 43 Stat. 253, which granted birthright citizenship to Native Americans born on tribal lands.

5 Carol Nackenoff & Julie Novkov, American by Birth: Wong Kim Ark and the Battle for Citizenship (2022), *cited in* the excellent essay by Professor Steven I. Vladeck, *Birthright Citizenship, "Invasions", and the Supreme Court* (Dec. 12, 2024); *see also* a thorough essay by David French, *Donald Trump Is Running Riot*, New York Times (Jan. 23, 2025), also citing Professor Vladeck's essay mentioned above.

6 James Madison, *The Report of 1800*, https://founders.archives.gov/documents/Madison/01-17-02-0202.

7 State of Washington v. Donald Trump, 765 F. Supp. 3d 1142 (W. Dist. Wash., 2025).

8 *Id.*

9 Trump v. Casa, Inc., 606 U.S. 831 (2025). *See also* Barbara v. Trump, 25-cv-244-JL-AJ (Dist. N.H., 2025) (granting class certification and ordering a nationwide preliminary injunction against President Trump's executive order suspending the Natural Born Citizen Clause).

PART I

Conclusion

In summary, Part I of this book has covered many topics within the domain of presidential "power." Against the backdrop of the philosophy of Locke, Hobbes, and Montesquieu, we see the Founders' deep concerns and mistrust of how too much power in a lone individual can lead to tyrannical rule in the hands of a president, as they witnessed from King George III and the British monarchy. Over time, the presidency as an institution has grown in prominence, power, and authority, resulting today with the current Supreme Court adopting a full-throated "Unitary Executive Theory" that would have been unheard of and unimaginable to the Founders.

This part on presidential power traced that growth in power through the selection of a "singular" president and the powers and authority set out explicitly or implied in Article II of the Constitution. In addition, we discussed the "powers" granted or delegated by Congress to the President, and powers acquired, inherited, or grabbed by successive presidents through inaction or acquiescence by Congress.

Even though the Founders clearly intended for Congress to predominate and have supremacy over the President, through the numerous checks and balances embedded in the Constitution, today we see a surge of more powers being claimed and asserted by presidents.[1] Examples include the President's power and authority to appoint and remove executive officers, the role the President plays in the administrative state, his Commander in Chief core responsibility over the military in international conflicts, wars, domestic disputes, and national emergencies. Another example of a president's exclusive powers is his power to grant pardons for federal criminal offenses. These powers are often exercised with or without consent or authorization from Congress.

[1] E. Thomas Sullivan & Richard S. Frase, Proportionality Principles in American Law: Controlling Excessive Government Actions (2009).

While "sharing" certain powers with Congress, a president also can be in competition with Congress, creating tensions that can flow as a result of a president exercising certain powers as a "checking function" on Congress – such as a presidential veto; a president's pocket veto; the President's power to impose tariffs and to sign executive agreements with foreign nations without congressional approval; and the President's power to appoint ambassadors and diplomats.

All of these have been discussed in this part of the book on presidential power. We now turn, in Part II, to the responsibilities of a president under the Constitution, the President's oath of office, and under Federal statutes.

PART II

Responsibility

Part I of this book is about the extent and limits of the powers of the President. Part II focuses on the President's obligation to use that power responsibly. The central focus here is the constitutional responsibility to "take care" that the laws are faithfully executed. This includes enforcement of the laws without regard to political affiliation, religious creed, race, or other irrelevant characteristics of those appearing before the federal government.

Responsible exercise of power is particularly important in foreign affairs where presidential power is at its zenith. The Supremacy Clause explicitly embraces the treaty obligations of the United States, making adherence to international law vitally important when the President acts as Commander in Chief.

The President is responsible for putting the interests of the country first, above the interests of his political party and above the financial interests of himself and his family. The President is also responsible for assuming that other Executive Branch officials do the same. Adherence to financial conflict of interest rules and other standards of conduct for federal employees was the function of the White House Ethics Office that one author of this book directed under President George W. Bush.

Finally, the President and Congress jointly exercise the constitutional power to manage, and preserve for future generations, the vast portions of US land owned by the federal government. Since the Teapot Dome scandal of the 1920s, faithful execution of this trust has been challenged by special interests seeking to exploit federal lands through undue influence in Congress or the Interior Department. The President's responsibility is to resist waste and desecration of federal land. This obligation of even greater importance in an age when pressure to increase natural resource extraction is intense and climate change threatens to destroy our natural habitats.

In sum, presidential responsibility is not about what the President has the power to do, but what a president should do and ought not do. Some of this responsibility is defined explicitly by law, but often the President has discretion to decide what is and is not a responsible use of power.

As Part III of this book, on accountability, will demonstrate, legal mechanisms for holding a president accountable for misuse of power are limited. Given the vast powers of the presidency and the limited accountability mechanisms to check presidential power, it is vitally important that American voters consider a candidate's personal commitment to responsible exercise of power as an overwhelmingly important value in choosing a president.

10

Responsibility and Duty under the "Take Care" Clause

President Trump's actions and inactions on January 6, 2021 have sparked renewed interest and debate in the Constitution's requirement that the President "shall take care that the Laws be faithfully executed."[1] The clause is original in the adoption of the Constitution in 1789. In this section, we explore the meaning of the language and application of (1) "shall take care," (2) "faithfully execute," and (3) "the laws." We discuss what kind of duty this imposes on a president,[2] whether it implies that it gives the President additional powers to carry out his duties, and whether it limits the "duty" of the President to only those laws passed by Congress.[3]

Clearly, however, to "faithfully execute" does not mean that the President is a lawmaker, that role is left to Congress.[4] Rather, the President is one that executes the enacted laws. We consider, also, whether "take care" means the President is required only to do his best, in a more passive role, rather than to *ensure* the faithful execution of the law.[5]

Regarding the term "laws," this would embrace federal laws passed by Congress, the Constitution, and Treaties of the United States. But does it also include Supreme Court opinions, interpretations, and policies issued by the Department of Justice, and rules passed by administrative agencies?[6]

1 U.S. Const. Article II, § 3.

2 Daniel A. Farber, How to Understand the Limits of Presidential Power: Contested Ground, 9–10, 51, 56 (2021).

3 *Id.*

4 *Id. See also* Heidi Kitrosser, Reclaiming Accountability, 144–46, 148, 156, 166, 254 (2014), *citing also* David M. Driesen, *Toward a Duty-Based Theory of Executive Power*, 78 Fordham L. Rev. 71, 83–94 (2015).

5 *Id. See also* Saikrishna Bangalore Prakash, The Living Presidency: An Originalist Argument Against Its Ever-Expanding Powers, 42 (2020).

6 *See* Lawrence H. Tribe, *Where Freedom Ends*, N.Y. Rev. of Books, 12–16 (Nov. 7, 2024). *See also* John Harrison, *The Constitution and the Laws of Nations*, 106 Geo. L. J. 1659 (2018) (arguing that the duty and responsibility only applied to laws passed by Congress); Frank H. Easterbrook, *Presidential Review*, 40 Case W. Reserve L. Rev. 905, 1988 (arguing that the

In addition, the President also takes an oath of office to "faithfully execute the Office of President … and … to the best of [his] ability, preserve, protect, and defend the Constitution of the United States."[7]

The early colonial and founding era charters, regarding the executive's responsibility to execute the laws, expressed language including "promise all due Submission and obedience,"[8] "shall be carefullie and duly observed, kept, performed, and putt in execucon, according to the true Intent and Meaning,"[9] and "exercise the executive power of government according to the laws."[10]

Legal scholars over time, and more recently, have debated the meaning of the "Take Care" Clause, having explained its breadth and limitations.[11] In a 2016 law review article, Professors Jack Goldsmith and John Manning discussed specific ways in which the Supreme Court has relied on the Take Care Clause in defining the broad extent, and occasionally the limits, of presidential power. Examples include:[12]

- Upholding the President's power to remove officers who do not follow the President's directives.[13]
- Limiting Article III standing (the power of a court to hear a case) for plaintiffs to sue the President for official actions (for example, the requirement that a plaintiff show causation of a *specific injury*), so that in most instances the President, rather than the judiciary, executes the laws and defines the legality of executive decisions.[14]

responsibility is broader to include the Constitution generally and also laws passed by Congress).

7 U.S. CONST. Art. II, § 8. *See also* PETER M. SHANE, DEMOCRACY'S CHIEF EXECUTIVE: INTERPRETING THE CONSTITUTION AND DEFINING THE FUTURE OF THE PRESIDENCY, 14 (2022); Sophia Shams, *Preserving Faithful Execution*, 20 GEO. J. L. & PUB. POLICY 805 (2022) (arguing that the clause imposes an affirmative duty on the President based on the definition of "take care" as used in the late 1700s and early 1800s to mean superintended, oversee, and keeping or securing) (citing Kendall v. United States ex rel. Stokes, 37 U.S. 524 (1838) holding that the "Take Care" Clause imposes an obligation on the President).

8 The Mayflower Compact (1620).

9 Massachusetts Bay Charter (1629).

10 Draft of the Virginia State Constitution (1776).

11 *Supra* at notes 5, 6, and 7.

12 Jack L. Goldsmith & John F. Manning, *The Protean Take Care Clause*, 164 U. PA. L. REV. 837 (2016).

13 *Id.* at 841–45 (discussing prior Supreme Court case law on presidential removal power). *See also* Seila Law v. Consumer Financial Protection Bureau, 591 U.S. 197 (2020) (decided by the Supreme Court after Goldsmith and Manning's article was published. *Seila Law* is discussed in Part I of this book on presidential power).

14 Goldsmith & Manning, *supra* note 12, at 1846–49, citing standing cases including Allen v. Wright, 468 U.S. 737, 751 (1984) (relying on the Take Care Clause in denying standing to African American schoolchildren who alleged the Internal Revenue Service (IRS) under President Reagan failed to revoke tax-exempt status of private schools that discriminated on the basis of race in admission); and Lujan v. Defenders of Wildlife, 504 U.S. 555 (1992) (denying standing to individual members of the Defenders of Wildlife to challenge the Interior Department regulation that allowed continued federal funding for overseas projects

- Upholding the President's prosecutorial discretion, which gives the President some ability to define the effective reach of laws enacted by Congress.[15]
- Recognizing the President's constitutional obligation to respect legislative supremacy, and the fact that the President does not have the power to suspend federal law (as the Court held when President Truman seized the steel mills to settle a labor dispute during the Korean War).[16]
- Recognizing presidential authority to take acts necessary to protect government operations even if no statutes give him explicit authority to do so.[17]

There continues to be debate about how far the President can go in defining how to "faithfully execute" the laws. For example, under President Obama, federal prosecutors deferred prosecution of certain lower-level narcotics offenses and diverted defendants to drug treatment programs.[18] President Obama also pardoned a large number of lower-level drug offenders, as did President Biden in January 2025.[19]

that endangered wildlife, the Court rejected plaintiffs' claim that they intended to return to two previously visited overseas sites to see the endangered species – the Nile crocodile and Asian elephant). The standing issue is also discussed further in Part III of this book, on Accountability.

15 Goldsmith & Manning, *supra* note 12, at 1849–50. Prosecutorial discretion became an issue of even greater importance under the Trump administration, and the Supreme Court later affirmed the President's near complete control over the Justice Department in Trump v. United States, 603 U.S. 593 (2024) (holding that the President has immunity from criminal prosecution for orders he gives the Justice Department officials).

16 Goldsmith & Manning, *supra* note 12, at 1851–52, discussing invocation of the Take Care Clause in Youngstown Sheet & Tube Co. v. Sawyer, 343 U.S. 579, 587–88 (1952) (the "steel seizure" case) ("In the framework of our Constitution, the President's power to see that the laws are faithfully executed refutes the idea that he [the President] is to be a lawmaker"). *Youngstown* is discussed in this book in Part I, Presidential Power.

17 Goldsmith & Manning, *supra* note 12, at 1853–54, citing In re Neagle, 135 U.S. 1, 63–64 (1890) (invoking the Take Care Clause, to find implied authority for the Attorney General to assign a deputy marshal to the task of protecting a Supreme Court justice). *Id.* at 1855, citing Wells v. Nickles, 104 U.S. 444 (1881) (holding that the Department of the Interior had the power to make rules to protect public land despite the lack of any specific statutory authorization). *See also* Henry P. Monaghan, *The Protective Power of the Presidency*, 93 COLUM. L. REV. 1, 61–63 (1993) (discussing how the Court has recognized "an executive power to preserve, protect, and defend the personnel, property, and instrumentalities of the national government"); Jack Goldsmith & John F. Manning, *The President's Completion Power*, 115 YALE L.J. 2280, 2302–03 (2006).

18 *How Obama Quietly Reshaped America's War on Drugs: Obama's Drug War Legacy Is Underappreciated. But It Now Hangs in the Balance – Thanks to Trump*, VOX (Jan. 19, 2017), www.vox.com/identities/2016/12/19/13903532/obama-war-on-drugs-legacy.

19 *See* Department of Justice, Archives, *Obama Administration Clemency Initiative*, Announced by former Deputy Attorney General James M. Cole on April 23, 2014, www.justice.gov/archives/pardon/obama-administration-clemency-initiative.

Even more controversial was President Obama's "Deferred Action for Childhood Arrivals" (DACA) program that deferred deportation of persons with no lawful immigration status after having entered the country as children with their parents. Also, President Obama's "Deferred Action for Parental Accountability" (DAPA) program is an example which deferred deportation of certain undocumented immigrants with children who are either American citizens or lawful residents.

Critics alleged both programs were unconstitutional departures from the President's duty to faithfully execute the laws.[20] Both were challenged in the courts. DAPA was struck down as exceeding the President's power under the Administrative Procedure Act by the Fifth Circuit in a 2015 decision which was upheld by the Supreme Court in a split 4–4 decision in *United States v. Texas*.[21] President Trump suspended DACA. Four years later President Biden issued an executive order on his first day in office reinstating DACA.[22] President Trump, upon assuming office again in January 2025, has stalled implementing DACA and may suspend it altogether.

Perhaps the most controversial issue today is whether the President can "take care" that the laws are effectively executed, while at the same time using prosecutorial discretion to go after political enemies. In *Trump v. United States*,[23] the Supreme Court affirmed that the President has near complete control over the Justice Department. But does this mean that the President can go so far as to order the Justice Department to prosecute a political enemy, or a personal enemy, for an alleged crime under circumstances where another person would not otherwise be investigated or prosecuted?

Arguably, a person charged with a crime in such circumstances would have grounds to challenge the indictment as selective prosecution in violation of the Fifth Amendment due process.[24] Still, courts are reluctant to grant discovery requests aimed at uncovering the motives for a criminal prosecution because, as

[20] Josh Blackman, *The Constitutionality of DAPA Part II: Faithfully Executing the Law (January 19, 2015)* 19 Texas Rev. of L. and Politics 215 (2015) (criticizing the constitutionality of DAPA under the Take Care Clause).

[21] United States v. Texas, 579 U.S. 547 (2016).

[22] Preserving and Fortifying Deferred Action for Childhood Arrivals (DACA), Memorandum for the Attorney General the Secretary of Homeland Security (Jan. 20, 2021), https://bidenwhitehouse.archives.gov/briefing-room/presidential-actions/2021/01/20/preserving-and-fortifying-deferred-action-for-childhood-arrivals-daca/.

[23] *See* Trump v. United States, 603 U.S. 593 (2024).

[24] Oyler v. Boles, 368 U.S. 448, 456 (1962) (to prove a selective prosecution claim, a defendant must show that the prosecutor's policy was motivated by a discriminatory purpose and had a discriminatory effect). Selective prosecution violates equal protection where prosecutors pursue a criminal case "directed so exclusively against a particular class of persons … with a mind so unequal and oppressive" that equal protection of the law has been negated by their efforts. United States v. Armstrong, 517 U.S. 456, 464–65 (1996). Most such cases to date have addressed alleged selective prosecution based on race or another similar category, not selective prosecution of an individual who happens to have provoked the ire of the President of the United States. *See generally* E. Thomas Sullivan & Toni Massaro, The Arc of Due Process in American Constitutional Law, xi–xiv, 218 (2013).

the Supreme Court recognized in *United States v. Armstrong*,[25] the President under the Take Care Clause has the discretion to direct the prosecutorial decisions of the Executive Branch.

As discussed in Part I of this book, other modern examples include President Nixon's impounding of congressionally authorized funds to undercut domestic programs he did not support. The Supreme Court, in 1975, ruled in *Train v. City of New York*[26] that the President could not ignore appropriation mandates passed by Congress, given his duty to execute the laws. The Congress, reacting to Nixon's impoundment of funds, followed through by enacting the Congressional Budget Impoundment Control Act[27] that limited a president's ability to impound budget appropriations authorized by Congress. Commentators called Nixon's impoundment "an unconstitutional version of a veto," noting that "[t]here is no authority for impoundment in the text of the Constitution."[28]

More recently, allegations have been made that President Trump violated the "Take Care" Clause when he failed to act in enforcing the law during a six-hour period on January 6, 2021 when he sat in the White House dining room watching television while over 1,000 people stormed the Capitol, causing chaos and damaging property in an attempt to prevent the constitutionally mandated certification of the 2020 Electoral College results.[29] Trump failed in his duty to take care that the laws governing free elections were faithfully executed, although Vice President Pence did his constitutional duty that day. He certified the 2020 election under threats to this own life. As discussed further in Part III of this book, in the end there was very little accountability for President Trump. As noted in Part I, in 2025 he used his pardon power to excuse this insurrection, the most violent attempt to overturn an election since the Civil War.

[25] United States v. Armstrong, 517 U.S. 456, 464 (1996) (refusing to request a defendant indicted for crack cocaine for discovery to support a claim of selective prosecution because they were Black). The *Armstrong* Court imposed a high bar for obtaining discovery, observing that federal prosecutors have "latitude because they are designated by statute as the President's delegates to help him discharge his constitutional responsibility to 'take Care that the Laws be faithfully executed.'"

[26] Train v. City of New York, 420 U.S. 35 (1975).

[27] Congressional Budget Impoundment Control Act of 1974, 2 U.S.C. §§ 601–88 (1974).

[28] David French, *Donald Trump Thinks He Won't Have Enough Power*, New York Times (Nov. 11, 2024), www.nytimes.com/2024/11/24/opinion/trump-recess-appointments-constitution .html.

[29] Patricia Zengerle & Richard Cowan, *Trump watched Jan. 6 U.S. Capitol Riot Unfold on TV, Ignored Pleas to Call for Peace*, Reuters (July 22, 2022), www.reuters.com/world/us/us-capitol-probes-season-finale-focus-trump-supporters-three-hour-rage-2022-07-21/.

11

Financial and Political Conflicts of Interest of the President

When considering presidential power, presidential "ethics" concerns also are relevant. Here we address two aspects of this problem – financial and political conflicts of interest of the President.

11.1 DOES THE FEDERAL FINANCIAL CONFLICT OF INTEREST STATUTE APPLY TO THE PRESIDENT?

The federal criminal code[1] makes it a crime for an Executive Branch official to participate in a federal government matter that directly affects a financial interest of the employee or the employee's spouse, including companies in which they are invested. But this statute does not apply to elected officials, including presidents, vice presidents, and members of Congress who throughout history have traded stocks in companies affected by bills pending in Congress.

An Office of Legal Counsel (OLC) opinion in 1975 stated that such a financial conflict of interest statute might be unconstitutional if applied to presidents and vice presidents. This was when questions arose over Vice President Nelson Rockefeller's financial conflicts of interest. The Justice Department sent the White House a memo opining that the criminal conflict of interest statute for Executive Branch employees could not constitutionally be applied to the President or the Vice President because it would constrain performance of their Article II duties.[2] The memo, written by Laurence Silberman, who was later appointed a Circuit judge by President Reagan, reflected an early stage of the evolving view within the Justice

1 18 U.S.C. § 208 (1962).

2 Memorandum for Richard T. Burress, Office of the President, from Laurence H. Silberman, Deputy Attorney General, Conflict of Interest Problems Arising out of the President's Nomination of Nelson A. Rockefeller to the Vice President under the Twenty-Fifth Amendment to the Constitution (Aug. 28, 1974).

Department that criminal laws could not be applied to official acts of the President, a view culminating fifty years later in the Supreme Court's immunity ruling in *Trump v. United States*, which is discussed in detail in Part III of this book.

Most presidents voluntarily have avoided financial conflicts of interest. President Jimmy Carter went so far as to sell his peanut farm. But as soon as President Trump was elected in 2016, the US Office of Government Ethics suggested he divest his hotel and golf club businesses. Trump reminded Americans that the conflict of interest statute does not apply to the President. In short, his argument was that a president is above the law – or at least this law.

For example, Presidents Washington and Jefferson owned large plantations with enslaved people. Was this financial conflict of interest "unethical" given their duties as President? In retrospect the answer is yes, both because the institution of slavery was morally wrong and because financial interest as well as racism discouraged presidents, many members of Congress, and the Supreme Court from doing anything to end the institution of slavery. Financial conflicts of interest also were part of the reason why so many of the Founders ignored the moral wrong of embedding the institution of slavery into the Constitution and laws of the United States. Clearly, financial conflicts of interest of elected officials, including presidents, have serious consequences for the United States.

With Trump's second presidency in 2025, his financial conflicts of interest were even greater than during his first term. The President and his family had begun new ventures in both social media and crypto currency. The President has his own "meme" coin, $Trump, as well as a very large interest in Liberty Financial, a crypto company that has attracted investors from around the world, including sovereign wealth funds.[3]

On July 9, 2025, one of the authors of this book testified before the US Senate Banking Committee about Trump's conflicts of interest in crypto currency that would affect Executive Branch regulation and enforcement under a crypto market structure bill then pending before Congress. Would investor protection and the stability of the financial system be the government's objective of regulating crypto or instead would the government be enabling a "pump and dump" of crypto currency at prices inflated by the appearance of regulation?[4] The broader question is whether the President can faithfully execute the laws of the United States if he is making money in industries regulated by those laws at the same time.

[3] Norman Eisen, Virginia Canter, & Richard W. Painter, A *Plane from Qatar? C'mon, Man*, New York Times (May 14, 2025), discussing conflicts of interest involving foreign governments, including billion-dollar sovereign wealth fund investments in Liberty Financial.

[4] Testimony of Richard W. Painter before the United States Senate Committee on Banking Hearing on July 9, 2025 titled "From Wall Street to Web3: Building Tomorrow's Digital Asset Markets," www.banking.senate.gov/imo/media/doc/painter_testimony_7-9-25.pdf.

11.2 DO FINANCIAL DISCLOSURE RULES APPLY TO THE PRESIDENT?

The Ethics in Government Act of 1978 imposes financial disclosure rules on senior officials in all three branches of government. Financial holdings of office holders and their spouses need to be disclosed. Also, all gifts received by the office holder, whether permissible or impermissible, need to be disclosed with very few exceptions. The Act requires disclosure of the "source" and "value of all gifts" that exceed the reporting threshold (currently $480).[5] For travel, this includes a "brief description (including a travel itinerary, dates and nature of any expenses provided) of reimbursements received from any source."[6]

These disclosure rules aren't always followed. As one of the authors of this book has pointed out, such disclosure lapses have been far worse in the case of at least one Supreme Court justice.[7]

Intentional omission of an item from a required financial disclosure filing can be a crime. Federal law imposes criminal penalties on "anyone who in a matter within the jurisdiction of the executive, legislative, or judicial branch of the Government of the United States, knowingly and willfully … makes or uses any false writing or document knowing the same to contain any materially false, fictitious, or fraudulent statement or entry."[8]

But in the case of presidents and Supreme Court justices, as well as members of Congress who leave free travel and other gifts off their disclosure forms, these lapses are attributed to "misunderstandings" of the disclosure requirements, forgetfulness, or other factors lacking criminal intent. Prosecutions of high-ranking officials are non-existent.

Another problem is that even if financial disclosure filings are technically correct, not all office holders' business interests are disclosed. President Trump, for example, like many wealthy office holders, owns and controls dozens of separately organized corporations and limited liability companies (LLCs) that do business with foreign persons and entities unknown. Very little about what goes on in the Trump Organization entities, however, was disclosed on Trump's annual public financial disclosure Form 278.[9] One of the authors of this book testified before the US House Oversight Committee and urged that more detailed disclosure of separately incorporated entities be required. Congress has yet to amend the disclosure

5 *See* Ethics in Government Act, 5a U.S.C. § 102(a)(2)(A) (1979).

6 5 U.S.C. §§ 13103(f)(11), 13101(10) (2022).

7 *See* Richard W. Painter, Conduct Unbecoming: The Ethics Crisis at the Supreme Court and How Legitimacy Can Be Restored (2026).

8 *See* 18 U.S.C. § 1001 (1948).

9 *See e.g.* Form 278 OGE, Public Financial Disclosure, of Donald J. Trump, President of the United States, dated July 31, 2020. www.documentcloud.org/documents/7012257-President-Donald-Trump-2020-financial-disclosure.html.

requirements.[10] President Trump's vast holdings in crypto currency, where transactions are almost always private, are very likely to make the problem worse.

11.3 DOES THE EMOLUMENTS CLAUSE APPLY TO THE PRESIDENT?

There are two separate "emoluments" clauses of the Constitution. The "foreign Emoluments Clause" applies to all federal office holders including the President. A "domestic Emoluments Clause" applies only to the President, prohibiting him from receiving profits from the federal government or the states more than the salary provided by Congress.

Article I, Section 9, Clause 8, the foreign Emoluments Clause, prohibits receipt of a gift, salary, or "emolument" (i.e., profit or benefit) from a foreign government without consent of Congress: "No Title of Nobility shall be granted by the United States: And no Person holding any Office of Profit or Trust under them, shall, without the Consent of the Congress, accept of any present, Emolument, Office, or Title, of any kind whatever, from any King, Prince, or foreign State."

As defined in Dr. Samuel Johnson's 1755 dictionary, the word "emolument" means "profit" or "advantage."[11] Simply put, the Emoluments Clause prohibits a federal officer from accepting any profit or advantage from a foreign government, or any entity controlled by a foreign government.

The intent of the Emoluments Clause is to prevent foreign financial influence of federal officials, falling short of that which can be proven to be bribery. Although the Emoluments Clause applies to all federal office holders, not just presidents, foreign influence over presidents was particularly feared by the Founders.[12] One of the constitutional requirements for the office of President is that the holder be a natural-born American citizen.[13]

Washington's farewell address, published in 1796, highlights several important themes, including a foreign policy of neutrality calling for the United States to avoid entanglement in alliances with foreign nations to protect the country's independence and order, the importance of national unity with concerns of "sectionalism" in

10 *See* Oral Testimony and Written Statement of Richard W. Painter before the United States House of Representatives Committee on Oversight and Government Reform, March 23, 2017 (hearing entitled "Legislative Proposals for Fostering Transparency").

11 Samuel Johnson, A Dictionary of the English Language 1755, 1773 (Beth Rapp Young, Jack Lynch, William Dorner, Amy Larner Giroux, Carmen Faye Mathes, & Abigail Moreshead eds., 2021).

12 Washington's Farewell Address to the People of the United States. Originally published in the Daily American Advertiser (Sept. 19, 1796). Published in the Senate Record at S. Doc. No. 106–21, at 27 (2000). David McCullough, John Adams, 557 (2001), Joseph J. Ellis The Cause, 208–09 (2021).

13 U.S. Const. Art. II, Sect. 1, Cl. 5.

the new country, a caution to the divisions within the country caused by partisanship that might lead to "despotism and foreign influences."[14]

In late 2016, one author of this book, with Norman Eisen and Laurence Tribe, wrote an essay on the intent of the Emoluments Clause:

> As careful students of history, the Framers were painfully aware that entanglements between American officials and foreign powers could pose a creeping, insidious risk to the Republic. The Emoluments Clause was forged of their hard-won wisdom. It is no relic of a bygone era, but rather an expression of insight into the nature of the human condition and the prerequisites of self-governance.[15] …
>
> Even as they celebrated the wisdom and invoked the teachings of England's unwritten constitution, colonists decried the King's success at subverting limits on his own power. As Professor Gordon Wood has observed, "Throughout the eighteenth century the Crown had slyly avoided the blunt and clumsy instrument of prerogative, and instead had resorted to influencing the electoral process and the representatives in Parliament in order to gain its treacherous ends." Having spent years scrupulously dissecting the King's use of gifts, offices, and other inducements to manipulate Parliament, early Americans were obsessed with the many species of corruption and figuring out how best to combat them. American observations of European politics – including its corrupt culture of gift-giving and back-scratching – only further accentuated their fear that foreign interests, deploying gifts and titles, would seek to cripple the new republic. In the 1790s, this was no hypothetical concern: foreign meddling could doom a young nation.[16]

Edmund Jennings Randolph, speaking at the Virginia Convention to ratify the Constitution, described the Emoluments Clause as applying to the President, and violation being grounds for impeachment:

> There is another provision against the danger mentioned by the honorable member, of the President receiving emoluments from foreign powers. If discovered he may be impeached. If he be not impeachable he may be displaced at the end of the four years … I consider, therefore, that he is restrained from receiving any present or emoluments whatever. It is impossible to guard better against corruption.[17]

[14] Washington's Farewell Address to the People of the United States, *supra* note 12.

[15] Norman L. Eisen. Richard W. Painter, & Laurence H. Tribe, *The Emoluments Clause: Its Text, Meaning, and Application to Donald Trump*, THE BROOKINGS INSTITUTION (Dec. 16, 2016).

[16] *Id.* at 5–6, citing GORDON WOOD, THE CREATION OF THE AMERICAN REPUBLIC, 1776–1787 33 (1969); ZEPHYR TEACHOUT, CORRUPTION IN AMERICA: FROM BENJAMIN FRANKLIN'S SNUFF BOX TO CITIZENS UNITED 37–40 (2014) (discussing scholarship by Gordon Wood and others); Zephyr Teachout, *The Anti-Corruption Principle*, 94 CORNELL L. REV. 341 (2009).

[17] DAVID ROBERTSON, DEBATES AND OTHER PROCEEDINGS OF THE CONVENTION OF VIRGINIA 345 (2nd ed. 1805), quoted and discussed in Eisen, Painter, & Tribe, *supra* note 15.

Ambassadors also were targets of foreign gift giving and were expected to comply with the Emoluments Clause. King Louis XVI of France, for example, bestowed on Benjamin Franklin, American Ambassador to France, a snuff box bearing a royal portrait surrounded by 408 diamonds. Franklin asked Congress for approval to keep the box.[18]

Today, Congress in the Foreign Gifts and Decorations Act has consented to some foreign gifts valued up to $480.[19] With very few exceptions, all else is prohibited. As mentioned above, this ban includes not just gifts but "emoluments," or profits and benefits, from foreign governments.

But the Emoluments Clause has not been enforced, at least with respect to the President. Other executive branch officials can be fired by the President or by their appointing officer for violating the Emoluments Clause, but only Congress can fire the President through impeachment. And that's not likely. There are no criminal penalties attached to violations of the Emoluments Clause. Congress could enact such a criminal statute but has not done so.

The Emoluments Clause was not controversial for the presidency until Donald Trump assumed office in 2017. No previous president had significant business dealings with foreign governments. On January 4, 2024, the House Oversight Committee Minority released a report documenting $7.8 million in payments from foreign governments to President Trump's hotel and apartment properties in Washington, DC, Las Vegas, and New York City while he was President.[20]

Saudi Arabia, Qatar, Kuwait, India, and Afghanistan were among the countries whose governments patronized Trump-owned properties. China alone paid more than $5.5 million to Trump's businesses. Qatar – the principal foreign funder of the Hamas terrorist organization – spent $456,744 at the Trump World Tower.[21] The House report said, "these countries spent – often lavishly – on apartments and hotel stays at Donald Trump's properties."[22] The payments did not go directly to Trump personally, but they went to businesses privately owned and controlled by him. Although the Trump administration took the position that only payments directly to a federal office holder are prohibited by the Emoluments Clause, this interpretation is difficult to reconcile with the constitutional intent, particularly if

[18] TEACHOUT, *supra* note 16 at 1–5. Article VI of the Articles of Confederation contained a similar foreign Emoluments Clause.

[19] 5 U.S.C. § 7342(a)(5)(A) (1967) (providing that "minimal value" of permitted foreign gifts shall be redefined in regulations prescribed by the Administrator of General Services to adjust for the consumer price index).

[20] White House for Sale: How Princes, Prime Ministers and Premiers Paid Off President Trump, Staff Report, Committee on Oversight and Accountability Democratic Staff, Rep. Jamie Raskin, Ranking Member, U.S. House of Representatives, January 4, 2024.

[21] *Id.* at 15–84.

[22] *Id.* at 10.

foreign governments make payments to a business majority owned by the President.

Another domestic provision of the Constitution, Article II, Section 1, Clause 7 prohibits the President from receiving emoluments from the United States government or from any of the individual states more than his salary: "The President shall, at stated Times, receive for his Services, a Compensation, which shall neither be increased nor diminished during the Period for which he shall have been elected, and he shall not receive within that Period any other Emolument from the United States, or any of them." This prohibits the President from receiving excess profits and benefits from the individual states as well as from the federal government. For example, if a state government or the federal government were to patronize a business owned by the President and pay an excessive price, that would likely be a violation of this domestic Emoluments Clause just as such patronage from a foreign government would violate the foreign Emoluments Clause.

Once again, enforcement is difficult if individual states give lucrative contracts to businesses owned by the President or the President causes executive branch agencies, such as the Secret Service, to contract with his businesses. For example, the Secret Service allegedly paid exorbitant rates – up to $1,185 a night per room – for agents to stay in Trump resorts at taxpayer expense.[23]

With no criminal law prohibiting violations of the Emoluments Clause, and no federal agency charged with enforcing compliance and investigating violations, each agency polices itself. This means that the President polices himself, or he doesn't. Civil litigation to enforce the Emoluments Clause has had mixed success.

In 2017, three separate groups of plaintiffs sued President Trump for his ongoing violations of the foreign and domestic Emoluments Clauses of the Constitution: (1) a suit in the Southern District of New York by Citizens for Responsibility and Ethics in Washington (CREW). One of the authors of this book (Painter) was vice chair and counsel, joined as plaintiff by businesses that compete with the Trump Organization; (2) a suit in the District of Maryland by the Attorney General of Maryland and the Attorney General of the District of Columbia, joined as plaintiffs by businesses that compete with the Trump Organization; and (3) a suit by virtually all of the Democrats in the House and Senate brought in the United States District Court for the District of Columbia.

Federal appeals courts eventually ruled on the legal standing of the plaintiffs in all three cases. Of these, only the individual businesses competing with the Trump Organization and state attorneys general suing on their behalf were held to have

[23] Barbara Sprunt, *Trump Hotels Charged His Secret Service Protectors "Exorbitant" Rates*, Nat'l Pub. Radio (Oct. 17, 2022), www.npr.org/2022/10/17/1129491352/trump-hotels-overcharged-secret-service-agents ("According to the documents, the Secret Service was charged as much as $1,185 per room per night, nearly five times the government rate, which is set by the General Services Administration").

standing (in the first and second of these cases). Public interest groups such as CREW were denied standing, as were members of Congress.[24]

The Department of Justice (DOJ) litigated all three of these cases on behalf of President Trump, defending his businesses' right to receive benefits from foreign governments, from the states, and from the federal government in violation of the Constitution. These legal services – DOJ defending Trump Organization emoluments at taxpayer expense – might themselves be a violation of the domestic Emoluments Clause because they constitute financial benefits to the President more than his salary.

President Trump appealed those rulings that gave standing to business groups to sue him under the Emoluments Clause, delaying the possibility of judicial enforcement of the clause until well past his first term in office. When Trump left office, the cases were dismissed by the Supreme Court as moot because the Emoluments Clause does not bind former presidents.[25] When Trump assumed office again in January 2025, the issue was no longer moot, although it remains to be seen whether any of the emoluments suits will be refiled.

11.4 DOES THE HATCH ACT APPLY TO THE PRESIDENT?

Most federal officials are prohibited from using their official position to influence a partisan election.[26] Federal employees must separate their personal capacity political involvement from their official capacity work for the government, avoiding use of government resources, their official government titles or the names of their departments, or their working hours for partisan political activity.

This is not true for the President. Most provisions of the Hatch Act do not apply to the President, or to members of Congress for that matter. Unlike other federal officers, the President, Vice President, and members of Congress must run for office, making strict separation of official and political capacities difficult. A president should not encourage a subordinate officer to violate the Hatch Act, and indeed the "Take Care" Clause of the Constitution implies that the President should affirmatively take steps to make sure that all officials comply with federal law.

How much care do presidents take to make sure their cabinet officials and high-ranking White House staff don't violate the Hatch Act? Perhaps not enough, as there

[24] *See also* Richard W. Painter, *Good Governance Paper No. 15*, *Enforcing the Emoluments Clause*, JUST SECURITY (Oct. 30, 2020) www.justsecurity.org/73148/good-governance-paper-no-15-enforcing-the-emoluments-clauses/ (discussing the procedural history of the emoluments cases in the Second, Fourth and District of Columbia Circuits).

[25] Order List: 592 US __ (Jan. 25, 2021), Trump, President of U.S. v. CREW et al., No. 20-330 ("The judgment is vacated, and the case is remanded to the United States Court of Appeals for the Second Circuit with instructions to dismiss the case as moot").

[26] *See* 5 U.S.C. § 7323 (1993) (providing that "Subject to the provisions of subsection (b), an employee ... may not ... use his official authority or influence for the purpose of interfering with or affecting the result of an election").

have been high-profile violations in just about every recent administration.[27] The Trump administration perhaps had the most frequent violations of the Hatch Act, some of which appeared to be encouraged by the President and high-ranking administration officials.[28] After an investigation by the Office of Special Counsel, Secretary Pompeo and others were later found to have violated the Hatch Act.[29]

The worst example of misuse of official position to influence an upcoming election was the scandal for which President Trump was impeached for the first time – withholding military aid to Ukraine to pressure the Ukrainian government into investigating Joe Biden and his son Hunter. State Department and Defense Department officials appeared to be under enormous pressure to use their official position to influence a partisan election, among other things a violation of the Hatch Act.

A common theme across all administrations, Democratic and Republican, is that many high-ranking White House officials, as well as cabinet officers, are engaged in "personal capacity" partisan political activity contemporaneously with their "official capacity" work leading the Executive Branch of the federal government. These roles are supposed to be separate. In practicality they blend in a way that encourages Hatch Act violations.

Since the Reagan administration there has been a White House Office of Political Affairs that advises the President on the political ramifications of his policy decisions, a legitimate official capacity concern, but where staff also in their "personal" capacity engage in political work for the President's re-election and/or other partisan elections for the President's political party. White House staff in this office often encourage cabinet members and other high-ranking officials to speak at political events, including fundraisers.[30]

[27] *See* U.S. Office of Special Counsel, Report of Prohibited Political Activity under the Hatch Act, O.S.C. File No. HA-12-1989 (Kathleen G. Sebelius) (reporting violations of the Hatch Act by Health and Human Services Secretary who in an official speech endorsed a Democratic Party primary candidate in North Carolina); Office of Special Counsel, Investigation of Political Activities by White House and Federal Agency Officials during the 2006 Midterm Elections at 33–34 (Jan. 2011).

[28] *See e.g. OSC Finds Kellyanne Conway Repeatedly Violated the Hatch Act, Recommends Removal from Federal Service*, USOSC: News (June 13, 2019), https://osc.gov/News/Pages/19-10-Kellyanne-Conway-Hatch-Act.aspx.

[29] *See* U.S. Off. of Special Counsel, Investigation of Political Activities by Senior Trump Administration Officials during the 2020 Presidential Election (Nov. 9, 2021) (finding Hatch Act violations of thirteen senior Trump administration officials prior to the 2020 election).

[30] *See* Richard W. Painter, Getting the Government America Deserves (2009), ch. 10 (discussing the White House office of Policial Affairs, which was headed by Karl Rove during the time the author was in the White House); Richard W. Painter, *The Separation of Politics and State*, New York Times (June 13, 2010), www.nytimes.com/2010/06/14/opinion/14painter .html (urging abolition of the White House Office of Political Affairs and restrictions on partisan political activity by senior White House officials); *The Hatch Act: The Challenges of Separating Politics from Policy, Hearing Before the H. Comm. on Oversight and Gov't Reform*, 112th Cong. 4 (June 21, 2011) (oral and written statements by Richard W. Painter) (urging similar reforms).

There are limits, however, on how much people can pressure federal employees, including political appointees, to engage in partisan political activity. Criminal provisions of the Hatch Act[31] prohibit anyone, including the President, from ordering or coercing any federal employee to engage in partisan political activity:

> It shall be unlawful for any person to intimidate, threaten, command, or coerce, or attempt to intimidate, threaten, command, or coerce, any employee of the Federal Government as defined in section 7322(1) of title 5, United States Code, to engage in, or not to engage in, any political activity, including, but not limited to, voting or refusing to vote for any candidate or measure in any election, making or refusing to make any political contribution, or working or refusing to work on behalf of any candidate. Any person who violates this section shall be fined under this title or imprisoned not more than three years, or both.

Unlike much of the Hatch Act, 18 USC § 610 is a criminal provision, and, this provision also applies to the President and Vice President.

Consider whether any of the following alleged conduct of President Trump in fall 2020 violated this statute:

> President Trump forced the State Department on Friday to commit to releasing at least some of Hillary Clinton's emails before next month's election, resurrecting a four-year-old issue in hopes that it would prove as helpful to his political prospects as it was when he defeated her in 2016.
>
> Trailing badly in the polls and eager to change the subject from the coronavirus, Mr. Trump succeeded in compelling Secretary of State Mike Pompeo to announce that he would make public the emails even as Attorney General William P. Barr resisted pressure from the President to prosecute Democrats like former Vice President Joseph R. Biden Jr., this year's Democratic nominee.[32]
>
> President Trump publicly pressured the Justice Department on Friday to move against his political adversaries and complained that Attorney General William P. Barr is not doing enough to deliver results of a probe into how the Obama administration investigated possible collusion between Russia and the 2016 Trump campaign.
>
> The delayed report is "a disgrace," and Trump's 2016 Democratic opponent, Hillary Clinton, should be jailed, Trump said in a rambling radio interview, one day after he argued on Twitter that his current Democratic opponent, Joe Biden, is a criminal who should be barred from running.[33]

[31] 18 U.S.C. § 610 (1993).

[32] Peter Baker, Maggie Haberman, Katie Benner, Lara Jakes, & Michael S. Schmidt, *Election Less Than a Month Away, Trump Leans on Barr and Pompeo for a Lift*, New York Times (Oct. 9, 2020).

[33] Anne Gearan Matt Zapotosky, Karoun Demirjian, & Josh Dawsey, *Trump, Lagging in Polls, Pressures Justice Dept. to Target Democrats and Criticizes Barr*, Wash. Post. (Oct. 9, 2020).

> Trump turned his frustration toward Secretary of State Mike Pompeo and Attorney General William Barr, lamenting that they had not done enough to speed the process of implicating his political opponents.
>
> "To be honest, Bill Barr is going to go down as either the greatest attorney general in the history of the country or he's going to go down as, you know, a very sad situation," Trump said. "I'll be honest with you. He's got all the information he needs. They want to get more, more, more. They keep getting more. I said, you don't need any more."[34]

One of the authors of this book (Painter) joined Professor Claire Finkelstein in filing a complaint with the Public Integrity Division of the Department of Justice about Trump's apparent violation of 18 USC Section 610.[35] This conduct, however, was never prosecuted. It might not have even been investigated. After the election, President Trump's political pressure on Executive Branch agencies, particularly the Justice Department, intensified in his effort to overturn the election result, leading to other criminal charges that eventually were brought against him in 2023.[36] The point here is that stricter enforcement of the Hatch Act, including the criminal provisions in 18 USC Section 610 before the election, might have discouraged the President's misuse of his official position after the election that targeted the democratic framework itself.

The problem is that the Hatch Act is enforced by Executive Branch agencies acting on investigations by the Office of Special Counsel. Criminal statutes are enforced by the Department of Justice, all under the command and control of the President. As discussed in Chapter 16 in this book, under the topic of investigating and prosecuting the President, the "unitary executive theory" under which the President controls the Executive Branch, including hiring and firing of senior officials, can make enforcement of the law extraordinarily difficult.

11.5 DO FEDERAL ELECTION LAWS APPLY TO THE PRESIDENT?

A president runs for reelection in his personal political capacity, not in his official capacity. The same federal election laws that apply to other federal candidates also apply to the President. No President has brought successfully an action challenging federal election laws as incompatible with Article II. However, President Trump defended his actions after the 2020 election as he argued that part of a president's Article II powers is to assure fair elections, and that a president can, in his official capacity, intervene to combat "voter fraud" and other irregularities in elections,

[34] Brett Samuels, *Trump Swipes at Barr, Pompeo, Wray in Return to Russia Investigation, Clinton Emails*, The Hill (Oct. 8, 2020).

[35] *See* Letter, dated Oct. 26, 2020, from Claire O. Finkelstein and Richard W. Painter to Mr. Corey R. Amundson, Chief, Public Integrity Section, United States Department of Justice.

[36] Trump v. United States, 603 U.S. 593 (2024).

including his own election.[37] There is nothing directly and specifically in the Constitution to support this election argument.

Part of the federal election laws binding on presidents, and other candidates, is the financial disclosure regime mandated by Congress and implemented by the Federal Election Commission. While the Supreme Court has struck down restrictions on spending by federal campaigns,[38] federal law still requires that campaign *contributions* and campaign *expenditures* be reported in publicly available reports.

This was the problem President Trump ran into shortly after winning the 2016 presidential election. His campaign finance reports for the fourth quarter of 2016 needed to disclose all expenditures by his campaign or by him personally in support of his campaign. This included expenditures in support of the campaign by the Trump Organization. The $120,000 payment to Stormy Daniels in October 2016, to persuade her to remain silent about her sexual affair with him just before the November election, was a campaign expenditure. It was not reported. Trump's lawyer, Michael Cohen, who secretly routed the payment to Daniels through his own bank account, was investigated and indicted in connection with the payment. Ultimately, he pleaded guilty and was sent to prison. Trump was not indicted, as he was President at the time.[39]

This is where New York Manhattan District Attorney Alvin Bragg picked up the case. He successfully prosecuted Trump for violation of New York laws prohibiting falsification of business records to conceal another crime – here the underlying federal campaign finance violation. We discuss in Part III of this book the promises and perils of states prosecuting presidents, and former presidents. The point here is that federal election laws apply to the President, and presidents who violate those laws presumably are subject to the same civil and criminal penalties that could be imposed on other candidates.

Once again, however, the unitary executive theory of presidential power could undermine evenhanded enforcement of election laws. The Federal Election Commission (FEC) is an independent Executive Branch agency with commissioners representing both political parties. The FEC is supposed to be the "umpire" in elections, calling "balls and strikes" in campaign finance, and disclosure compliance, without regard to partisan politics. But the FEC is often deadlocked, and thus unable to make decisions, or dominated by a majority aligned with the President's political party.

In Chapter 1 of this book, we discussed the power of the President to remove his own appointees in Executive Branch agencies. For now, statutory arrangements

[37] Trump v. United States, 603 U.S. 593 (2024). Indeed, Article I, Section 4 of the Constitution states that the "Times, Places, Manner" of federal elections shall be established by the legislature.

[38] Buckley v. Valeo, 424 U.S. 1 (1976). *See also* Citizens United v. FEC 558 U.S. 310 (2010).

[39] *See* discussion in Part III of this book of the DOJ's refusal to indict a sitting president. After he left office, the DOJ pursued other charges against him but not this one.

protecting members of independent agencies from removal without cause are constitutional.[40] But the Supreme Court is increasingly hostile to the statutory constraints on removal power.[41] If the Court overturns *Humphrey's Executor* and applies the unitary executive theory – that is, unrestrained presidential removal power – to members of independent agencies, the President's power and control over the FEC will be complete.

[40] *See* Humphrey's Executor v. Federal Trade Commission, 295 U.S. 602 (1935) (upholding statute creating the FTC with commissioners only removable for cause).

[41] *See* Seila Law v. Consumer Financial Protection Bureau, 591 U.S. 197 (2020) (holding unconstitutional the statutory provision that the director of the CFPB could only be removed for cause).

12

Corruption in the Presidency

Corruption is an ancient problem.[1] Edmund Burke, as a member of the English Parliament, denounced the corrupt influence on government by corporations, particularly the East India Company.[2] After the 1773 Tea Act granted that company a monopoly on sale of tea in America, colonists dumped their tea into the Boston harbor, an event that became known as the Boston Tea Party. Americans in the past and now are deeply concerned with being governed by money.

The corruption issue is vitally important to discussion of presidential power, which is particularly dangerous when it is used corruptly. Much of this book considers whether the President could make himself a king, the opposite of what the Framers intended. This section is about whether the twenty-first-century American President, who has acquired some of the powers and immunities of a king, will act like a corrupt king. Today restraints on presidential corruption are minimal, and getting narrower since the presidential immunity case of *Trump v. United States*.

Chapter 11 of this book discussed the Founders' fear of corruption, particularly by foreign governments. The solution they saw in the Constitution's Emoluments Clause prohibited federal officers from receiving profits and benefits from foreign governments. But the Framers omitted one thing: other than impeachment, there is no specific mechanism in the Constitution for enforcement.

Even criminal prosecution of a president for corruption is now exceedingly difficult due to the Supreme Court's decision in 2024 that a president is entitled

[1] The late Judge John T. Noonan of the Ninth Circuit Court of Appeals recorded the history of bribery in his seminal book *Bribes*, published shortly after President Reagan appointed him to the Ninth Circuit Court of Appeals. John T. Noonan, Jr., Bribes (1986).

[2] Mr. Burke's Speech, On the 1st December 1783 [Upon the Question for the Speaker's Leaving the Chair, in Order for the House to Resolve Itself into a Committee on Mr. Fox's East India Bill] (describing the East India Company's abuse of global monopoly powers bestowed on it by Parliament).

to a presumption of immunity from criminal prosecution for official acts, and even in a trial for crimes in a president's personal capacity – such as receiving a bribe – evidence of the President's motives for official acts are now inadmissible.[3]

Furthermore, presidents, unlike other officers and employees of the Executive Branch, are not subject to the criminal statute prohibiting official acts that conflict with personal financial interests.[4] Financial disclosure rules do require the President to file a financial disclosure report every year.[5]

12.1 THE SUPREME COURT NARROWS THE DEFINITION OF CORRUPTION

The first problem is that the Supreme Court has narrowed considerably the reach of anti-corruption statutes. This has occurred at the same time as several of the Justices have had ethics scandals of their own.[6]

This current trend of narrowing criminal liability by the Court started in the criminal prosecution of Enron Corporation's Chief Financial Officer Jeffrey Skilling. The Court, in 2010, ruled for Skilling, limiting the reach of the federal Theft of Honest Services statute to bribery and "kickback" schemes, not other types of self-dealing and conflicts of interest. The Court said that the language of the criminal statute otherwise would be unconstitutionally vague.[7]

Next, the Governor of Virginia, Robert McDonnell, was convicted of exchanging official meetings for gifts to himself and his wife. In *McDonnell v. United States*,[8] the Court in 2016 held that an "official act" for purposes of the federal bribery statute is an action that "involves a specific exercise of formal governmental power."[9] Agreeing to a meeting in exchange for a gift or contacting another official on behalf of the gift giver is insufficient to be an "official act" under the bribery statute, according to the Court. Buying access to a public official, apparently, is legal so long as the public official does not promise to do a specific official act in exchange for the bribe.

More recently, in 2024, the Court ruled in favor of James Snyder, the former mayor of Portage, Indiana, who had been convicted for receiving a large payment from a city contractor *after* he approved the contract. The Court distinguished bribery, which is criminalized in every state and at the federal level, from a gratuity (a "thank you" gift to a public official *after* an official act) which is a lesser crime in

[3] Trump v. United States, 603 US 593 (2024).

[4] 18 U.S.C. § 208 (1962). (applying to all Executive Branch employees except the President and Vice President).

[5] *See* discussion of the financial disclosure requirements in Chapter 11.

[6] *See* Richard W. Painter, *SCOTUS House: Can a Supreme Court Ethics Lawyer and Inspector General Help Get this Fraternity under Control*, XXXVII Georgetown Journal of Legal Ethics, 347 (2024).

[7] Skilling v. United States, 561 U.S. 358 (2010).

[8] United States v. McDonnell, 579 U.S. 550 (2016).

[9] *Id.*

some jurisdictions and is not a crime at all in others.[10] The current federal criminal code, 18 USC § 201(b), provides that the crime of bribery occurs whenever anyone "directly or indirectly, corruptly gives, offers or promises anything of value to any public official … with the intent to influence any official act." 18 USC § 201(c), by contrast, prohibits "gratuities," which is the acceptance of a reward *after* an official act even if there is no corrupt intent before the official act, but is considered a lesser crime. But those statutes don't apply directly to state and local government officials. The Court in *Snyder v. United States* ruled that a separate federal criminal statute does not apply to gratuities received by state and local officials. 18 USC § 666(a)(1)(B) only prohibits bribes and not gratuities, which are left to regulation under state laws.[11] Some states don't prohibit gratuities at all.

What do these cases have to do with presidential power? A lot, unless the United States wants to return to the days of the Grant administration when many of the President's appointees as well as state and local government officials were allegedly on the take.[12] Anti-corruption laws were passed by Congress in the late nineteenth and twentieth centuries to deal with this problem. But if the Supreme Court continues to interprets them as narrowly as possible, perhaps we are back where we started on a lack of enforcement. The definition of "bribery" in federal criminal statutes, which now requires an express quid pro quo, is considerably narrower than the Founders' understanding of the word "bribery" which appears in the Impeachment Clause of the Constitution.[13] Yet as discussed in Part III of this book impeachment as an accountability mechanism for abuse of presidential power has been largely ineffective.

12.2 CAMPAIGN FINANCE

The greatest damage the Supreme Court has done to the battle against corruption is in campaign finance.

[10] 18 U.S.C. § 201 (1962).

[11] Snyder v. United States, 603 U.S. _ (2024), Slip Op. at 4: "Importantly, because bribery can corrupt the official act, Congress treats bribery as a far more serious offense than gratuities. For example, if a federal official accepts a bribe, federal bribery law provides for a 15-year maximum prison sentence. *See* 18 U.S.C. §201(b). By contrast, if a federal official accepts a prohibited gratuity, federal gratuities law sets a two-year maximum prison sentence. *See* § 201(c)." In Snyder, the Court ruled that a separate federal criminal statute was applicable to state and local officials, 18 U.S.C. § 666(a)(1)(B), only prohibits bribes and not gratuities, which are left to regulation under state laws.

[12] *See* Corruptions of the Grant Ring, Speech of Hon. John F. Farnsworth, United States Congressman (R–IL), Reviewing the Corruption and Abuses of the Grant Administration (1872).

[13] For discussion of the difference between quid pro quo bribery as understood in judicial construction of modern criminal statutes and the Founders' broader understanding of corruption, *see* Richard W. Painter, *Bribery Law: Is Anything Left?*, 46 CARDOZO L. REV. 1775 (2025); and ZEPHYR TEACHOUT, CORRUPTION IN AMERICA: FROM BENJAMIN FRANKLIN'S SNUFF BOX TO CITIZENS UNITED, 110–11 (2016).

Congress in 1907, during the Theodore Roosevelt administration, passed the Tillman Act[14] that prohibits donations from corporate treasuries to political campaigns. Ever since then, political operatives have exploited loopholes to get around the law, with the Supreme Court lending a helping hand.

The most notorious of these cases is *Citizens United v. Federal Election Commission*,[15] in which the Court, in 2010, struck down an act by Congress that it said unconstitutionally interfered with corporations' First Amendment right to spend money on electioneering communications. The Court held that corporations, just like billionaires, are people too and have the constitutional right to spend as much money as they want influencing elections. In other words, money is speech. The Court held there was insufficient evidence of a traditional *quid pro quo* between political spending and politicians benefiting from such largess to show a compelling state interest in regulating this form of "speech." Subsequent Court of Appeals decisions have used similar reasoning to allow unlimited expenditures on Super PACs (Political Action Committees).[16]

This book is not the place to dissect the logic or illogic of the *Citizen United* decision.[17] But the Court's reasoning in *Citizens United* is based on the premise that a *quid pro quo* relationship justifying federal regulation of campaign finance cannot easily be shown. *Quid pro quo* must be proven, not assumed, even to allow regulation designed to prevent corruption in the first place. This is an extremely high bar to meet, making it virtually impossible to regulate corruption of elected officials, including presidents, by way of political expenditures.

Although some restrictions on direct contributions to campaigns and political parties have been upheld by the Court,[18] unlimited expenditures both by campaigns and by dark money organizations are constitutionally protected. As Justices Sandra

[14] 34 Stat. 864 (1907).

[15] Citizens United v. FEC, 558 U.S. 310 (2010). For the claim that "money is speech," *see also* Buckley v. Valeo, 424 U.S. 1 (1976).

[16] *See* Lieu et al. v. FEC, No. 19-5072 (D.C. Cir., 2019), Order (dismissing suit brought against the FEC by Rep. Ted Lieu, Rep. Walter Jones, Senator Jeff Merkley, State Senator John Howe, Zephyr Teachout, and Michael Wager asking the Circuit Court to overturn its decision in SpeechNow.org v. FEC, 599 F.3d 686 (D.C. Cir. 2010) (en banc), cert. denied, 562 U.S. 1003 (2010) (interpreting the Citizens United holding to allow unlimited spending on Super PACs). *See also* Buckley v. Valeo, 424 U.S. 1 (1976).

[17] *See* Richard W. Painter, *Taxation only with Representation: The Conservative Conscience and Campaign Finance Reform* (Take Back our Republic 2016); Edmond and Lily Safra Center for Legal Ethics, Harvard University, Seminar 2014–15, https://ssrn.com/abstract=2733787. *See also* Len Niehoff & E. Thomas Sullivan, Free Speech: From Core Values to Current Debates, 160–61 (2022).

[18] *See* Buckley v. Valeo, 424 U.S. 1 (1976) (holding that dollar limitations on contributions by individuals to campaigns do not violate the First Amendment but that limitations on spending by political campaigns do violate the First Amendment); McConnell v. Federal Election Commission. 540 U.S. 93 (2003) (upholding limits on soft money contributions used to register voters and increase attendance at the polls); McCutcheon v. FEC, 572 U.S. 185 (2014) (striking down aggregate limits on donor contributions to multiple candidates).

Day O'Connor and John Paul Stevens famously wrote in *McConnell v. Federal Election Commission*, one of the few cases upholding campaign finance laws, "money, like water, will always find an outlet."[19] And so it does.

Presidential elections, of course, are the most expensive. In 2020, for example, the federal election cost almost $14 billion, double the previous presidential election cycle; $6.6 billion was spent on the presidential race alone and $7.2 billion for the House and Senate races combined.[20] After all this spending every four years, one can wonder who really chose the President? Where do the President's true loyalties lie?

12.3 CORRUPTION AND THE ARMS TRADE

Part I of this book already discussed President Eisenhower's worries about the political influence of the "military industrial complex" and its significant role in driving the defense budget up close to a trillion dollars in 2025. Without restating the specifics, it is important to note here, in Part II of this book, that constraining wasteful defense spending is an important responsibility of the President. Insistence that the Defense Department strictly adhere to ethics rules is part of that responsibility. This means limiting the revolving door of senior officials between the Department and military contractors. Refusing or limiting contracts with companies that spend excessive amounts on PACs, electioneering communications, and other ways of influencing elections might help break down the link between campaign finance and defense spending.

There are other foreign arms sales that are not included in the defense budget but also consistently subsidized by the taxpayer when a portion of the cost is underwritten by the United States government. Military aid, for example, in 2024 was provided to Ukraine and Israel. Because these expenditures usually require the consent of Congress, the issue is not one of presidential power alone. However, regardless of the merits of the arms sale, it is not irrelevant that the defense industry has a powerful voice in Washington.

Substantive issues involving the arms trade and defense spending are discussed in Chapter 3 of this book. The issue addressed here is that part of the President's responsibility as Commander in Chief is not just to spend money on armaments because he can, or because Congress authorizes it, but to make sure that the arms industry, through campaign contributions, lobbying, and the revolving door between corporations and government, is not adding unnecessarily to an annual defense budget already approaching $1 trillion dollars.

[19] McConnell v. Federal Election Commission, 540 U.S. 93 (2003).

[20] *The Most Expensive Race Ever*, Brennan Center for Justice (Nov. 11, 2020), www.brennancenter.org/our-work/analysis-opinion/most-expensive-election-ever (citing statistics from Open Secrets).

12.4 PRESIDENTIAL MOTIVE AS A FACTOR IN THE USE OF POWER

Is the President's motive for an official act relevant to assessment of presidential power and accountability? In some cases, it is difficult to ascertain the President's motive. But it is also unrealistic to discount entirely the President's motive when assessing the validity of a particular act.[21]

Incorporating evidence of the President's motive can be difficult for a court that is trying to articulate broad parameters of power, responsibility, and accountability for all presidents, not just the President in the case presently before the court. But broad principles in specific cases are applied to facts, and evidence of the President's motives is among the relevant facts. Only two members of the Supreme Court (Justices Sotomayor and Jackson) have been judges in federal trial courts where legal rules are routinely applied to particular facts. Most of the Justices do not have this experience and, for this or other reasons, often discount factual evidence of the President's motive in a case. They fall back on broad formulaic principles of presidential power.

Consider, for example, the Supreme Court's ruling in *Trump v. Hawaii*.[22] The Court gave little weight to overwhelming evidence of what President Trump was really trying to do with his travel ban targeting six predominantly Muslim countries by excluding immigrants because of their religion.[23]

The Court recognized that the President's motives were suspect:

> At the heart of plaintiffs' case is a series of statements by the President and his advisers casting doubt on the official objective of the Proclamation. For example, while a candidate on the campaign trail, the President published a "Statement on Preventing Muslim Immigration" that called for a "total and complete shutdown of Muslims entering the United States until our country's representatives can figure out what is going on." That statement remained on his campaign website until May 2017. Then-candidate Trump also stated that "Islam hates us" and asserted that the United States was "having problems with Muslims coming into the country." ... One week after his inauguration, the President issued EO-1. In a television interview, one of the President's campaign advisers explained that when the President "first announced it, he said, 'Muslim ban.' He called me up. He said, 'Put a commission together. Show me the right way to do it legally.'" Shortly before the release of the Proclamation, he stated that the "travel ban ... should be far

[21] Constitutional law scholar Alan Rozenshtein suggests that courts and Congress should consider the character of a particular president when determining the scope of the President's power. Alan Rozenshtein, *The Virtuous Executive*, 108 MINN. L. REV. 605 (2023). Given the practical difficulties with assessing a president's character and then incorporating a meaningful assessment of character into case law on presidential power, we have narrowed the discussion here to focus on the President's motives for a particular act.

[22] Trump v. Hawaii, 585 U.S. 667 (2018).

[23] Rozenshtein, *supra* note 21 (discussing the Court's refusal to inquire into the President's motive in Trump v. Hawaii).

larger, tougher, and more specific," but "stupidly that would not be politically correct." More recently, on November 29, 2017, the President retweeted links to three anti-Muslim propaganda videos. In response to questions about those videos, the President's deputy press secretary denied that the President thinks Muslims are a threat to the United States.[24]

But the Court then discounted the value of this evidence of President Trump's motive when applying a "rational basis" standard, the lowest level of scrutiny, in its constitutional review of the travel ban under the First Amendment:

> Plaintiffs argue that this President's words strike at fundamental standards of respect and tolerance, in violation of our constitutional tradition. But the issue before us is not whether to denounce the statements. It is instead the significance of those statements in reviewing a Presidential directive, neutral on its face, addressing a matter within the core of executive responsibility. In doing so, we must consider not only the statements of a particular President, but also the authority of the Presidency itself.
>
> … The Proclamation, moreover, is facially neutral toward religion. Plaintiffs therefore ask the Court to probe the sincerity of the stated justifications for the policy by reference to extrinsic statements – many of which were made before the President took the oath of office …
>
> [The rational basis] standard of review considers whether the entry policy is plausibly related to the Government's stated objective to protect the country and improve vetting processes. As a result, we may consider plaintiffs' extrinsic evidence, but will uphold the policy so long as it can reasonably be understood to result from a justification independent of unconstitutional grounds.[25]

The Court thus based its decision principally on abstract concepts of presidential power, and the executive order's facial neutrality toward religion. This abstract approach to jurisprudence, focusing on legal rules and giving relatively little weight to motives and other characteristics of the persons involved in a particular case, has been criticized,[26] but is common with appellate courts.

Trump v. Hawaii is perhaps a case where the Supreme Court went too far. It seemed clear to many people in America, including Trump's supporters who wanted him to ban Muslim immigration, that he was doing exactly what he had said he would do during the campaign. It is also clear to most constitutional lawyers that a per se "Muslim ban" would be unconstitutional under the First Amendment. Calling it something else simply to arrive at a different conclusion strained the credibility of the Trump administration and of the Supreme Court that bought that argument.

[24] Trump v. Hawaii, 585 U.S. 667 (2018) (citations to the record omitted).

[25] *Id.* at 705 (citations omitted).

[26] *See* John T. Noonan, Jr., Persons and Masks of the Law, xvii (1975) (criticizing this abstract approach to legal decision-making).

Yet another example of the Court turning a blind eye to "motive" is *Trump v. United States*,[27] the 2024 immunity decision discussed in Part III. There, the Court not only bestowed immunity from criminal prosecution on the President for official acts but also ruled that evidence of the President's motive for an official act cannot be inquired into in a criminal trial for a personal capacity act, for example accepting a bribe in exchange for the official act. Evidence of the President's motive for an official act cannot even be introduced, the Court held. As explained in more detail in Part III, such an exclusionary rule could make prosecution for bribery or other personal capacity crimes very difficult.

The more general problem is that the motive for a president's official act – whether a ban on immigrants or an official act aimed at overturning an election result – is in the record in each of these cases. It is relevant even if its weight is ultimately downplayed or ignored by the Court. Courts routinely inquire into the motives of official acts of other government officials, for example a police officer in making a traffic stop or a state university in denying tenure to a professor. Why should courts be more reticent to inquire into the motive for official acts of the President?

The answer to this question turns on a theme that has arisen repeatedly throughout this book – presidential exceptionalism. This is the concept that the President somehow needs to be treated differently under the law to carry out his duties under Article II of the Constitution. And here we return to the fears of the Founders discussed in the Introduction: Having too weak a president is dangerous for national security and weakens the internal functioning of the federal government. But having a president who is beyond the reach of the law is a danger to the Republic itself and a direct threat to the rule of law.[28] A president whose motives cannot be inquired into by a court falls in the latter category. We ask whether the Court's recent decisions in the two *Trump* cases will lead to an "imperial presidency" with much greater presidential power than the Founders intended.[29]

[27] 603 U.S. 593 (2024).

[28] E. Thomas Sullivan & Toni M. Massaro, The Arc of Due Process in American Constitutional Law, 1, 3–12, 33, 34 (2013).

[29] Arthur M. Schlesinger, Jr., The Imperial Presidency (1973).

13

Taking Care of Federal Lands

The President not only has the enumerated constitutional powers of Commander in Chief, and head of the Executive Branch, but also is the largest property manager in the United States, and apart from Russia and China, the world. The President shares with Congress management of federal land and collection of rents, royalties, and other fees for commercial uses of federal land.

When there are competing uses of federal land – mining, timber, oil and gas extraction, recreation, wildlife protection, housing, and conservation of land for future generations – the President and Congress share power and responsibility to decide who and what gets priority.

13.1 THE INTERIOR DEPARTMENT

The federal government owns about 640 million acres of land, between a quarter and a third of the total land in the United States.[1] Under the United States Constitution, Congress holds this land in trust.[2] Public lands may only be disposed of with congressional authorization.[3] But Congress has delegated many decisions

[1] This section is based on prior testimony provided by one of the authors before the United States House of Representatives. *See* Testimony of Richard W. Painter before the United States House of Representatives Committee on Natural Resources, Subcommittee on Oversight and Investigations, Hearing on April 30, 2024.

[2] Article IV, Section 3, Clause 2 provides: "The Congress shall have Power to dispose of and make all needful Rules and Regulations respecting the Territory or other Property belonging to the United States; and nothing in this Constitution shall be so construed as to Prejudice any Claims of the United States, or of any particular State."

[3] The Supreme Court has held that the power of Congress is exclusive. United States v. Fitzgerald, 40 U.S. (15 Pet.) 407, 421 (1841); Utah Power & Light Co. v. United States, 243 U.S. 389, 403-04 (1917), although in the absence of congressional action courts often defer to the executive branch. United States v. Midwest Oil Co., 236 U.S. 459, 469 (1915). Congress has from time to time reasserted control over federal lands. *See e.g.* 43 U.S.C. §315. Grazing districts; establishment; restrictions; prior rights; rights of way; hearing and notice; hunting or fishing rights. Pub. L. No. 94-579, § 704(a), 90 Stat. 2792 (1976).

concerning federal lands to the Department of the Interior. Because the Interior Department controls such vast swaths of federal land, and much of the US's natural resources, attempts to corrupt the Department and get preferential access to federal lands are persistent. The Interior Department has had multiple scandals for over a century.

In April 1922, Senator John Kendrick (D-WY) demanded investigation of a secret deal in which Interior Secretary Albert Fall, without competitive bidding, leased the US Naval Petroleum Reserve at Wyoming's Teapot Dome to a private oil company. Senator Robert La Follette (R-WI) and the Senate Committee on Public Lands investigated. Prosecutions soon followed. Fall was the first former cabinet officer to go to prison.[4]

More recently, in 2005, lobbyist Jack Abramoff faced criminal charges for corrupt dealings with clients and the government. Much of his activity centered on the Department of the Interior and misuse of statutes and rules intended to allow Native American tribes specific privileges in lobbying the government about use of tribal land and federal land. Abramoff used – indeed abused – these federal laws to make profits for himself and the casino industry. J. Steven Griles, former Deputy Secretary of the Interior, was sentenced to ten months in prison for obstruction of the US Senate's investigation into Abramoff.[5]

The Inspector General's report on an Interior Department program that managed oil and gas royalties from federal lands found:

> That eight officials in the royalty program accepted gifts from energy companies whose value exceeded limits set by ethics rules including golf, ski, and paintball outings; meals and drinks; and tickets to a Toby Keith concert, a Houston Texans football game and a Colorado Rockies baseball game … Several of the officials "frequently consumed alcohol at industry functions, and used cocaine and marijuana, and had sexual relationships with oil and gas company representatives."[6]

During the Trump administration, Interior Secretary Ryan Zinke faced allegations that he misused his position to advance a commercial development project in his Montana hometown and he may have lied to an agency ethics official about his involvement. He was also accused of making false statements during a probe of a Native American casino development.[7] Zinke was the subject of over a dozen

4 Albert B. Fall v. United States, 49 F.2d 506 (D.C. Cir. 1931) (conviction affirmed).

5 *See* Department of Justice Press Release, *Former Interior Deputy Secretary Steven Griles Sentenced to 10 Months in Prison for Obstructing U.S. Senate Investigation into Abramoff Corruption Scandal* (June 26, 2007), www.justice.gov/archive/opa/pr/2007/June/07_crm_455.html.

6 Charles Savage, *Sex, Drug Use and Graft Cited in Interior Department*, New York Times (Sept. 10, 2008), www.nytimes.com/2008/09/11/washington/11royalty.html.

7 The OIG found that Zinke used his office and taxpayer resources for personal gain, used a personal email account to communicate information, and may have lied to the OIG about it. *See* www.washingtonpost.com/national/health-science/interior-secretary-zinke-resigns-amid-investigations/2018/12/15/481f9104-0077-11e9-ad40-cdfd0e0dd65a_story.html and www.washingtonpost.com/climate-environment/2022/08/24/ryan-zinke-misled-investigators-watchdog-report/.

investigations by either the Interior Department Office of the Inspector General (OIG), the Government Accountability Office (GAO), or the Office of Special Counsel (OSC). No criminal charges were filed. None of these allegations has been proven in court.

Zinke's successor, Interior Secretary David Bernhardt, disclosed over two dozen former clients and employers who presented potential conflicts of interest.[8] Bernhardt's appointment is just one example of the longstanding close ties between senior Interior Department officials and private industry.

On May 19, 2022, the Interior Department OIG released a report of its investigation into whether Bernhardt violated the Lobbying Disclosure Act of 1995 when he represented Westlands Water District as a lobbyist before and after serving as Interior Secretary.[9] Bernhardt refused to be interviewed. The OIG was not able to make a determination. On January 19, 2023, OIG issued a report on whether Bernhardt violated the Ethics Pledge and conflict of interest rules by participating in matters involving the California Central Valley Project, a large federal water project under the jurisdiction of the Bureau of Reclamation.[10] Once again, Bernhardt declined to be interviewed. OIG did not reach a determination.

On May 11, 2022, Committee Democrats made a criminal referral to the Department of Justice outlining evidence of a *quid pro quo* between Trump administration officials, including Bernhardt, and real estate developer Mike Ingram, the owner of El Dorado Holdings, which proposed to build the Villages at Vigneto (Vigneto), a large housing and commercial development near the endangered San Pedro River in Benson, Arizona. At the same time as the Army Corp of Engineers permit for the project was reopened, Ingram and other Arizona donors gave about a quarter of a million dollars to the Trump Victory Fund and the Republican National Committee. The question, not yet proven one way or the other, is whether this donation was in exchange for the US Fish and Wildlife Service changing its position about a Clean Water Act permit for Vigneto.[11]

8 Marc Rehmann, *David Bernhardt Is President Trump's Most Conflicted Cabinet Nominee*, American Progress (Mar. 15, 2019), www.americanprogress.org/article/david-bernhardt-president-trumps-conflicted-cabinet-nominee/.

9 Office of Inspector General, Former Secretary's Alleged Lobbying Disclosure Act Violation before Joining the U.S. Department of the Interior as Deputy Secretary, Report No. 20-0393, Department of the Interior (May 19, 2022), www.oversight.gov/sites/default/files/documents/reports/2022-05/WebRedactFormerSecretarysAllegedLDAViolation.pdf.

10 Office of the Inspector General, Allegations of Ethics Violations by Former U.S. Department of the Interior Secretary Were Not Substantiated, Report Number: 19-0313, Department of the Interior (Jan. 19, 2023), www.doioig.gov/sites/default/files/2021-migration/WebRedacted_AllegationsofEthicsViolationsbyFormerDOISecretaryWereNotSubstantiated.pdf.

11 House Committee on Natural Resources, Letter of Criminal Referral to U.S. Department of Justice, U.S. House of Representatives (May 11, 2022), https://democrats-naturalresources.house.gov/download/grijalva-porter-to-doj-regarding-villages-at-vigneto&download=1.

In none of these instances has criminal wrongdoing been proven. Nonetheless, there have been far too many allegations backed up by substantial evidence about corruption in the Interior Department.

Yet another problem is the growing influence of foreign corporations, some with ties to foreign governments. For example, mining conglomerates controlled by foreign billionaires seek to open sulfide mines near the Boundary Waters and Lake Superior watershed. In 2017, one of these mining companies, PolyMet, arranged a land swap with the Interior Department to acquire federal land for sulfide mining. Litigation by environmental groups against the Interior Department continued throughout the Biden Administration.[12] PolyMet (now NorthMet) is controlled by Swiss mining conglomerate Glencore, founded by a tax cheat Marc Rich, who was pardoned by President Clinton. Glencore recently has had close ties with Russian oligarchs, and in 2017 Glencore's CEO Ivan Glasenberg received the Presidential Medal of Friendship from Vladimir Putin.[13] The Trump Administration in 2025 plans accelerated approval of the NorthMet mine, although the permitting process under Minnesota environmental laws will continue to be contentious.[14]

A different sulfide mine on a lease of federal land, adjacent to the Boundary Waters, was championed by federal officials in the Trump administration. This mine would be controlled by Antofagasta, a corporation owned by a billionaire from Chile. The same billionaire in 2017 also leased an expensive house he had purchased in Washington, DC to Jared Kushner and Ivanka Trump.[15] The Trump administration supported this mine, although that decision was reversed during the Biden administration.[16]

[12] *See* Center for Biological Diversity v. Haaland (D. Minn.) Case No. 22-cv-181 (PJS/LIB) (seeking an Order of the Court voiding the land exchange between the Forest Service and PolyMet; setting aside and vacating the various reports, opinions, and assessments created by defendants).

[13] *See* Jack Farchy, *Putin Awards Glasenberg Order of Friendship After Rosneft Deal*, Bloomberg (Apr. 10, 2017), www.bloomberg.com/news/articles/2017-04-10/putin-awards-glasenberg-order-of-friendship-after-rosneft-deal?embedded-checkout=true.

[14] *See* Executive Order, Immediate Measures to Increase American Minerals Production, March 20, 2025; and The White House, Press Release, Trump Administration Boosts Domestic Mineral Production – Adding 10 More Critical Mineral Production Projects to the Federal Permitting Dashboard, May 2, 2025 (listing specific projects including NorthMet).

[15] Mark Maremont, *Ivanka Trump's Landlord Is a Chilean Billionaire Suing the U.S. Government*, Wall Street Journal (Mar. 8, 2017), www.wsj.com/articles/ivanka-trumps-landlord-is-a-chilean-billionaire-suing-the-u-s-government-1489000307.

[16] U.S. Department of the Interior, Press Release: *Interior Department Takes Action on Mineral Leases Improperly Renewed in the Watershed of the Boundary Wates Wilderness* (Jan. 26, 2022), www.doi.gov/pressreleases/interior-department-takes-action-mineral-leases-improperly-renewed-watershed-boundary. The Trump administration in 2025 again seeks to help Twin Metals open this mine, and the tariffs on imported copper announced in July 2025 may make it even more lucrative.

In sum, vast portions of the United States owned by the federal government are important sources of resource extraction, including minerals, timber, oil, and gas, by private enterprise under leases and similar arrangements with the federal government. Much of it is important to the US economy, even to the national security. Yet the question today is the same as during the Teapot Dome scandal 100 years ago. Should appointees of the President in the Interior Department, who have been entrusted with stewardship of this land by Congress, make decisions based on the national interest or their own personal interest?

Then there is the even more pressing problem of climate change. There is a risk that corruption of federal agencies beyond the Interior Department could slow the public response.[17] Fossil fuel companies utilize the floodgates of political spending opened by the Supreme Court's decision in *Citizens United*. But they also take advantage of the revolving door in and out of government, when the President appoints industry offices, directors, lobbyists, or lawyers to high-level posts in the Interior Department, Department of Energy, and Environmental Protection Agency. Existing ethics rules only limit participation in matters in which a former employer is an identifiable party. An example is an oil-drilling permit or a lease of federal land in which the party was previously involved.[18] These ethics rules do not prevent participation in industry-wide regulation – or deregulation – that affects a former employer.

The President's appointment power, discussed in Section 1.4, is embedded in the Constitution. The President's removal power has been read into the Constitution by the Supreme Court. If the President favors the fossil fuel industry, for whatever reason, much of the regulatory machinery of the Executive Branch may soon follow.

13.2 THE FEDERAL LAND POLICY MANAGEMENT ACT

The Federal Land Policy Management Act (FLPMA) of 1976 expressly states a policy that the "public lands be retained in Federal ownership."[19] The Act gives the

[17] Testimony of Richard W. Painter before the United States Senate, Committee on the Budget, Hearing "Democracy Distorted: Unraveling the Consequences of Fossil Fuel Dark Money in Politics" (June 21, 2023), www.budget.senate.gov/imo/media/doc/Mr.%20Richard%20Painter%20%20Testimony%20-%20Senate%20Budget%20Committeel.pdf.

[18] *See* 5 C.F.R. 2635.502 (Office of Government Ethics impartiality rule) (requiring prior authorization for an executive branch employee to participate in a particular party matter in which a former employer within the past year is a party or represents a party). Presidents Obama, Trump, and Biden each issued executive orders on ethics that lengthened this recusal period to two years or longer for appointees of the President. These ethics rules, however, do little to prevent federal officials from participating in regulatory matters that affect their previous employers' industry. The only legal requirement is that they divest their financial interest in the industry and sever employment with the former employer during their term in office. *See* 18 U.S.C. Section 208 (financial conflicts of interest for executive branch employees).

[19] 43 U.S.C. § 1701(a) (1976).

Interior Department's Bureau of Land Management (BLM) authority to manage public lands for mining, grazing, recreation, and other multiple uses. BLM's mandate is for mixed use of federal land, including livestock grazing and mineral development as well as conservation and wilderness protection.

Under the FLPMA. Congress is the primary decision-maker on the question of which lands can be withdrawn from commercial use. The President can temporarily withdraw federal lands from development, but congressional approval is needed for more substantial and permanent withdrawals.[20]

The FLPMA also requires the President to consider input from the public and from state and local governments. The President through BLM submits recommendations to Congress regarding areas considered for wilderness designation. However, the President cannot alone by executive order designate wilderness areas under the Act.[21]

13.3 THE ANTIQUITIES ACT

The FLPMA did not repeal the 1906 Antiquities Act. That law gives the President considerably more power to act unilaterally in restricting use of federal land for the purpose of designating a national monument.

Congress passed the Antiquities Act to allow the President to prevent destruction of Native American sites on federal lands, but the language is very broad. Under the Act, the President has the power to:

> [D]eclare by public proclamation historic landmarks, historic and prehistoric structures, and other objects of historic or scientific interest that are situated on land owned or controlled by the Federal Government to be national monuments … The limits of the parcels shall be confined to the smallest area compatible with the proper care and management of the objects to be protected.[22]

This power has been used dozens of times by presidents for over a century. Sites such as Devils Tower National Monument, Agate Fossil Beds National Monument, and Montezuma Castle National Monument have been protected. National monuments can be created by the President alone, but creation of a national park requires separate legislation by Congress.[23] Some national monuments later become national parks. The Grand Canyon, Olympic, Acadia, and Grand Tetons national parks were originally designated as monuments under the Antiquities Act.

[20] Before FLPMA, the President had considerably more power over designation of federal lands as national forests under the Forest Service Organic Act of 1897, ch. 2, 30 Stat. 34 (1897).

[21] *See* 43 U.S.C. § 1702(i); 43 U.S. Code § 1782(b) ("A recommendation of the President for designation as wilderness shall become effective only if so provided by an Act of Congress").

[22] 54 U.S.C. § 320301 (2014).

[23] 54 U.S.C. § 100101 *et seq.* (2014).

The original focus of the Antiquities Act was the historic, cultural, or scientific interest of a site; national parks were created for purposes of scenic or recreational value, or to protect wildlife. However, presidents also have designated national monuments for natural preservation purposes and some of those monuments have been very large areas. This invites the criticism that presidents interpret the Antiquities Act expansively to bypass Congress and to protect federal land from commercial uses.

There is considerable controversy about how far a president can go in designating a national monument under the Antiquities Act. This question comes in three parts. First, how liberally can a president construe the term "objects of historic or scientific interest" in the Act? Second, how much federal land can be designated as a monument under the Act which specifically says that the monument "shall be confined to the smallest area compatible with the proper care and management of the objects to be protected." Third, what restrictions on commercial use of the federal land are reasonable under the Act? Is there an implicit requirement that the President only impose restrictions necessary to protect the monument?

Courts generally have deferred to the President on all these questions. In *Cameron v. United States*,[24] a suit by the United States to enjoin a miner from using a lode-mining claim in the Grand Canyon, the Supreme Court affirmed the President's authority under the Antiquities Act. President Theodore Roosevelt had designated the 800,000-acre Grand Canyon National Monument in 1908. Justice Van Devanter, writing for the Court in 1920, observed that "[i]t is the greatest eroded canyon in the United States, if not in the world, is over a mile in depth, has attracted wide attention among explorers and scientists, affords an unexampled field for geologic study, is regarded as one of the great natural wonders, and annually draws to its borders thousands of visitors."[25] The Court in *Cameron* upheld the power of the President as the authority to unilaterally act in 1908 to make the Grand Canyon a national monument, even though Congress in 1919 also made the Grand Canyon a national park.

The President's designation of a national monument should not be arbitrary and capricious. A federal district court in Wyoming in 1945 observed that

> if a monument were to be created on a bare stretch of sage-brush prairie in regard to which there was no substantial evidence that it contained objects of historic or scientific interest, the action in attempting to establish it by proclamation as a monument, would undoubtedly be arbitrary and capricious and clearly outside the scope and purpose of the Monument Act.[26]

Yet the same court noted that in the case before it, the court was bound by the testimony of the government's experts on the rationale for the monument even if

[24] Cameron v. United States, 252 U.S. 450 (1920).
[25] *Id.* at 454–56.
[26] State of Wyoming v. Franke, 58 F. Supp. 890, 896 (D. Wyo. 1945).

that testimony did not establish by the preponderance of the evidence the government's contention.[27] Other legal challenges to national monument designations also have been unsuccessful.[28]

The DC Circuit Court of Appeals more recently held that "objects of historical or scientific significance" under the statute may include "ecosystems and scenic vistas."[29] Arguably, such an expansive interpretation of the Antiquities Act blurs the difference between establishing a national monument and establishing a national park or a national forest which would require the consent of Congress.

Thus far the federal courts have not interpreted the "smallest area compatible" requirement in the Antiquities Act. In concurring with denial of a cert petition in an Antiquities Act case, however, Chief Justice John Roberts expressed concern that the language is ignored by presidents designating monuments covering vast areas of land and water.[30]

Marine national monuments in coastal waters were not created during the first century after the Antiquities Act. Yet, as Chief Justice Roberts has noted, "since 2006, presidents have established five marine monuments alone whose total area exceeds all other American monuments combined."[31] The Northeast Canyons and Seamounts Marine National Monument, 130 miles off the coast of Cape Cod, was created by President Obama. Its size and the restrictions on commercial fishing were reduced by President Trump. Thereafter, the original size and restrictions were reinstated by President Biden. It "contains three underwater canyons and four undersea volcanoes" and "[t]he 'objects' to be 'protected' are the 'canyons and seamounts themselves,' along with 'the natural resources and ecosystems in and around them.'"[32] The courts have not ruled definitely on whether the Antiquities Act allows a marine national monument to be created. Yet no court to date has held that a president cannot create a marine monument. Even one such as this, which covers an area of ocean the size of the State of Connecticut.

A separate question is whether Congress in the Antiquities Act bestowed power going only in one direction, where the President can designate a monument, but once it is designated it can only be undesignated or reduced in size by an act of Congress. If so, that's not the practice at the present time.

[27] *Id.*

[28] *See e.g.* Cappaert v. United States, 426 U.S. 128 (1976) (Devil's Hole National Monument); Tulare County. v. Bush, 306 F.3d 1138 (D.C. Cir. 2002) (Grand Sequoia National Monument); Mountain States Legal Found. v. Bush, 306 F.3d 1132 (D.C. Cir. 2002) (Grand Canyon-Parashant, Canyons of the Ancients, Cascade-Siskiyou, Hanford Reach, Ironwood Forest, Sonoran Desert National Monuments); Utah Ass'n of Counties v. Bush, 316 F. Supp, 2d 1172 (D. Utah 2004) appeal dismissed Utah Ass'n of Counties v. Bush, 455 F.3d 1094 (10th Cir. 2006) (Grand Staircase-Escalante National Monument).

[29] Tulare County v. Bush, 306 F.3d 1138, 1142 (D.C. Cir. 2002).

[30] Massachusetts Lobstermen v. Raimondo, cert denied, 141 S.Ct. 979 (2021) (statement of C. J. Roberts).

[31] *Id.*, citing the certiorari petition at 7–8.

[32] *Id.* (quoting Presidential Proclamation No. 9496, Oct. 8, 2021).

Consider the back and forth among Presidents Obama, Trump, Biden, and now Trump again over a 1.3-million-acre area in Utah surrounding two buttes which Native Americans had referred to as the "Bears Ears." President Obama in his December 2016 proclamation of the Bears Ears National Monument, one month before he left office, observed:

> For hundreds of generations, native peoples lived in the surrounding deep sandstone canyons, desert mesas, and meadow mountaintops, which constitute one of the densest and most significant cultural landscapes in the United States. Abundant rock art, ancient cliff dwellings, ceremonial sites, and countless other artifacts provide an extraordinary archaeological and cultural record that is important to us all, but most notably the land is profoundly sacred to many Native American tribes, including the Ute Mountain Ute Tribe, Navajo Nation, Ute Indian Tribe of the Uintah Ouray, Hopi Nation, and Zuni Tribe.[33]

This Bears Ears National Monument severely restricted mining, oil, and gas development in a wide part of southern Utah, angering local businesses and politicians. Bears Ears was reduced in size by 85 percent in a 2017 executive order by President Trump. But President Biden redesignated to it its original size in October 2021.[34] Bears Ears very likely will be reduced again in a second Trump administration. If this pattern of conflicting executive orders continues, the Bears Ears National Monument will be over six times as large during Democratic administrations than when the White House is controlled by Republicans.[35]

President Trump also has reduced the restrictions on commercial activity in national monuments created by his predecessors. He did just that in his executive order allowing commercial fishing in the Northeast Canyons and Seamounts Marine National Monument.[36]

Meanwhile conservative groups, such as the Heritage Foundation, have long sought repeal of the Antiquities Act,[37] a proposal also embodied in Project

[33] Proclamation 9558 of December 28, 2016 by President Obama establishing the Bears Ears National Monument.

[34] *See* Proclamation 9681 December 4, 2017, by President Trump reducing the size of Bears Ears. On October 8, 2021, President Biden restored the Monument to its original size in Proclamation 10285.

[35] Compare Proclamations 9558 and 9681. Proclamation 9558 established the Bear Ears National Monument on approximately 1.35 million acres. Proclamation 9681 reduced the size of the monument to approximately 201,000 acres.

[36] Proclamation 10049 (Modifying the Northeast Canyons and Seamounts Marine National Monument to remove the restrictions on commercial fishing (June 5, 2020). Multiple parties challenged Proclamation 10049 in federal court, asserting that it exceeded President Trump's authority under the Antiquities Act. President Biden restored the original restrictions in Presidential Proclamation No. 9496 (Oct. 8, 2021). If President Trump again reverses these restrictions in his second term, litigation may resume over whether he is permitted do so under the Antiquities Act.

[37] Nicholas D. Loris, *The Antiquated Act: Time to Repeal the Antiquities Act*, Heritage Foundation (Mar. 2015).

2025.[38] Their argument is that the President alone should not have the power to withdraw federal lands from commercial use. Under the Constitution and laws of the United States, except the Antiquities Act, this is a power reserved for Congress.

13.4 TAKING CARE OF FEDERAL LANDS FOR FUTURE GENERATIONS

In summary, the President and Congress share responsibility for management of federal lands, deciding who gets to use those lands, including how much to charge for rents, royalties, and other fees for that use.[39] Over a century of scandal in the Interior Department has shown that persons and industries with an interest in resource extraction on federal land will use political influence, and sometimes outright bribes, to get priority over other users.

The Constitution clearly contemplates that Congress and the President exercising powers delegated by Congress will hold federal land in trust not only for today's citizens, but for future generations. But those future generations don't vote now and, perhaps more importantly, don't contribute to campaigns for public office. History shows some users of federal land get priority over others.

Like trustees of a family trust, Congress and the President jointly have responsibility to take care of federal lands and not to squander trust assets, but unlike the typical private trust, the beneficiaries of this public trust have limited recourse when they believe this trust has been violated. Courts defer almost always to the President and even more so to Congress. The President is bound by the "Take Care" Clause of the Constitution,[40] but in areas where Congress has given the President considerable discretion, he and his appointees in the Executive Branch can all too easily abuse it. The political process is supposedly a check on abuses by the President and Congress, but the Supreme Court's blessing on nearly the unlimited role of money in politics[41] means that commercial interests that want priority use of federal lands can find a way – other than paying rents and royalties – to buy it.

[38] Mandate for Leadership: The Conservative Promise, Chapter 16, The Department of the Interior, at 532 (urging repeal of the Antiquities Act), https://static.project2025.org/2025_MandateForLeadership_CHAPTER-16.pdf.

[39] Jedediah Britton-Purdy, *Whose Land? Which Public? The Shape of Public-Lands Law and Trump's National Monument Proclamations*, 45 Ecology L. Quarterly 921 (2019).

[40] U.S. Const. Art. II, § 3.

[41] Citizens United v. Federal Election Commission, 558 U.S. 310 (2010).

PART II

Conclusion

Part I of this book was about the extent and limits of the powers of the President. Part II addressed the President's obligation to use that power responsibly. The central focus here was the constitutional responsibility of the President to "take care" that the laws are faithfully executed. While some legal scholars see this responsibility as a rationale for expanding presidential power, many see in the "take care" clause recognition of the capacity of law itself to constrain the President. That law is the Constitution, the federal statutes and treaties of the United States.

While the President has some discretion in deciding how to enforce the law, there are limits on how far discretion can go. Some exceptions to immigration law that Presidents Obama and Biden carved out were too much for some federal courts to accept. President Trump's excesses in the other direction, such as enforcing immigration laws to deport natural-born citizens and detaining documented immigrants because of their political speech, conflict with judicial precedent and have now run into trouble in the courts. The common theme is that law enforcement can vary somewhat from administration to administration, but not so much that it fundamentally changes the law itself, unless and until Congress changes the law.

Another theme in Part II was ethics, including the obligation of the President to avoid financial conflicts of interest with official duties. Even when the financial conflict of interest statute technically doesn't apply to the President, the President's oath of office clearly requires him to put his country first. Compliance with the Emoluments Clause of the Constitution is another part of this responsibility. The President's responsibility includes insisting that presidential appointees also conduct themselves ethically, an important function of the White House ethics office.

The corruption problem in government is not a subject addressed in detail in this book, but it has been touched upon in Part II because corruption is a serious problem, exacerbated by the US campaign finance system. Part of a president's responsibility is to minimize the adverse impact of corruption on discretionary spending and policy decisions in federal agencies.

Regarding war powers, the subject of Chapter 3, we emphasized in this part the obligation of the President to use those powers responsibly. This includes not only the decision about when to go to war, discussed at length in Chapter 3, but also the amount of money spent on defense, now a trillion-dollar budget. Presidents should do more in their capacity as Commander in Chief to assure that the budget is not bloated by financial conflicts of interest of government officials, campaign contributions by defense contractors, and other factors unrelated to national security,

Finally, the President has enormous responsibility in taking care of federal lands, an area where special interests constantly have sought unfair advantage through influence on the Interior Department and other parts of the administration. The President shares with Congress trusteeship over these lands for the benefit of future generations. Although the President does not have plenary power over the entire globe, a responsible approach of the United States to climate change is needed to address that global challenge. Proper use of the executive power of the presidency is a necessary, if not sufficient condition, for making that happen.

PART III

Accountability

Thus far this book relates presidential power with presidential responsibility. But what happens when a president uses his power irresponsibly in the general sense, and also in violation of the responsibilities required under the Constitution, the oath of office, and laws of the United States?

The three branches of government were designed to function as checks and balances on each other – such was an important component of political theory at the time of the Founding in the writings of Montesquieu and also in the Federalist Papers. This concept is embedded in Articles I, II, and III of the Constitution.

For a president there are no effective checks and balances without accountability. This part of our book is about the accountability of a president in the Constitution, the oath of office, and in subsequent statutes and case law. We probe whether those accountability mechanisms are sufficient to constrain an irresponsible, reckless, and perhaps criminal president.

14

Impeaching and Removing the President

On the eve of the first impeachment of Donald Trump in late 2018, constitutional law scholars Laurence Tribe and Joshua Matz published an insightful book[1] emphasizing the critically important role of impeachment in establishing checks on abuse of power in the presidency. The authors' vision, much like that of the Framers, was that the threat of impeachment can stop the worst abuses by a president. For reasons we explore here, it has not always worked out that way. Nonetheless, the proper role of impeachment in the US constitutional framework, including what the House and Senate should do to carry out their responsibilities in an impeachment proceeding, is important to discuss here.

Impeachment in the United States and England has had a long history. The first impeachment by Parliament in England dates back to 1376. Two of the King's ministers, William Latimer and Richard Lyons, were impeached and convicted by the House of Commons, during the reign of Edward III, for an abuse of power due to corruption and financial mismanagement. The remedy was prison.[2] The instrument of impeachment was used to challenge the King's powers, and "discipline and

[1] Laurence Tribe & Joshua Matz, To End a Presidency: The Power of Impeachment (2018).

[2] John Hatsell, Precedent of Proceedings in the House of Commons, Vol. 9, 50–51, 62–71 (1776); T. F. T. Plucknett, *The Impeachment of 1376*, 1 Trans. Royal Hist. Soc. 153–54 (1951); Jill Lapore, *"You're Fired". A Short Account of the Long History of Impeachments*, The New Yorker (Oct. 28, 2019), 25–31. *See also* Michael J. Gerhardt, The Federal Impeachment Process, at 3–21 (2019); Michael J. Gerhardt, The Law of Impeachment, at xiii, xiv, xix–xx, 9 (2024) ("In the United States, 20 people have been impeached, including 14 federal judges. Only eight of these have been convicted by the Senate and removed from office, each being a federal judge. Three presidents have been impeached (Andrew Johnson, William Clinton, and Donald Trump – twice. Richard Nixon resigned the presidency on the eve of being impeached." *Id.* at 21). At the time of this writing, Secretary of Homeland Security, Alejandro Mayorkas, was impeached by the House in April 2024 and quickly the Senate dismissed the charges without a trial).

remove the King's Ministers."[3] It has been noted as "the most powerful weapon in the political Armory, short of war."[4]

The English practice of impeachment was not confined to criminal conduct, but swept into a significant abuse or misuse of power and the lack of public trust in a public official.[5] An underlying crime was "neither necessary nor sufficient" in England or in the colonies in North America.[6] Egregious wrongdoing was the early historical focus. Impeachment itself was considered an essential and foundational process to ensure the success of a republican form of government, especially if the nation state could be considered endangered.[7] As one distinguished historian has noted, "impeachment [as a checking function] was forged to counter a terrible power: the despot who deems himself to be above the law."[8] Another distinguished scholar has concluded that "impeachment and removal from office were the ultimate check on presidential power. Shall any man be above justice?"[9]

When the delegates came to Philadelphia in 1787 for the Constitutional Convention, they were aware of the English historical and colonial-era understanding of impeachment. They began to discuss early whether the soon-to-be-drafted Constitution should adopt an impeachment clause.[10] History records that it was unlikely that the Constitution would have been ratified without an impeachment clause to provide accountability and serve as a check on the presidency and its powers as envisioned under Article II.[11]

3 Tom Ginsburg, Aziz Huq, & David Landau, *The Comparative Constitutional Law of Presidential Impeachment*, 88 U. CHICAGO L. REV. 88, 109 (2021). *See also* FRANK O. BOWMAN III, HIGH CRIMES AND MISDEMEANORS, 3–4, 22–23 (2019).

4 T. F. T. Plucknett, *Presidential Address*, 3 TRANS. ROYAL HISTORICAL SOCIETY, 145 fn12 (1953). *See also* CHARLES BLACK JR. & PHILLIP BABBITT, "IMPEACHMENT": A HANDBOOK, NEW EDITION, 30–37 (2018); CHARLES BLACK, JR., IMPEACHMENT: A HANDBOOK, 49 (1974); CASS R. SUNSTEIN, IMPEACHMENT: A CITIZEN'S GUIDE, 34–36 (2019).

5 BLACK JR. & BABBITT, *supra* note 4, at 34, 55, 60.

6 *Id.* at 39. Sunstein, *supra* note 4. *See also* RICHARD A. POSNER, AN AMERICAN AFFAIR: THE INVESTIGATION, IMPEACHMENT, AND TRIAL OF PRESIDENT CLINTON, 98–99, 100 (1999), citing PETER CHARLES HEFFER & N. E. H. HALL, IMPEACHMENT IN AMERICA, 1635–1805, 101–02, 118–19 (1984).

7 BLACK JR. & BABBITT, *supra* note 4, at 40. Sunstein, *supra* note 4.

8 Lapore *supra* note 2, at 25, 28 ("An impeachable offense is an abuse of power of the office that violates the public trust counter to the national interest and undermines the Republic").

9 THE HOUSE INTELLIGENCE COMMITTEE, THE IMPEACHMENT REPORT: THE HOUSE INTELLIGENCE COMMITTEE'S REPORT ON ITS INVESTIGATION INTO DONALD TRUMP AND UKRAINE, v (2019) (reprinted by Crown Publishing with Foreword by Jon Meacham) (Jon Meacham at 3, quoting George Mason).

10 Sunstein *supra* note 4, at 34. *See also* Posner *supra* note 6, at 96–97, citing PETER CHARLES HOFFER & N. E. H. HALL, IMPEACHMENT IN AMERICA, 1635–1803 (1984).

11 Sunstein, *supra* note 4, at 2. In the view of Benjamin Franklin and Alexander Hamilton, Sunstein says, "the power to impeach was core to the establishment of good government." Sunstein observed that "without the power to impeach, We the People would probably have refused to ratify the constitution in the first place ... it was central 'to balance the defining republican commitments to liberty, equality, and self-rule with the belief in a strong, energetic national government'" with its many checking safeguards between the President and Congress.

Impeachment comes in two stages. First, Article I, Section 2, Clause 5 of the Constitution grants the sole power of impeachment to the House of Representatives. Then Article I, Section 3, Clause 6 provides: "The Senate shall have the sole Power to try all Impeachments. When sitting for that Purpose, they shall be on Oath or Affirmation. When the President of the United States is tried, the Chief Justice shall preside: And no Person shall be convicted without the Concurrence of two thirds of the Members present."[12]

In addition, under Article I, Section 3, Clause 7, upon conviction by the Senate, the President or any other impeached and convicted federal officer shall be removed from office, and with the Senate's discretion it can deny and disqualify the convicted President from holding public office in the future.[13] Importantly, the Constitution is clear that once convicted, the impeached officer is subject to indictment, trial, judgment, and punishment under the law.[14]

The legal basis for conviction and removal from office during an impeachment trial in the Senate is based on a finding of "Treason, Bribery, or other high Crimes and Misdemeanors."[15] The Constitution defines treason as "levying War against the [United States], or in adhering to the [United States'] Enemies, giving the Enemies Comfort."[16] Additionally, the federal criminal code codifies the language of the Constitution on treason.[17]

Bribery is also a basis for impeachment with a history that includes both offering a bribe and receiving a bribe.[18] Today, under federal law, a distinction is drawn between bribes and "gratuities."[19] In order for the exchange of a thing of value, such as cash or gold bars, and an official act to rise to the level of bribery the exchange must occur *before* the official act and there must be a clear connection between the exchange and the act.[20] On the other hand, if the valuable good was given after the official act or there is a more generalized connection between the valuable good and the act it is more likely to be viewed as a gratuity.[21] It seems clear that the state of both the person offering the bribe and the person receiving the bribe are material to proving an illegal bribe either attempted or completed.[22] The focus, then, is on the "benefit offered, and the value created."[23]

[12] U.S. CONST. Art. I, § 2, cl. 5; § 3, cl. 6.
[13] *Id.* at § 3, cl. 7.
[14] *Id.* at § 3, cl. 7.
[15] U.S. Const. Art. II, § 4.
[16] U.S. CONST. Art. III, § 3, cl. 1; BLACK JR. & BABBITT, *supra* note 4, at 24–25, 37.
[17] 18 U.S.C. § 2381 (1948).
[18] 18 U.S.C. § 201 (1962). *See also* McDonnell v. United States, 579 U.S. 550 (2016).
[19] *Id. See* Snyder v. United States, 603 U.S. 1 (2024) (concerning the use of federal bribery statute over state and local officials and the difference between "gratuities" made after a government action and a quid pro quo where the bribe is made before a government action).
[20] 18 U.S.C. § 201 (1962).
[21] *Id.*
[22] BLACK JR. & BABBITT, *supra* note 4, at 25.
[23] *Id.*

The Impeachment Clause, however, predates federal bribery statutes, and the Supreme Court's even more recent decisions narrowing the reach of these criminal statutes, as discussed in Chapter 12 of this book. The Founders' understanding of bribery, and related corruption crimes, was based on English common law and was considerably broader in scope. For example, payment in exchange for access to a public official probably would have been considered a bribe by the Founders even if it is not a bribe under modern criminal law interpretation.[24]

The third charge under the Impeachment Clause focuses on "other high crimes and misdemeanors," suggesting other offenses – a reference to wrongs and abuses against the public interest and public trust.[25] At its best, most readers would agree that this vague phrase is open to substantial interpretation. It was debated only briefly by the Founders, and just a mere nine days before the Constitution was signed on September 17, 1787. We know that the phrase does not include "maladministration," as that term was rejected later in the debates. Nor did it include an actionable offense of merely an "inefficient administration," or a dislike of the President and his policies and politics.[26]

Again, the weight of the historical scholarship suggests that the phrase "other Crimes and Misdemeanors" would include "many great and dangerous offenses," broadly defined.[27] While treason and bribery are statutory or common law crimes, the term "other" may connote additional large or small crimes of the same kind but may not also require per se criminal conduct.[28] Rather, it may include serious, substantial abuses of power that might "corrupt or subvert the political governmental process."[29]

In summary, we see that the substantive offense of impeachment under Article II, Section 4 was derived from the text and close reading of English precedents and from the colonies' understanding of the English tradition that resulted in the colonies' own interpretation as seen through the development of their own common law of impeachment. Accordingly, the Founders envisioned an expanded definition of impeachment as a checking function by the legislature over the executive for substantial abuses of power.[30]

[24] *See* Richard W. Painter, *Bribery Law: Is Anything Left?*, 46 Cardozo L. Rev. 1775 (2025) (contrasting the Supreme Court's holding in McDonnell v. United States, 579 U.S. 550 (2016) (holding that payment only for a meeting with the governor is not a bribe under federal law) with the "XYZ Affair" in which Thomas Jefferson and others expressed anger at French Foreign Minister Talleyrand demanding payment from American diplomats in exchange for a meeting).

[25] Black Jr. & Babbitt, *supra* note 4, at 27–28, 31–32; Sunstein *supra* note 4, at 45, 48.

[26] Black Jr. & Babbitt, *supra* note 4, at 27–28.

[27] *Id.* at 27.

[28] *Id.* at 32–37, 43, 55, *See also* Bowman *supra* note 3, at 45, 47–49, 50–67, 70–75.

[29] Bowman, *supra* note 3, at 49.

[30] *Id.* at 4, 23, 45, 71, 75.

14.1 IMPEACHMENT AND THE CONSTITUTIONAL CONVENTION OF 1787: AN ORIGINALIST POINT OF VIEW

During the Constitutional Convention of 1787, the question of impeachment was split into two distinct questions. First, the delegates debated whether a president should be impeachable at all.[31] Early in the debates, delegates arguing against impeachment believed that the political process should be the ultimate determination of a president's abuse of power, and that removal from office by losing an election was an appropriate guardrail on abuses of power.[32] In response to this argument, George Mason of Virginia and Benjamin Franklin of Pennsylvania argued that no man is above justice and that the President as head of state with an immense array of powers was uniquely suited to abuse that power.[33] Therefore, accountability for presidential abuses of power through impeachment became the focus of the debate.

Further, Franklin argued that in the absence of a formal mechanism for holding the President accountable, such as impeachment, Americans would take matters into their own hands and political violence and assassination of the President would be the natural consequence.[34] Franklin viewed this as unacceptable as it would deprive the President of both his life and a means of vindicating his character.[35] Also, James Madison was concerned that without impeachment as a means of presidential accountability the President would "pervert his administration into a scheme of peculation or oppression" such that the political process could not work as designed to vote a president out of office. Ultimately, those opposed to including impeachment in the Constitution came around to view it as necessary. The debates continued on *who* should try a presidential impeachment trial and what would constitute an impeachable offense.

The debate over who should try an impeached president centered on whether the Supreme Court or the Senate should try the President. Those in favor of the Supreme Court trying the impeachment, such as James Madison and Thomas Pinckney, believed that putting the entire impeachment process in the legislative branch would make the President improperly dependent on a co-equal branch of government.[36] Hugh Williamson of North Carolina was also concerned that the Senate would be too lenient, rather than too rigorous, during an impeachment trial because of the frequency with which the President and the legislature must work

[31] Notes of James Madison from the Constitutional Convention (July 20, 1787), reprinted in The Records of the Federal Convention of 1787, Vol. 2., 64 (Max Farrand ed., 1911).

[32] *Id.*

[33] *Id.* at 65.

[34] *Id.*

[35] *Id.*

[36] *Id.* at 551.

together to sign legislation into law. In other words, the Senate would be likely to acquit to stay in good favor with the President.[37]

In contrast, delegates in favor of impeachment trials in the Senate made two arguments. First, they argued that unlike the Senate, which at the time of ratification would have had twenty-six members, the Supreme Court only had six members at the time of ratification.[38] The difference in size between the two bodies led Gouverneur Morris to believe that the Court was more likely to be corrupted or influenced by the executive and not be a truly impartial body during an impeachment trial.[39] Second, Roger Sherman shared Morris's concerns, and believed that Supreme Court Justices were especially likely to be deferential to the President because they would be appointed by him.[40] Ultimately a motion to strike the words "by the Senate" from the Impeachment Clause failed 9–2.[41] Today impeachment trials of a president are held in the Senate and presided over by the Chief Justice of the Supreme Court.

The original language of the Impeachment Clause only provided for impeachment of a president for two specific crimes – bribery and treason.[42] Drawing on the lessons of English history, specifically the attempt by William Hastings in the 1480s to usurp the crown, some delegates believed that these two enumerated bases for impeachment would not adequately cover all the possible ways a president may abuse his power.[43] In response, George Mason proposed that a third basis for impeachment, "maladministration," be added.[44] Unlike bribery and treason, the maladministration amendment drew criticism for being too broad. James Madison was concerned that such a vague term would lead to the President serving at the pleasure of the Senate and that any policy disagreement between Congress and the President would lead to impeachment.[45] In response, the maladministration language was struck and replaced with "other high Crimes and Misdemeanors."[46]

This description of the history of the debates surrounding the Impeachment Clause and its final wording does not tell the full story. In part, the issue is that while the Convention discussed what an impeachable offense is, the matter received surprisingly little debate. The lack of an extended record on these impeachment debates makes it difficult to ascertain what exactly the delegates intended by "other high Crimes and Misdemeanors." Despite this ambiguity, two canons of construction can help in bringing clarity to this ambiguous phrase.

37 *Id.*
38 *Id.*
39 *Id.* at 551.
40 *Id.*
41 *Id.* at 552.
42 *Id.* at 550.
43 *Id.*
44 *Id.*
45 *Id.*
46 *Id.*

The first canon of construction is known as *ejusdem generis* ("of the same kind"). This canon of construction is used when a drafter has tacked on a catchall phrase at the end of an enumerated list of specific things.[47] For example, a sign prohibiting "cars, trucks, and other vehicles" from entering the park would likely also prohibit motorcycles and all-terrain vehicles from entering the park because they are of the same type of motorized vehicles as cars and trucks, but not bicycles or wheelchairs. In the case of impeachment, we have two enumerated crimes, bribery and treason, followed by the catchall phrase. These two preceding crimes likely would have been understood by a reader in the 1780s as a large-scale abuse of distinctly presidential powers.[48] Therefore, the language of "other high Crimes and Misdemeanors" should be seen as a catchall for other types of presidential conduct that are neither bribery nor treason but are still a gross abuse of a presidential power that betrays the country in some way.

Another way to approach the "other high Crimes and Misdemeanors" puzzle is to take an intratextual look at similar clauses in the Constitution. "Crime" is used as a catchall in three other clauses throughout the Constitution. First, the Interstate Extradition Clause[49] refers to persons "charged in any State with Treason, Felony, or other Crime." Unlike the Impeachment Clause, the Interstate Extradition Clause refers to crime generally rather than just "high Crimes," indicating that high crimes are a unique category of criminal conduct. Second, the Speech and Debate Clause[50] provides congressional immunity from arrest "in all Cases, except Treason, Felony, and Breach of Peace." This clause, in comparison to the Impeachment Clause, enumerates felonies rather than high crimes, indicating the two are distinct. Finally, the Grand Jury Clause of the Fifth Amendment guarantees a right to a grand jury when someone is "held to answer for a capital, or otherwise infamous crime." Thus, taken together, these four clauses of the Constitution indicate that a "high Crime" is different than normal criminal conduct and, taken together with the *ejusdem generis* canon, a "high Crime" should naturally be read as an extreme abuse of presidential authority.

The debate over the scope of impeachment did not end at the Convention. After the Convention, delegates went home to convince both state leadership and the public that this new Constitution was a good idea. The debates surrounding ratification give further clues about how the Impeachment Clause should be understood. *Federalist* 65 argued that trials of impeachment should arise from "those offenses which proceed from the misconduct of public men, or, in other words, from the abuse or violation of some public trust. They are of a nature which may with peculiar propriety be denominated POLITICAL, as they relate chiefly to

[47] ANTONIN SCALIA & BRYAN GARNER, READING LAW: THE INTERPRETATION OF LEGAL TEXTS, ch. 32 (1st ed. 2011).

[48] Cass R. Sunstein, *Impeaching the President*, 147 U. PA. L. REV. 279, 283 (1998).

[49] U.S. CONST. Art. IV, § 2, cl. 2.

[50] U.S. CONST. Art. I, § 6, cl. 1.

injuries done immediately to society itself."[51] This excerpt from Hamilton's argument bolsters the idea that high crimes and misdemeanors must be beyond and distinct from a criminal act. Rather, they must be injurious to the country and the national character.

14.2 IMPEACHMENT AND HISTORICAL PRACTICE

Another approach to understanding the Impeachment Clause is to consider how it would have been understood at the time of drafting in 1787. The practice of governing in the 236 years that have followed must be given considerable weight as well. Since the Constitution was ratified in 1789, four presidents have had articles of impeachment brought against them. This list includes Presidents Andrew Johnson (1868), Nixon (1973), Clinton (1988), and Trump (2020 and 2021).

In a 1998 law review article, Professor Cass Sunstein argued that the infrequency of impeachment proceedings represents a legislative understanding that impeachment is appropriate only in the most extraordinary cases of abuse of a distinctly presidential power.[52] Further, Sunstein outlines eight cases where presidents have run afoul of the law, and Congress *could* have brought articles of impeachment but ultimately chose not to because the wrongful conduct was not an abuse of a distinctly presidential power. Sunstein's eight instances of possibly impeachable conduct include President Nixon's tax evasion, President Reagan and Vice President Bush's involvement in the Iran–Contra Affair, President Franklin Roosevelt's shipment of illegal weapons to England during World War II, President Eisenhower's lies to the American public about a spy plane that was shot down over Soviet airspace, President Ford's pardon of Nixon and rumors of a backroom deal between the two men, President Kennedy's alleged affair with a woman who had connections to organized crime, and President Lincoln's suspension of habeas corpus during the Civil War.[53]

The "distinctly presidential power" standard carries its own ambiguity. Where should a line be drawn, if one should be drawn at all, between the official duties of a president and his personal conduct.[54] One illustrative case

[51] The Federalist No. 65 (Hamilton), emphasis original.

[52] Sunstein, *supra* note 48, at 294.

[53] *Id.* at 296–98. *See also* Craig Unger, Den of Spies: Reagan, Carter, and the Secret History of the Treason that Stole the White House (2024) (recall the "October surprise" asserting that Reagan's 1980 presidential campaign discussed with Iran delaying the release of US hostages until after Reagan had been sworn in as president to sabotage President Carter's reelection bid).

[54] *See* Trump v. United States, 603 U.S. 593 (2024) (establishing for purposes of criminal prosecution of a president, but not impeachment, that there are three categories of presidential conduct entitled to different levels of immunity. For acts that are exclusive constitutional powers such as pardons, the President enjoys absolute immunity. For official acts outside of the President's constitutional powers there is a presumption of immunity. For unofficial acts, or when the President acts in his personal capacity, there is no immunity).

that Sunstein explores was allegations that President Nixon was involved in income tax evasion. In the lead-up to articles of impeachment being drafted against President Nixon, the House of Representatives considered adding an additional charge that included these allegations. However, those charges were not ultimately brought because they concerned President Nixon's personal conduct rather than an abuse of his presidential authority.[55]

In contrast to the Nixon income tax case is the impeachment of President Clinton. Viewed through one lens, the impeachment of President Clinton involved purely personal matters, sexual in nature, one before he was president and one while he was the president in office.[56]

This analysis, however, is incomplete. His perjury charges, statements made twice while president before a Grand Jury and in a civil court deposition before a federal judge, arguably were impeachable, even though the subject matter concerned personal conduct. Under Article II, the President has an obligation to see that the laws of the United States are faithfully executed. By committing perjury twice, under oath, the President, arguably, violated that obligation and hence abused a presidential power.

Another approach that Sunstein considers is how impeachment has been used against other non-presidential officers. Article II, Section 4 of the Constitution allows for impeachment of all civil officers including the Vice President, cabinet heads, and judges for high crimes and misdemeanors.[57] The identical language of impeachment for civil officers and the President indicates that the same standard of impeachable conduct applies for both the President and civil officers. But as we will see, the impeachment of federal judges has a lower threshold of burden in practice for judges to be impeached.

The most helpful point of comparison here is how impeachment has been used against federal judges. Of the fifteen federal judges who have been impeached, the vast majority involve a gross abuse of judicial power and the unfair administration of justice. The charges have ranged from refusing to hear witnesses, to wrongfully disbarring lawyers, to threatening jurors.[58]

Two important points from these judicial impeachments stand out. First, judicial impeachments almost always involve some misuse of a distinct judicial

55 *See* House Impeachment Hearing, 105th Cong. (statements from Congresswoman Elizabeth Holtzman (D-NY), former Congressman Robert Drinan (D-MA) former Congressman Wayne Owens (D-UT)) (noting that because it was personal rather official misconduct, Nixon's tax evasion was not impeachable).

56 *See generally* Kenneth Starr, Referral from Independent Counsel Kenneth W. Starr Independent Counsel Transmitting a Referral to the United States House of Representatives Filed in Conformity with the Requirements of Title 28, United States Code, Section 595(c) 132 (1998).

57 U.S. Const. Art. II, § 4.

58 Sunstein, *supra* note 48, at 301. (Thirteen federal judges had been impeached at the time Sunstein wrote this article.)

power. Drawing the comparison to presidential impeachment, Sunstein argues that the history of judicial impeachment for abuse of judicial power implies that a president may be impeached only for an abuse of a presidential power and not for personal conduct. Second, in practice, judges are subject to a lower standard of impeachable offenses compared to the President. The basis for this argument is that federal judges enjoy lifetime tenure and are not subject to the will of the political process through elections in the same way that presidents are. Because of lifetime tenure, a lower threshold for impeachment is necessary for judges because otherwise the nation and its system of justice would be stuck with corrupt and self-dealing judges through their life tenure.

14.3 THE IMPEACHMENT OF ANDREW JOHNSON

The first president to be subject to impeachment in 1868 was Andrew Johnson. He became president in 1865 after the assassination of President Lincoln. He faced the daunting task of reuniting a nation after four years of bitter and bloody war. At the end of the Civil War, the thirty-ninth Congress, which was sworn in on March 4, 1865, was controlled by Lincoln's Republican Party with supermajorities in both the House and the Senate. As a Southern Democrat and former slaveholder, Johnson faced considerable political headwinds when he assumed the presidency following Lincoln's death.

Two of the largest points of contention between Johnson and congressional Republicans were the scope of presidential authority and how Reconstruction should proceed. As discussed in Part I of this book, President Lincoln believed firmly in the power of the President to act unilaterally, and Johnson shared many of Lincoln's views on this topic.[59] Johnson asserted Lincoln's view that the task of Reconstruction was his alone. He repeatedly denied attempts by Congress to participate in the process and used the power of the presidency to obstruct the Republicans' plans to use Reconstruction to fundamentally restructure the South.[60] This view on presidential authority was unacceptable to congressional Republicans who believed that the legislative branch had the proper authority to make laws governing the reentry of the former confederacy into the union.

The fight between Congress and the President over Reconstruction was not simply a matter of procedure. Rather, it reflected sharp policy differences on the conditions that should be imposed on the Southern states during this time. In Johnson's view, Reconstruction was a matter of reintegrating the Southern states

59 Michael Les Benedict, *From Our Archives: A New Look at the Impeachment of Andrew Johnson*, 113 Pol. Sci. Q. 493, 495 (1998).
60 *Id.*

with maximum speed and minimum disturbance to the institutions and governing bodies of the South beyond the abolition of slavery.[61] The practical effect of this policy was that former Confederates would be able to maintain their grip on power and formerly enslaved people would be subjected to "black codes" that among other things prohibited interracial marriage,[62] criminalized unemployment for African Americans,[63] criminalized firearm ownership for African Americans,[64] and allowed farmers to "hire" incarcerated African Americans to work in their fields.[65]

In other words, while the formerly enslaved would be liberated under the Thirteenth Amendment, the "black codes" purposefully were designed to ensure that the formerly enslaved would be treated as second-class citizens. In contrast, congressional Republicans viewed Reconstruction as an opportunity to free the enslaved populations of the South and to grant them full citizenship under the law and provide them with all of the opportunities and privileges that come with citizenship. This fight over Reconstruction culminated in the passage of the Civil Rights Act of 1866 over Johnson's veto and the eventual passage of the Fourteenth Amendment that incorporated many of the protections of the 1866 Act.[66]

Early in 1867 a small group of congressional Republicans began to consider bringing articles of impeachment over what they viewed as Johnson's stonewalling of their vision of Reconstruction.[67] However, the radical Republicans arguing for impeachment quickly ran into resistance from more conservative Republicans who believed that the "other high crimes and misdemeanors" language of the Impeachment Clause should be construed narrowly. The conservative Republicans' argument against impeachment of Johnson was both pragmatic and legal. First, they feared that impeaching a president during a time of incredible national fragility risked undoing much of the work that already had been done to reunite the country.[68] Second, they believed that impeachment for high crimes and misdemeanors must be limited only to those actions that are a violation of a criminal law.[69]

For the radical Republicans this view was far too narrow. They looked to both English history before the ratification and the impeachment of civil officers prior to 1868. They found that in both cases officers had been impeached and removed from office for noncriminal conduct.[70] In their view, Johnson's use of discretionary power

[61] *Id.*
[62] *Laws of the State of Mississippi* (Jackson, Miss: J. J. Shannon & Sons, 1866), 82.
[63] *Id.* at 91.
[64] *Id.* at 165.
[65] *Acts of the General Assembly of the State of South Carolina* (Columbia, SC: Julian A. Selby, 1866), 44.
[66] Civil Rights Act of 1866, 14 Stat. 27–30 (1866).
[67] Benedict, *supra* note 59, at 496.
[68] *Id.* at 498.
[69] *Id.*
[70] *Id.*

against the will of Congress, although not criminal in nature, was enough to bring articles of impeachment.

The tension between Johnson and Congress finally boiled over in 1867 when Johnson attempted to fire and replace his radical Republican Secretary of War, Edwin Stanton, with Major General Lorenzo Thomas. In Congress's view this attempted removal by Johnson was a violation of the Tenure in Office Act that prohibited the President from dismissing an executive officer who previously had been confirmed by the Senate without the Senate's approval. The attempted replacement of Stanton with Thomas outraged Republicans because it represented an attempt by Johnson to replace a pro-Reconstruction Secretary of War with one more aligned with Southern interests.

In response to Stanton's attempted removal, House Republicans drafted eleven articles of impeachment against Johnson. Eight of the eleven articles alleged violations of the Tenure in Office Act, one article alleged unlawful control of money apportioned by Congress to the Department of War, one article alleged violations of the Command of Army Act, and the remaining article alleged that Johnson had acted with "a loud voice, certain intemperate, inflammatory, and scandalous harangues, and did therein utter loud threats and bitter menaces ... against Congress."[71] Together, congressional Republicans argued, these eleven counts constituted high crimes and misdemeanors.

Two days after the articles were introduced the House voted, for the first time in American history, to impeach a president by a vote of 126 to 47.[72] Of the eleven articles, five received a straight party line vote of 127 to 42, and the most divisive article received a vote of 88 to 44.[73] At the Senate trial the impeachment managers from the House argued that Johnson explicitly had violated the Tenure in Office Act and that even if Johnson believed the law was unconstitutional he still had an obligation to follow the law until the Supreme Court found it to be unconstitutional. Johnson argued that his removal of Stanton was not a violation of the Tenure in Office Act, and that even if it were, it was not criminal in nature and thus not a high crime or misdemeanor. The basis of the defense's argument on the violation of the Act was that Stanton was appointed by Lincoln, rather than Johnson. Therefore, because Johnson did not appoint Stanton he was outside of the purview

[71] Journal of the House of Representatives of the United States, 40th Cong., 2nd sess., 440–50, 464–65 (1868). Slightly different voting results appear in "Impeachment of the President," Remarks in the House, Congressional Globe 39, 1616–18, 1642 (Mar. 2 and 3, 1868); and Asher C. Hinds, Hinds' Precedents of the House of Representatives of the United States, Vol. III, 863–69 (1907).

[72] *Impeachment of the President – Again, Remarks in the House,* Congressional Globe, 39, 1400 (Feb. 24, 1868).

[73] Note: the vote counts authorizing impeachment and for the different articles of impeachment are not the same because different numbers of members of Congress abstained from each of the votes. For the sake of clarity, abstaining votes have been removed from the vote count in this book.

of the Tenure in Office Act and he was able to remove him without the consent of the Senate.

Ultimately, the Senate by just one vote acquitted Johnson, with a final vote of 35 to 19.[74] History has not been kind to the efforts by the Republicans to impeach Johnson. Historian James Schouler described it as "a solemn theatrical fiasco."[75] The prevailing view among historians today is that Johnson's impeachment was a political, rather than a constitutional, exercise of power. This view of Johnson's impeachment was reinforced in 1926 in *Myers v. United States*,[76] when the Supreme Court held that the Tenure in Office Act had been unconstitutional because it infringed on the President's unilateral removal power.

After the conclusion of Johnson's impeachment, it would be over 100 years until a president again would be impeached.

14.4 PRESIDENT NIXON AND THE WATERGATE SCANDAL

In January of 1972 the Committee for the Re-election of the President (CRP) devised a scheme to break into the headquarters of the Democratic National Committee (DNC) at the Watergate complex to photograph sensitive memos prepared by the DNC and install wiretaps of phones in offices in the headquarters.[77] On June 17, 1972, when the operation was taking place, police arrested five men who were carrying sophisticated burglary tools, $2,300[78] in sequential $100 bills, and police radio scanners.[79] The next day an explosive report by the Associated Press tied one of the men arrested, James McCord, to the CRP. Thus began one of the greatest scandals in American political history. Over the following weeks and months investigative reporting would uncover a complex web of financial and personnel ties that led back to the Nixon campaign and the Nixon White House.

In early 1973, five days before Nixon's second inauguration, and following President Nixon's forty-nine-state victory over his opponent Senator George McGovern, the Senate opened an investigation into what had become known as the Watergate Scandal.[80] In May 1973, the Senate began to televise their hearings,

74 Edmund G. Ross, The Impeachment of Andrew Johnson, 105 (2012). Note: Conviction by the Senate requires a two-thirds majority rather than a bare majority.

75 William F. Swindler, *High Court of Congress: Impeachment Trials, 1797–1936*, 267 Popular Media (1974), https://scholarship.law.wm.edu/cgi/viewcontent.cgi?article=1262&context=popular_media.

76 Myers v. United States, 272 U.S. 52 (1926).

77 *The Unraveling of the Watergate Affair: Shock by Shock*, New York Times (Dec. 30, 1979), www.nytimes.com/1979/12/30/archives/the-unraveling-of-the-watergate-affair-shock-by-shock.html.

78 $17,294 as of April 2024 adjusted for inflation.

79 Bonnie Berkowitz & Dylan Moriarty, *How the Watergate Scandal Broke to the World: A Visual Timeline*, Wash. Post. (June 13, 2022), www.washingtonpost.com/history/interactive/2022/timeline-watergate-scandal-revelations/.

80 *Id.*

and on May 18 the Attorney General appointed Archibald Cox as special prosecutor.[81] During a July 16 hearing, a junior White House aide, Alexander Butterfield, stated that Nixon had installed a secret taping system in the Oval Office and that several of the tapes implicated the President directly in the underlying crimes and the cover-up.[82] During subsequent hearings, White House Counsel John Dean testified that he discussed the operation and the cover-up with the President on at least thirty-five occasions.[83]

Nixon, however, refused to turn over the implicating tapes, citing executive privilege. Nixon's claims of executive privilege over the tapes reached the Supreme Court, and in *United States v. Nixon*[84] the Court held that executive privilege is not absolute, no person is above the law, and that "the fundamental demands of due process of law in the fair administration of justice" required the President to hand over the tapes to the special prosecutor. Without a specific injury or need for the protections of executive privilege, a generalized need is insufficient and would effectively establish presidential primacy over the judiciary. In determining whether to grant executive privilege, courts will consider the need of the President to receive candid advice from advisors without fear of their discussion reaching the public against the needs of investigators to develop facts for criminal investigations.[85] After his battle with the Court, Nixon sought to release a "summary" of the tapes, but the special prosecutor refused to accept only the summaries.

This showdown between Nixon and Cox led to what would become known in October 1973 as the "Saturday Night Massacre." Nixon, furious that Cox wouldn't accept the summaries, ordered his Attorney General, Elliot Richardson, to fire Cox. Richardson refused and resigned in protest. When Richardson's deputy, William Ruckelshaus, also refused to fire Cox, Ruckelshaus resigned as well. Finally, Nixon was able to find a willing participant in Solicitor General Robert Bork, who fired Cox. Twelve days after Cox's firing a new special prosecutor, Leon Jaworski, was appointed to replace Cox.

The Supreme Court's decision requiring Nixon to turn over the incriminating tapes, a growing controversy of hundreds of thousands of dollars in unpaid taxes, and the public outcry over the Saturday Night Massacre put the President on the defensive in the court of public opinion. In an attempt to regain control of the narrative of these overlapping scandals, President Nixon gave a freewheeling press

81 *Id.*
82 *Id.*
83 Michael Gerhardt, The Law of Presidential Impeachment: A Guide for the Engaged Citizen, 69 (1st ed. 2024).
84 United States v. Nixon, 418 U.S. 683 (1974).
85 *Id.* at 711–12.

conference in, of all places, Walt Disney World.[86] During the press conference, Nixon discussed topics such as who made the secret recording system he installed in the Oval Office, whether milk price increases were the result of campaign contributions by the dairy industry, and what his personal plans were after leaving office.[87] The most famous answer, however, came in response to a question on Nixon's personal wealth. Replying to a question on whether he had profited improperly from his time as Vice President and President, Nixon stated "I've made my mistakes … but in all my years of public life I've never profited from public service. I've earned every cent. I'm not a crook."[88] The odd language of Nixon's answer, "I'm not a crook," would come to be one of the defining episodes of the Watergate saga.

In July 1974 the Supreme Court ordered the President to turn over an additional sixty-four tapes to Jaworski that were deemed relevant to the inquiry. Among the newly released recordings was White House Tapes Conversation 741-002.[89] This "smoking gun" tape directly implicated the President in the cover-up of the scandal. Three days after tape 741-002 was released to the House Judiciary Committee, it voted to adopt three articles of impeachment against the President. All three articles of impeachment alleged high crimes and misdemeanors by the President.

The first article impeachment alleged violations of the presidential office and violations of the President's constitutional duty under Article II to take care that the laws be faithfully executed.[90] Among the complaints lodged in the first article were that the President personally had and through close subordinates designed a scheme to gain unlawful entry into the DNC headquarters, that the President had made false or misleading statements to investigative officers, that he had withheld relevant information to investigators, that he had misused the Central Intelligence Agency (CIA) in furtherance of the scheme, and that he had abused the powers of the presidency by promising pardons in exchange for the silence and false testimony of his co-conspirators.[91]

The second article of impeachment alleged a variety of abuses of executive branch power. These abuses included using the Internal Revenue Service (IRS) and IRS audits in a discriminatory manner to harass the President's enemies, using the FBI and the Secret Service to electronically surveil private citizens without any basis, establishing a secret investigative unit within the White House funded by

[86] R. W. Apple Jr., *Nixon Declares He Didn't Profit from Public Life*, New York Times (Nov. 18, 1973), www.nytimes.com/1973/11/18/archives/nixon-declares-he-didnt-profit-from-public-life-predicts-both.html.

[87] *Id.*

[88] *Id.*

[89] Richard Nixon Presidential Library, *"Smoking Gun": Richard Nixon and Bob Haldeman Discuss the Watergate Break-in, June 23, 1972*, www.youtube.com/watch?v=ehKRQoN-dIg.

[90] Articles of Impeachment Adopted by the House of Representatives Committee on the Judiciary, www.presidency.ucsb.edu/documents/articles-impeachment-adopted-the-house-representatives-committee-the-judiciary.

[91] *Id.*

campaign contributions, and interfering with the Federal Bureau of Investigation (FBI) and Department of Justice's internal processes for his own personal and political gain.[92]

The third article of impeachment directly addressed Nixon's alleged obstruction of justice during the Senate hearings on the Watergate Scandal. Throughout the Senate's investigation, Nixon on four occasions ignored subpoenas by Congress to produce relevant papers and records. Taken together, these three articles of impeachment painted a damning picture of a president who regularly abused his uniquely executive powers to further his own personal and political ambitions.

The articles of impeachment, however, would never receive a vote before the House of Representatives. After the "smoking gun" tape was released, Nixon's support both in Congress and in his administration almost immediately collapsed. Vice President Ford told Nixon that while he would continue to support the President's policies, he would no longer defend his actions regarding Watergate.[93] Similarly, Republican leaders in Congress, including 1964 Republican nominee for President and United States Senator Barry Goldwater, Senate Minority Leader Hugh Scott, and House Minority Leader John Rhodes indicated that there were enough senators to convict the President and for the good of the country he should resign.[94] The following morning, on August 8, 1974, Nixon addressed the nation and announced that he would be resigning on noon the following day.[95]

14.5 PRESIDENT CLINTON AND PERJURY

The origins of the Clinton impeachment, which occurred in late 1998 and early 1999, date back to a land investment President Clinton made in 1978 when he was the Arkansas Attorney General. In 1978, Clinton contributed money to a joint venture with Arkansas businessman James McDougal to purchase 220 acres in the Ozarks to develop vacation homes through their new business, the Whitewater Development Corporation.[96] In the same year Clinton entered into the agreement with McDougal, he was elected Governor of Arkansas.

Because of the historically poor economic conditions of the late 1970s there was little market appetite for vacation homes. While the Whitewater Development Corporation tried to wait for economic conditions to improve, Clinton continued

[92] *Id.*

[93] GERALD FORD, A TIME TO HEAL: THE AUTOBIOGRAPHY OF GERALD R. FORD, 20–21 (1st ed. 1979).

[94] Dan Nowicki, *In 1974, Goldwater and Rhodes Told Nixon He Was Doomed*, ARIZ. CENTRAL (Aug. 2, 2014), www.azcentral.com/story/azdc/2014/08/03/goldwater-rhodes-nixon-resignation/13497493/.

[95] Carroll Kilpatrick, *Nixon Resigns*, WASH. POST. (Aug. 9, 1974), www.washingtonpost.com/wp-srv/national/longterm/watergate/articles/080974-3.htm.

[96] *Whitewater Timeline*, WASH. POST. (1998), www.washingtonpost.com/wp-srv/politics/special/whitewater/timeline.htm.

to contribute money to the corporation for interest payments on loans and other overhead expenses. When Clinton lost his gubernatorial reelection bid in 1980, McDougal purchased a local bank. It was renamed Madison Guaranty.[97]

In 1984 and 1985 Madison Guaranty began to draw regulatory attention for alleged insider lending, overcompensation to McDougal and his close associates, and other questionable lending practices.[98] Additionally, in 1985 McDougal personally drew scrutiny from investigators when he allegedly used depositor funds to help pay off a Clinton campaign debt.[99] This pattern of allegedly using Madison Guaranty to improperly enrich McDougal and his allies continued throughout the 1980s until 1989, when Madison ultimately collapsed. McDougal was indicted for, but ultimately cleared of, federal fraud charges.[100]

In 1992, as Clinton was running for President, the Federal Resolution Trust Corporation, which was examining the cause of the collapse of Madison, sent a referral to the Department of Justice that identified Clinton as a potential beneficiary of illegal activity at Madison.[101] In January 1994, then Attorney General Janet Reno, who had been appointed by Clinton, appointed Robert Fiske as special counsel to investigate any potential criminal involvement between Whitewater and Clinton.

Just seven months into the investigation, Fiske was replaced when a three-judge federal panel found that under the newly enacted independent counsel statute he was not adequately independent because he had been appointed by Clinton's Attorney General.[102] Fiske was replaced with Kenneth Starr, who previously had served as solicitor general for President George H. W. Bush and as a federal judge on the DC Circuit. As independent counsel, Starr dramatically widened the scope of the investigation from the Arkansas land deal to include statements made by Clinton as part of an ongoing, but unrelated, sexual harassment claim.

The investigation by the special counsel concluded in 1998 with what has become known as the "Starr Report." In the report, Starr concluded that there were eleven grounds to impeach the President, with nine of the eleven charges relating to alleged obstruction of justice and false statements made during the sexual harassment lawsuit.[103] While the Starr Report found no wrongdoing by the Clintons regarding the Whitewater deal that was the original basis for the special counsel's

[97] *Id.*

[98] *Id.*

[99] *Id.*

[100] *Id.*

[101] *Id.*

[102] Sara Fritz, *Fiske Ousted in Whitewater Case; Move is Surprise: Investigation: Federal Three-Judge Panel Names Kenneth Starr as New Special Counsel. Switch Is Seen as Prolonging Probe. The Action Stuns Clinton's Advisers*, Los Angeles Times (Aug. 6, 1994), www.latimes.com/archives/la-xpm-1994-08-06-mn-24261-story.html.

[103] H.R. Rep. No. 105–795, at 5–6 (1998).

investigation, it would ultimately serve as the basis for the impeachment articles against Clinton.

When the House of Representatives brought forward articles of impeachment against President Clinton, they included two articles for high crimes and misdemeanors.[104] The first article alleged that the President had violated his oath of office to preserve, protect, and defend the Constitution and violated his constitutional duty to take care that the laws be faithfully executed.[105] In support of this article, the House alleged that President Clinton had lied to a federal grand jury regarding his relationship with Monica Lewinski, that he had given false testimony in a federal civil rights case brought against him by Paula Jones, that he had allowed his attorney to make similarly false statements in the *Jones* case, and that he had attempted to persuade witnesses to give false testimony to provide cover for his wrongful acts.[106] The articles of impeachment alleged that these acts by the President were impeachable high crimes and misdemeanors because he "undermined the integrity of [the] office, ha[d] brought disrepute on the Presidency ... betrayed his trust as President, and ha[d] acted in a manner subversive to the rule of law and justice, to the manifest injury of the people of the United States."[107]

The second article of impeachment also alleged a violation of his oath of office and violations of the Take Care Clause.[108] Like the first article, Article II focuses on several misleading and false statements made during the civil suit brought by Paula Jones.[109] Identical to the language of Article I, Article II alleges that the President's actions undermined the integrity of his office, betrayed the trust in the presidency, and was a manifest injury to the public.[110]

When the House of Representatives voted on the two articles of impeachment, both passed along near party line votes. The first article of impeachment passed 228–206, with five Republicans voting against it and five Democrats voting in favor.[111] Of the five Democrats to vote in favor of the first article, four were conservative Southern Democrats, three of whom eventually switched parties and become Republicans. The second article passed along a similar near-party line vote of 221–212, with twelve Republicans voting against and the same five Democrats voting in favor.[112]

When the impeachment reached the Senate, it received a similarly partisan vote. For one week in January 1999, House impeachment managers made their case for impeachment and counsel for the President defended it on the grounds that the case

[104] H.R. Res. No. 611 (1998).
[105] *Id.*
[106] *Id.*
[107] *Id.*
[108] *Id.*
[109] *Id.*
[110] *Id.*
[111] 144 Cong. Rec. 28110 (1998).
[112] 144 Cong. Rec. 28111 (1998).

against Clinton was unsubstantiated and did not rise to the constitutional level of impeachment.[113] The deliberations of the two articles would take three days. On the second day of deliberations, Senate Democrat Dianne Feinstein (D-CA) introduced a resolution with the support of a bipartisan group of thirty-seven other senators to censure President Clinton rather than convicting.[114] This resolution never gained any real traction. The following day the Senate voted on the articles of impeachment. On the first article, the Senate returned a "not guilty" verdict, with forty-five Republicans voting for a guilty verdict, and all forty-five Democrats plus ten Republicans voting "not guilty."[115] The vote on the second article was even more partisan, with fifty Republicans voting "guilty," and all Democrats plus five Republicans voting "not guilty."[116] Thus, the Senate failed to reach the two-thirds majority vote necessary to convict.

In the aftermath of Clinton's impeachment and acquittal he was more popular than before the Starr Report was released. In a Pew Research poll, Clinton had a 55 percent approval rating when the Starr Report was released, 71 percent approval rating when the House approved the two articles of impeachment, and a 63 per cent approval rating after the final Senate vote.[117] This change in public opinion is likely a general reflection of public opinion of the impeachment of Clinton. A *Washington Post* opinion poll taken just prior to the House vote to impeach found that just over one-third of Americans believed that Clinton should be impeached and a nearly identical proportion found that the articles of impeachment being put forward were politically motivated.[118]

Putting aside the votes in the House and Senate, the debate continues whether Clinton's perjurious actions were truly impeachable under the Constitution. Some scholars believe that impeachment was inappropriate for Clinton's perjury. The argument in support of this position is twofold. First is that lying under oath in a civil suit alleging tortious conduct that occurred prior to his time in office had no connections to his duties or authority as President.[119] Second, without a connection to the misuse of a distinctly presidential authority the action is not impeachable.

[113] *See generally* THE IMPEACHMENT AND TRIAL OF PRESIDENT CLINTON: THE OFFICIAL TRANSCRIPTS, FROM THE HOUSE JUDICIARY COMMITTEE HEARINGS TO THE SENATE TRIAL (Michael R. Beschloss intro.; Merrill McLoughlin ed., 1st ed. c1999).

[114] S. Res. 44, 106th Congress (1999).

[115] *How the Senators Voted on Impeachment*, CNN (Feb. 12, 1999 12:51 PM), www.senate.gov/legislative/LIS/roll_call_votes/vote1061/vote_106_1_00017.htm.

[116] *Id.*

[117] Drew Desilver, *Clinton's Impeachment Barely Dented His Public Support, and It Turned Off Many Americans*, PEW RESEARCH CENTER (Oct. 3, 2019), *a* www.pewresearch.org/short-reads/2019/10/03/clintons-impeachment-barely-dented-his-public-support-and-it-turned-off-many-americans/.

[118] David Morin & Claudia Deane, *Public Against Impeachment, but Clinton Support Has Limits*, WASH. POST. (Dec. 14, 1998), www.washingtonpost.com/wp-srv/politics/special/clinton/stories/poll121598.htm.

[119] GERHARDT, *supra* note 83, at 101.

On the other hand, some argue that the act of perjury is a distinct violation of the President's constitutional responsibility to see that the laws be faithfully executed and to his oath of office. For those who subscribe to this theory, it does not matter whether the conduct that led to the perjurious statements were official actions or not. Rather, all that matters is that Clinton had made the misleading and false statements twice under oath that were perjurious.

Another way to consider the question of impeachment for perjury is to consider the history of impeachment. Prior to Clinton's impeachment, two federal judges had been impeached for perjury in 1985 and 1989.[120] As discussed in Section 14.1, this raised further questions about the extent impeachment of federal judges should draw comparisons to presidential impeachments. While federal judges in practice are generally subject to a lower bar for impeachable offenses,[121] they are almost always related to some official judicial act. The written words in the Constitution on impeachment make no distinction on the legal burden of proof between federal judges and the President.

14.6 PRESIDENT TRUMP'S FIRST IMPEACHMENT

The first impeachment of President Trump involved a phone call between the President and Ukrainian President Volodymyr Zelenskyy. During the summer of 2019, as the 2020 presidential campaign was getting into full swing, Trump called Zelenskyy and insinuated that if Ukraine wished to receive congressionally appropriated foreign assistance, Zelenskyy should open an investigation into Joe Biden's son's business dealings in Ukraine.[122] The substance of the call came to the attention of Congress when a whistleblower filed a complaint soon after the call was made.

In the month after the whistleblower complaint, Congress, specifically House Democrats, were hesitant to bring articles of impeachment against the President out of concern that the political blowback would threaten their fragile and newly obtained majority in the House. However, a group of seven freshman Democratic members of Congress from battleground districts changed the political calculus of impeachment. In a September 23 *Washington Post* opinion column, these seven members of Congress, all of whom are either veterans or former national security experts, argued that if the allegations in the whistleblower's complaints were true, then the President had threatened national security and corrupted the office of the President.[123] In the view of these seven members, the President's actions had reached the level of an impeachable offense.

[120] *Id.* at 99.

[121] *Id.*

[122] Memorandum of Telephone Conversation with President Zelenskyy of Ukraine (July 25, 2019). Available online in unclassified form at https://d3i6fh83elv35t.cloudfront.net/static/2019/09/Unclassified09.2019.pdf.

[123] Gil Cisneros, Jason Crow, Chrissy Houlahan, Elaine Luria, Mikie Sherrill, Elissa Slotkin, & Abigail Spanberger, *Opinion | Seven Freshman Democrats: These Allegations Are a Threat to All*

One day after the opinion column was published, Speaker of the House Nancy Pelosi announced a formal impeachment inquiry against the President.[124] For the next two and a half months, six committees of the House of Representatives heard from a range of witnesses including White House officials, ambassadors, and members of the President's National Security Council. The House Judiciary Committee ultimately voted along party lines to bring two articles of impeachment against the President.[125] The vote was 13–9.

The articles of impeachment brought against President Trump included a charge of abuse of power and a charge of obstruction of Congress.[126] According to the House, both of these acts constituted a high crime and misdemeanor. As in the Clinton impeachment, both articles of impeachment brought against the President were based on a violation of his oath of office and violations of the Take Care Clause. Article I of the impeachment tied directly into the President's pressure campaign to have Ukrainian President Volodymyr Zelenskyy publicly announce an investigation into then-candidate Joe Biden's son's dealings in Ukraine in exchange for the release of military aid that Congress had already authorized.[127] Article I alleges that this quid pro quo was in pursuit of his personal reelection rather than the national interest, that it compromised national security, it undermined the integrity of the democratic process, and was injurious to the national interest.[128]

Article II of the impeachment was similar to Article III of the Nixon impeachment in that it alleged high crimes and misdemeanors in the form of obstruction of a congressional inquiry.[129] During the lead-up to voting on the articles of impeachment, Congress sought documents from the Executive Branch and testimony from current and former Executive Branch officers. In response to these subpoenas, President Trump on ten separate occasions ordered his staff to defy the subpoenas and to withhold the production of relevant documents.[130] The article also alleges that this obstruction was part of a consistent pattern by President Trump to obstruct investigations throughout his presidency into foreign election interference. In obstructing a constitutionally authorized investigation, the House argued that President Trump violated separation of powers and placed his own personal interest above that of the nation.

We Have Sworn to Protect, WASH. POST. (Sept. 23, 2019, 9:00 AM), www.washingtonpost.com/opinions/2019/09/24/seven-freshman-democrats-these-allegations-are-threat-all-we-have-sworn-protect/.

124 Domenico Montanaro & Susan Davis, *Pelosi Announces Formal Impeachment Inquiry into President Trump*, NAT'L PUB. RADIO (Sept. 24, 2019, 11:22 AM), www.npr.org/2019/09/24/763700264/trumps-ukraine-call-may-be-game-changer-on-impeachment.

125 H.R. REP. NO. 116-346 (2019).

126 H.R. RES. 755, 116th Cong. (2019).

127 *Id.*

128 *Id.*

129 *Id.*

130 GERHARDT, *supra* note 83, at 197.

When the two articles of impeachment were brought before the House of Representatives, they both received a near completely party-line vote of 230–197 in favor of impeachment. Article I received "yea" votes from all but three Democrats and "nay" votes from every Republican in the House.[131] Among the Democrats to vote against Article I were Collin Peterson (D-MN), who represented a heavily Republican district, Jeff Van Drew (D-NJ), who would switch to the Republican Party the day after the impeachment vote, and Tulsi Gabbard (D-HI) (voting "present") who would leave the Democratic Party in 2022 and be appointed by President Trump as Director of National Intelligence in 2025. The second article of impeachment received a nearly identical vote of 299–198 to impeach, with only moderate Jared Golden (D-ME), joining the "nay" votes.[132]

By the time impeachment reached the Senate for trial, it was clear that it would be viewed through a partisan lens. During an interview following the President's impeachment in the House, Senate Majority Leader Mitch McConnell (R-KY) said, "I'm not an impartial juror. This is a political process … The House made a partisan political decision to impeach. I would anticipate we will have a largely partisan outcome in the Senate. I'm not impartial at all about this at all."[133] Similar sentiments were echoed by Senator Lindsey Graham (R-SC), who stated that he's "not trying to pretend to be a fair juror."[134] These statements were made even though each Senator was required as the trial opened to take a separate oath under the Constitution to be impartial during the impeachment trial.

Given the indications by senators leading up to the trial, the final vote was both surprising and unsurprising. On both articles of impeachment, every Democrat voted "guilty."[135] On Article II every Republican voted to acquit.[136] However, on Article I, despite the toxic partisanship of the trial, Senator Mitt Romney (R-UT) became the first Senator in United States history to vote "guilty" for a president of his own party. The final vote was forty-eight votes to convict and fifty-two votes to acquit on Article I and forty-seven votes to convict and fifty-three votes to acquit on Article II.[137]

[131] 165 Cong. Rec. H12205 (daily ed. Dec. 18, 2019).

[132] *Here's How the House Voted on Trump's Impeachment*, Politico (Dec. 18, 2019, 12:07 PM), www.politico.com/interactives/2019/trump-impeachment-vote-count-house-results/.

[133] Kelsey Snell, *McConnell: "I'm Not Impartial" about Impeachment*, Nat'l Pub. Radio (Dec. 17, 2019, 3:06 PM), www.npr.org/2019/12/17/788924966/mcconnell-i-m-not-impartial-about-impeachment.

[134] Colby Itkowitz, *Sen. Graham: "Not Trying to Pretend to Be a Fair Juror,"* Wash. Post. (Dec. 14, 2019, 4:48 PM), www.washingtonpost.com/politics/lindsey-graham-not-trying-to-pretend-to-be-a-fair-juror-here/2019/12/14/dcaad02c-1ea8-11ea-b4c1-fd0d91b60d9e_story.html.

[135] 166 Cong. Rec. S937–S938 (2020) (Rollcall Vote Nos. 33 and 34).

[136] 166 Cong. Rec. S938 (2020) (Rollcall Vote No. 34).

[137] Gerhardt, *supra* note 83, at 128.

14.7 PRESIDENT TRUMP'S SECOND IMPEACHMENT, FOR JANUARY 6, 2021

The most recent presidential impeachment followed in the aftermath of the attack on the United States Capitol on January 6, 2021. Following Donald Trump's loss in the 2020 presidential election, he began a campaign to discredit the results of the election based on debunked claims of "election fraud," including over sixty lawsuits, a call to the Georgia Secretary of State to "find votes," and generally casting doubt on the legitimacy of the election. This campaign culminated with a speech by the President on January 6, 2021, where he warned the crowd assembled that "if you don't fight like hell you're not going to have a country anymore." It was followed by over 1,000 of his supporters storming the Capitol in an attempt to prevent Congress from certifying the votes from the Electoral College. During and after the attack on the Capitol, over 1,000 protesters were arrested and charged for criminal conduct on that day.

The reaction to the attack on the Capitol was swift. Just five days after the assault on the United States Capitol, a single article of impeachment for high crimes and misdemeanors was brought against the President. As in President Clinton's impeachment and President Trump's first impeachment, this article of impeachment alleged high crimes and misdemeanors for violating the oath of office and violating the Take Care Clause.[138] Additionally, it alleged high crimes and misdemeanors by inciting violence against the government of the United States.[139] However, unlike those two prior impeachments, this article also alleged a violation of Section 3 of the Fourteenth Amendment which prohibits those who have engaged in insurrection or rebellion against the United States from holding office.[140]

This article of impeachment was based on two claims. First, it alleged that President Trump repeatedly issued false public statements about voter fraud in the 2020 presidential election in an attempt to wrongfully steal the election. According to the article, these statements included his speech at the Ellipse in Washington, DC the morning before Congress met to certify the election. The President's statements were an attempt to sow doubt on the integrity of the electoral process. They foreseeably led to the ensuing violence at the Capitol a few hours later. The second part of the allegation was that on January 2, 2021 President Trump urged the Georgia Secretary of State to "find" enough votes to overturn the state's result in President Trump's favor.

Despite the overwhelming condemnation of the January 6 attacks, the vote to impeach the President broke down largely along party lines. When the impeachment vote was taken in the House one week after the attack on January 13, 2021, it

[138] H.R. Res. 24, 117th Cong. (2021).
[139] *Id.*
[140] U.S. CONST. AMEND. XIV, § 3.

was adopted by a vote of 232–197.[141] All 222 House Democrats were joined by ten House Republicans in voting for impeachment.[142] The remaining 197 House Republicans voted against the article of impeachment.[143] The large vote in the House against impeachment was perhaps rooted in political survival of House Republicans rather than a principled belief that the President hadn't committed high crimes and misdemeanors. Of the ten Republican members of the House to vote for impeachment, only two were reelected the following term.[144]

By the time the trial began in the Senate, former President Trump had left office. This fact raised the question of whether Trump could be tried at all for impeachment as a *former* president. Prior to opening arguments, Senator Rand Paul (R-KY) brought a motion to dismiss the article of impeachment, arguing that it had been mooted.[145] The motion was defeated 55–45.[146] Despite the motion brought by Senator Paul, it was not the first time the Senate had taken jurisdiction over impeachment after an officer had left office. On six prior occasions, the Senate had voted to convict federal judges who already had resigned.[147] The final vote on the article of impeachment was 57–43, with seven Republicans joining all fifty Senate Democrats in voting guilty. A conviction failed for a lack of two-thirds of the Senate voting in favor.

These majority fifty-seven votes to convict were both the largest number (but not the largest percentage) of votes in history to convict in the Senate and the largest percentage of votes to convict by Senators of the President's own party. As with the vote in the House, the electoral prospects for Republicans who voted to convict was dim. Of the seven Republicans, three retired at the end of their terms in office, one Senator left the Senate to pursue other work, two won reelection in 2020 and are up again in 2026, and another won reelection in 2022.[148]

141 167 CONG. REC. H191 (daily ed. Jan. 13, 2021).

142 *Id.*

143 *Id.*

144 Liz Cheney (R-WY), Jaime Herrera Beutler (R-WA), Peter Meijer (R-MI), and Tom Rice (R-SC) lost their primary elections in 2022. Anthony Gonzalez (R-OH), John Katko (R-NY), Adam Kenzinger (R-IL), and Fred Upton (R-MI) chose to retire from Congress when their term expired in 2023. Dan Newhouse (R-WA) and David Valadao (R-CA) were able to win reelection in 2022.

145 Kadia Goba, *Most Senate Republicans Join Rand Paul Effort to Dismiss Trump's 2nd Impeachment Trial*, AXIOS (Jan. 26, 2021), www.axios.com/2021/01/26/trump-impeachment-trial-vote-to-dismiss.

146 *Id.*

147 GERHARDT, *supra* note 83, at 151.

148 The list of senators who voted to convict includes Richard Burr (R-NC) (retired in 2023), Pat Toomey (R-PA) (retired in 2023), Mitt Romney (R-UT) (retired at the end of his current term in 2025), Ben Sasse (R-NE) (resigned from the Senate to become President of the University of Florida in February 2023), Susan Collins (R-ME), and Bill Cassidy (R-LA) (won reelection in 2020, next up for reelection in 2026), and Lisa Murkowski (R-AK) (won reelection in 2022 with 53.7 percent of the vote).

Following President Trump's acquittal, even those who voted to acquit made known their displeasure with the former President's actions on January 6. Shortly after voting to acquit, Senator Mitch McConnell (R-KY) said that "there's no question, none, that President Trump is practically and morally responsible for provoking the events of the day" and that the former president's actions amounted to "a disgraceful, disgraceful dereliction of duty."[149] Similarly, Senator Chuck Grassley (R-IA), who also voted to acquit, said that "time is going to take care of that [referring to the attacks of January 6] some way or another.[150]

These four instances of Senate acquittal of impeachment make a larger point about Madisonian views of government and the balance of power between Congress and the President. In all four instances, party loyalty, rather than loyalty to the institutional powers of Congress, prevented a president from receiving the high two-thirds vote in the Senate necessary to convict. When party loyalty and polarization override a constitutional responsibility to check abuses of power, the entire scheme of impeachment as a check on presidential abuse becomes a toothless and political exercise.[151] The fear is that future impeachment will be used not as a method to prevent abuse of power, but instead as another political tool by Congress to express its dissatisfaction with a president's policy choices.

14.8 THE TWENTY FIFTH AMENDMENT AND REMOVAL OF A PRESIDENT

An alternative to impeachment, and not yet discussed, is removal of a president on account of physical or mental incapacity. The original Constitution did not provide for removal in such circumstances. But the incapacity of President Woodrow Wilson in the last year of his presidency, the assassination of President Kennedy, and the advent of nuclear weapons brought more urgency to the question of presidential succession.

The possibility that a mentally incapacitated president could destroy human civilization featured prominently in the 1964 election, with President Johnson's famous Daisy Girl television ad suggesting a mentally imbalanced president would start a nuclear war. Some mental health experts weighed in (negatively) on the fitness of the Republican nominee, Senator Barry Goldwater. The ensuing controversy led professional associations of psychiatrists to impose the "Goldwater Rule" prohibiting their members from diagnosing or offering a professional opinion on the

[149] Alan Fram, *GOP's McConnell: Trump Morally Responsible for Jan. 6 Attack*, Associated Press (Feb. 14, 2021, 9:04 AM), https://apnews.com/article/mitch-mcconnell-donald-trump-impeachment-c9a38d7492feea56821f4e0930914b61.

[150] *Id.* Andrew Kaczynski & Melanie Zonona, *In Days after January 6, McCarthy Said Trump Admitted Bearing Some Responsibility for Capitol Attack*, CNN (Jan. 14, 2022 12:18 PM), www.cnn.com/2022/01/14/politics/kfile-kevin-mccarthy-donald-trump-january-6/index.html.

[151] Gerhardt, *supra* note 83, at 156.

mental health of a public figure without evaluation and authorization from the patient.[152]

Regardless of what psychiatrists should be allowed to say publicly about a president or a candidate for the presidency, this controversy regarding mental health and the presidency after the 1964 election also underscored the urgency of addressing on a constitutional level what process should be in place if a president were mentally incapacitated, and potentially dangerous. Through the constitutional amendment process, the Twenty Fifth Amendment was ratified by the states in 1967. The Twenty Fifth Amendment, Section 4 provides:

> Whenever the Vice President and a majority of either the principal officers of the executive departments or of such other body as Congress may by law provide, transmit to the President pro tempore of the Senate and the Speaker of the House of Representatives their written declaration that the President is unable to discharge the powers and duties of his office, the Vice President shall immediately assume the powers and duties of the office as Acting President.
>
> Thereafter, when the President transmits to the President pro tempore of the Senate and the Speaker of the House of Representatives his written declaration that no inability exists, he shall resume the powers and duties of his office unless the Vice President and a majority of either the principal officers of the executive department or of such other body as Congress may by law provide, transmit within four days to the President pro tempore of the Senate and the Speaker of the House of Representatives their written declaration that the President is unable to discharge the powers and duties of his office. Thereupon Congress shall decide the issue, assembling within forty-eight hours for that purpose if not in session. If the Congress, within twenty-one days after receipt of the latter written declaration, or, if Congress is not in session, within twenty-one days after Congress is required to assemble, determines by two-thirds vote of both Houses that the President is unable to discharge the powers and duties of his office, the Vice President shall continue to discharge the same as Acting President; otherwise, the President shall resume the powers and duties of his office.

Removal of a President under the Twenty Fifth Amendment is extraordinarily difficult and challenging. The process does not even begin unless initiated by the "Vice President and a majority of either the principal officers of the executive departments." This means that the majority of the President's Cabinet must deem him unfit for office. Recall from Part I of this book that under the unitary executive theory cabinet officers are removable at will by the President. Any Cabinet officer who questions the President's mental capacity likely will be terminated by the President. A president aware that his own mental health is an issue can through

[152] *See* Jacob M. Appel & Akaela Michels-Gualtieri, *Goldwater after Trump*, 30 Cambridge Q. of Healthcare Ethics 651–61 (Oct. 2021) (observing that since the election of Donald Trump in 2016 "a significant number of psychiatrists have either violated or criticized the rule openly" while arguing for its rescission).

unitary executive removal power assure that he has a Cabinet unlikely even to initiate the Twenty Fifth Amendment removal process. If the majority of the Cabinet does initiate the Twenty Fifth Amendment process, the President when he transmits to Congress "his written declaration that no inability exists" and resumes his powers can also fire the Cabinet, making it virtually impossible that the next step will follow in which the Vice President and "a majority of either the principal officers of the executive department … transmit within four days to [Congress] their written declaration that the President is unable to discharge the powers and duties of his office."

Congress could fix this problem by providing for another body to initiate this process – for example a panel of medical experts, former presidents or some other combination of experts – but Congress has not done so.[153]

A second problem is that even were the Twenty Fifth Amendment removal process to be pursued, if the President insists that he is mentally competent to hold office, the final decision rests with the Congress. The required threshold to remove the President – two-thirds of each House – is very high. In fact, higher than for impeachment, where only a majority of the House is required to initiate the process although two-thirds of the Senate must agree to convict. This means that even if somehow the Vice President and the majority of the Cabinet were to initiate the removal process and continue it in Congress, Congress would be very unlikely to follow through with removal except in the most extraordinary case.

[153] *See* Norman Eisen & Richard W. Painter, *Interpreting and Implementing the Twenty-Fifth Amendment, in* The Dangerous Case of Donald Trump: 37 Psychiatrists and Mental Health Experts Assess a President (Bandy X. Lee ed., 2019) (recommending legislation that would establish an appointed panel to evaluate the President's mental fitness for office instead of relying on the Cabinet to perform this role).

15

Suing the President

Impeachment by Congress is the principal Article I check on the presidency. Presidents also can be held accountable in federal courts and sometimes by state courts. These include suits for injunctive relief against the President such as the famous *Youngstown Steel* case.[1] More recent cases include *Boumediene v. Bush*[2] and *Biden v. Nebraska*.[3] A separate category is when a president or former president is personally sued for money damages. In these scenarios we consider what special rules, if any, apply when the President is a defendant?

15.1 CAN A PRESIDENT BE CIVILLY SUED FOR OFFICIAL ACTS?

This question was addressed in *Nixon v. Fitzgerald*.[4] Arthur Ernest Fitzgerald, an Air Force civilian contractor, blew the whistle on a $2.3 billion cost overrun for the Lockheed C-5 aircraft. He subsequently testified before Congress. President Nixon ordered him fired. Fitzgerald was not a presidential appointee subject to removal at will, so he sued claiming wrongful discharge. One of the defendants was Nixon himself, who by the time of suit was a former president.

Most federal and state officials enjoy some form of qualified immunity from civil suit for "official acts." The defense of qualified immunity bars actions for damages against government officials, unless the defendant meets a very high standard of culpability. Violating a clear statutory or constitutional mandate of which a reason-

1 Youngstown Sheet & Tube Co. v. Sawyer, 343 U.S. 579 (1952).

2 Boumediene v. Bush, 553 U.S. 723 (2008) (granting a writ of habeas corpus for a prisoner at the military prison in Guantanamo Bay, Cuba).

3 Biden v. Nebraska, 600 U.S. 477 (2023) (striking down an executive order forgiving federally guaranteed student loans).

4 Nixon v. Fitzgerald, 457 U.S. 731 (1982).

able person would have known is an example.[5] Qualified immunity is a well-established legal doctrine, allowing civil suits for the most egregious behavior to go forward, but allowing immunity for public officials who believe they are acting within the bounds of the law and their authority.

Nixon, however, claimed absolute immunity from civil suit for official acts as President. Absolute immunity bars any suit against a public official even if a higher standard of culpability is met.

The Court already had bestowed broad immunity on federal officials in suits brought at common law.

> In exercising the functions of his office, the head of an executive department, keeping within the limits of his authority, should not be under an apprehension that the motives that control his official conduct may at any time become the subject of inquiry in a civil suit for damages. It would seriously cripple the proper and effective administration of public affairs as entrusted to the executive branch of the government, if he were subjected to any such restraint.[6]

Subsequent decisions interpreted statutes allowing public officials immunity.[7]

The Court in *Nixon* held that a former president has absolute immunity from civil suit for his official acts in office.

> Applying the principles of our cases to claims of this kind, we hold that petitioner, as a former President of the United States, is entitled to absolute immunity from damages liability predicated on his official acts. We consider this immunity a functionally mandated incident of the President's unique office, rooted in the constitutional tradition of the separation of powers and supported by our history.[8]

The Court also rejected the argument that Nixon's actions were not within his official responsibility because they were illegal. "This construction would subject the President to trial on virtually every allegation that an action was unlawful, or was taken for a forbidden purpose. Adoption of this construction thus would deprive absolute immunity of its intended effect."[9] A president's absolute immunity thus

5 Lawrence Rosenthal, *Defending Qualified Immunity*, 72 S.C. L. Rev. 547 (2021). *See also* Gregory C. Sisk, *How Qualified Immunity Condones Rogue Behavior by Government Officers*, U of St. Thomas (Minnesota) Legal Studies Research Paper No. 22-12, https://ssrn.com/abstract=4048427.

6 Spalding v. Vilas, 161 U.S. 483, (1896) (affirming immunity from common law civil suit for the Postmaster General of the United States).

7 Subsequent decisions have interpreted statutes to allow public officials immunity. For example Pierson v. Ray, 386 U.S. 547 (1967) held that common law principle that judicial immunity from liability for judicial acts was not abolished by 42 U.S.C. § 1983. Similarly, in Scheuer v. Rhodes, 416 U.S. 232 (1947) the Supreme Court held that in varying scope qualified immunity is available to executive branch officers depending on the scope of discretion, the responsibility of the office, and the circumstances as they appeared at the time of the action for which liability is being sought.

8 Nixon v. Fitzgerald, 457 U.S. 731 (1982) at 749.

9 *Id.* at 756.

extends to all acts within the "outer perimeter" of his duties of office both while in office or after the completion of his term.[10]

In a footnote in *Fitzgerald*, the Court distinguished civil liability from criminal liability: "The Court has recognized before that there is a lesser public interest in actions for civil damages than, for example, in criminal prosecutions."[11] Immunity from criminal prosecution was not addressed in *Fitzgerald* or subsequently until the Court decided *Trump v. United States* in 2024.[12]

15.2 CAN A SITTING PRESIDENT BE CIVILLY SUED FOR PERSONAL CONDUCT?

This question was addressed by the Supreme Court in *Clinton v. Jones*.[13] Paula Jones, as an Arkansas state employee, alleged that Bill Clinton, as Governor, had used his position to demand sex from her. Her lawsuit had the support of many prominent conservatives who disliked Clinton, including billionaire Richard Mellon Scaife, who funded the "Arkansas project" seeking to investigate, discredit, and ultimately impeach Clinton after he was elected President.

Liberals rallied to Clinton's defense. This led to a paradigmatic shift in perspectives on presidential accountability. With the abuses of the Nixon administration over two decades in the past, liberal politicians focused more on the short-term objective of protecting Clinton from accountability than the long-term dangers of an unaccountable president. The *Jones* case was the first test. Many of Clinton's defenders argued that a sitting president should not be sued in civil court for anything, even personal conduct.

Extrapolating from *Nixon v. Fitzgerald*, Clinton, with the support of the Justice Department, argued that a civil suit, even for personal conduct, would be too much of a burden on the presidency and should be postponed until after a president leaves office.

Some liberal academics followed suit. In a *Harvard Law Review* article, Professor Akhil Reed Amar of Yale Law School and Neal Kumar Katyal, then a law student at Yale, argued that Article II of the Constitution required that a president be immune from civil suit before leaving office.[14]

[10] *Id*. at 755–57.

[11] *See* United States v. Gillock, 445 U.S. 360, 371–73 (1980); *cf*. United States v. Nixon, 418 U.S. at 711–12, and fn 19 (basing holding on special importance of evidence in a criminal trial and distinguishing civil actions as raising different questions not presented for decision).

[12] Trump v. United States, 603 U.S. 593 (2024). This case is discussed at length in Chapter 16 of this book.

[13] Clinton v. Jones, 520 U.S. 681 (1997).

[14] Akhil Reed Amar & Neal Kumar Katyal, *Executive Privileges and Immunities: The Nixon and Clinton Cases*, 108 Harv. L. Rev. 701 (1995).

The Supreme Court rejected these and similar arguments in a unanimous decision in *Clinton v. Jones*.[15] Clinton argued he was too busy being President to deal with a civil suit. This defense fell on deaf ears. Most telling was this colloquy between the President's lawyers and Justice Scalia in oral argument:

JUSTICE SCALIA. But we see Presidents riding horseback, chopping firewood, fishing for stick fish, playing golf and so forth and so on. Why can't we leave it to the point where, if and when a court tells a President to be there or he's going to lose his case, and if and when a President has the intestinal fortitude to say, "I am absolutely too busy," so that he'll never be seen playing golf for the rest of his Administration, if and when that happens, we can resolve the problem.

MR. DELLINGER. Justice Scalia –

JUSTICE SCALIA. But, really, the notion that he doesn't have a minute to spare is, is just not credible.[16]

History records that what followed next was some of the political chaos that Clinton's defenders had predicted in arguing for presidential immunity from civil suit, although much of this chaos came not from the suit itself but because Clinton, in a deposition in the *Jones* case, chose to lie under oath about his affair with another subordinate, White House intern Monica Lewinsky. This lie, not the *Jones* case itself, gave Republicans the opportunity to try to take down the President. That investigation is discussed in the next chapter, where we address the independent counsel statute. Clinton's subsequent impeachment is addressed in the previous chapter (Section 14.5).

15.3 THE DIFFERENCE BETWEEN OFFICIAL AND PERSONAL CONDUCT OF THE PRESIDENT

If presidents are immune from suit for "official acts," but can be sued for personal capacity acts, some presidents will be tempted to argue that everything they do is "official."

Carroll v. Trump,[17] a sexual abuse case, was filed during the Trump presidency. It quickly became a defamation case when Trump responded in 2019 by calling Carroll a liar. The Department of Justice – under Trump and surprisingly also under Biden – filed briefs with the court arguing that Trump's allegedly defamatory statements about Carroll were made in an "official capacity." Thus they were not

[15] *Id.*

[16] *Excerpts from Arguments before the Supreme Court in Clinton Case*, NEW YORK TIMES (Jan. 14, 1997), www.nytimes.com/1997/01/14/us/excerpts-from-arguments-before-the-supreme-court-in-clinton-case.html.

[17] E. Jean Carroll v. Donald J. Trump, 22-cv-10016 (S.D.N.Y. 2023).

amenable to suit for money damages under *Nixon v. Fitzgerald*, the aforementioned case in which the Court held a president is not liable for money damages for *official* acts. Carrol, of course, disagreed: How can slandering a woman who claims sexual assault be an official act? The willingness of the Biden Justice Department to side with defendant Trump on this issue in a sexual abuse case shows how deeply ingrained the concept of presidential privilege is in administrations of both political parties. Ultimately the federal courts refused to extend immunity to Trump in the Carroll case because the lawsuit did not involve his official conduct as president.[18]

Most recently, a series of civil lawsuits brought against President Trump as a private citizen for his role in the January 6, 2021 assault on the Capitol has brought new wrinkles to the distinction between official and personal conduct. Eight separate lawsuits, brought by police officers and members of Congress who were at the Capitol that day, allege a variety of claims including incitement to riot, civil rights violations, battery, assault, and other claims.[19]

Unlike the four criminal cases brought against President Trump, that have all but ended following his reelection in 2024, these eight civil cases have continued because, unlike the criminal cases, these civil cases have survived immunity reviews by courts. In 2022, a federal district court ruled that Trump's speech near the White House hours before the Capitol was attacked constituted personal conduct because there was no connection between the speech and the President's official duties.[20] This decision was later upheld in 2024 by a federal court of appeals.[21]

While it is unclear, at this writing, if these eight civil cases will survive Trump's reelection, at this time they represent a stark contrast to the outright dismissal of the criminal cases brought against Trump.

15.3.1 *Who Can Get an Injunction against the President?*

What if a president exceeds the parameters of presidential power discussed in Part I of this book? Who can stop him by suing in the courts? The short answer to this question is that most people can't.

The first question that must be addressed is "standing." Not every plaintiff has standing to sue the President, or an agency of the federal government for that matter. The plaintiff must show a unique injury that is different from an alleged injury to the public at large. Article III of the Constitution requires that a plaintiff suffer an

[18] *See* Carroll v. Trump, 23-793 (2nd Cir., June 13, 2025) (denying hearing en banc of an appellate panel's denial of President Trump's appeal to set aside the $5 million verdict against him), https://storage.courtlistener.com/recap/gov.uscourts.ca2.60504/gov.uscourts.ca2.60504.199.0_3.pdf.

[19] Alan Feuer, *As Jan. 6 Criminal Cases against Trump Fizzle, Civil Cases Plod Ahead*, New York Times (Dec. 6, 2024), www.nytimes.com/2024/12/06/us/politics/trump-jan-6-civil-cases.html.

[20] *Id.*

[21] United States v. Trump, 91 F.4th 1173, (D.C. Cir. 2024).

injury "in fact" — a concrete and imminent harm to a legally protected interest, like property or money, that is traceable to conduct likely to be redressed by the court.[22] Some lawsuits brought against the President for alleged abuse of power are never decided on the merits because the plaintiffs lack standing. In fact, it may be very hard to find plaintiffs who do have standing.

This almost happened in the 2023 student loans case, *Biden v. Nebraska*.[23] The Department of Justice argued that the states had no standing to sue over President Biden's executive order forgiving hundreds of billions of dollars in student loans. The Court ultimately ruled that at least one state agency in Missouri had standing because it could show a unique injury to its interests – the Higher Education Loan Authority of the State of Missouri (MOHELA), a nonprofit government corporation created by Missouri to participate in the student loan market, credibly alleged that it would lose an estimated $44 million a year in fees because of the President's loan forgiveness plan.[24] The Court then decided the case on the merits, striking down the plan as exceeding Biden's statutory authority.[25]

The suits brought against President Trump under the Emoluments Clause of the Constitution stalled for three years over standing issues. The merits of those suits are addressed in Chapter 12 of this book on financial conflicts of interest of the President, but the merits were not addressed until standing issues were resolved. By that time Trump had left office, and the Supreme Court dismissed in 2021 the suits as moot. The public interest group Citizens for Responsibility and Ethics in Washington (CREW) was ruled not to have standing to sue Trump for violation of the Emoluments Clause,[26] and even a large group of Democrats in Congress were also ruled not to have standing,[27] but restaurants and hotels competing with Trump were deemed to have standing to sue on the theory that Trump's unconstitutional foreign emoluments gave him an unfair competitive advantage.[28] Interestingly, the Emoluments Clause was not put in the Constitution to protect public officials' business competitors, rather to protect the public from a particularly dangerous type of public corruption. Standing under Article III, as interpreted by the federal courts, nevertheless, does not extend in most cases to the general public, public interest organizations, or even Members of Congress, but rather only to those persons who can show a unique and identifiable injury in fact.

Standing, again, was the ground for dismissal of one of the most important First Amendment cases decided by the Court in 2024. In *Murthy v. Missouri*,[29] the Court

22 Lujan v. Defenders of Wildlife, 504 U.S. 555, 560–61 (1992).
23 Biden v. Nebraska, 600 U.S. 477 (2023).
24 *Id.*
25 *Biden v. Nebraska* is discussed in further detail in Part I of this book.
26 Citizens for Responsibility & Ethics in Wash. v. Trump, 276 F. Supp. 3d 174 (S.D.N.Y. 2018).
27 Blumenthal v. Trump, 949 F.3d 14 (D.C. Cir. 2020).
28 Citizens for Responsibility & Ethics in Wash. v. Trump, No. 18-474-cv (2nd Cir. 2020).
29 Murthy v. Missouri, 603 U.S. 43 (2024).

addressed First Amendment challenges to the Biden administration's "soft pressure" on social media companies to take down harmful or misleading content. The Court did not decide the case on the constitutional merits. Rather, the Court dismissed the case arguing that the plaintiff lacked standing to sue the Biden administration.

The Court required a threshold showing that a particular defendant federal agency pressured a particular social media platform to censor a particular topic *before* that platform suppressed a particular plaintiff's speech on that topic. The plaintiff needed to demonstrate that the platform acted due to government *coercion*, rather than acting on its own judgment.[30] The standing requirements imposed by the Court, however, make it very unlikely that future plaintiffs will sue successfully over these or similar federal interventions with social media platforms over content moderation policies. For practical purposes, this means that the Court did much the same thing as deciding the case on the merits. Present and future administrations likely will be permitted to put considerable soft pressure on social media platforms without a particular plaintiff showing a connection between that pressure and censorship of their speech by social media companies sufficient to have standing to sue.

This standing problem is even more salient with respect to presidential war powers. As discussed in Part I of this book, presidents acted at the very "outer limits" of their constitutional powers, sometimes exceeding those powers, for well over a century. But one reason presidents have used war powers so broadly is that courts don't intervene because almost nobody has standing to sue. For example, courts were flooded with petitions to end the Vietnam War and again the war in Iraq after 9/11, but they were dismissed because of lack of standing.[31]

There are some exceptions, however. For instance, these include the case overturning President Truman's wartime seizure of steel companies to resolve a labor dispute[32] and habeas corpus petitions brought by a US citizen detained as a suspected terrorist after 9/11.[33] But these cases involve persons *uniquely* impacted by an act of the President or his subordinates, not persons *generally* impacted by the President's decisions to go to war, or whether to conduct a particular military operation. These decisions, if they are challenged at all, will be challenged in the voting booth, not the federal courts.

In conclusion, a lot of presidential power may never be challenged in the courts because standing requirements for plaintiffs are sufficiently narrow that the most important presidential decisions that affect everybody never get adjudicated.

30 *Id.*

31 *See e.g.* Alden B. Campen et al., Plaintiffs, v. Richard M. Nixon et al., Defendants, 56 F.R.D. 404 (N.D. Cal. 1972) (suit challenging legality of Vietnam War dismissed where plaintiffs only claim of standing to raise the issue was that they were citizens and taxpayers).

32 Youngstown Sheet & Tube Co. v. Sawyer, 343 U.S. 579 (1952).

33 Hamdi v. Rumsfeld, 542 U.S. 507 (2004).

A related question to "standing" is when do courts refuse to decide questions about presidential power because they are too "political"? The "political questions" doctrine is a common reason for lawsuits against the President to be dismissed.

Under this doctrine, the courts' jurisdiction under the Constitution must extend to "cases and controversies" between specific parties. Matters that are under separation of powers principles should be resolved by other branches of government. As Chief Justice Marshall wrote, "[q]uestions, [which are] in their nature political, or which are, by the constitution and laws, submitted to the executive, can never be made in this court."[34]

The criteria used to determine whether a dispute presents a nonjusticiable "political question" are: (1) a textually demonstrable constitutional commitment of the issue to a coordinate political department; (2) a lack of judicially discoverable and manageable standards for resolving it; (3) the impossibility of deciding without an initial policy determination of a kind clearly for nonjudicial discretion; (4) the impossibility of a court's undertaking independent resolution without expressing lack of the respect due coordinate branches of government; (5) an unusual need for unquestioning adherence to a political decision already made; or (6) the potential of embarrassment if multiple branches or departments of government answer the question in different ways.[35] Even one of these factors can indicate the existence of a political question.[36] The political questions doctrine is particularly likely to be invoked in cases that involve foreign relations.[37]

[34] Marbury v. Madison, 5 U.S. 1 (1 Cranch) 137, 170 (1803). *See* Baker v. Carr, 369 U.S. 186, 210 (1962) (the nonjusticiability of political questions is based on separation of powers, where a matter under the Constitution is committed to another branch of government); Powell v. McCormack, 395 U.S. 486, 518 (1969); Japan Whaling Ass'n v. Am. Cetacean Soc'y, 478 U.S. 221, 230 (1986) (the doctrine "excludes from judicial review those controversies which revolve around policy choices and value determinations constitutionally committed for resolution to the halls of Congress or the confines of the Executive Branch").

[35] Baker v. Carr, 369 U.S. 186, 217 (1962).

[36] Rucho v. Common Cause, 588 U.S. 684 (2019) (holding in a 5-4 decision that partisan claims of gerrymandering raise political questions that are not reviewable by the courts, but that gerrymandering may be "incompatible with democratic principles.")

[37] *See e.g.* Oetjen v. Central Leather Co., 246 U.S. 297, 302 (1918) (foreign relations "is committed by the Constitution to the executive and legislative – 'the political' – departments of the government, and the propriety of what may be done in the exercise of this political power is not subject to judicial inquiry or decision"); Haig v. Agee, 453 U.S. 280, 292 (1981) (foreign relations is "exclusively entrusted to the political branches ... [and] immune from judicial inquiry or interference"); United States v. Curtiss-Wright Exp. Corp., 299 U.S. 304, 319 (1936) ("The President is the sole organ of the nation in its external relations, and its sole representative with foreign nations").

16

Prosecuting the President

16.1 INDICTING A SITTING PRESIDENT

It's one thing to say a sitting president can be civilly sued for personal capacity conduct, as the Court held in *Clinton v. Jones*.[1] It's quite another to say that a sitting president can be indicted for a crime. Or are they so different? The courts have never addressed this question. The Department of Justice (DOJ) in three Office of Legal Counsel memos (1974, 2000, and 2019) answered in the negative. Other lawyers and legal scholars disagree.[2]

The Constitution is silent on this topic. It provides in Article I, Section 3, Clause 7 that: "Judgment in Cases of Impeachment shall not extend further than to removal from Office, and disqualification to hold and enjoy any Office of honor, Trust or Profit under the United States: but the Party convicted shall nevertheless be liable and subject to Indictment, Trial, Judgment and Punishment, according to Law."

Some scholars have argued that this provision requires impeachment and conviction to come before criminal indictment and trial, that unless and until a president is impeached and removed from office, criminal charges cannot be brought.[3] The problem is that this clause applies to impeachment of any federal officer, not just presidents. There is ample precedent of impeachable federal officers, such as cabinet members and federal judges, being criminally indicted without

[1] Clinton v. Jones, 520 U.S. 681 (1997).

[2] *See* Claire O. Finkelstein & Richard W. Painter, *Presidential Accountability and the Rule of Law: Can the President Claim Immunity if He Shoots Someone on Fifth Avenue?* 24 UNIV. OF PENN. J. OF CONST. L. 93 (2022); Laurence H. Tribe, *Yes, the Constitution Allows Indictment of the President*, LAWFARE (Dec. 20, 2018) (explaining that the language in Article 1, Section 3, Clause 7 was intended to avoid the ban on double jeopardy which otherwise could preclude criminal proceedings after impeachment and conviction).

[3] Cass R. Sunstein, *A Sitting President Can't Be Prosecuted*, BLOOMBERG QUINT (Aug. 1, 2017); Philip Bobbitt, *Can the President Be Indicted? A Response to Laurence Tribe*, LAWFARE (Dec. 17, 2018).

impeachment. For example, Seventh Circuit Judge Otto Kerner only resigned from the bench a week before he was required to report to prison on a bribery conviction. Even the Office of Legal Counsel (OLC) memos disfavoring indictment of a sitting president reject the argument that Article I, Section 3, Clause 7 requires impeachment to precede an indictment or criminal trial.[4]

Instead, the OLC memos assert that indictment and trial of a *sitting* president unconstitutionally would interfere with Article II powers of the President. The time commitment required of the President to defend a criminal trial is one factor. Another is the risk of a politically motivated criminal indictment specifically intended to hinder the presidency. Yet another problem is that the threat of criminal indictment could be used to coerce the President in his decisions. Finally, the OLC considered the national security risks of allowing a criminal case to proceed against the Commander in Chief. For a range of reasons, OLC concluded that indictment of a sitting president was unconstitutional.

Critics of the OLC memos, including one of the authors of this book and Professor Claire Finkelstein, have argued that all of these problems with indicting and even trying a sitting president should be addressed by federal courts on a case-by-case basis rather than a categorical assumption that indicting a sitting president is per se unconstitutional.[5] For example, a court overseeing the trial of a sitting president could accommodate the President's schedule, as observed in the *Clinton* case, for depositions and the trial itself, and also protect the executive privilege against unwarranted intrusion by prosecutors.

Most important, the argument is that criminal accountability of a sitting president is essential in view of the difficulties of impeachment, a topic discussed in Chapter 14. Given the highly political nature of impeachment proceedings, and the two-thirds majority vote required to convict in the Senate, leaving impeachment as the only constraint on a criminal president is potentially dangerous.[6] The prospect of voting a criminal president out of office also is an unappealing alternative, given that elections are only every four years and an incumbent president is virtually assured his party's nomination. In a functioning democracy, rooted in the principles of the rule of law, a president must be accountable under the criminal law like everyone else.

There is, however, a different view. Presidential immunity was embraced by some liberal constitutional law scholars at the time of President Clinton's legal peril at the hands of special prosecutor Kenneth Starr. Akhil Amar in 1997 argued that after the

[4] Amenability of the President, Vice President, and Other Civil Officers to Federal Criminal Prosecution While in Office, Op. Office of Legal Counsel (OLC) (Sept. 24, 1973) at 7. The two subsequent OLC opinions on immunity are A Sitting President's Amenability to Indictment and Criminal Prosecution, Op. O.L.C. (Oct. 16, 2000), and Memorandum for the Attorney General, Review of the Special Counsel's Report (Mar. 24, 2019).

[5] *See* Finkelstein & Painter, supra note 2.

[6] *Id.*

Court granted presidents immunity from civil suit for official acts, this same logic should extend to criminal prosecution and that a sitting president could not be criminally indicted: "[the President's] temporary privilege from prosecution is less of a threat to the rule of the law than the immunity given to presidents acting in their official capacities. President Nixon said that 'if the President does it, it's not illegal' and the Supreme Court, in the case of *Nixon v. Fitzgerald* essentially agreed with him."[7]

The fact that supposedly some liberal constitutional law scholars agreed with Nixon on presidential immunity shows the impact the Clinton presidency had in undermining what appeared to be the post-Watergate consensus that the President should be constrained by the rule of law and the constitutional requirement of accountability through the doctrine of checks and balances.

For conservatives, it was the Trump presidency that brought back the Nixonian perspective on presidential immunity. Justice Samuel Alito, dissenting in *Trump v. Vance* in 2020, describes the parade of horribles that he envisioned following even from a state grand jury subpoena for the President's personal papers:

> If a sitting President were charged in New York County, would he be arrested and fingerprinted? He would presumably be required to appear for arraignment in criminal court, where the judge would set the conditions for his release. Could he be sent to Rikers Island or be required to post bail? Could the judge impose restrictions on his travel? If the President were scheduled to travel abroad – perhaps to attend a G-7 meeting – would he have to get judicial approval? If the President were charged with a complicated offense requiring a long trial, would he have to put his Presidential responsibilities aside for weeks on end while sitting in a Manhattan courtroom? While the trial was in progress, would aides be able to approach him and whisper in his ear about pressing matters? Would he be able to obtain a recess whenever he needed to speak with an aide at greater length or attend to an urgent matter, such as speaking with a foreign leader? Could he effectively carry out all his essential Presidential responsibilities after the trial day ended and at the same time adequately confer with his trial attorneys regarding his defense? Or should he be expected to give up the right to attend his own trial and be tried in absentia? And if he were convicted, could he be imprisoned? Would aides be installed in a nearby cell?[8]

We ask: what did the Founders think on this issue? The answer is not entirely clear.

As discussed in the Finkelstein and Painter law review article, among others, the legislative history of the Constitution reveals little discussion of whether a sitting president can be subjected to criminal prosecution. The most on-point discussion of this hypothetical occurred after ratification of the Constitution in the Senate

[7] Akhil Reed Amar & Brian C. Kalt, *The Presidential Privilege against Prosecution*, 2 Nexus 11, 16 (1997).

[8] Trump v. Vance, 591 U.S. 786 (2020) (J. Alito dissenting).

cloakroom during the First Congress. William Maclay, Senator from Pennsylvania, kept a diary while in Congress, and recounted a debate he had with Vice President John Adams and Senator Oliver Ellsworth on whether the President was subject to judicial process from federal courts:

> [Adams and Ellsworth] said the President, personally, was not the subject of any process whatever; could have no action whatever brought against him; was above the power of all judges, justices, etc. For what, said they, would you put it in the power of a common justice to exercise any authority over him and stop the whole machine of government? I said that, although President, he is not above the laws. Both of them declared you could only impeach him, and no other process whatever lay against him . . . I put the case: "Suppose the President committed murder in the street. Impeach him? But you can only remove him from office on impeachment. Why, when he is no longer President you can indict him. But in the meantime, he runs away. But I will put up another case. Suppose he continues his murders daily, and neither House is willing to impeach him?" Oh, the people would arise and restrain him. "Very well, you will allow the mob to do what legal justice must abstain from." Mr. Adams said I was arguing from cases nearly impossible. There had been some hundreds of crowned heads within these two centuries in Europe, and there was no instance of any of them having committed murder. Very true, in the retail way, Charles IX of France excepted. They generally do these things on a great scale. I am, however, certainly within the bounds of possibility, though it may be improbable.[9]

Maclay was an ardent anti-Federalist, very critical of President Washington, and presidential power in general. There is no separate verification of the views attributed to John Adams, although Adams was aligned with the Federalist vision of presidential power and a strong central government.

The President's accountability under the criminal law also arose in more general terms during the ratification debate. James Iredell told the North Carolina legislature that in Great Britain a privy council was needed to constrain the monarch:

> In that country, the executive authority is vested in a magistrate who holds it by birthright. He has great powers and prerogatives, and it is a constitutional maxim, *that he can do no wrong*. We have experienced that he can do wrong, yet no man can say so in his own country. There are no courts to try him for any high crimes; nor is there any constitutional method of depriving him of his throne. If he loses it, it must be by a general resistance of his people, contrary to *forms* of law, as at the revolution which took place about a hundred years ago.[10]

9 William Maclay, Diary of Senator William Maclay, United States Senator from Pennsylvania, 1789–91 (Edgar S. Maclay ed., 1890).

10 Elliot, Jonathan, ed., The Debates in the Several State Conventions on the Adoption of the Federal Constitution as Recommended by the General Convention at Philadelphia in 1787, 5 vols. (2nd ed. 1888).

The President of the United States, however, is different:

> Under our Constitution we are much happier . . . No man has an authority to injure another with impunity. No man is better than his fellow-citizens, nor can pretend to any superiority over the meanest man in the country. If the President does a single act by which the people are prejudiced, he is punishable himself, and no other man merely to screen him. If he commits any misdemeanor in office, he is impeachable, removable from office, and incapacitated to hold any office of honor, trust, or profit. *If he commits any crime, he is punishable by the laws of his country, and in capital cases may be deprived of his life*. This being the case, there is not the same reason here for having a council which exists in England.[11]

Professors Finkelstein and Painter argue that this speech, and others made to convince the states to ratify the Constitution, suggest that the Framers never intended that the President be outside the reach of criminal prosecution.[12]

Regardless of the intent of the Framers, the intent of the Justice Department is set forth clearly in the 1973, 2000, and 2019 memos, and the Justice Department decides who to prosecute for federal crimes. A sitting president will not be indicted by federal prosecutors, according to the DOJ. To change that, OLC would have to reverse its position in the memos, which is highly unlikely when senior OLC lawyers are appointees of the President. A more likely solution would be for Congress to reauthorize the independent counsel statute, a topic we discuss in a separate section below, and then specifically provide that the independent counsel can indict a sitting president. At that juncture, a president who was indicted could challenge the constitutionality of the indictment.

The Supreme Court, ultimately, might have to decide whether the arguments in the OLC memos against indicting a sitting president truly rise to constitutional proportions such that, even if Congress provides for it, indictment and trial of a sitting president is prohibited. Justice Kavanaugh, before he joined the Court, published an article on this issue and emphasized the interference a prosecution would have with presidential duties. But he stopped short of saying that prosecution of a sitting president would be per se unconstitutional. When criminal prosecution and sometimes even investigation of a sitting president is postponed, "[t]he point is not to put the President above the law or to eliminate checks on the President, but simply to defer litigation and investigations until the President is out of office."[13]

[11] *Speech by James Iredell at the North Carolina Ratifying Convention 28 July 1788*, in The Debates in the Several State Conventions on the Adoption of the Federal Constitution as Recommended by the General Convention at Philadelphia in 1787, 4:108–10 (Jonathan Elliot ed., 1888), reprinted *by* University of Chicago Founders Documents (emphasis added).

[12] Finkelstein & Painter, *supra* note 2.

[13] Brett Kavanaugh, *Separation of Powers during the Forty- Fourth Presidency and Beyond*, 93 Minn. L. Rev. 1454, 1462 (2009). Justice Kavanaugh served in President George W. Bush's administration before being appointed to the federal bench.

Unless and until a prosecutor charges a sitting president, however, this question will be unanswered.

A related issue is whether a person who was previously indicted before becoming president can be prosecuted while serving as president. The Justice Department in late 2024 decided the answer is no. An indicted sitting president cannot be brought to trial. Special Counsel Jack Smith thus requested the dismissal of the criminal case he had brought in 2023 against Donald Trump in the District of Columbia for his role in the effort to overturn the 2020 election.[14] The Special Counsel also withdrew his appeal of a judge's order dismissing another criminal case against Trump in Florida for taking classified documents in 2021.[15] To support this decision, Smith cited the DOJ's longstanding position that a sitting president cannot be subject to criminal prosecution,[16] set forth in the 1973, 2000, and 2019 OLC memoranda discussed earlier in this chapter. The DOJ's policy against indicting a sitting president also had been cited by Special Counsel Robert Mueller as a factor in his 2019 determination not to prosecute Donald Trump in the Russia investigation.[17] Again, this was a factor in the decision by Special Counsel Robert Hur in his 2023 determination not to prosecute President Biden for the unauthorized removal and retention of classified documents between 2017 and 2021.[18]

[14] United States v. Donald Trump, Opinion filed November 25, 2024 (D. D.C. Criminal Action 23-257) (dismissing the case without prejudice because "immunity afforded to a sitting President is temporary, expiring when they leave office"), www.documentcloud.org/documents/25402573-chutkan-ruling-on-trump-dismissal/.

[15] United States v. Donald J. Trump, Waltine Nauta, and Carlos De Oliveira (11th Cir.), Case No. 24-12311, Order filed Nov. 26, 2024 (granting motion to dismiss appeal as to defendant Trump only), www.courtlistener.com/docket/68955302/81/2/united-states-v-donald-trump/.

[16] United States v. Donald Trump, Government's Motion to Dismiss filed November 25, 2024 (D. D.C. Criminal Action 23-257) ("It has long been the position of the Department of Justice that the United States Constitution forbids the federal indictment and subsequent criminal prosecution of a sitting President. But the Department and the country have never faced the circumstance here, where a federal indictment against a private citizen has been returned by a grand jury and a criminal prosecution is already underway when the defendant is elected President. … After careful consideration, the Department has determined that OLC's prior opinions concerning the Constitution's prohibition on federal indictment and prosecution of a sitting President apply in this situation"), www.govinfo.gov/content/pkg/USCOURTS-dcd-1_23-cr-00257/pdf/USCOURTS-dcd-1_23-cr-00257-16.pdf.

[17] U.S. Department of Justice, Office of Special Counsel, Report on the Investigation into Russian Interference in the 2016 Presidential Election (Mueller Report), Part II (discussing evidence that President Trump had obstructed justice in the investigation, and declining to prosecute because of the DOJ's longstanding position that a sitting president cannot be indicted) (Apr. 18, 2019), www.govinfo.gov/app/details/GPO-SCREPORT-MUELLER.

[18] U.S. Department of Justice, Office of Special Counsel, Report on the Investigation into Unauthorized Removal, Retention, and Disclosure of Classified Documents Discovered at Locations Including the Penn Biden Center and the Delaware Private Residence of President Joseph R. Biden, Jr. (Feb. 5, 2024), at 1 (stating that Department of Justice policy forecloses indictment of a sitting president and citing in fn 2 the DOJ's 2000 memorandum reaching the same conclusion), www.justice.gov/storage/report-from-special-counsel-robert-k-hur-february-2024.pdf.

Trial of a previously indicted president, however, is different. Professor Claire Finkelstein and one of the authors of this book explained in a law review article,[19] before it was known that Trump would be elected president again, another argument that is critical to consider. First, the indictment itself is not an interference with the powers of the presidency, because the indictment was filed against a person who was not yet president. This is particularly true for an indictment filed before a person is elected president.[20] Second, while an indicted defendant who is a political candidate may claim that the indictment was politically motivated, this is a separate issue from whether the indictment interferes with the powers of the presidency. In fact, many candidates for public office have been indicted.[21] Third, when voters elect an already indicted candidate as president, it is difficult to argue that the criminal case is an attempt to overturn the results of the election.[22]

For these and other reasons, the federal criminal cases against President Trump, arguably, should have gone to trial. However, Smith faced another reality entirely apart from DOJ's legal position on indicting and trying a sitting president – the President has the power to appoint senior officials in the Department of Justice and the power to order those officials to fire a special prosecutor. The Supreme Court reiterated the President's "unitary executive theory" control over the DOJ in *Trump v. United States*.[23] If the criminal cases against Trump had not been withdrawn in 2024, Trump surely would have ordered his appointees in the Justice Department to fire Smith in early 2025. The DOJ would have sought dismissal of the indictments soon thereafter.

A related question, whether a state court can proceed to sentencing someone already convicted of a crime before that person becomes president, also never arose in American history until after the 2024 election. In late 2024, a New York trial court indefinitely postponed sentencing President-elect Trump on his felony convictions a Manhattan jury had handed down against him earlier that year. Trump's New York conviction also was appealed, and Trump has sought dismissal of the case or its removal to federal court.[24] Then, after the US Supreme Court refused Trump's request to postpone his sentencing, the New York court in early 2025 proceeded with

[19] Claire O. Finkelstein & Richard W. Painter, *When an Indicted Candidate Wins the Presidency: What Happens to the Trials If Donald Trump Wins the Election?*, 98 S. Cal. L. Rev. Postscript 1 (Oct. 2024), https://scholarship.law.umn.edu/cgi/viewcontent.cgi?article=2097&context=faculty_articles.

[20] *Id.*

[21] *Id.*

[22] *Id.*

[23] Trump v. United States, 603 U.S. 593 (2024), slip op. at 8 (discussing the President's constitutional power to remove his own appointees in the Executive Branch).

[24] "Letter from Todd Blanche, attorney for Donald Trump, to Judge Juan M. Merchan, dated November 19, 2024, re: People v. Trump, No. 71543/23 (NY Supreme Court, Criminal Term) (seeking dismissal under the United States Constitution, the 1963 Presidential Transition Act and the interests of justice), www.nycourts.gov/LegacyPDFS/press/PDFs/BlancheLaw_112024.pdf.

the hearing at which Trump appeared by Zoom to be sentenced to "unconditional discharge," meaning there would be no punishment entered for his crimes.

Meanwhile, the ill-fated criminal case against Trump in Georgia faces an uncertain future. After delays because of a scandal in the prosecutor's office unrelated to the merits of the case,[25] and after the 2024 election, Trump sought dismissal on the same premise that it is unconstitutional to prosecute a sitting president.[26] Now the DOJ may intervene on his behalf. With a Republican Attorney General in Georgia, and a conservative state judiciary, it is unlikely that the case will proceed to trial.

The drama surrounding all four Trump criminal cases, and the sharp reversal of his legal position after the 2024 election, demonstrates the extraordinary power of the presidency over the criminal justice system. The possibility of a future president using the office for criminal purposes, or to protect himself from prosecution for past crimes, or even initiate criminal prosecutions of his political enemies, is an unintended consequence of the President's control over the DOJ under the "unitary executive theory" adopted by the Supreme Court. But this is also a consequence of which we are aware, however inconsistent it may be with the intent of the Framers that "no man is above the law." The United States, perhaps, should have a more independent DOJ. But that is not where we are right now. It is precisely the opposite of the Founders' intent for clear lines for checks and accountability of a president.

16.2 DOES A CRIMINAL CONVICTION BAR A PERSON FROM BECOMING PRESIDENT?

The short answer to this question is no. A criminal conviction is not a per se bar to assuming the presidency. There are only two exceptions. The first would be a president who was impeached by the House, convicted by the Senate, and also barred by the Senate from assuming future office, a process discussed in Chapter 14 on impeachment. The second exception would be a president who engaged in insurrection or rebellion within the meaning of the Fourteenth Amendment Section 3, the post-Civil War disqualification provision intended to prohibit known insurrectionists from assuming any public office, not just the presidency. A criminal conviction for insurrection or sedition, crimes which closely match the disqualification language of Section 3, could disqualify a person from the presidency or any other federal office.

[25] Richard W. Painter, *Step Aside, Fani Willis Recusal Is the Right Course for the Fulton County District Attorney, even if the Judge Rules in Her Favor*, THE ATLANTIC (Feb. 18, 2024), www.theatlantic.com/ideas/archive/2024/02/fani-willisfultun-trump/677506/.

[26] Donald John Trump v. State of Georgia, Court of Appeals of the State of Georgia, Interlocutory Appeal, Docket No. A24A1599, President Trump's Notice of Jurisdictional Issue Indictment and Prosecution of Sitting President of the United States, filed December 4, 2024 (seeking dismissal), www.democracydocket.com/wp-content/uploads/2023/08/2024-12-04-Trumps-notice-of-jurisdictional-issue-WM.pdf.

The Fourteenth Amendment, Section 3, which was ratified after the Civil War, expressly bars from public office anyone who, previously having sworn an oath of loyalty to the United States, participated in an insurrection or gave "aid or comfort" to an insurrection. This includes a president, whether he gave aid or comfort to a rebellion during his presidency or thereafter.

Once again, however, the Constitution is unclear about how this provision is triggered for enforcement. The Fourteenth Amendment, Section 3 provides that Congress by a two-thirds vote can lift this ban on holding public office for a particular individual, but nowhere specifies a process for imposing the ban. Could the provision be triggered and applied by a majority vote by Congress? Would a criminal conviction for sedition or insurrection be necessary to trigger the ban?

The Supreme Court in 2024 addressed Fourteenth Amendment Section 3 in *Trump v. Anderson*.[27] The Court unanimously held that states could not determine eligibility for federal office, including the presidency, under Section 3 of the Fourteenth Amendment. The majority of the Justices stated that Congress alone can determine the disqualification of candidates for federal office who were alleged to have engaged in insurrection. In other words, without legislation or other enabling action by Congress barring a candidate under Section 3 of the Fourteenth Amendment, the states alone have no power to enforce the disqualifications of the Amendment.

Other than these two exceptions, there is no bar on a person convicted of a crime, even a serious crime, assuming the presidency. That decision is left to the voters.

16.3 IS A FORMER PRESIDENT IMMUNE FROM CRIMINAL PROSECUTION FOR OFFICIAL ACTS?

In 2024, the Supreme Court in *Trump v. United States* ruled, by a vote of 6–3, along ideological and party lines, that a president is absolutely immune from prosecution for acts within core constitutional powers of the President. In addition, he is entitled to a presumption of immunity for other "official acts."[28] The Court remanded the case to the trial court to determine which acts of President Trump charged in his indictments fell into one of the following three categories: (1) core constitutional responsibilities where he enjoys absolute immunity from prosecution; (2) official acts falling outside a core constitutional responsibility where the President is at least

[27] Trump v. Anderson, 601 U.S. 100 (2024). For a different interpretation of the Fourteenth Amendment, *see* William Baude & Michael Paulsen, *The Sweep and Force of Section Three*, 172 U. Pa. L. Rev. 605 (2024) (arguing that Section Three is self-executing, operating as an immediate disqualification from office, without the need for additional action by Congress, and that Section 3 disqualifies President Donald Trump because of his participation in the attempted overthrow of the 2020 presidential election).

[28] Trump v. United States, 603 U.S. 593 (2024).

entitled to a presumption of immunity; or (3) personal capacity conduct. Chief Justice Roberts wrote for the majority:

> We conclude that under our constitutional structure of separated powers, the nature of Presidential power requires that a former President have some immunity from criminal prosecution for official acts during his tenure in office. At least with respect to the President's exercise of this core constitutional powers, this immunity must be absolute. As for his remaining official actions, he is also entitled to immunity. At the current stage of proceedings in this case, however, we need not and do not decide whether that immunity must be absolute or instead whether a presumptive immunity is sufficient.[29]

With respect to the first category, the core constitutional powers of the President, the Court explained:

> Congress cannot act on, and courts cannot examine, the President's actions on subjects within his "conclusive and preclusive" constitutional authority. It follows that an Act of Congress – either a specific one targeted at the President or a generally applicable one – may not criminalize the President's actions within his exclusive constitutional power. Neither may the courts adjudicate a criminal prosecution that examines such Presidential actions. We thus conclude that the President is absolutely immune from criminal prosecution for conduct within his exclusive sphere of constitutional authority.

This category of core constitutional authority includes, among other things, the President's pardon power, power to remove federal officers appointed by the President in the executive branch, and the power "to control recognition determinations" of foreign nations.[30] This category of core constitutional authority also includes "commanding the Armed Forces of the United States."[31]

The second category, other official acts of the President, the Court describes as follows:

> As Justice Robert Jackson recognized in *Youngstown*, the President sometimes "acts pursuant to an express or implied authorization of Congress," or in a "zone of twilight" where "he and Congress may have concurrent authority." 343 U.S., at 635, 637 (concurring opinion). The reasons that justify the President's absolute immunity from criminal prosecution for acts within the scope of his exclusive authority therefore do not extend to conduct in areas where his authority is shared with Congress ... [W]e conclude that the separation of powers principles explicated in our precedent necessitate at least a *presumptive* immunity from criminal prosecution for a President's acts within the outer perimeter of his official

[29] *Id.*

[30] *Id.* at 609, citing United States v. Klein, 13 Wall. 128, 139–41 (1872) (pardon power), Seila Law LLC. v. Consumer Financial Protection Bureau, 591 U.S. 197, 204 (2020) (removal power), Zivotofsky v. Kerry, 576 U.S. 1, 32 (2015) (power to recognize foreign nations).

[31] *Id.* citing U.S. Const. Art. II, § 1, cl. 1.

> responsibility. Such an immunity is required to safeguard the independence and effective functioning of the Executive Branch, and to enable the President to carry out his constitutional duties without undue caution ... At a minimum, the President must therefore be immune from prosecution for an official act unless the Government can show that applying a criminal prohibition to the act would pose no "dangers of intrusion on the authority and functions of the Executive Branch."[32]

The third and final category is "personal capacity" conduct of the President that the Court, and indeed both parties in *Trump v. United States*, conceded is not entitled to any presumption of immunity.[33]

The Court was not willing to determine which of Trump's alleged conduct in the case fell in which category. That determination was left for the trial court on remand.

Justice Barrett, who was nominated to the Court by President Trump, in a concurring opinion, wrote that some of the conduct alleged in the Trump indictment involving the 2020 election, namely the fake elector scheme, contacts with state legislators, and what Trump said at his political rally on January 6, 2021, was clearly personal capacity conduct. She observed that the Supreme Court should have so ruled rather than leaving that for further litigation in the courts below, which, of course, would mean further delay of the court proceedings.

For many readers of the majority opinion, including the dissenting Justices, the most frightening aspect of the Court's decision in *Trump v. United States* is not what Trump did in connection with the 2020 election, but what he or any future president could have done and gotten away with under the newly announced shield of immunity. In oral argument in the Court of Appeals and in the dissenting opinion in the Supreme Court, the hypothetical was presented in which a president orders Seal Team Six to assassinate a political rival. Command of the military is a core constitutional responsibility of the President, meaning military orders are per se entitled to absolute immunity from criminal prosecution under the majority's ruling. A criminal law prohibiting premeditated murder cannot override that, and accordingly the President would be entitled to immunity according to Justice Roberts's majority opinion. The same is true for a president who orders the military to conduct a coup after losing an election, the option that President Trump did not pursue, but that a future president might, knowing that the sphere of immunity around the presidency is as broad as the Court has said it is.

Justice Sotomayor in her dissent, however, observed:

> Looking beyond the fate of this particular prosecution, the long-term consequences of today's decision are stark. The Court effectively creates a law-free zone around the President, upsetting the status quo that has existed since the Founding ... The

[32] Trump v. United States, 603 U.S. 593 (2024).

[33] *Id.*

> President of the United States is the most powerful person in the country, and possibly the world. When he uses his official powers in any way, under the majority's reasoning, he now will be insulated from criminal prosecution. Orders the Navy's Seal Team 6 to assassinate a political rival? Immune. Organizes a military coup to hold onto power? Immune. Takes a bribe in exchange for a pardon? Immune. Immune, immune, immune.[34]

What impact does presidential immunity have on the military chain of command? This problem was addressed in an amicus brief filed with the Court on behalf of over a dozen retired senior military officers who were very concerned about the implications of immunity. The authors of this brief, Professors Finkelstein and Painter, summarized their views in an op-ed in *The Atlantic*:

> Imagine a President who orders U.S. troops to engage in a massacre such as famously occurred in My Lai, Vietnam, in 1968. In such a case, every service member must assess for him or herself the risk of illegality of such an order and thus the weight to accord the general duty to obey orders. Where the order is patently illegal, such as with My Lai had the massacre occurred pursuant to orders, no service member could carry out such a command without risking major sanctions following trial by court-martial … If he merely thinks the order is illegal but the order is in fact legal, he is virtually certain to be convicted for refusal to obey.
>
> Against that backdrop, presidential immunity for criminal use of Commander-in-Chief authority is untenable. While the duty of obedience on the part of subordinates does not extend to patently illegal orders, an order issued by the President himself would exert considerable pressure on servicemembers. If everyone in the chain of command except the President knows he or she can be prosecuted both for failure to obey a legal order and for obeying an illegal order, and if presidential orders cannot be presumed to be legal, military service would be fraught with peril.[35]

The Court in *Trump v. United States* went out of its way to rule 5–4 that evidence of the motivation behind an official act of a president is inadmissible even in a criminal trial of the President for "personal capacity" crimes. Justice Barrett also departed from the majority on this point in her concurring opinion.[36]

Consider the implications of this new evidentiary exclusion rule for prosecution of a bribery case against the President. Presumably taking something of value – a bribe – in exchange for an official act is personal capacity conduct still subject to prosecution. However, without admissible evidence that the official act was in exchange for the bribe, the prosecution almost certainly will fail.

34 *Id.* (Sotomayor J., dissenting).

35 Claire O. Finkelstein & Richard W. Painter, *Trump's Presidential-Immunity Theory Is a Threat to the Chain of Command: Subordinates Need to Know That the Commander in Chief Is Bound by the Same Laws as Everyone Else*, The Atlantic (Apr. 15, 2024), www.theatlantic.com/politics/archive/2024/04/presidential-immunity-supreme-court-trump/678050/.

36 Trump v. United States, 603 U.S. 593 (2024) (Barrett J., concurring in part).

The majority opinion in a footnote tried to save the prosecution of a bribery case under its ruling:

> Justice Barrett disagrees, arguing that in a bribery prosecution, for instance, excluding "any mention" of the official act associated with the bribe "would hamstring the prosecution." But of course, the prosecutor may point to the public record to show the fact that the President performed the official act. And the prosecutor may admit evidence of what the President allegedly demanded, received, accepted, or agreed to receive or accept in return for being influenced in the performance of the act. *See* 18 U.S.C. § 201(b)(2). What the prosecutor may not do, however, is admit testimony or private records of the President or his advisers probing the official act itself. Allowing that sort of evidence would invite the jury to inspect the President's motivations for his official actions and to second-guess their propriety. As we have explained, such inspection would be "highly intrusive" and would "seriously cripple" the President's exercise of his official duties. And such second-guessing would "threaten the independence or effectiveness of the Executive.[37]

The majority, however, ignored what should be obvious: if the President did take a bribe, the real reason for the President's official act is not likely to be stated in the public record, which is prepared in the Executive Branch by officials who were appointed by the President and report to him. The majority believes that the prosecution can proceed excluding "testimony or private records of the President or his advisers probing the official act itself" but having the public record be the only evidence of motive for an official act that is admissible in a bribery case will likely doom the prosecution, as any experienced judge or prosecutor knows.

Even worse, this evidentiary ruling might doom prosecution not only of the President for bribery, but of "advisors" who in exchange for a bribe influence an official act of the President. The majority rules that the motivations for an official act of the President are off-limits in a criminal trial, and presumably in any criminal trial. If the prosecution in a bribery case cannot introduce evidence of what was said to the President about an official act, and by whom, the President's senior advisors also might have de facto immunity from prosecution.

In sum, the majority opinion in *Trump v. United States* is highly controversial and troubling in many respects. First, by issuing a fully embraced endorsement of presidential immunity from criminal prosecution, it ignored the constitutional history that the Founders were deeply concerned between a too-powerful presidency on the one hand, and on the other hand ineffective leadership authority they experienced under the Articles of Confederation.

Although they wanted a strong and energetic executive under Article II, they feared the return of a tyrannical, dictatorial, and authoritarian leader, who would

[37] Trump v. United States, *supra* note 32 (internal citations omitted).

attempt to seize and control more power.[38] At its core, the intent of the Framers was to have a Congress, the legislative branch, have superiority over the presidency and to build into the presidency a strong sense of accountability as seen through its extensive network of checks and balances within the doctrine of separation of powers.[39]

The design of a "preeminent" legislative branch over the presidency was intended to make clear the importance of the "rule of law," that Congress's power "to make law" was to be the "supreme power,"[40] as an essential part of the separation of powers doctrine.[41]

Further evidence of the Founders' deep concern over concentrated power in the presidency is seen in the constitutional debate over impeachment and the Electoral College as the ultimate accountability check over a president. As noted in Chapter 14, it is unlikely that the Constitution would have been approved by the Constitutional Convention but for the impeachment provision under Article I, Section 3.[42] The history and the doctrinal development of impeachment from its English origins to the present-day interpretation are that it was an accountability check on the President for an egregious abuse of "power" and thus a loss of trust in leadership.

This constitutional check on power was meant to serve as a deterrent on presidents' excessive, irresponsible, and reckless abuse of presidential power. There could be no effective checks and balances without accountability. Impeachment, as a checking function, was forged to counter a terrible power: the despot who deems himself to be above the law.[43] Another scholar has concluded that "removal from office w[as] the ultimate check on presidential power: Shall any man be above justice?"[44] The Constitution also expressly provides in Article I, Section 3, Clause 7 that a president or any other officer who is impeached and removed from office shall also "be liable and subject to Indictment, Trial Judgment and Punishment, according to Law." There is no mention of immunity from criminal prosecution for official acts, and in fact this language strongly suggests the opposite. A close reading of this important history and the doctrinal legal development could hardly be

38 Theodore J. Lowi, Benjamin Ginsberg, Kenneth A. Shepsle, Stephen Ansolabehere, & Hahrie Han, American Government: Power and Purpose (17th ed. 2023).

39 *Id. See also* Federalist 51 (Madison).

40 Lowi et al., *supra* note 38 at 111.

41 *See* Federalist 51 (Madison) for the argument that divided power between the branches of government would serve as a "checking function" on each other. Hence, it would be an accountability mechanism to avoid concentrated power.

42 Cass R. Sunstein, Impeachment: A Citizen's Guide, 34 (2019); Richard A. Posner, An American Affair: The Investigation, Impeachment, and Trial of President Clinton, 96–97 (1999).

43 Jill Lapore, *"You're Fired": A Short Account of the Long History of Impeachments*, The New Yorker (Oct. 28, 2019), 25–31.

44 Jon Meacham, And There Was Light: Abraham Lincoln and the American Struggle, 372 (2022).

considered consistent with the Supreme Court's immunity opinion in *Trump v. United States*.

Likewise, considering the Founders' reasons and justifications for the Electoral College, however flawed that reasoning might be, a subject we discuss in the Epilogue of this book, the Founders did not want direct election of the President because they feared enabling a demagogue whose power rested on popular appeal. If original intent means anything, it is hard to imagine the same Founders bestowing on the President immunity from prosecution for crimes he commits in office.

Contrary to the Framers' abhorrence of concentrations of power and abuse of power in the presidency, the Supreme Court's holding in *Trump v. United States* would, nonetheless, make clear that impeachment proceedings, such as those against President Nixon, who resigned on the eve of an impeachment by the House, will be extremely difficult if not impossible if the President can obstruct the proceedings by criminal acts. This could include threatening members of Congress, intimidating witnesses, destroying official documents, or anything else to prevent the impeachment from going forward. This conclusion is clear given the Court's broad and far-reaching precedent of absolute and presumptive immunity, even when there is a "corrupt intent and criminal purpose."[45] As the Court held, a president or former president cannot be prosecuted for conduct that was within the "core" constitutional powers of his office, and other official acts that do not fall within the "core" are still entitled to a presumption of immunity.[46]

As Judge Stephen Trott recently observed in an essay, this new "imperial power [created by the Supreme Court] is difficult to reconcile with an explicit Constitutional responsibility in Article II of the Constitution to 'take care that the laws be faithfully executed.'"[47] Moreover, the Impeachment Clause of Article I, Section 3 of the Constitution is clear that a president is subject to indictment, trial, judgment, and punishment according to the law. Even Alexander Hamilton, a leading Founder advocating for a unitary authority figure and a strong presidency, said that the President "would be liable for prosecution and the punishment in the ordinary course of the law."[48]

More recently, we can look at the statements and understanding of Presidents Nixon and Clinton regarding the potential for indictment and subsequent criminal trial when Nixon was resigning his office and when he accepted a pardon from

[45] Stephen S. Trott, *Why the Supreme Court's Immunity Ruling Is Untenable in a Democracy*, WASH. POST. (Oct. 8, 2024), www.washingtonpost.com/opinions/2024/10/07/trump-immunity-justices-ellsberg-nixon-trott/. Judge Trott is a senior judge on the United States Court of Appeals for the 9th Circuit. He was nominated to the bench by President Ronald Reagan.

[46] Trump v. United States, 603 U.S. 593 (2024).

[47] Trott, *supra* note 45. *See also* U.S. CONST. Art. II, § 3.

[48] THE FEDERALIST NO. 69 (Hamilton).

President Ford, and when Clinton accepted a "plea deal" after the resolution of his impeachment proceedings.[49]

Furthermore, Republican Minority Senate Leader Mitch McConnell, a lawyer himself, stated forcefully on the Senate floor, on February 13, 2021, after the second impeachment trial of President Trump was completed, his understanding of the state of settled law and the expectations of the people as he quoted from Justice Story. Former officials, he firmly stated, are "still liable to be tried and punished in ordinary tribunals of justice. We have a criminal justice system in this country. We have civil litigation in this country. And former presidents are not immune from being held accountable by either one."[50]

Finally, we can see in the majority opinion in the *Trump* immunity decision how the Court rejected well-established, settled law and constitutional precedent dating back to the Greeks through the British system.[51] Its holdings and dicta severely undercut the long-established rule of law in the United States. In *United States v. Lee*[52] the Supreme Court in 1882 stated:

> No man in this country is so high that he is above the law. No officer of the law may set that law at its defiance with impunity. All the officers of the government, from the highest to the lowest, are creatures of the law and are bound to obey it. It is the only supreme power in our system of government, and every man who by accepting office participates in its functions is only the more strongly bound to submit to that supremacy, and to observe the limitations while it imposes upon the exercise of authority which it gives.[53]

More recently, three of the justices in the majority in the *Trump* immunity case affirmed their belief, during their confirmation hearings before the Senate Judiciary committee, in the canonical principle of the rule of law. In 2005, the present Chief Justice and the author of the majority opinion in *Trump* stated: "I believe that no one is above the law under our system and that includes the President. The

49 *See* David Stout, *Clinton Reaches Deal to Avoid Indictment and to Give Up Law License*, New York Times (Jan. 19, 2001). Clinton's agreement to this deal was an acknowledgment that he could have been prosecuted for conduct that included some official acts, for example obstructing government witnesses in the Special Counsel Investigation.

50 167 Cong. Rec. S735–36 (daily ed. Feb. 13, 2021) (statement of Sen. McConnell).

51 *See* Aristotle, Politics, 3:16 (trans. Benjamin Jowett, 2017) (1st ed. 1885): "And the rule of the law, it is argued, is preferable to that of any individual. On the same principle, even if it be better for certain individuals to govern, they should be made only guardians and ministers of the law."

52 United States v. Lee, 106 U.S. 96 (1882).

53 *Id.* at 871. *See* E. Thomas Sullivan & Toni M. Massaro, The Arc of Due Process in American Constitutional Law, 1–2, 6–10, 34 (2013); Tom Bingham, The Rule of Law, 3–33 (2010); Brian Z. Tamanaha, On the Rule of Law: History, Politics, Theory, 7–31 (2004); James R. Silkenat & Gerold W. Libby, Building the Rule of Law: Firsthand Accounts form a Thirty-Year Global Campaign (2021). *See also* Trott, *supra* note 45 at 3.

President is fully bound by the law, the Constitution and the statutes."[54] Justice Alito in his 2006 confirmation hearing proclaimed: "there is nothing that is more important for our republic than the rule of law. No person in this country no matter how high or powerful is above the law."[55] Justice Kavanaugh also affirmed: "no one's above the law in the United States, that's a foundational principle ... we are all equal before the law ... The foundation of our Constitution was that ... the presidency would not be a monarchy ... the President is not above the law, no one is above the law."[56]

In response to the majority's near total immunity for a president's criminal behavior, Justice Sotomayor, in her dissent in *Trump*, offered a withering attack: "The relationship between the President and the people he serves has shifted irrevocably. In every use of official power, the President is now a king above the law."[57]

Another troubling aspect of the *Trump* case is the procedural setting of the decision. As reported in the *New York Times*, on February 22, 2024, the Chief Justice sent a confidential memorandum to each of the Justices shortly after the case was appealed by Trump's counsel from the decision of the United States Court of Appeals for the District of Columbia that rejected Trump's immunity defense. The memorandum, as reported by the *New York Times*, "offered a scathing critique of [the] lower court's decision [in its rejection of an immunity defense] [and went on to preview] how the High Court would later rule." In addition, the memorandum discussed whether the Court should take the case and when, either before the 2024 election or after.[58]

Surprisingly, the Chief Justice's memorandum preceded receiving the full briefings by the counsel on both sides and before legal arguments were scheduled and heard.[59] Oral arguments were scheduled for April 25, 2024. The final decision by the Court was issued in the first week of July 2024 with a remand to the Federal District Court. Interestingly, in 2013, nine years earlier, Chief Justice Roberts is reported to have said, "when we get on the bench, it

54 Confirmation of Chief Justice John Roberts, Hearing before the Senate Judiciary Committee, 152 (Sept. 13, 2005), www.congress.gov/supreme-court/GPO-CHRG-ROBERTS.pdf.

55 Confirmation of Justice Samuel Alito, Hearing before the Senate Judiciary Committee, 56 (Jan. 9, 2006), www.govinfo.gov/content/pkg/GPO-CHRG-ALITO/pdf/GPO-CHRG-ALITO.pdf.

56 Confirmation of Justice Brett Kavanaugh, Hearing before the Senate Judiciary Committee, 233 (Sept. 5, 2018), www.govinfo.gov/content/pkg/CHRG-115shrg32765/pdf/CHRG-115shrg32765.pdf.

57 Trump v. United States, 603 U.S. 593 (2024) (J. Sotomayor dissenting).

58 *See* an excellent analysis of the Court's immunity decision at Heather Cox Richardson, *Letters from an American* (July 2, 2024); Trump v. United States, 603 U.S. 593 (2024) (Sotomayor J., dissenting, joined by Kagan J. and Jackson J.).

59 Jodi Kantor & Adam Liptak, *How the Chief Justice Shaped Trump's Supreme Court Winning Streak*, New York Times, 1, 24–25 (Sept. 15, 2024).

really is the first time we start to get some clues about what our colleagues think."[60]

Since the *Trump* decision, one of the United States' most distinguished historians has written "*Trump v. United States* [is] the most sweeping judicial reconstruction of the American presidency in history."[61] He cited Chief Justice John Marshall in 1811 that "nothing is more to be deprecated than the transfer of party politics to the seat of justice."[62] Professor Wilentz concluded that the *Trump* immunity decision "[in] effect invests the presidency with quasi-monarchial powers, repudiating the foundational principles of the rule of law."[63]

In summary, the country is left to ponder, after the *Trump* decision, James Madison's aphorism that "an elective despotism was not the government we fought for."[64] An excellent new book by Professor Minh Ly argues that by creating an executive privilege of immunity, the Court rejects democratic norms of accountability that are critically essential for self-government in a constitutional republic and for the rule of law to succeed. Presidential immunity, he argues, makes a mockery of the "duty of oversight by the people, who are the sovereign gatekeepers of democratic accountability."[65] Such accountability by the citizens over the government is essential in a self-governing regime.[66]

We pose the question from this thoughtful critique: do we have democratic accountability, through the rule of law, after *Trump v. United States*?

The Supreme Court in the summer of 2024 decided another case arising out of the upheaval of January 6, 2021. *Fischer v. United States*[67] interpreted a federal

[60] Adam Liptak, *A Most Inquisitive Court? No Argument There*, NEW YORK TIMES (Oct. 7, 2013) ("When we get out on the bench, it's really the first time we start to get some clues about what our colleagues think") (quoting Chief Justice Roberts).

[61] Sean Wilentz, *The Dred Scott of Our Times*, NEW YORK REVIEW OF BOOKS, 33–34 (Aug. 15, 2024).

[62] *Marshall to Timothy Pickering, February 28, 1811, in* THE PAPERS OF JOHN MARSHALL (Charles F. Hobson ed., digital edition 2014), rotunda.upress.virginia.edu. *See also* Wilentz, *supra* note 61. Comparing the *Trump* immunity case to the "shame reserved until now for the Roger B. Taney court that decided the case of *Dred Scott v. Sanford* in 1857." 60 U.S. 393 (1857). *See also* SEAN WILENZ, THE RISE OF AMERICAN DEMOCRACY: JEFFERSON TO LINCOLN, xvii–71 (2005) ("The Framers of the Constitution tried to balance the imperatives of popular sovereignty against the fear of excessive democracy"), 30. Professor Wilentz is the winner of the Bancroft Prize and a Pulitzer Prize finalist.

[63] *Id.* at 33, *citing* THE PAPERS OF JOHN MARSHALL, *supra* note 62.

[64] Madison was quoting Thomas Jefferson's notes on the State of Virginia. (*See* FEDERALIST 48 (Madison)). MINH VY LY, ANSWERING TO US: THE RIGHT OF DEMOCRATIC ACCOUNTABILITY, 38 (2025). *See also* BOB PEPPERCORN TAYLOR, LIBERAL EDUCATION AND DEMOCRACY (2025) (On the important relationship between a liberal education and the maintenance and advancement of democracy).

[65] *Id.*

[66] *Id. See also* an excellent analysis of constitutional accountability, HEIDI KITROSSER, RECLAIMING ACCOUNTABILITY: TRANSPARENCY, EXECUTIVE POWER, AND THE U.S. CONSTITUTION (2015).

[67] Fischer v. United States, 603 U.S. 480 (2024).

statute criminalizing obstruction of an official proceeding. The criminal code[68] imposes criminal liability on anyone who "corruptly . . . (1) alters, destroys, mutilates, or conceals a record, document, or other object, or attempts to do so, with the intent to impair the object's integrity or availability for use in an official proceeding; or (2) otherwise obstructs, influences, or impedes any official proceeding or attempts to do so." Subsection (2), if read independently of subsection (1) describes what the January 6 rioters did when obstructing Congress's counting of the electoral votes in the presidential election.

The Supreme Court, nonetheless, relied on the more specific language of subsection (1) to limit the reach of "otherwise" in subsection (2), holding that to prove a violation the government must establish that the defendant "impaired the availability or integrity for use in an official proceeding of records, documents, objects, or other things used in an official proceeding or attempted to do so." Breaking into the Capitol and other physical interference with an official proceeding was not what this statute was about, according to the Court. Fischer and other January 6 defendants who broke into the Capitol could be charged under other criminal laws, but not this one.

What would this have meant for the criminal case against Donald Trump if the Department of Justice had not sought dismissal of the charges after his reelection?[69] To the extent Trump engaged in his "personal capacity" in conduct as a presidential candidate, he is not entitled to immunity under *Trump v. United States*. The Court's decision in *Fischer* also probably does not impede this aspect of the case against Trump, because Trump was charged with a plan to obstruct Congress's counting of the electoral votes that did involve official records. Trump's actions, including his participation in the "fake elector" scheme, impaired the availability of the *records* – the vote of the presidential electors when they met on December 14, 2020 in their respective states – that were vitally important for the official proceeding in Congress on January 6, 2021. At the time of this writing, the case against Trump has been dismissed during his second presidency. If the case were ever revived after he leaves office, the application of the *Trump* and *Fischer* cases would need to be reviewed by the lower federal courts.

16.4 CAN A STATE PROSECUTE A FORMER PRESIDENT FOR OFFICIAL ACTS?

A state prosecuting a president for official acts raises additional issues. Never before has there been such a case. In 2024 Donald Trump was convicted by a New York jury for falsification of Trump Organization business records in 2017 while he was in the White House, but this was a crime committed in his personal capacity. Although

[68] 18 U.S.C. § 1512(c).

[69] 18 U.S.C. § 1521(c) is one of the criminal statutes that the former President was accused of violating in the criminal case in the District of Columbia.

the falsified business records pertained to Trump's 2016 campaign for the presidency, they were not connected with his official duties as President. In another case, technically still pending in Georgia, Trump faces multiple counts of criminal conspiracy and racketeering under Georgia law. These charges pertain to his 2020 campaign as candidate Trump, not his duties as President. This case also faces an uncertain future as the Georgia appellate courts, dominated by conservative judges, will probably take the position that Georgia should not prosecute a sitting president. Had this case proceeded to trial, the Georgia courts, perhaps, would have had to adjudicate another question: Whether any of the alleged crimes were official acts, and whether a state can prosecute a president for official acts that violate state law.

The first issue is preemption – would the state criminal law under which the prosecution is brought conflict with Article II or federal statutory provisions defining the duties of the President? Similar issues would arise if a state were to prosecute any federal official for performance of official duties. Imagine what would have happened if after *Brown v. Board of Education*,[70] Southern states had brought criminal charges against federal officials – including Presidents Eisenhower and Kennedy – who enforced desegregation decrees of federal courts.

A second issue is the potential for prosecutorial abuse if state prosecutors – almost all of whom are elected – can use state criminal statutes to prosecute a president for official acts that are unpopular in the state. Even if federal law does not preempt a state criminal statute, arguably Article II of the Constitution precludes prosecution of a president for official acts that do not also violate federal law because the threat of state prosecution could interfere with performance of official duties. Federal officials, other than the President, if threatened with state prosecution can argue that they were simply carrying out the orders of the President, or a political superior appointed by the President, implicitly raising the federal preemption issue, under Article VI of the Constitution, if the orders are lawful under federal law. A president, who takes orders from nobody except the law itself, could argue that only federal criminal law can constrain his performance of official duties. Allowing state criminal law to fill a vacuum when federal law is silent would perhaps unduly constrain the presidency.

The problem with this argument is that at the time the Constitution was drafted and ratified almost all criminal law was state law. It's difficult to imagine that the Founders would have wanted a president unrestrained by state law prohibiting such crimes as murder or theft under the argument that the President was acting in his official capacity. A president who orders federal officers to kill a political rival, to burn down his house, or to steal his property must be held accountable like anyone else under the doctrine of the "rule of law." At the time of the Founders at least there was no federal statute to prohibit many such crimes. State prosecution, or no prosecution at all, may have been the only alternatives.

70 Brown v. Board of Education of Topeka, 347 U.S. 483 (1954).

17

Investigating the President

There are different types of investigations of the President: congressional investigations, federal criminal investigations, state criminal investigations, civil suits in state courts, and if the United States were to submit to jurisdiction, potentially even proceedings before international tribunals. The discussion in the preceding chapters focused on impeachment and criminal prosecution. But first must come an investigation. Some investigations have neither impeachment nor prosecution in mind, at least at the outset. Yet investigations of all types can be an effective check on presidential power.

The effectiveness of congressional investigations often turns on which political party controls Congress, whether there is divided government in Washington, and whether Congress can induce or compel testimony and document production from the Executive Branch. The subject of presidential "privilege" is addressed separately below in Section 17.2.

17.1 CAN A PRESIDENT FIRE A SPECIAL PROSECUTOR?

There are two scenarios to consider. The first is what happens if Congress specifically provides for a special prosecutor who cannot be fired by the President, as Congress did for twenty years from 1979 to 1999. The second is where Congress does not specifically provide for job protection for a special counsel, but one is appointed pursuant to Justice Department regulations.

Federal criminal investigations are conducted by the Justice Department, under the command of an Attorney General who can be removed at will by the President. Going back to the Saturday Night Massacre of October 1973 and the firing of Watergate special prosecutor Archibald Cox, this has been a problem. Congress passed the Independent Counsel statute in 1978, which was upheld by the Supreme

Court in *Morrison v. Olson.*[1] But the law was allowed to expire in 1998 amid dissatisfaction in both political parties with independent counsels investigating Iran–Contra under President Reagan and then Whitewater during the Clinton administration, which morphed into an investigation into Clinton lying about White House sex. Today, we are essentially back where we were under Nixon, with special prosecutors, such as Robert Mueller, appointed pursuant to a Department of Justice (DOJ) regulation and subject to removal by an attorney general who reports to the President.

Morrison v. Olson[2] addressed the issue in which there is an independent counsel statute or similar law prohibiting the President from removing a prosecutor. The Court held that the independent counsel law then in force did not unconstitutionally infringe the President's removal power under the unitary executive theory:

> This case does not involve an attempt by Congress itself to gain a role in the removal of executive officials other than its established powers of impeachment and conviction. The Act instead puts the removal power squarely in the hands of the Executive Branch; an independent counsel may be removed from office "only by the personal action of the Attorney General, and only for good cause."[3]

Justice Scalia dissented, saying the statute violated the Framers' intent about the separation of powers:

> This is what this suit is about. Power. The allocation of power among Congress, the President, and the courts in such fashion as to preserve the equilibrium the Constitution sought to establish – so that "a gradual concentration of the several powers in the same department," can effectively be resisted. Frequently an issue of this sort will come before the Court clad, so to speak, in sheep's clothing: the potential of the asserted principle to effect important change in the equilibrium of power is not immediately evident, and must be discerned by a careful and perceptive analysis. But this wolf comes as a wolf.[4]

Justice Scalia and subsequent critics of the *Morrison* decision argue that an earlier Supreme Court case, *Myers v. United States*[5] had affirmed the President's right to remove appointees in the executive branch. But the *Myers* case upheld only the President's power to remove a postmaster.[6] If the Court today were to agree with Justice Scalia, and the President wants to fire a member of the Executive Branch, including a prosecutor, no ordinary legislation can stop him.

In 2018 Senate testimony, Yale Law School Professor Akhil Amar said that *Morrison v. Olson* was probably wrongly decided in 1988 (even though at the time

[1] Morrison v. Olson, 487 U.S. 654 (1988).

[2] *Id.*

[3] *Id.* at 686.

[4] *Id.* at 699, (Justice Scalia, dissenting) citing FEDERALIST No. 51, p. 321 (J. Madison).

[5] Myers v. United States, 272 U.S. 52 (1926).

[6] *Id.*

Justice Scalia was the lone dissenter). Amar also testified that President Trump had the constitutional right to order the firing of Robert Mueller.[7] Others disagreed.[8]

This issue without an independent counsel statute arose both before and after the Independent Counsel Statute. Special counsels vulnerable to removal on orders of the President have been many, some of the most well-known being the Watergate Special Prosecutor (1973–1974) as well as more recent special counsels including Robert Mueller (for the Russia investigation from 2017 to 2019), Jack Smith (for the January 6, 2021-related indictment of former President Trump as well as the classified documents case against Trump), and Robert Hur (for the classified documents investigation of President Biden). We consider here what happens if the President orders the special prosecutor to be fired? This is, of course, exactly what President Nixon did in the infamous "Saturday Night Massacre" of October 1973.

The answer to this question is that probably nothing will happen if the President orders the firing of a special counsel. The *Trump v. United States* opinion makes it clear that the President could not be prosecuted for obstruction of justice, because the firing would be an official act.[9] The only hope is that Congress, as both Republicans and Democrats did with Nixon in 1973, would express outrage and threaten impeachment if another special prosecutor is not appointed. In today's hyper-partisan environment, a Congress controlled by the President's political party is not likely to do anything at all.

Trump never fired Mueller, although he did eventually fire his Attorney General Jeff Sessions, putting Attorney General William Barr in charge of the roll-out of the release of the Mueller Report in 2019. This brings up a second question of how much the Attorney General, who is appointed by the President and can be removed by the President, can or will control the work of a special prosecutor who is appointed pursuant to DOJ regulations without an independent counsel statute.

17.2 CAN A PRESIDENT UNDER SUBPOENA INVOKE EXECUTIVE PRIVILEGE?

Consider two different issues. The first is whether the subpoena comes from a federal or state prosecutor. The second is whether the subpoena is issued by Congress.

A sitting president clearly can be investigated. Criminal subpoenas can be enforced. *United States v. Nixon* upheld a federal prosecutor's subpoena of White

[7] *See* Special Counsels and the Separation of Powers, Hearing Before the Senate Committee on the Judiciary, 115th Cong. 1-2 (2017) (statement of Akhil Reed Amar, opining that Trump had the right to fire Special Counsel Mueller under the constitutional removal power).

[8] Claire Finkelstein & Richard Painter, *"You're Fired": Criminal Use of Presidential Removal Power*, 25 NYU J. Legis. and Pub. Pol'y 307, (2023), at 317, 343–57 (noting Amar's testimony but arguing such removal of a special prosecutor could be criminal obstruction of justice).

[9] Trump v. United States, 603 U.S. 593 (2024).

House tapes.[10] *Trump v. Vance* upheld a state prosecutor's subpoena of the President's tax returns in an investigation that ultimately led to Trump's indictment in 2023 by the same prosecutor's office.[11] But how far can prosecutors, particularly state prosecutors, go in investigating a sitting president? Will federal courts at some point enjoin investigations until after a president leaves office?

Congress is different. Courts are somewhat more skeptical of congressional subpoenas because of the very real possibility that they are politically motivated. Some presidents and former presidents cooperated with congressional investigations and some presidents and former presidents refused to cooperate. These include Harry Truman, who as a former president, refused to comply with a subpoena from the House Un-American Activities Committee. Donald Trump cited Truman's example in refusing to cooperate with the House January 6 Committee.[12]

"Executive privilege" is the first line of defense by the White House against an investigation. The broader the privilege the more difficult it is for anyone to get the evidence needed to investigate the President and his administration. The narrower the privilege the easier it is for someone – Congress, a prosecutor, or a private plaintiff – to investigate. In some situations, disclosure of information about the President's deliberative process may hinder him from doing his job. The privilege also, arguably, is important if it encourages presidents and their advisors to honestly discuss sensitive matters without fear of political embarrassment.

The law on presidential privilege has been murky to say the least. *United States v. Nixon*[13] rejected an assertion of an absolute privilege from prosecutorial subpoena of the White House tapes. But the Court indicated that the result might have been different if the subpoenaed tapes concerned national security. Since then, high-ranking Executive Branch officials have refused to comply with congressional subpoenas, and sometimes even refused to cooperate with DOJ investigations, citing executive privilege.

Federal criminal investigations, however, usually can bypass executive privilege claims on the core theory that the Justice Department is part of the Executive Branch and thus there is no separation-of-powers issue. In a case involving the government attorney–client privilege, the United States Court of Appeals for the District of Columbia Circuit in *In re Lindsey*[14] held that communications between the President and White House Counsel cannot be kept from a review by an independent counsel. Moreover, there is an important "crime–fraud" exception to

[10] United States v. Nixon, 418 U.S. 683 (1974).

[11] Trump v. Vance, 591 U.S. 786 (2020).

[12] *See* The Presidents and Ex-Presidents Subpoenaed before Trump, THE WASH. POST. (Oct. 13, 2022) (discussing among other subpoenas of presidents, former President Truman's refusal to testify for the House Un-American Activities Committee).

[13] United States v. Nixon, 418 U.S. 683 (1974).

[14] In re Lindsey, 158 F.3d 1263 (D.C. Cir. 1998).

the attorney–client privilege when the attorney–client relationship is used to obstruct an investigation or to commit some other crime or fraud.[15]

Under the Bush administration, former White House Counsel Harriet Miers refused to comply with a congressional subpoena for testimony, citing the privilege.[16] Attorney General Eric Holder did the same under President Obama.[17] In both instances, litigation to enforce the congressional subpoenas was so protracted that the issue became moot before it was definitively resolved.

On June 12, 2024 the US House voted to hold Attorney General Merrick Garland in contempt of Congress for refusing to turn over to Congress videotaped interviews of President Biden by Special Counsel Robert Hur. Hur had investigated Biden's alleged misappropriation of classified documents after his term as Vice President in 2017. A written report by Hur was turned over along with Hur's conclusions and decision not to pursue any charges. House Republicans were investigating, among other things, Biden's apparent memory loss during the interview. After President Trump again took office in 2025, the Justice Department released this tape of the Biden interview with Hur.

President Trump had several subpoena contests with Congress during and after his presidency. In *Trump v. Mazars*[18] the Supreme Court held that congressional subpoenas, in that case of a president's personal records, could not be enforced without a clearly demonstrated congressional purpose such as an impeachment investigation or a specific need for new, corrective legislation. "Indeed, from President Washington until now, we [The Supreme Court] have never considered a dispute over a congressional subpoena for the President's records."[19]

The subpoenaed documents were much the same documents that the Supreme Court in *Trump v. Vance*,[20] another case decided at the same time, held could be subpoenaed by a New York State grand jury.[21] The Court thus upheld a subpoena in a state criminal investigation but refused to enforce a congressional subpoena for substantially the same documents. One rationale for this discrepancy is that the President is at high risk of harassment by a hostile Congress, whereas a grand jury subpoena has a narrower focus and is subject to judicial oversight.

[15] *Id.* at 1287.

[16] *See* Comm. On the Judiciary, U.S. House of Representatives v. Harriet Miers, 558 F. Supp. 2d 53, 62 (D.D.C. 2008).

[17] *See* Comm. On Oversight and Gov't Reform, U.S. House of Representatives v. Eric Holder, 979 F. Supp. 2d 1, 3 (D.D.C. 2013) (Berman Jackson, J.) ("The fact that this case arises out of a dispute between two branches of government does not make it non-justiciable; Supreme Court precedent establishes that the third branch has an equally fundamental role to play, and that judges not only may, but sometimes must, exercise their responsibility to interpret the Constitution and determine whether another branch has exceeded its power").

[18] Trump v. Mazars USA, LLP, 591 U.S. 848 (2020).

[19] *Id.* at 863–66.

[20] Trump v. Vance, 591 U.S. 786 (2020).

[21] *See also* Claire O. Finkelstein & Richard W. Painter, *Trump's Bid to Stand Above the Law*, New York Times (May 8, 2020) (discussing the *Vance* case).

Yet another intriguing question is whether a former president can assert executive privilege even if his successor chooses to waive it. *Trump v. Thompson*[22] was a case brought by former President Trump to stay enforcement of a subpoena of former White House officials by the House January 6 Committee. Two justices of the Supreme Court (Thomas and Kavanaugh) suggested the answer might be yes, that a former president had such a right to assert executive privilege. But Justice Kavanaugh agreed that the January 6 Committee had met the *U.S. v. Nixon* standard anyway, so he concurred with the majority in refusing to stay the subpoena.

Presidents nearly always seek to protect the privilege – including the privilege of their predecessors of the opposing political party. The Biden Justice Department has gone to court to protect the privilege of the Trump administration from subpoenas issued by congressional Democrats – including a subpoena for General Services Administration (GSA) documents concerning the Trump Hotel. This suggests that for many presidents the power of the presidency is an even more powerful political motivator than political partisanship.

17.3 IS CONGRESSIONAL SUBPOENA POWER BROADER IN AN IMPEACHMENT INVESTIGATION?

Initiating an impeachment investigation makes it more likely that courts will enforce a congressional subpoena of the President. In *Trump v. Mazars*[23] the Court declined to enforce a House subpoena of Trump's tax returns but suggested that if there had been an open impeachment investigation the result might have been different. Congress could take advantage of an open impeachment inquiry to obtain as much information as possible. In this context, the objective of the impeachment process may not necessarily be removal of the President, which is almost impossible for reasons explained in Chapter 14, but using subpoena power to obtain information that otherwise might not be available to Congress.

As Professor Claire Finkelstein has argued, the House may have moved too quickly to impeach Trump over the Ukraine scandal in early 2020, in the first of his two impeachments.[24] Trump used his power as President to block witnesses from testifying and to withhold incriminating documents and other evidence.[25] Instead of issuing subpoenas for additional documents and testimony, the House rushed too

22 Trump v. Thompson, 142 S. Ct. 680 (2022).

23 Trump v. Mazars USA, LLP, 591 U.S. 848 (2020).

24 Claire O. Finkelstein, *This Question Is More Important Than Removing Trump*, New York Times (Jan. 27, 2020), www.nytimes.com/2020/01/27/opinion/trump-obstruction-impeachment.html.

25 *See* Charlie Savage, *Trump Vows Stonewall of "All" House Subpoenas, Setting Up Fight over Powers*, New York Times (Apr. 24, 2019). Professor Claire Finkelstein wrote in the *New York Times* in January 2020 that a vote in the House to subpoena witnesses "would strike at the heart of the president's efforts – which continue to this day – to impede his own removal from office." Finkelstein, *supra* note 24.

soon to file articles of impeachment based on the limited evidence they had.[26] The Senate could have confronted Trump under its own impeachment rules, which provide that "the Senate shall have power to compel the attendance of witnesses" and to "enforce obedience to its orders."[27] Instead, Senate Republicans blocked any attempt to call witnesses, much less compel them to testify. Trump was acquitted in the Senate along party lines.

[26] *Id.*

[27] Rules of Procedure and Practice in the Senate When Sitting on Impeachment Trials [Revised pursuant to S. Res. 479, 99-2, Aug. 16, 1986], www.govinfo.gov/content/pkg/SMAN-104/pdf/SMAN-104-pg177.pdf.

18

Presidential Term Limits

Today we take for granted that when a candidate for President wins the election he will run for reelection in four years. If they win reelection, a new president will be sworn in at the end of the current President's second term. However, for most of American history, until the ratification of the Twenty Second Amendment in 1951, this cycle of presidents serving for at most two terms was governed by tradition and norms, rather than law. In this section we explore the historical debate on presidential term limits, the long-standing tradition of two-term presidents, the passage of the Twenty Second Amendment, and ongoing attempts to repeal or modify the Amendment.

18.1 PRESIDENTIAL TERM LIMITS: A CONTENTIOUS CONVENTION DEBATE

During the Constitutional Convention of 1787, the debate over how long a presidential term should be and whether a president should be eligible for reelection was lengthy, contentious, and drew out ideological and philosophical differences between the Federalists and Anti-Federalists. The debate exposed the contradictions of the Convention's desire to rectify the errors of the Articles of Confederation by establishing a strong national government in contrast to the fear that a strong Executive Branch would make the President a king in all but title.

One of the earliest plans considered that the President should be elected by Congress.[1] This plan was rooted in the practice of many of the states at the time whose state legislatures elected the Governor.[2] This idea, however, was quickly voted down by the delegates of the Convention, who feared that selection of the

[1] 2 The Records of the Federal Constitution, 29 (Max Farrand ed., 1911).

[2] *Id.*

President by Congress would violate their carefully architected plans for separation of powers and make the President beholden to the whims of Congress.[3]

Having decided that the President should be elected by the general population, the debate then turned to how long the President should be able to hold office. From the Convention, two initial plans emerged. First, James Wilson proposed a term of three years, provided that the President would be eligible for reelection.[4] In contrast, Charles Pickney proposed that the President should only be eligible to serve for a single seven-year term.[5] Initially, the Convention voted for Pickney's seven-year plan but continued to debate the question throughout the Convention.[6] Among the plans proposed were a twenty-year, fifteen-year, eight-year, six-year terms, and indefinite service during "good behavior."[7]

The critical issue that emerged from the Convention with these plans for longer or indefinite terms was that it would "destroy the great motive to good behavior, the hope of being rewarded by a reappointment."[8] When the question was brought before the Committee of Eleven in August 1787, it proposed a four-year term with no bar to reelection.[9]

Although the final draft of the Constitution included a four-year term with no limits on reelection, the debate continued while the Constitution was being ratified in the states. This debate is best represented by the debates in the Federalist and Anti-Federalist papers. Writing under the pseudonym "Cato" Anti-Federalist George Clinton argued that "the greatness of the power [of the executive] must be compensated by the brevity of the duration; and that a longer time than a year would be dangerous."[10] As Clinton viewed it, the inherent powers of the presidency as well as the potentially indefinite term of the President presented a unique danger that threatened to turn the United States into a monarchy.

In contrast, Alexander Hamilton in *Federalist Papers* 69 and 71 argued that the four-year term with no limits on reelection was closer to a state governor than a king. Defending the Constitution's design, Hamilton wrote that

> [the President] is to be elected for four years; and is to be re-eligible as often as the people of the United States shall think him worthy of their confidence. In these circumstances there is a total dissimilitude between him and a king of Great Britain, who is a hereditary monarch, possessing the crown as a patrimony descendible to his heirs forever; but there is a close analogy between him and a governor of

3 *Id.* at 31–32, 34.
4 1 The Records of the Federal Constitution, 68 (Max Farrand ed., 1911).
5 *Id.*
6 *Id.* at 69.
7 2 The Records of the Federal Constitution, 33, 35, 100, 102, 112 (Max Farrand ed., 1911).
8 *Id.* at 33.
9 *Id.* at 497.
10 The Anti-Federalist papers, No. 4 (Cato/George Clinton) (citing Montesquieu).

New York, who is elected to three years, and is re-eligible without limitation or intermission.[11]

In Hamilton's view, a three-year term as governor of New York was insufficient to establish a "dangerous influence" over a single state. He went on to reason that a four-year term, in comparison, was appropriate because it was unlikely that a president could establish a dangerous influence over the much larger United States during that time.[12]

Responding to Clinton's argument, Hamilton also argued that a lengthy term of four years was a feature of the presidency, and not an inherent danger. As an advocate of an "energetic executive," Hamilton believed that it was important that a president have both the wisdom and power to move the nation forward. In Hamilton's view, a four-year term was the correct length because it insulated the President from the whims of the national mood and allowed him to make unpopular, but necessary, decisions while being insulated by time from voters.[13]

Ultimately the Federalists would win the national debate. When the Constitution was ratified in June 1788 Article II gave the President a four-year term with no limits on how many times he may be reelected.[14]

18.2 THE LONG ROAD TO PRESIDENTIAL TERM LIMITS

As the election of 1792 approached, Washington was coy about whether he intended to seek a second term. While he viewed his first term a success in establishing a national government, he was frustrated with the limitations of the office and believed that his age and infirmity would limit his potential in a second term.[15] While President Washington never announced he would run for a second term, he also declined to say he was retiring. In the election of 1792 he was unanimously reelected for a second term. Throughout Washington's second term his health continued to decline. He published a letter in September 1796, known today as Washington's Farewell Address, in which he announced he would not seek a third term.[16]

For nearly eighty years President Washington's decision to decline a third term acted as a norm that prevented presidents from seeking a third term. In 1880 President Grant sought a third term in office.[17] However, Grant's ambitions were

[11] THE FEDERALIST, NO. 69 (Hamilton).

[12] *Id.*

[13] THE FEDERALIST, NO. 71 (Hamilton).

[14] U.S. CONST., Art. II, § 1.

[15] FORREST MCDONALD, THE PRESIDENCY OF GEORGE WASHINGTON, 139, 164–65 (1974).

[16] George Washington, Washington's Farewell Address to the People of the United States, S. Doc. No. 106-21, at 1 (2000).

[17] Joan Waugh, *Ulysses S. Grant: Life after the Presidency*, UNIVERSITY OF VIRGINIA MILLER CENTER, https://millercenter.org/president/grant/life-after-the-presidency.

stopped when the Republican Party could not decide on a candidate to nominate for the presidency. Ultimately James Garfield was selected as a compromise.

Thirty-two years later President Theodore Roosevelt would also seek a third term in office in 1912. Unlike Grant, who sought the election of his party, Roosevelt created his own "Bull Moose" party that was ideologically rooted in the progressive politics of his "Square Deal."[18] While Roosevelt was able to win six states and over 27 percent of the vote, his campaign for a third term ultimately split the Republican vote, allowing Woodrow Wilson to win forty of forty-eight states with just under 42 percent of the vote.[19]

In 1940 President Franklin Roosevelt was able successfully to run for and be elected to an unprecedented third term. Much like Grant and Theodore Roosevelt's decision to run for a third term, Franklin Roosevelt's decision drew swift criticism from the press, in part because of rumors during his second term that he would not seek a third term.[20] However, Roosevelt reneged on his promise when it appeared that the US would be drawn into World War II.[21] He then won a fourth term in 1944 after the United States had been at war for almost three years.

Two years after President Roosevelt's death in 1945 Congress passed and proposed to the states the Twenty Second Amendment. It was ratified by the states in 1951.[22] However, this effort was not the first time that Congress had considered similar amendments. In the 1870s, 1900s, and 1910s Congress introduced proposed amendments that would have established Washington's norm as a firm limit of presidential tenure.[23]

The language of the Twenty Second Amendment is brief. It states in part that "[n]o person shall be elected to the office of the President more than twice, and no person who has held the office of President, or acted as President, for more than two years of a term to which some other person was elected President shall be elected to the office of the President more than once."[24] From the ratification of the Twenty Second Amendment, the nation has had five presidents serve two terms. No president has tried to circumvent the limits of the Amendment.

[18] Sid Milkis & Carah Ong, *Transforming American Democracy: TR and the Bull Moose Campaign of 1912*, University of Virginia Miller Center, https://millercenter.org/transforming-american-democracy-tr-and-bull-moose-campaign-1912.

[19] *Id.*

[20] *Roosevelt Won't Choose to Seek Third Term: So to State Jan. 20, Says Lawrence*, New York Times (Jan. 16, 1940), www.nytimes.com/1940/01/16/archives/roosevelt-wont-choose-to-seek-third-term-so-to-state-jan-20-says.html.

[21] *1940: Roosevelt Wins Third Term*, New York Herald Tribune (Nov. 6, 1940), https://archive.nytimes.com/iht-retrospective.blogs.nytimes.com/2015/11/05/1940-roosevelt-wins-third-term/. *See* Richard Moe, Roosevelt's Second Act (2013). Roosevelt won his fourth term in 1944, defeating Thomas Dewey. No other president has won a fourth term.

[22] Thomas H. Neale, *Presidential Terms and Tenure: Perspectives and Proposals for Change*, Cong. Research Service, 19 (Apr. 15, 2019), https://sgp.fas.org/crs/misc/R40864.pdf.

[23] *Id.* at 4.

[24] U.S. Const., Amend. XXII, § 1.

18.3 REPEAL OF THE TWENTY SECOND AMENDMENT AND THE DEBATE TODAY

While no president has sought publicly to repeal the Twenty Second Amendment, supporters of Presidents Nixon, Reagan, and Clinton have sought its repeal. Repealing an amendment to the Constitution is itself neither unconstitutional nor unprecedented. The Eighteenth Amendment, which prohibited manufacture, sale, and transport of liquor, was repealed by the Twenty First Amendment in 1933.[25] In 1973, supporters of Nixon argued that his successes in ending the war in Vietnam, reaching arms control agreements with the Soviet Union, and normalizing relations with the People's Republic of China would make a third term good for the nation's health after the turbulent 1960s.[26] However, the revelations of the Watergate scandal halted any momentum for repeal. Similarly, the Iran–Contra scandal in 1986 and President Clinton's impeachment in 1999 killed efforts to repeal the Amendment.[27] During the twenty-first century, there has been no serious interest in Congress to repeal presidential term limits.

The question of the Twenty Second Amendment has drawn renewed interest in 2024 and 2025 following President Trump's reelection to a second nonconsecutive term. In a meeting with House Republicans in November 2024, President Trump said: "I suspect I won't be running again unless you say, 'He's so good we've got to figure something else out.'"[28] While it is unclear if President Trump was serious about seeking a third term, some of his allies have pounced on his comment and attempted to construct theories about how to make it a reality. In a December 2024 dinner with the New York Young Republican Club, former White House Chief Strategist and Trump ally Steve Bannon argued that Trump could run for a third term because his two terms were nonconsecutive.[29]

This interpretation, however, is contrary to the plain language of the Amendment. The Amendment states that no person shall be elected more than twice. It does not make any exception for nonconsecutive terms. Recall, also, that President Grover Cleveland was the only other president, besides President Trump, to serve two nonconsecutive terms. This historical fact was well known at the time the Twenty Second Amendment was ratified in 1951.

The current suggestion, however, raises another constitutional issue. The Twenty Second Amendment states that no person shall be *elected* more than twice. The

[25] U.S. Const. Amend. XXI.

[26] Neale, *supra* note 22.

[27] *Id.*

[28] Annie Karni, *As Trump Refers to Third Term, Democrat Wants to Leave No Constitutional Loophole*, New York Times (Nov. 13, 2024), www.nytimes.com/2024/11/13/us/politics/congress-resolution-22nd-amendment-loophole.html.

[29] Hugo Lowell, *Trump allies Float Extreme Ideas, Including Trump Third Term, at Gala*, The Guardian (Dec. 16, 2024), www.theguardian.com/us-news/2024/dec/16/trump-allies-extreme-policies-third-term.

underlying issue is whether a person may become President without being elected to the office. This question implicates the Twelfth and Twenty Second Amendments as well as the Presidential Succession Act of 1947.

Under the Presidential Succession Act of 1947, if the President dies or is incapacitated, the order of presidential succession is the Vice President, the Speaker of the House of Representatives, the President Pro Tempore of the Senate, and then various cabinet secretaries.[30] Additionally, the Twelfth Amendment provides that "no person constitutionally ineligible to the office of President shall be eligible to that of Vice-President of the United States."[31] Together, the Act and the Twelfth Amendment raise a series of important questions.

But what if a former two-term president is subsequently the Speaker of the House, President Pro Tempore of the Senate, or the ranking cabinet secretary?[32] Could a former two-term president become President for a third term? Arguably, if the Twelfth Amendment incorporates the 22nd Amendment, then a two term president could only become President for a third term by being in line for the presidency through the Presidential Succession Act and being neither President nor Vice President at the time.

So, any lingering question would turn on the key term "no person shall be *elected*." While the Court has not decided the question, there remains a question of whether a person would be barred from serving another term through the Presidential Succession Act, under the Twenty Second Amendment, or if it only bars a person from being *elected* to a third term. Given the requirements of these successive offices, the scenario of a president serving a third term without being elected seems highly unlikely.

30 Presidential Succession Act, Pub. L. 80-199.

31 U.S. Const. Amend. XII.

32 The Presidential Succession Act of 1947 establishes the line of succession if the President and Vice President cannot serve in the order of the Speaker of the House, the President Pro Tempore, and the ranking cabinet member.

PART III

Conclusion

Part III addressed presidential accountability. Given the broad, and expanding, presidential powers addressed in Part I of this book, one would think holding the President accountable would be that much more important. As discussed earlier in this part, some of the Founders thought so. For example, future Supreme Court Justice James Iredell, in his speech to the North Carolina ratifying convention, explicitly said that the United States did not need a privy council to restrain the President because the President would be accountable under the law like anyone else. In a well-balanced constitutional framework, broad presidential power should mean robust presidential transparency and accountability.[1]

But such is not the case. Removal of a president under impeachment requires a supermajority in the Senate that has never been achieved once in American history. Senators of the President's political party are simply too loyal to him to convict. The President's control over the Department of Justice under the unitary executive theory allows him to remove senior officials, and potentially even to remove special prosecutors. The independent counsel statute was allowed to expire twenty-five years ago in 1999, and even if another independent counsel law were to be enacted, the Court might hold it to be unconstitutional under the unitary executive theory. Moreover, Senate rules do not prescribe the burdens of proof required to convict a president. That decision is left up to each individual senator. Thus, political considerations often factor into the verdict in the Senate, even though the senators' constitutional duty in the trial is to answer two questions: (1) is the impeachment charge an impeachable offense? And if so, (2) did the President in fact commit the impeachable act?

Even former presidents may escape criminal prosecution or be able to delay it indefinitely. The Court's 2024 holding in *Trump v. United States* is an example. The

[1] *See* Minh Vy Ly, Answering to Us: The Right of Democratic Accountability, 38 (2025). *See also* Heidi Kitrosser, Reclaiming Accountability: Transparency, Executive Power, and the U.S. Constitution (2015).

holding gives a former president absolute immunity from prosecution for official acts within core constitutional powers, but also creates powerful presumptions in favor of the legality of all official presidential acts that in many cases will make prosecution difficult. Meanwhile, even constitutional provisions designed to rein in conflicts of interest, such as the Emoluments Clause, are difficult to enforce with respect to the President. Finally, the President's control over the Executive Branch can, and has, been used to bolster his chances of reelection, and in one case (Trump in 2020 and early 2021) tried to reverse the result of an election that the President had lost.

It is important also to note that investigations of presidents by international tribunals, such as the International Criminal Court (ICC), are not an effective constraint on presidential power. This is because the United States has not joined the Rome Statute which created the ICC and has not submitted to the jurisdiction of the ICC. In the current political environment, the United States is not likely to do so for the foreseeable future. Some other countries whose constitutions grant broad immunity from domestic criminal prosecution to their presidents and even former presidents, including France, have nonetheless submitted to the jurisdiction of the ICC, which could be a deterrent for the most egregious official capacity crimes, such as war crimes.[2] This is not true in the United States.

In sum, accountability mechanisms are weak. They are probably too weak for a president who has more power over a far larger federal government than existed at the time of the Founders. Increasing the level of presidential accountability to be commensurate with the extraordinary increase in presidential power over the past century will be difficult without constitutional amendment making it easier for Congress to remove a president through impeachment or an independent Department of Justice. Both are unlikely. More modest adjustments would be Congress passing a law restoring the office of independent counsel (assuming it is constitutional), a law enforcing the Emoluments Clause of the Constitution, and perhaps laws providing for more transparency.

As pointed out in Part I, however, a lot of presidential power comes from the enormous size of the federal agencies created and funded by Congress.

Congress may want to impose additional constraints on presidential power in the statutory framework governing areas as far-reaching as national defense, commerce, and the environment. The Court's reversal of the *Chevron* Doctrine in 2024 will mean less judicial deference to executive branch agencies, increasing the power of Congress to constrain the President, and greater judicial review over congressional delegation of agency powers and less agency discretion in exercising expertise. Presidents who want to reverse judicial interpretations of federal statutes more often will have to go back to Congress to seek amendments. In return, Congress, if it wants, can use its power to impose constraints on presidential power.

[2] Jacob Bourgault, *Presidents, Power, and Immunity: A Comparative Analysis Post-Trump v. United States* (Nov. 16, 2024), https://ssrn.com/abstract=5023568 or http://dx.doi.org/10.2139/ssrn.5023568 (discussing presidential immunity from prosecution for official acts under the French constitution but also France's submission to jurisdiction of the ICC).

Epilogue

This book has discussed the power, responsibility and accountability of the US President, examining the Founders' intentions and the very different presidency we have today. The President is more powerful and less accountable than the Founders ever imagined. Responsible exercise of presidential power today depends more than ever on the character of the person who occupies the presidency. Americans for good reason have less confidence in the constitutional checks and balances the Founders anticipated would restrain abuse of presidential power.

With so much depending on who the President is, this book would be incomplete without mention of the peculiar process by which Americans choose their President. The Electoral College is not a democratic institution. The Founders believed we would elect a better president, one less likely to abuse presidential power or to curry popular favor, by avoiding direct democracy in selecting the President.

In most presidential elections, the Electoral College has not made a difference because the same candidate won both the popular vote and the Electoral College. But in five presidential elections the winner of the presidency lost the nationwide popular vote: John Quincy Adams in 1824, Rutherford B. Hayes in 1876, Benjamin Harrison in 1888, George W. Bush in 2000, and Donald Trump in 2016. Perhaps the 1824 election illustrated the Founders' point. Adams's populist opponent Andrew Jackson would have to wait four years to gain the presidency by winning in 1828 both the popular vote and the Electoral College. Jackson's use of the office typified much of what the Founders' feared.[1] But the steady expansion of presidential power over

[1] Among other things, President Jackson is the only President to have ignored an order of the United States Supreme Court. The Court in Worcester v. Georgia, 31 U.S. (6 Pet.) 515 (1832), expressly held that the Cherokee Indians were a nation holding sovereign powers that could not be intruded upon by Georgia. Jackson ignored the Court and allowed, indeed encouraged, the Georgia militia to keep Worcester and other missionaries as prisoners and to forcibly remove the Cherokee from their land. During the Civil War, President Lincoln defied a federal district court order issued by Chief Justice Roger Taney in *Ex Parte Merryman*, 17 F. Cas. 144 (C.C.D.

the next two centuries, culminating in controversy in both the George W. Bush and Donald Trump administrations, among others, has made it harder to defend a system in which the majority of voters do not get to decide who the President is.

First, we consider in more detail what the Founders feared, which is why we have the Electoral College system. Then we ask perhaps the more important question of whether the Electoral College does anything to prevent presidential power being amassed in the hands of a demagogue or whether it may make the problem worse.

The Founders intended the Electoral College to be yet another designed check on the President to ensure that a direct election would not give too great a power to the President consistent with the doctrine of separation of powers.[2] The Framers were balancing this new office of the presidency, created to address the failures of inefficiency and a lack of an Executive Branch in the Articles of Confederation, with their fears of too powerful a president replicating what they experienced during their colonial days under a very powerful monarchial, executive rule by King George III.[3] For the Founders, a direct election of the President might create "excessive democracy" with too close a relationship of the President to the public, resulting in enhancement of powers of a popular president.[4] The election through the Electoral College "afforded the President a measure of independence from the people" and, at the same time, the ability to "withstand democratic pressures"[5] from "a popular majority" that could lead to abusive power in a democracy.[6] The indirectness of the election process through chosen electors in the states was a central defense against a more monarchial or tyrannical executive with a political separation of powers mantra of checks and balances, each holding the other branch of government accountable.[7] This could be accomplished by limiting the President's power, and avoiding a more autocratic authority to ensure the protection of the liberty of the people.[8]

Md. 1861), the habeas corpus case discussed in Chapters 1 and 3, but the Supreme Court never reviewed that case. Congress later granted the consent to suspend habeas corpus that had been required under the original order.

2 Theodore J. Lowi, Benjamin Ginsberg, Kenneth A. Shepsle, Stephen Ansolabehere, & Hahrie Han, American Government: Power and Purpose, 54 (17th ed. 2023).

3 *Id.* at 291. *See also* Federalist 67 (Hamilton) regarding the powers of the Executive and the fear of extending presidential powers; Federalist 69 (Hamilton) comparing presidential and monarchical powers; Joseph J. Ellis, Founding Brothers: The Revolutionary Generation: The Record of the Federal Convention of 1787, 4 vols. (Max Farrand ed., revised ed. 1966).

4 Lowi et al, *supra* note 2, at 54.

5 *Id.* at 57–58.

6 *Id.* at 69.

7 *Id.* at 63, 68.

8 *Id.* at 69–70.

As James Madison noted, in creating political order, abuse of power and concentration of power would be curtailed by internal constitutional checks.[9] Hamilton, in *Federalist* 68, agreed, and expressed fear that without an indirect election of the President, the "general population would be vulnerable to demagogues, the whims of the population, and too much domestic popular influence and politician's overreach."

For these reasons, unlike most modern democracies where a candidate for head of state simply needs to win more votes than their opponents, the United States has adopted a unique system with the Electoral College rooted in federalism. Under the Electoral College each state and the District of Columbia receive a total number of votes in the Electoral College equal to the state's number of members of Congress for a total of 538 votes (although the District of Columbia does not have a voting representative in the House or Senators it is still apportioned three votes in the Electoral College as if it had a representative in the House and two senators). To win a presidential election, a candidate must receive a majority, not just a plurality, of the votes in the Electoral College.

If no candidate wins a majority of votes in the Electoral College, the Twelfth Amendment provides that the House of Representatives shall elect the President and the Senate shall elect the Vice President.[10] Under the 12th Amendment each *state* in the House casts a single vote from among the three candidates with the most electoral college votes. In the Senate, each Senator casts a single vote from among the two candidates with the most Electoral College votes.[11] Additionally, unlike in the Electoral College, the District of Columbia receives no votes in either the House or the Senate during a contingent election.

The possibility of a contingent election in modern times raises interesting possibilities. For example, the assumption today is that during a contingent election Representatives and Senators would vote with their party's candidate even if they lost the vote in the state the member of Congress represents. This could result in a situation where the House chooses a president from one party, and the Senate chooses a vice president from another party.

The Electoral College system has several problems.[12] First, it is antidemocratic in instances (including two of the past seven presidential elections) in which the winner of the popular vote loses the Electoral College. Second, candidates have an incentive to campaign mostly in a handful of "swing states" where the outcome is uncertain. In a political environment where most states are predictably Republican or Democratic, this means that most states get ignored in the general election.

9 *Id.* at 70, 78, 81, citing Federalist 51 (Madison). *See also* Federalist 68 (Hamilton); Heather Cox Richardson, *Letters from an American* (Juy 2, 2024).

10 U.S. Const. Amend. XII.

11 *Id.*

12 Jesse Wegman, Let the People Pick the President: The Case for Abolishing the Electoral College (2020).

Third, even if the Founders intended the Electors to exercise independent judgment and occasionally support someone other than the winner in their state, the Supreme Court in the "faithless elector" case[13] ruled that they couldn't do that. We ask why have the Electoral College to begin with, and pretend that the electors are some type of buffer between the people and the presidency, if electors don't have any discretion whatsoever? Fourth, the system can invite mischief, even criminal election fraud, for example if "fake electors" were to conspire to cast a state's electoral votes for someone other than the winner of that state, which is what happened in several states in 2020. Democracy advocates, including Larry Lessig, have urged reform of the Electoral College.[14]

The system could be changed by constitutional amendment, although it's difficult to imagine three-fourths of the states agreeing to ratify such an amendment. Even without a constitutional amendment, more states could proportionately allocate their electoral votes between the candidates instead of using a winner-take-all system. Nebraska and Maine allocate their electoral votes in this manner. Finally, some states could by statute provide that their electors must vote for the winner of the nationwide popular vote regardless of who wins in that state. If several swing states enacted such a law, the likelihood of the Electoral College vote deviating from the popular vote would be reduced substantially.

But unless this system is changed, there remains the possibility that in the twenty-first century yet more presidents could be elected without the popular vote. It would be ironic if despite the extensive constitutional measures the Founders put in place to create checks on the presidency, as discussed throughout this book, the Electoral College ultimately has the most impact.

***

As this book is published, in 2025, the United States inaugurated another President, the forty-seventh. It is not a conventional time in history. It is a difficult and challenging period in America, with political polarization, partisan infighting, divided government in Congress, and social discontent. The mood of the country is unsettled.

One distinguished historian, Theodore H. White, has observed that "most Presidents come to the White House as finished portraits," but noted that "it takes years to evaluate any President."[15] Another leading historian, Arthur M. Schlesinger Jr., in a later period, wrote that "[t]he historic idea of a unifying American identity is now in peril in many arenas – in our voluntary organizations, our churches, our language."[16] This same author warned us in 1992, over three decades ago, about

[13] Chiafalo v. Washington, 591 U.S. 578 (2020) (ruling unanimously that states can enforce an elector's pledge to vote according to state law).

[14] *See* Lawrence Lessig, They Don't Represent Us: Reclaiming Our Democracy (2019) (recommending democracy reforms including reform of the Electoral College).

[15] Theodore H. White, The Making of the President 1968, 427 (1969).

[16] Arthur M. Schlesinger Jr., The Disuniting of America: Reflections on a Multicultural Society, 17 (1992). *See also* Robert D. Putnam, Bowling Alone: The

"The Imperial Presidency" given the expansion and abuse of presidential power. He asked whether this development was an aberration in the country's history and trajectory.[17] He quoted the Founders' concern of "concentrating authority in a single institution" and their solution of separation of power that would disperse power and authority among three independent branches of government. Quoting Madison's writing in *Federalist* 51, he emphasized the importance of a checks and balances system with the "necessary constitutional means and personal motives to resist encroachments of the others."[18] His conclusion was that: "The American democracy must discover a middle ground between making the President a czar and making him a puppet. The problem is to devise means of reconciling a strong and purposeful presidency with equally strong and purposeful forms of democratic control. Or, to put it succinctly, we need a strong presidency – but a strong presidency *within the Constitution*."[19]

His impressive historical scholarship tells us that to understand American history we need to understand the "Cycles of American history." And that includes the cycles of the American presidency. He leaves us with a quote from Walt Whitman, the "ever hopeful poet of American democracy" who wrote in his poem *The Great City* that a great city is:

> Where the populace rise at once against the never-ending audacity of elected persons,
> Where fierce men and women pour forth as the sea to the whistle of death pours its weeping and unript waves,
> Where outside authority enters always after the precedence of inside authority,
> Where the citizen is always the head and ideal, and President, Mayor, Governor and what not, are agents for pay. . .
> There the great city stands.[20]

Historians tell us history is about telling stories, among other matters.[21] This book tells the story of how the presidency through history, law, and politics has grown in power far from the Founders' original intent. Through numerous checks and accountability provisions, based on separation of powers, the Founders favored the

COLLAPSE AND REVIVAL OF AMERICAN COMMUNITY (2000); ROBERT D. PUTNAM, THE UPSWING: HOW AMERICAN CAME TOGETHER A CENTURY AGO AND HOW WE CAN DO IT AGAIN (2020).

17 ARTHUR M. SCHLESINGER JR., THE IMPERIAL PRESIDENCY (1973).

18 *Id.* at vii. (citing THE FEDERALIST 51 (Madison)).

19 *Id.* at x.

20 ARTHUR M. SCHLESINGER JR., THE CYCLES OF AMERICAN HISTORY, 336 (1999) (quoting Walt Whitman, *Song of the Broad-Axe*, LEAVES OF GRASS; Schlesinger Jr., *supra* note 16, at 407, 419, quoting Walt Whitman ("There is no week, nor day, nor hour when tyranny may not enter upon this country if the people lose their supreme confidence in themselves – and lose their roughness and spirit of defiance . . . Tyranny may always enter; there is no charm no bar against it. The only bar against it is a large, resolute breed of men").

21 DAVID MCCULLOUGH, THE AMERICAN SPIRIT: WHO WE ARE AND WHAT WE STAND FOR, 113, 114 (2017) (quoting Barbara Tuchman and Samuel Eliot Morrison, "We ought to read history because it will help us behave better").

Congress to predominate over the presidency. But a significant power shift occurred in the last 236 years of the republic, especially during the twentieth century.

We trace this remarkable transformation from the Founders' intent, the common understanding at the time, and their written words until the most recent Supreme Court interpretations through 2024. The title and flow of this book tie together the three interrelated foundational constitutional principles that define and limit the presidency – power, responsibility, and accountability.

In each part of this book, we discern the Framers' intent and understanding, followed by Supreme Court opinions interpreting the central issues core to the power, responsibility, and accountability, and we include a diverse and expansive sampling of past and current scholarly commentary. In this way, the reader can weigh the credible evidence, the historical record, and balance the competing viewpoints.[22] We show how history, politics, and the law can, and have, informed the present state of the law today. We ask whether over time the right balance has been struck between "sharing" of powers between the President and Congress, and how and when the Supreme Court has weighed in to ultimately decide the boundaries of power, responsibility, and accountability.

We also expose the reader to an understanding of the difference between the powers of the President and the responsibility to use that power wisely. Whether the power should or should not be exercised is the critical decision.

Finally, this book pairs the questions of power and responsibility with a discussion of accountability of the President when there is an abuse of power resulting in a lack of trust by the people. The responsible exercise of power and discretion by a president is fundamental to the country's deep history in upholding the rule of law and democratic accountability. In the end, we return to the question that confronted the Founders – are there sufficient, effective checking mechanisms in the Constitution and understood by the Supreme Court today for holding a president accountable for misuse of power, enough for our constitutional republic to be sustained, as Benjamin Franklin warned at the creation of the country and the signing of the Constitution in Philadelphia in 1787.[23] Franklin's refrain bespoke of the fragility of a republic that depends on the people's engaged vigilance and consent in the exercise of their sovereignty in governing in order to throw off and prevent a tyrannical form of leadership that undermines and rejects democratic principles, values, and norms.

[22] The authors acknowledge there is a wealth of extensive scholarship and writing on the presidency from which we have benefited, but because of space limitations could not discuss in this book.

[23] During the final session of the Constitutional Convention, Mr. Franklin was asked whether we have a "republic or a monarchy?" His reply was "A republic, if you can keep it."

Index

For EU product safety concerns, contact us at Calle de José Abascal, 56–1°, 28003 Madrid, Spain or eugpsr@cambridge.org.

www.ingramcontent.com/pod-product-compliance
Lightning Source LLC
LaVergne TN
LVHW011808200926
848484LV00005B/1104

* 9 7 8 1 0 0 9 5 2 1 9 8 7 *